FROM THE KITCHEN OF

IT'S A NO GRAINER
COOKBOOK

IT'S A NO GRAINER
COOKBOOK

OVER 180 DELIGHTFULLY GLUTEN-FREE, GRAIN-FREE, LOW-CARB,
PALEO- AND KETO-FRIENDLY RECIPES FOR A HEALTHIER YOU

BARBARA HANKEY-ROGERS

Two Pups Press
PALM DESERT · CALIFORNIA

This book details the author's personal experiences with and opinions about eliminating gluten and grains from your diet and personal benefits received. The author is not a healthcare provider. You understand that this book is not intended as a substitute for consultation with a licensed healthcare or nutrition practitioner, or your physician. Before you begin any healthcare or dietary nutrition program, or change your lifestyle in any way, you will consult your physician or another licensed healthcare practitioner to ensure that you are in good health and that the information contained in this book will not harm you. The author and the publisher have no responsibility for any adverse effects arising directly or indirectly as a result of the information in this book.

Throughout this book, trademarked names are used. Rather than put a trademark symbol after every occurrence of a trademarked name, names are used in an editorial fashion only and to the benefit of the trademark owner, with no intentions of infringement of the trademark.

Published by Two Pups Press

It's a No Grainer Cookbook
Copyright © 2022 by Barbara Hankey-Rogers

All rights reserved.
No part of this publication may be reproduced or distributed in any form or by any means, electronic or mechanical, or stored in a database or retrieval system, without prior written permission from the publisher.

Food Shoot Art Direction: J. Alex Gomez
Photography: David Fox, Ethan Kaminsky, J. Alex Gomez, Hector R. Gomez, and Fernando Acevedo

Cover Photography:
Author Photography: John Decindes, Cool Breeze Photo
Hair and Make-up: Sandy Navarro
Food Photography: Hector R. Gomez
Food Stylists: Chloe Bean, Lisa Knox

Editor: Nancy Hancock

Publisher's Cataloging-In-Publication Data
(Prepared by The Donohue Group, Inc.)

Names: Hankey-Rogers, Barbara, author.
Title: It's a no grainer cookbook : over 180 delightfully gluten-free, grain-free, low-carb, paleo- and keto-friendly recipes for a healthier you / Barbara Hankey-Rogers.
Description: First edition. | Palm Desert, California : Two Pups Press, [2022]
Includes bibliographical references and index.
Identifiers: ISBN 9781736360552 (paperback) | ISBN 9781736360576 (ebook)
Subjects: LCSH: Gluten-free diet—Recipes. | Low-carbohydrate diet—Recipes. | Ketogenic diet—Recipes. High-protein diet—Recipes. | Food combining. | Hankey-Rogers, Barbara—Health. | LCGFT: Cookbooks.
BISAC: COOKING / Health & Healing / Gluten-Free.

Classification: LCC RM237.86 .H36 2022 (print)
LCC RM237.86 (ebook) | DDC 641.5/6393--dc23

FIRST EDITION
Printed in the United States of America by Courier Graphics Corporation, Arizona

www.ItsANoGrainerLife.com

"80% of all health care costs are driven by chronic disease where the dominant factor is diet and lifestyle."
—Dr. Joseph E. Scherger, Centers for Disease Control

To my late son, Taylor Rogers.
This book was to be his legacy,
but his life ended too soon,
halfway during the writing of this book.
I felt like giving up, but I heard his voice
encouraging me to keep going.
I love you, Taylor!

acknowledgements

To Dr. Joseph Scherger who inspired me to write this book. His expertise in functional medicine helped me understand how important it is to prevent diseases by eating the proper foods and living a healthy lifestyle.

To my brother, Don Hankey, who never let me forget I needed to lose weight while growing up. Most importantly, you set an excellent example as a father figure to me, due to our father's passing away early on. This book could not have been written without your guidance and financial influence.

To Alex, my marketing director, for your blood, sweat, and tears! We finally made it! Are we really finished, Alex? What's next? Thank you for putting up with me.

To Alex's team, Lisa Knox, perfect food stylist and now a dear friend and to our amazing photographer, Hector Gomez, for all his great food photos.

To Gary Geske, my other half, who tirelessly ran to the market for food items we needed.

To my friend and angel, Ronda Giangreco, who at the last minute proofed the entire book as a favor to me, making important improvements for my book *It's a No Grainer Cookbook*.

contents

Preface 1

Introduction No Grainer Basics 3
    What Gluten Does 5
    Glycemic Index and Our Bodies 7
    Replacing and Balancing Ingredients 10
    Answers to Diet Choices 16
    The 41 Most Nutrient-Dense Foods on Earth 20

Part One Benefits of Living Gluten and Grain Free ... 23

Part Two Kitchen Needs 28
    Utensils, Cookware, and Appliances 29

Part Three Yummy Recipes! 30
    Breakfast 32
    Appetizers and Beverages 54
    Salads 88
    Soups 112
    Small Plates 126
    Pasta Dishes 142
    Main Dishes 154
    Seafood and Fish 200
    Side Dishes 224
    Sauces 256
    Baked Goods 264
    Desserts 300

Endnotes 324
Index 325

preface

Life is amazing when you savor how you live, how you work and how you eat. Find a path that empowers you and all facets of your life are impacted.

While I'm not an expert cook, a dietician or a medical professional, I have learned from experience that what you eat has enormous effect on how you feel. Like most people, I tried many diets and never achieved the results I had hoped for. When I eliminated grains, however, my health, weight, energy and overall vibrancy improved dramatically.

It is my hope that the information and recipes I've provided in this book will start you on a journey to a long, healthy and active life.

Yours in Health!

Barbara Hankey-Rogers

introduction:
no grainer basics

My journey has taught me how and what to eat. I have tried almost every approach known to man including Atkins, fat free, low carbs, no carbs, all vegetable, Weight Watchers, liquid protein, and others. But, science has shown us that nutrients, minerals, and vitamins are best sourced from plants. I discovered that there are so many modified foods that lack the total nutrient package they had in the past.

It took a while to get the hang of replacing grains and other food items that contain gluten. I had already made the effort to eat fresh whole foods and to eat better in general. I found some foods dragged me down and sapped my energy. Many of my friends joked about their "food coma," especially around the holidays when we packed on heavy meals to sustain us over the winter. Of course, that often means packing on the pounds too.

I have also learned that for optimal balance in the health of our bodies, we need proper amounts of proteins, carbohydrates,

What Gluten Does 5

Glycemic Index and Our Bodies 7

Replacing and Balancing Ingredients 10

Answers to Your Diet Choices 16

The 41 Most Nutrient-dense Foods on Earth 20

and fat to run efficiently. An important part of this was learning portion control. The point is that you can control your choices to meet your individual goals.

To set yourself up for success, you need to consider what you want to accomplish. Personally, I started by reading the book, *Grain Brain* by Dr. David Perlmutter, and then Dr. Joseph Scherger's book, *Lean and Fit,* which explained "why" eliminating grains was so important. Also, very helpful was Dr. William Davis' book, *Wheat Belly, 10-Day Grain Detox,* because it explained and identified all the grains. Many people don't understand grains and their impact on our bodies. Then, I moved toward learning about this marvelous biological machine—my body. I became very familiar with the intimate details of what my system needed to operate efficiently and at an optimal state.

As with any changes you decide to make, I earnestly advise you to check with your personal doctor before beginning or changing your dietary practices. If you decide to start exercising or modulating your form of fitness with any newfound energy, make sure your physician is aware and lets you know that you are fit for it.

what gluten does

Gluten (from Latin gluten, "glue") is a composite of storage proteins termed prolamins and glutelin that are stored together with starch in the endosperm (which nourishes the embryonic plant during germination) of various cereal (grass) grains. It is found in wheat, barley, rye, and related species and hybrids (such as spelt, Khorasan wheat, emmer, einkorn, triticale, kamut, etc.), as well as products derived from these grains (such as breads and malts).

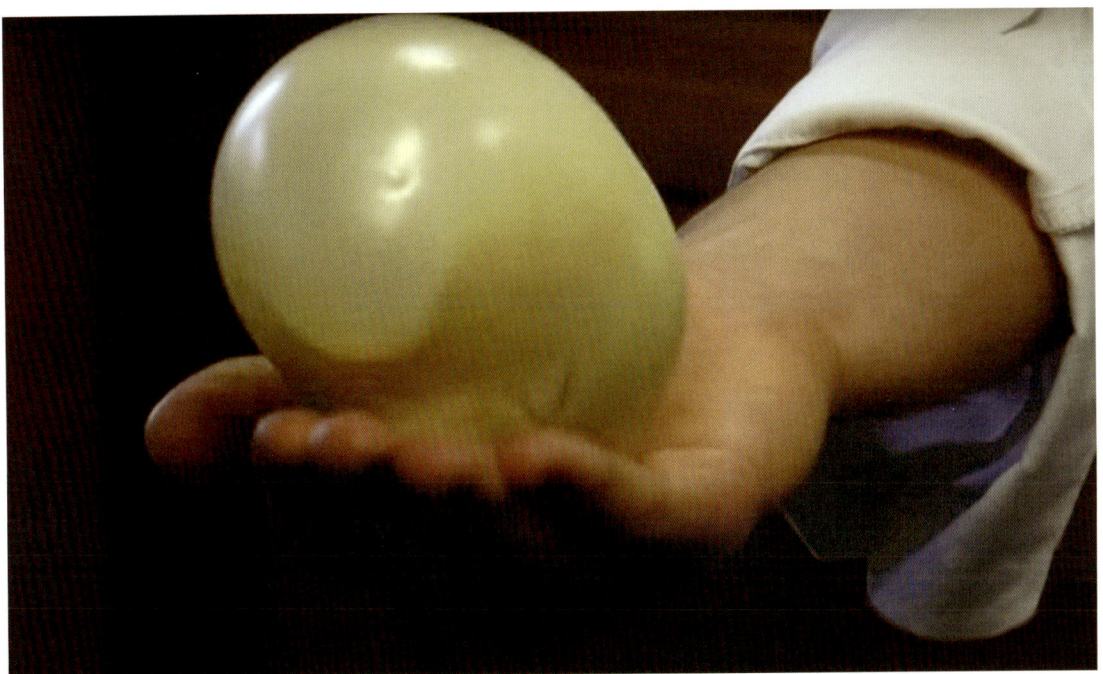

Science: What is Gluten? Here's How to See and Feel Gluten", America's Test Kitchen, Jun 19, 2013

Gluten is mostly made of two chemical components, Glutenin and Gliadin. Glutenin is the major protein in wheat flour and accounts for 47% of the total protein content. Gliadin, a type of prolamin, is a class of proteins present in wheat and several other cereals within the grass genus *triticum*. Gliadins, the other components of gluten, are essential for giving bread the ability to rise properly during baking.

There are three main types of gliadin (α, γ, and ω), to which the body is intolerant in coeliac (or celiac) disease. It can also be found in wheat varieties such as spelt, kamut, farro, and durum as well as in bulgur and semolina. Other grains where it is present are barley, rye, triticale, and oats. Certain types of rice and corn also contain amounts of gluten.

So, you ask, what does gluten do? In wheat flour–based foods, gluten gives elasticity to the dough of bread and creates air bubbles within the breads and cakes. I found it interesting that 1 in 133 people in the US have celiac disease. For them, gluten triggers an autoimmune response that attacks the lining of the small intestine.[1] The body cannot absorb nutrients into the bloodstream properly, leading to anemia, delayed growth, and weight loss, among other things, and may result in inflammation, leading to further damage.

It also helps to note that gluten will lead to weight gain when consumed in excess, especially around the waist. Some studies have suggested that wheat and wheat products can contribute to the early onset of Alzheimer's disease, dementia, and Parkinson's disease. For some people, it may elevate the blood sugar and can contribute to the development of type 2 diabetes.

glycemic index and our bodies

The measuring of how fast blood sugar rises after we eat is referred to as the glycemic index (GI). According to Harvard University,[2] "The glycemic index ranks foods containing carbohydrates from 0–100. Depending on how fast it will raise your blood sugar will matter in relation to the glycemic index (GI) of the foods." The GI is set at 100, meaning that anything at the top of the scale will give you that "sugar rush" that makes you feel nauseous. If you have ever done the blood sugar test where you have to drink glucose, you know exactly what that feels like.

The GI of white and wheat bread are both very high and come in at around 70 on the GI scale. When these breads are digested, they convert to glucose almost immediately, causing blood sugar to spike dramatically. Foods that rank around 50 are considered medium, meaning they still raise your blood sugar, but not as impactful as 70 or more. Foods at 35 or less on the GI scale are considered low.

The benefit of foods that are low on the GI scale (predominately non-grains) lead to a much lower risk for heart disease, stroke, type 2 diabetes, depression, chronic kidney disease, formation of gall-stones, formation of uterine fibroids, and cancer of the breast, prostate, and pancreas according to Dr. Scherger and others.

Low Glycemic Foods List 0 – 55	Medium Glycemic Foods List 56 – 70	High Glycemic Foods List 70+
Most non starchy vegetables <15	Canned kidney beans 52	Bagel 72
Peanuts <15	Kiwifruit 52	Corn chips 72
Low-fat yogurt, no sugar <15	Orange juice 52	Watermelon 72
Tomatoes 15	Banana 53	Honey 73
Cherries 22	Potato chips 54	Mashed potatoes 73
Peas 22	Special K 54	Cheerios 74
Plum 24	Sweet potato 54	Puffed wheat 74
Grapefruit 25	Brown rice 54	Doughnuts 75
Pearled barley 25	Linguine 55	French fries 76
Peach 28	Oatmeal cookies 55	Vanilla wafers 77
Can peaches, natural juices 30	Popcorn 55	White bread 79
Soy milk 30	Sweet corn 55	Jelly beans 80
Baby lima beans 32	Muesli 55	Pretzels 81
Fat-free milk 32	White rice 56	Rice cakes 82
Low-fat yogurt, with sugar 33	Pita bread 57	Mashed potatoes, instant 83
Apple 36	Blueberry muffin 59	Cornflakes 84
Pear 36	Bran muffin 60	Baked potato 85
Whole wheat spaghetti 37	Hamburger bun 61	Rice, instant 91
Tomato soup 38	Ice cream 61	French bread 95
Carrots, cooked 39	Canned apricots, light syrup 64	Parsnips 97
Apple juice 41	Macaroni and cheese 64	Dates 100
All-Bran 42	Raisins 64	
Canned chickpeas 42	Couscous 65	
Custard 43	Quick-cooking porridge 65	
Grapes 43	Rye crsip bread 65	
Orange 43	Table sugar (sucrose) 65	
Canned lentil soup 44	Instant porridge 66	
Macaroni 45	Pineapple 66	
Pineapple juice 46	Taco shells 68	
Banana bread 47	Whole wheat bread 68	
Long-grain rice 47		
Bulgur 48		
Canned baked beans 48		
Grapefruit juice 48		
Green peas 48		
Oat bran bread 48		
Old-fashioned porridge 49		

Compiled by www.LowGIHealth.com.au from various sources

It has been documented that 80% of all health-care costs are driven by chronic disease where the dominant factor is diet and lifestyle. This gives you an idea of how vital it is to eat a very low-carb diet and eliminate grains.

Grains are hidden in so many foods. Different factors can also impact the GI scale, such as how food is prepared, the combination of ingredients, and balancing vegetables, fruit, and nuts or seed-based foods. For example, adding lemon juice or vinegar can lessen the affect of what you eat on the GI scale. Also, the longer you cook pasta, the higher the GI becomes. The riper a banana, the higher the GI becomes. Foods eaten at the same time can impact the affects of higher glycemic foods; for example, combining high glycemic foods, like beets, with lower ones, like cucumbers, can lessen the effects of higher glycemic foods.

Your age, how active you are, and how you digest food also affects how your body reacts to carbs and sugar spikes. We now know that inflammation causes disease and inflammation can be caused by grains and gluten. When our body experiences constant blood sugar spiking during the day, it tends to build up inflammation. Too much inflammation results in a leaky gut. When that occurs, it is the direct cause of so many autoimmune diseases. Even allergies and many more problems increase when we indulge in a high-glycemic diet, not to mention the most common problem of all—obesity.

replacing and balancing ingredients

On my journey to improve my nutrition, I discovered how to replace grains with seeds and greens, manage my portions, replace sugars with other sweeteners to improve blood sugar levels, and replaced wheat flours with plant-based ingredients.

seeds

Our ancestors lived on seeds and nuts of all sorts. The plants that produce them flourish and provide proteins and nutrients that our bodies know how to process. Most seeds and nuts are great sources of fiber and essential oils to promote good vascular and digestive health.

meat

While some of my friends chose to become vegetarians, many of us have learned how to balance our consumption of beef, pork, and other available meats. The key is portion control, knowledge of cuts, and the balance of fat we consume in our lives. Meat is hard to digest, and studies show meat eaters have a higher risk of some cancers. I wish I could eliminate meat entirely and become a vegetarian, but it's quite difficult, especially being a foodie. So, I have personally chosen to eat meat as a side dish and in very small portions. Observing meatless days has become a goal of mine. I've replaced the meat with wild-caught fish and feel the health benefits just by doing that. I offer many delicious fish and seafood recipes in this book for you to enjoy if you are making this change in your diet.

my love affair with bacon

Growing up, the aroma of bacon wafting through my kitchen was the most alluring smell that I can remember. It meant it was either a Saturday or Sunday, certainly not a school day. School mornings were so hurried that there was no time for cooking bacon, but the perfect time for a bowl of cereal. The aroma of bacon brings back so many fond memories of family and friends gathering for holidays, beginning the mornings with bacon, eggs, toast, orange juice, and of course—another dear friend of mine—a cup of joe. Then all of a sudden, back in 1967, the sugar industry actually paid its researchers to say that fat was the culprit, not sugar. Shortly thereafter, there was fat-free this, fat-free that—so my wonderful friend, bacon, became

the enemy. The government sold us a bill of goods by telling us that fat was killing all of us but not mentioning sugar whatsoever.

The tide really started to turn when doctors wrote books about fat being healthy and that the added sugar was the bad guy. Dr. William Davis, a cardiologist, was having good results with patients suffering from diabetes and weight gain by eliminating grains. Other doctors were proclaiming how important fat was to our health and that we needed to ditch the sugar! Once again, bacon became my friend and I was delighted. Bacon enhances almost every food I can think of, it's even in some chocolate bars. Just make sure the bacon is uncured, which means no nitrates, antibiotics, or other additives. There are so many on the market now, and I promise you, the taste is not compromised!

Changing over from one lifestyle to another is never easy. I knew that if I added bacon, which I do in many of my recipes, it might help entice more readers to get excited about the changeover.

The easiest way to cook bacon is to place each slice on a rack over a baking sheet lined with aluminum foil, bake (never having to turn the bacon over) 15-20 minutes at 400°F (204°C). The foil lined baking sheet makes cleanup much easier.

chicken

Chicken is versatile and there are many recipes you can make with chicken. The healthiest chickens I have found are organic and hormone-free. It tastes the same to me as the other chicken, but as I have said, choosing to eat as clean as you can will promote overall health and balance.

seafood and fish

So much has happened to our lakes, rivers, and oceans. You have to do your homework on what types of fish to consume and learn about the regions where your fish come from. Beware of levels of mercury and other harmful chemicals that, over time, will negatively impact your health. I go for wild-caught fish. The same with other seafood. Crustaceans and shellfish, such as shrimp, lobster, crab, oysters, clams, and mussels all have varieties that, depending on how they are caught, frozen, stored, and cooked, have a way of impacting our health.

oils

As much as we work to maintain balance with what we cook, there are benefits when you vary and moderate the oils and fats in which you use to cook. Watch out for hydrogenated oils as the side effects of using can lead to higher risks for cardio vascular disease. Plant-based oils like avocado, coconut, and olive have a lot of benefits beyond seed-based oils. Avocado oil is becoming widely used as it contains antioxidants and healthy fats. Coconut oil has a unique set of fatty acids that provide healthful benefits like boosting fat loss, heart health, and brain function. Olive oil is one of the best alternatives to grain-based oils. The biggest reason is its concentration of a monounsaturated fat called oleic acid, making up 73% of the total oil content. Oleic acid reduces inflammation and may even have beneficial effects on genes linked to cancer according to the National Institutes of Health. The bottom line is read the label, know your oils, and manage your use so that you have a variety of tastes and benefits.

hidden sugars

Check with your physician to see if your blood sugar is elevated. Are you pushing prediabetic levels? Grains produce those hidden sugars that we forget about because they aren't listed on nutritional labels. The sugar in breads like sourdough, French baguette, and whole wheat is listed at about 2–3 grams. They don't tell you about the hidden sugars. The next time you're in the market, check out the nutrional label on other foods you are consuming, such as skim milk. It has 12–13 grams of sugar. Yet, cream has none. Whole milk is very high also.

We know sugar is a huge problem in cancer because cancer feeds on sugar. Other awful diseases are a result of too much sugar. Foods that contain hidden sugars raise our blood sugar throughout the day to dangerous levels.

Here's a quick easy way to make your own erythritol syrup to replace sugar, corn syrup or honey. It's my preferred keto syrup and it's easy to do!

Just set a saucepan on the stovetop over medium heat.

Add 1 cup of water.

Bring to nearly boiling or when you begin to see steam rising.

Turn off flame and add 1½ cups of erythritol and stir to dissolve as the water cools.

Fill your syrup bottle or a 24-ounce glass jar.

Lasts 1-2 weeks in the fridge.

Note: You can replace erythritol with xylitol or Swerve to make your keto syrup.

answers to your diet choices

Keto, paleo, vegetarian, vegan, Mediterranean, pescatarian—what's the answer to all of these choices? In all my research I've narrowed it down to these main factors.

keto versus paleo

A ketogenic diet is the elimination of grains, gluten, and refined sugar. The primary goal when doing keto is to put your body in ketosis. Ketosis occurs when your body uses fat instead of carbohydrates as a main energy source. The diet is high fat and low in carbs and is similar to the Atkins diet. It consists of 80% fat and little to no carbs. The difference is, Atkins has a gradual increase in carbs, and the keto diet is low carbs all the time. Staples of the keto diet are fish, meat, eggs, dairy, oils, and green vegetables. Pasta, rice and some other grains, and some fruit are strictly forbidden. It's very similar to paleo as both are low in carbs.

Most of the recipes in this book are paleo-friendly which includes some keto. For those that are not, I have provided the option to make them keto-friendly. The ones that are keto-friendly already are noted with a (KF). Both keto and paleo do not allow grains and don't advocate legumes, but for different reasons. Keto doesn't allow legumes because of the high carb count they have. According to the paleo approach, legumes can cause digestive problems.

The keto diet is also very structured. Fruit is forbidden on keto, except for berries. God forbid should you have an apple or a banana. High-starch veggies are also eliminated. Keto also manipulates the three macronutrients: fat, carbs, and protein. I believe being so restrictive will lead you to not following through in the long run and cause you to give up. Too strict and too fast generally doesn't work. Also, because of how strict it is, one will tend to consume too much meat. I don't think eating meat every day is necessary. Vegetables and some fruits are the winners here. For all you keto followers, it certainly does work, and I am not discouraging you from following that way of eating. It's just that if you are new to making big changes in your lifestyle, you may want to consider going paleo as a good starting point.

Paleo does not manipulate the macronutrients. You get to make your choices as to the amount of protein or fat you prefer. Low carb is always a factor when doing paleo.

Keto uses erythritol and/or stevia in place of honey or maple syrup. The banana breads in this book would not be allowed on keto, so I have given you an option. You may use banana extract as a substitute as you'll see in my recipe in the Baked Goods recipe section. If you eliminate grains and refined sugar, you are well on your way to losing weight and feeling wonderful.

The Mediterranean diet makes sense and certainly works. My problem is that it does allow some grains and therefore may cause some weight gain.

vegan or vegetarian? what's the difference?

Vegans do not eat animal products. Vegetarians don't eat animals but may eat products that come from animals, such as dairy products and eggs. Both diets can be healthy but may lack certain nutrients. Vegans have to get really creative to ensure they get enough protein, calcium, iron, and vitamin B12. Vegetarians find these nutrients in eggs and dairy. Vegans rely solely on plant sources. I found being a vegan was very difficult. I tried it and gave up. It's very disciplined and, for foodies, almost out of the question. It's been stated that they now have proven in at least one study that they tend to live longer.

The term Blue Zone first appeared in a November 2005 *National Geographic* magazine cover story, "The Secrets of a Long Life" by Dan Buettner.[3] Blue Zones are regions of the world where Buettner claims people live much longer than average. In the Blue Zones, which are Okinawa, Japan, Sardinia, Italy, Nicoya, Costa Rica, Icaria, Greece, and right here in California in Loma Linda, people live much longer lives. Diet is a major component as well as other factors such as exercise, stress, and air quality. Why is Loma Linda a Blue Zone and not another area in California or the United States? There's a community of 9,000 Adventists in Loma Linda. They are the core of America's Blue Zone. Their longevity can be attributed to vegetarianism and regular exercise plus they do not smoke or drink alcohol.

the pescatarian diet

Pescatarian is one way to go. But avoid farm-raised fish. With so many healthy fish choices, you can get creative with recipes and styles of cooking to vary what you consume. My main protein source is from wild-caught fish. You'll find many recipes featuring these with delicious blends of flavors and textures.

how do these diets differ from eliminating gluten and grains

As I stated in the introduction of the book, I have been on a dietary journey and believe that this way of nourishing your body can provide better results for a healthy life and avoiding chronic disease.

Hippocrates was so right on with his belief that "food is thy medicine." There are many foods to buy now that you can easily take with you, such as grain-free crackers, breads, even tortilla chips, which is my favorite junk food. It is a somewhat difficult challenge to eliminate grains, but I find it becomes easier in time, and I think you'll find that many of the recipes in this book will help you make this transition with flavorful meals to cook for years to come.

As I mentioned earlier, the three great books that helped me were *Grain Brain* by Dr. David Perlmutter, *Lean and Fit* by Dr. Joseph Scherger and *Wheat Belly 10-Day Grain Detox* by Dr. William Davis. Dr. Scherger's book opened my eyes as to why giving up grains was important for my functional health. Dr. Davis' book explains how to begin the process in depth. The desire for grains dissipates in time as it did for me.

the 41 most nutrient-dense foods on earth

FOOD FOR THOUGHT I poured through many studies on nutrition and health that now serve as the basis to what has become my It's A No Grainer Life website (www.ItsANoGrainerLife.com) as well as this book.

I found an article based on a study by Jennifer Di Noia, PhD—who specializes in public health—called "Defining Powerhouse Fruits and Vegetables: A Nutrient Density Approach."[4] In this study, Dr. Di Noia ranked fruits and vegetables based on nutrient measures to determine which ones were considered a "powerhouse." Essentially, she defined a powerhouse as those "most strongly associated with reduced chronic disease." Each fruit and vegetable was measured for their content of seventeen nutrients that are very important to our health. Her findings were very interesting and some of the powerhouses included the following: watercress, Chinese cabbage, chard, beet green, spinach, red pepper, carrots, lemons, strawberries, oranges, grapefruit, blackberries, leeks, sweet potatoes, iceberg lettuce, and romaine lettuce. Please note that leafy greens appeared in the top fifteen spots on this list. (See rankings chart opposite page.)

The exact formula for density scoring (which can be found at www.cdc.gov/pcd/issues/2014/13_0390.htm), it turns out romaine lettuce ranked ninth on the list with a density score of 63.48. Who knew romaine lettuce was so nutritious! Maybe that is why we enjoy Caesar salad so much (just eliminate the croutons)!

Well, there you have it!

Sharing is caring—and my goal here is to share these wonderful possibilities for improved living and a healthy body. I can tell you this: replacing foods that no longer supported my personal goals was much easier than I thought it would be.

part one: benefits of living gluten and grain free

Why should any of us follow a gluten-and-grain-free life? Remember if it's grain-free, it's automatically gluten-free; if it is gluten-free, it is not always grain-free. Many people have benefited from this approach, also referred to as paleo-and-keto-inspired. Many intestinal discomforts and diseases can be prevented or reversed, eliminating the need for medication that treats diseases such as hypertension, type 2 diabetes, and allergies.

This way of life is not a fad. Today many people are discovering what I found on my own journey through the years. Studies have validated what I suggest with *It's a No Grainer Cookbook*. People have found that by eliminating foods that bother them, they are reducing their inflammation, bloating, low energy, and even turning back the clock on aging. I found I can support the normal function of my immune system and eat my way to improved health.

This way of feeding ourselves is composed of nutrients, minerals, vitamins, proteins, and fiber that have proven to be anti-inflammatory. It is believed that gluten sensitivity can be an emerging factor in autoimmune diseases. According to the National Institutes of Health, "autoimmune disease occurs when the immune system attacks self-molecules as a result of a breakdown of immunologic tolerance to autoreactive immune cells. Many autoimmune disorders have been strongly associated with genetic, infectious, and/or environmental predisposing factors."[5] Autoimmune diseases impact everything in your body that oftentimes have to be managed with pharmaceuticals. When you start to look at the source of many diseases, they come from what we consume and the lifestyles we follow. Most people, by culture or custom, only scratch the surface in truly feeding themselves.

We have been taught to eat until we are full, and we are filling ourselves with starchy, grain-based foods that run counter to what our body needs to run efficiently for the long term.

Gluten has become so concentrated in our diets that we are, in a sense, overdosing our bodies with it. Most people who become sensitive to gluten start to experience increased intestinal permeability, more commonly known as leaky gut, which can contribute to autoimmune diseases. Other factors that can play a role in causing autoimmune disease are genetics, previous infections, some forms of chemical exposure, environmental factors, lack of sleep, and stress. If you think about it, our bodies are like a fiberoptic network. When we do sleep, our bodies have the mechanics to recharge, repair, and reenergize. Sleep deprivation can be connected to what we eat, and can cause inflammation to rise, even at a very young age. While, we can control the stress of everyday life sometimes, we always have control over what we eat.

Type 2 diabetes in adults and children is also on the rise in this country. This has been attributed to the alarming rate of obesity in the United States. Back in the 1980's the incidences of children with type 2 diabetes were almost unknown. Nowadays, one in three adults are considered pre-diabetic which means their blood sugar is very high but not high enough to be classified as a diabetic. In time diabetes will certainly manifest itself if they don't make lifestyle changes.

Some of the foods that have been found to contribute to autoimmune conditions are soy, whole grains, and low-fat dairy. Practicing moderation and portion control help in managing weight. Limiting or eliminating grains altogether improve wellness management.

This book will provide recipes that can fulfill your desires for delightfully tasty foods by exchanging grains and gluten for cleaner nutrients that enable your body to function well.

The list of diseases that are impacted by diet and lifestyle is long: diabetes, allergies, migraines, colitis, irritable bowel syndrome,

Alzheimer's disease, Crohn's disease, celiac disease, leaky gut, hypertension, and more. Dr. Dale Bredesen, a neurologist from Tiburon, California, is reversing Alzheimer's as I write this, having reversed over 100 patients.[6] He's worked on this for over twenty years. Almost as a last resort, he finally decided to concentrate on diet and lifestyle. Diet plays a huge role, as well as other factors, such as hormones, vitamins, and toxic metals. There is a test available to see where you stand in the probability of developing Alzheimer's. It's called a *cognoscopy* test, which includes blood work and an MRI on the hippocampus.

I was fortunate enough to have one done and feel very happy that I am in the eighty-seventh percentile of not acquiring the disease. Evidently, people are coming down with the disease at a much younger age. It's vital to eat the right foods and exercise as much as possible. You can look this up in his book, *The End of Alzheimer's,* and read about the paradigm shift Dr. Bredesen is causing in this area.

Much of what is on the internet is focused on dieting, some on giving up meats, others on going paleo, vegan, or strict vegetarian. Many provide insight on selecting the foods that support overall health in the short-term and true body health for the long-term. That has been my focus in cooking for myself, as well as for my family and friends.

It is important to note that we each have a unique body and that everybody possesses the power to change or transform what we consume. As autoimmune diagnoses are on the rise, I invite you to consider my paleo- and keto-inspired recipes and foods. I certainly have enjoyed curating them for this book. If I accomplish anything with *It's a No Grainer Cookbook,* it is my hope that you see the importance of eliminating grains and the terrible effects grains can have on our bodies. One of my favorite books is *The End of Illness* by Dr. David Agus. In his book he mentions often that if we treat our microbiome well by feeding it healthy foods, we can prevent many diseases.

The joy of life is greatly affected by our culinary desires. I truly wish that you find health and happiness exploring your path to healthy eating and a healthier you for the long haul.

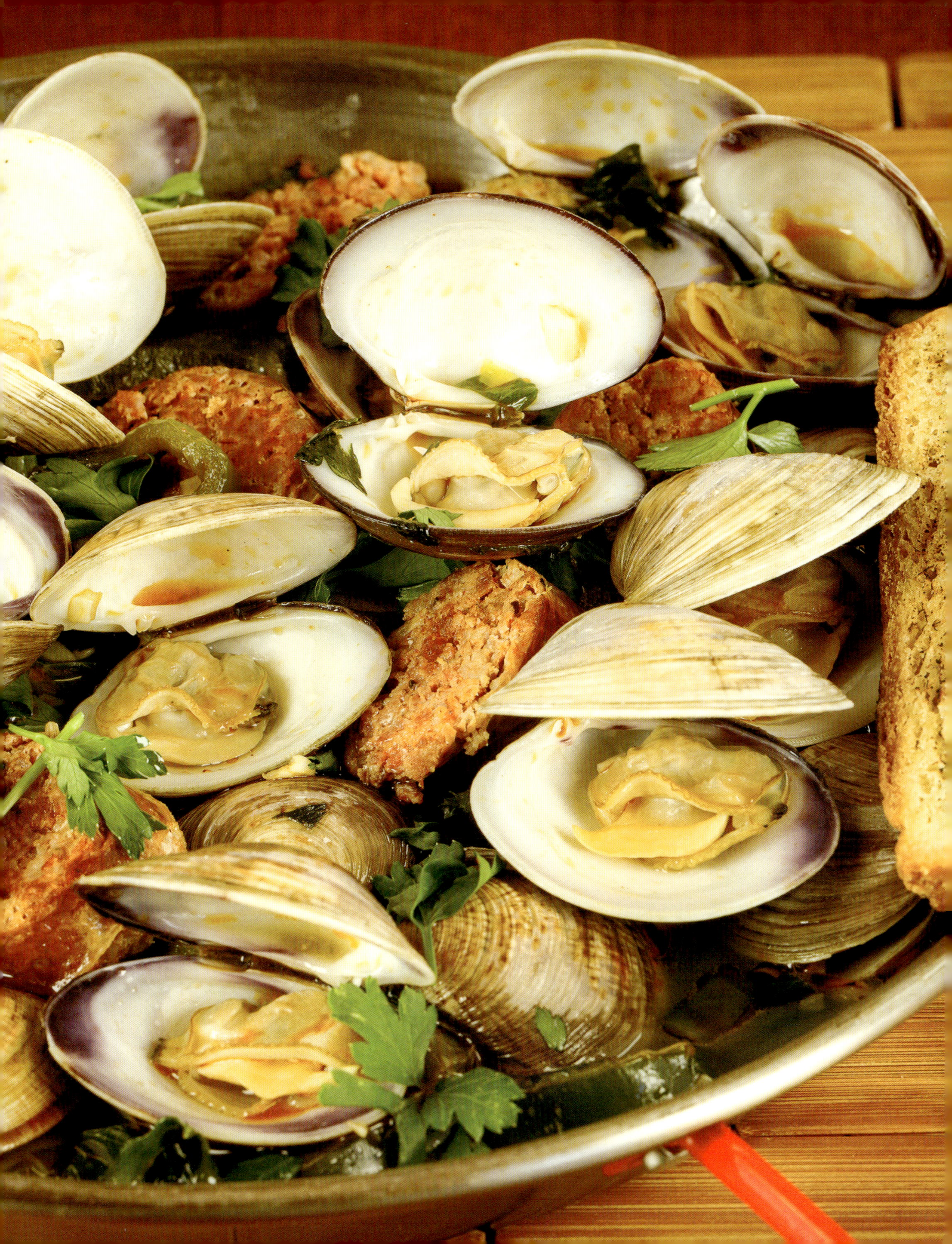

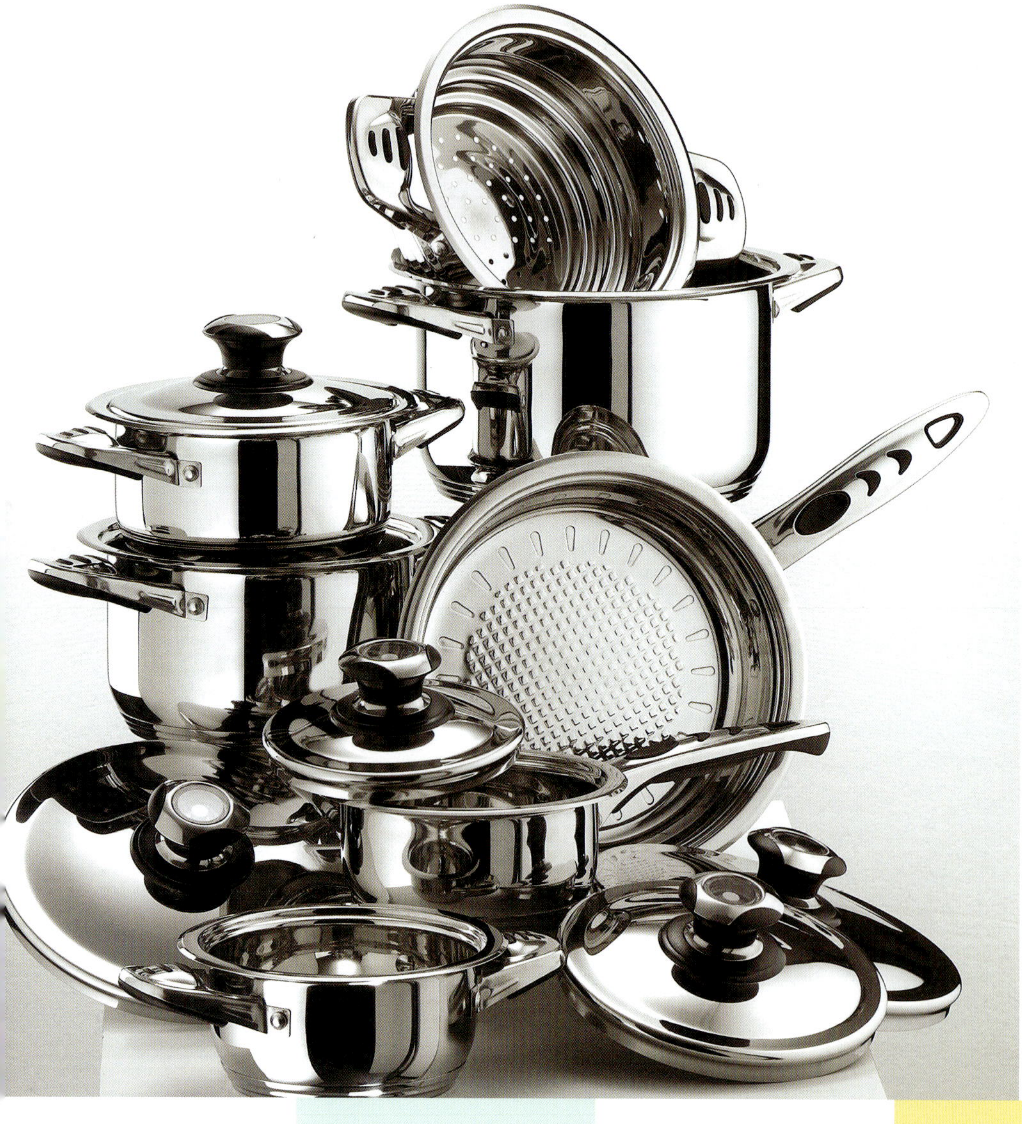
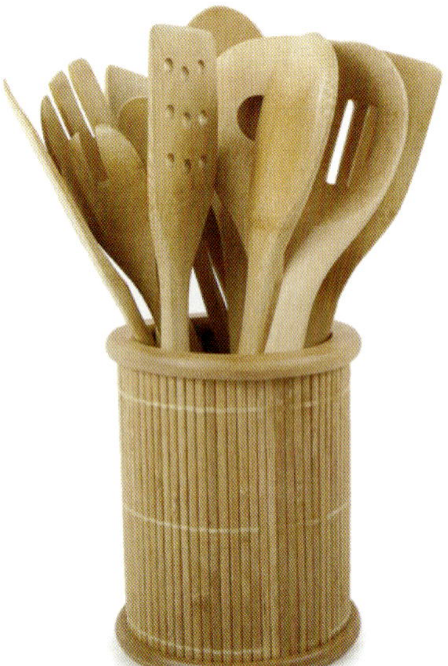

part two: kitchen utensils, cookware, + appliances

Having the right tools in the kitchen can make cooking much more fun and creative. Imagine if you were working on some home improvement project, and you lacked the tools. You would be running to the home improvement center, time and again, to purchase the next tool.

I have found that knives, cooking spoons, wooden spoons, strainers, and the like in some households need updating. You don't have to spend extravagantly to have a nice set of kitchen utensils and cookware to make the recipes in this or just about any cookbook you may have.

A good mix can be found at your favorite kitchen store, discount stores, or online. The point is that you do not have to have a drawer full of utensils that won't see the light of day. But, as you venture on your culinary journey, you will expand your collection and see your favorites get more use than others. You should also have good kitchen knives. Some people spend over $3,000 on really good knives with a sharpener, but you can get a reasonably serviceable set for around $200. Again, you'll want to have a set that works well for various uses whether you are slicing, dicing, paring, chopping, or cutting.

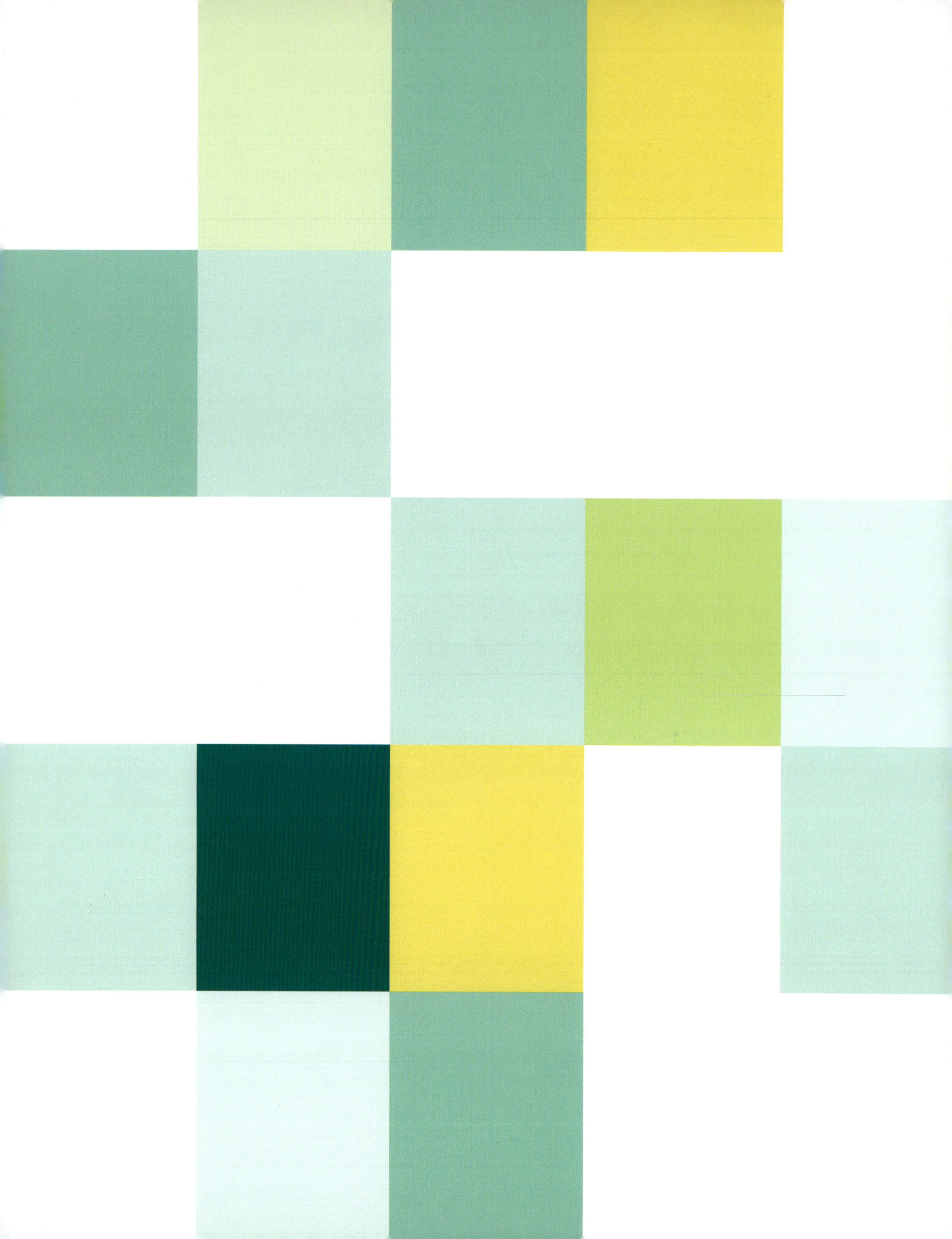

part three:
yummy recipes!

Breakfast 32

Appetizers and Beverages 54

Salads 88

Soups 112

Small Plates 126

Pasta Dishes 142

Main Dishes 154

Seafood and Fish 200

Side Dishes 224

Sauces 256

Baked Goods 264

Desserts 300

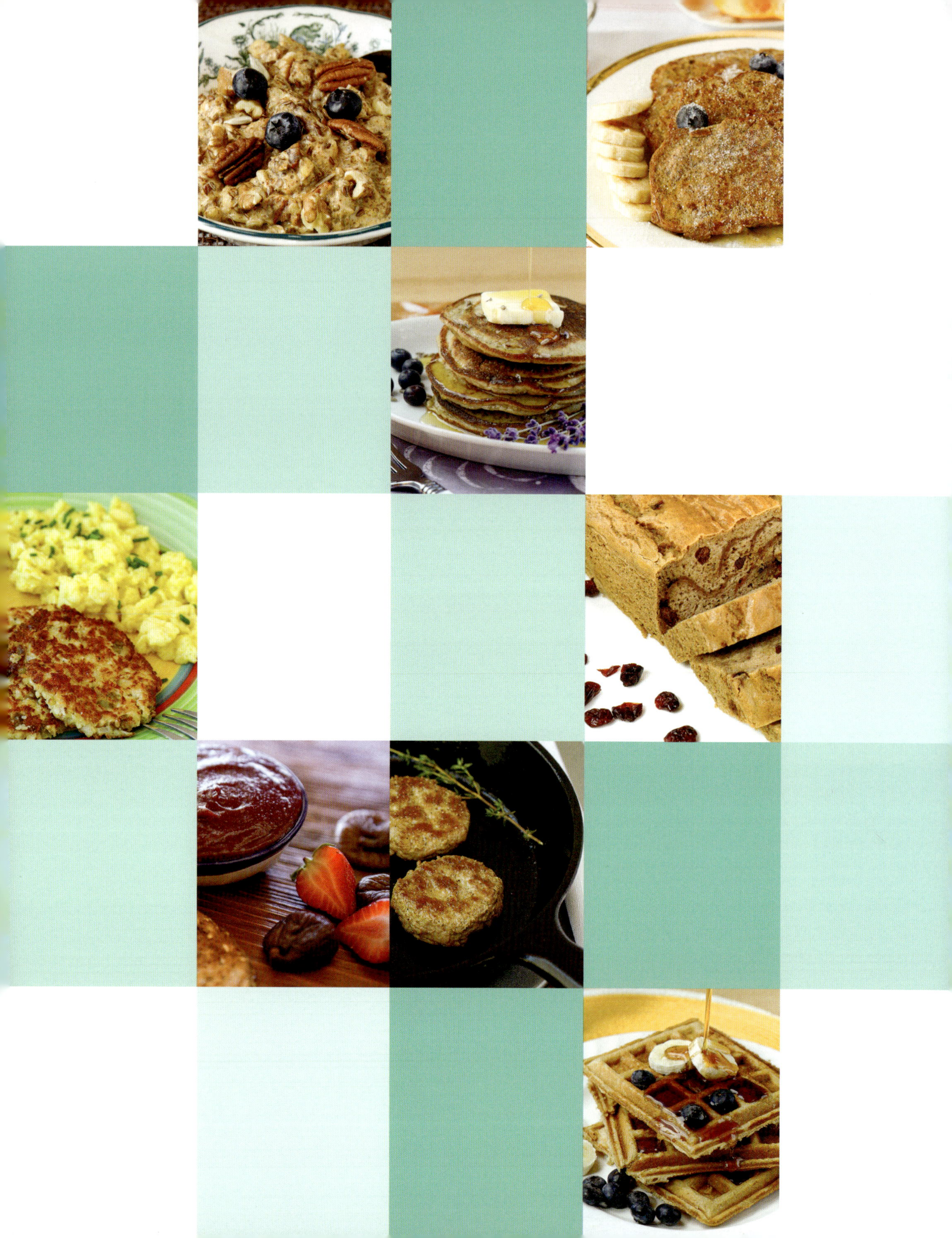

breakfast

When it comes to breakfast, many people will stop at their favorite coffee place and grab one of those decadent sugar laced muffins, sweet breads or bagels. What they do not realize is that they're spiking their blood sugar level first thing in the morning and this will cause cravings for sugars during the day. In order to fuel your engine, you should consider having nutritious foods that contain minimal sugar but are high in antioxidants and vitamins. There are a variety of recipes in this section that could accomplish that for you. My breakfast items are good for your belly and won't end up on your waistline.

KF Denotes that recipe can be made or is keto-friendly.

Almond Butter Cereal 34

Avocado Cheese Breakfast Soufflé 36

Banana and Egg Pancakes 45

Banana Coconut Pancakes with Lavender Sprinkles 38

Barbara's Nutty Bark 40

Cinnamon Craisin Breakfast Bread 42

Coconut Flour Pancakes 44

Country Hash Brown Mock Potatoes 46

Fig and Strawberry Jam 48

French Toast 41

Green Chile and Egg Casserole 49

Homemade Breakfast Sausage 50

Maple Candied Bacon 51

Pumpkin Smoothie 37

Waffles 52

almond butter cereal

makes 1–2 servings

⅓ cup almond or coconut milk, unsweetened

3 tablespoons almond butter

2 tablespoons raw flax seeds

3 tablespoons raw pecans, chopped; may use another nut

3 tablespoons raw walnuts, chopped; may use another nut

2 tablespoons raw sunflower seeds

KF *Who doesn't like breakfast, especially if you have something wholesome and nutty? This will put a smile on your face for breakfast that will carry you throughout the day.*

Add your choice of almond or coconut milk with the almond butter in a bowl or cup and blend with a fork or spoon. Add flax seeds, chopped pecans, chopped walnuts, and sunflower seeds and mix.

Heat in a microwave for about 30 seconds or until warm.

Serve with fresh berries of your choice.

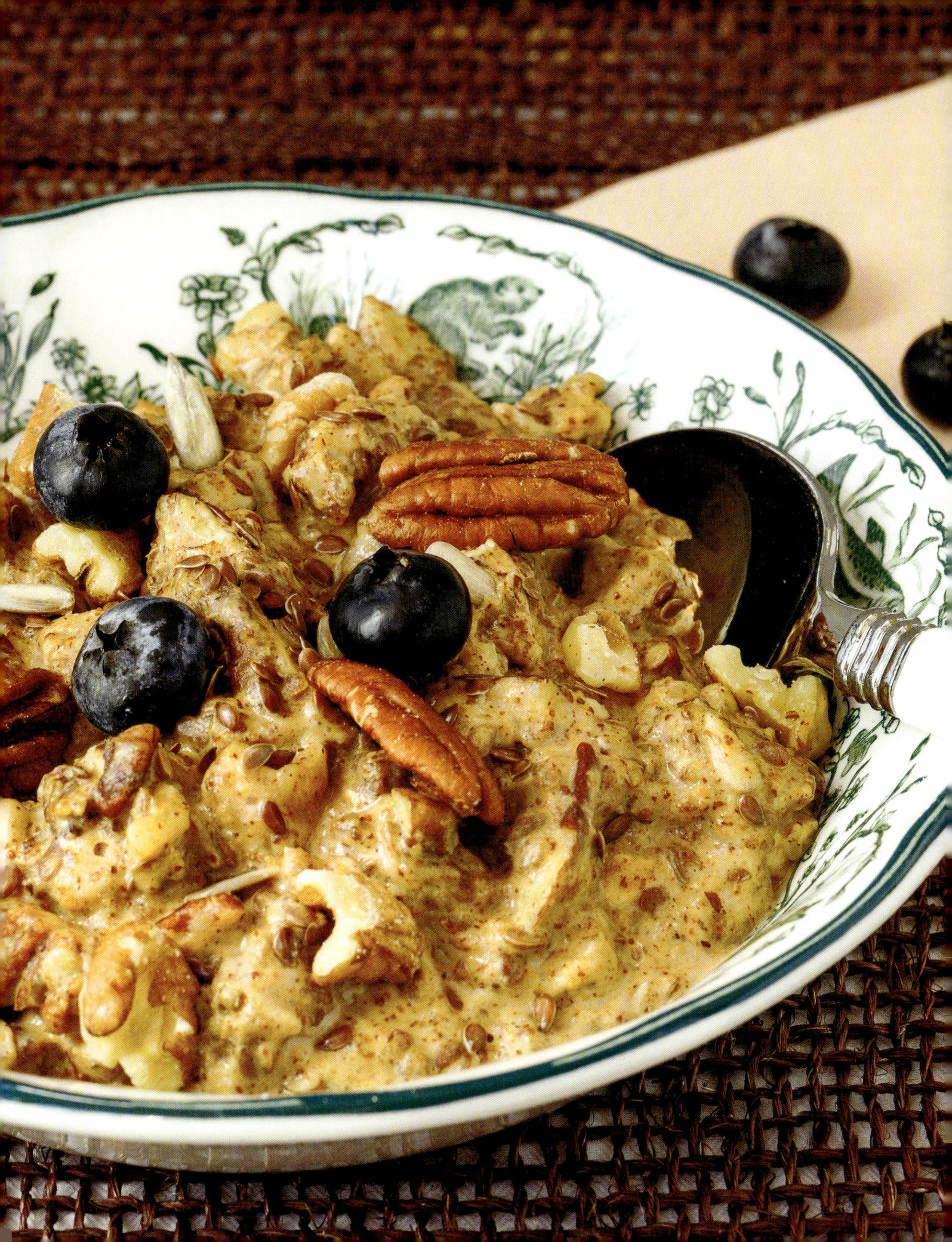

avocado cheese breakfast soufflé

serves 1–2

KF *Here's a yummy keto-friendly breakfast soufflé that you can serve to family or eat by yourself. It also stores very well for up to 3 days in the refrigerator.*

- 3 egg whites, with 3 egg yolks, separated
- ½ cup Gruyère cheese; may use your cheese of choice
- ½ avocado, diced
- 2 tablespoons pickled jalapeño juice (optional)
- Sea salt and pepper to taste
- 3 tablespoons crème fraiche; may use sour cream
- Cooking spray

Preheat oven to 425°F (218°C).

Separate the egg whites and the egg yolks into two separate bowls.

Beat the egg yolks until blended, then add the crème fraiche. Blend until mixed, set aside.

Dice the avocado and add a pinch of salt and set aside in a bowl.

If using, add the two tablespoons of the jalapeño juice to the avocado.

Now add the Gruyère cheese and avocado to the egg yolks and crème fraiche. Stir to combine.

Beat egg whites until soft peaks appear, then fold into the egg yolks being careful not to over-fold.

Add salt and pepper to taste.

Place ingredients into a small, 6-inch oven-proof skillet and bake for 10–12 minutes.

It looks beautiful and appetizing and tastes even better, so I recommend sharing this dish.

pumpkin smoothie

What better way to say "I love you" than with a pumpkin smoothie! This one even includes hemp seeds. Did you know that hemp seeds are one of nature's super foods? They have the most concentrated balance of proteins, essential fats, vitamins, and enzymes, combined with a relative absence of sugar, starches, and saturated fats.

Add all ingredients to a blender. Start to blend on low speed, gradually increasing as you watch for desired thickness.

Add ice to thicken if you'd like.

serves one

½ frozen banana, peeled (if not frozen, add 3 ice cubes)

½ cup almond or coconut milk, unsweetened

2–3 tablespoons canned pumpkin

½ teaspoon vanilla extract

1 teaspoon honey

1 teaspoon hemp seeds

½ teaspoon ground cinnamon

½ teaspoon ground cloves

¼ teaspoon ground nutmeg

tip: Be sure and peel the banana before you freeze it. You'll just find it so much easier.

37 breakfast

banana coconut pancakes with lavender sprinkles

serves 3–4

2 overripe bananas

6 eggs

6 tablespoons almond or coconut milk, unsweetened

Splash of vanilla extract

½ teaspoon sea salt

1 teaspoon baking powder

6 tablespoons coconut flour

¼ cup coconut oil, melted

1 tablespoon lavender (organic edible lavender flower can be found in the baking section of most grocery stores or online)

2 tablespoons maple syrup or honey (optional)

Here's is a fun way to get the flavor of lavender in your pancakes with this delightful recipe. Yummy!

Add all ingredients except for coconut oil, lavender, and syrup together in a high-speed blender and mix until well combined. Let the batter stand about 5 minutes to allow the coconut flour to absorb everything.

Mix one more time.

Brush or coat a skillet with coconut oil and place over medium heat.

Cook pancakes in the skillet. Flip when you notice little bubbles starting to pop up in the batter. Don't be tempted to turn up the temperature—you'll just end up burning them! Slow and low heat is better for coconut flour.

Finish cooking on the other side, about 3 minutes, until the pancakes are fluffy and set.

Brush more coconut oil to your pan after each pancake is done.

Serve with maple syrup and garnish with lavender sprinkles.

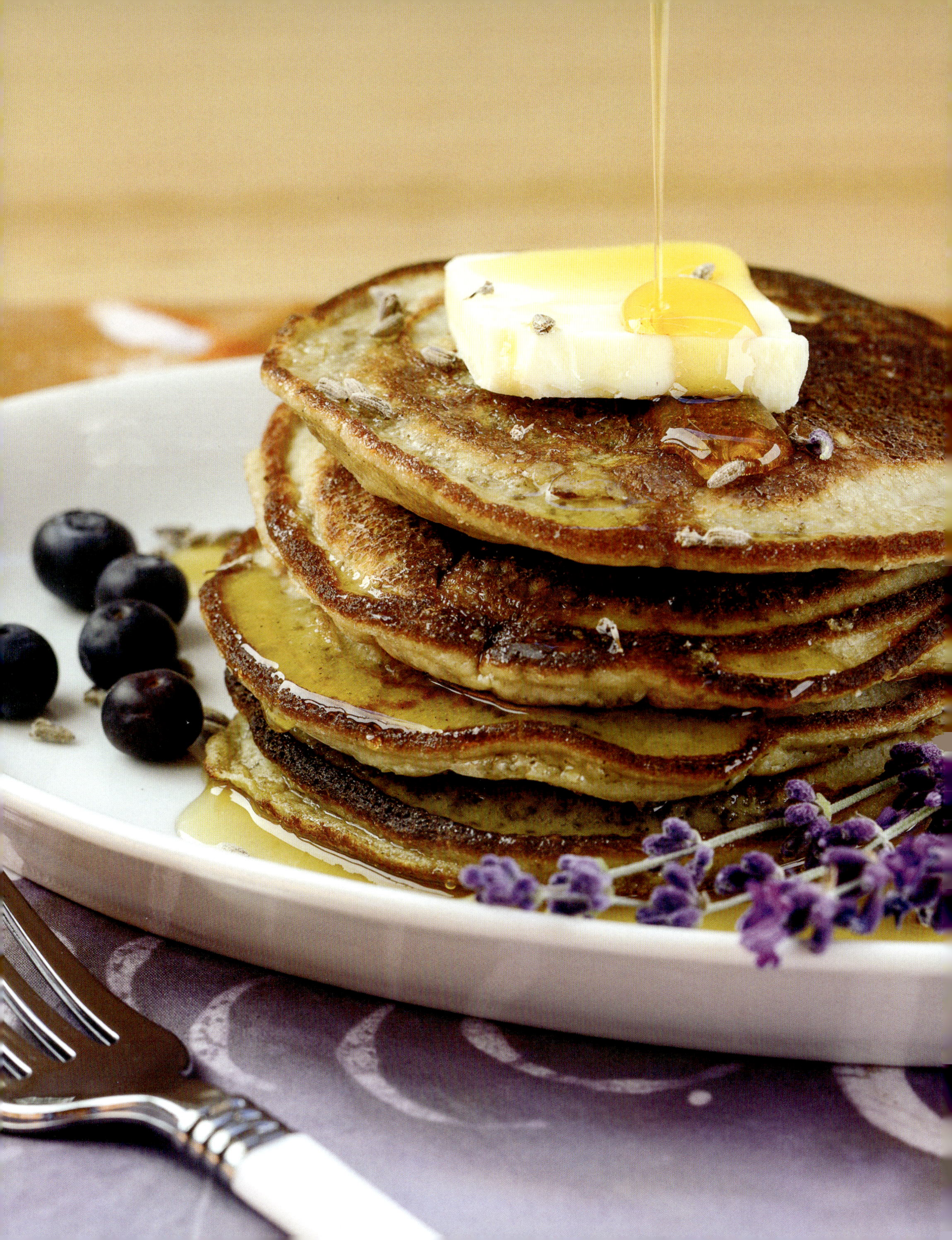

barbara's nutty bark

18–20 servings

At the beginning, the most difficult part of eliminating grains for me was in the morning. I absolutely adore cereal, and of course, it's not allowed, except you can make homemade granola—such a great substitute! Whenever you buy it in the stores, they still add too much sugar. I know there's a keto cereal out now, but I haven't tried it yet. Many of us are hooked on having some form of bread, especially in the morning. I switched to scrambled eggs and omelets because I missed having my bread sopped up in the fried eggs. Oh, the sacrifices we have to make. Now I don't miss it at all.

- 2 cups coconut flakes, unsweetened
- 2 cups sliced almonds or mixed nuts of your choice, such as pecans, walnuts, and macadamia nuts
- 1 cup shelled raw pumpkin seeds
- ½ cup sesame seeds
- 2 tablespoons chia seeds (optional)
- ½ teaspoon kosher salt
- ½ teaspoon ground cinnamon
- ⅛ teaspoon ground cardamom
- ½ cup honey
- 2 tablespoons olive oil or coconut oil
- 1 teaspoon vanilla extract

Preheat oven to 300°F (149°C).

Toss coconut flakes with nuts, seeds, salt, cinnamon, and cardamom in a large bowl.

In a small saucepan, cook honey, coconut or olive oil over medium heat, stirring occasionally until hot, about a minute. Pour over nut mixture and stir to combine.

Spread mixture evenly on a parchment-lined baking sheet. Place in oven.

Bake for 12 minutes and stir with wooden spoon. Bake for 13–15 more minutes until golden brown and crisp.

Once cooled, use a pizza slicer or knife to make into squares or bars.

Store in a tightly covered container at room temperature.

french toast

What a tasty and delicious way to enjoy French toast, especially if you made it with my grain-free bread.

Cut the bread into ½-inch thick slices. My loaf will yield 6 slices, including the ends.

In a medium-sized mixing bowl, add the two eggs and beat lightly. Add cinnamon, pinch of sea salt, coconut milk, and vanilla. Mix well until completely blended.

Dip each of the slices into the mixture and let them soak for 3–5 minutes, longer if possible, turning the slices every minute or so. It may be easier to do two slices at a time.

Preheat your skillet over medium to medium-low flame and grease with the butter. Using a slotted spatula, remove soaked slices of bread and place into skillet, one or two at a time. Cook on each side for 3–4 minutes until browned.

Remove from skillet and plate. Add butter and maple syrup to taste, along with your favorite berry or other fruit.

serves 2–3

Loaf of Barb's Sandwich Bread, recipe on page 273

2 eggs

½ tablespoon cinnamon

Pinch sea salt

4 tablespoons coconut or almond milk, unsweetened

1–2 tablespoons butter

½ teaspoon vanilla

Pure maple syrup to taste

tip: Store any leftovers wrapped in plastic wrap or in a sealed container in the fridge for up to 5 days.

cinnamon craisin breakfast bread

serves 8–10

- 7 large eggs
- ¾ cup almond milk, unsweetened
- 4 teaspoons apple cider vinegar
- 2 ½ cups whole cashews, about 17.5 ounces
- 6 tablespoons coconut flour
- 1 ½ tablespoons baking soda
- ½ tablespoon sea salt
- 3 tablespoons cinnamon or more if desired
- 1 tablespoon erythritol
- 1 teaspoon water
- ¾ cup craisins or more if desired, eliminate if doing keto
- Cooking spray for greasing

tip: Heat in the microwave when ready to eat along with some butter! Yummy.

KF OPTIONAL *You can give up the sugar bomb from those frosted cinnamon rolls for this nice breakfast bread with cinnamon, cranberry raisins, and no wheat or refined sugar. Make this keto-friendly by taking out the craisins.*

Preheat oven to 325°F (163°C).

Place a heatproof dish filled with 2 inches of water on the bottom rack of an oven.

Lightly grease the inside of a large loaf pan 12 x 4.5 inches with cooking spray.

Place a piece of parchment paper into the bottom with flaps that hang over the sides of the pan.

Place all of the ingredients, except the craisins, cinnamon, and erythritol, into a high-speed blender and process on low for 15 seconds. Scrape down the sides and process again on high for 1–30 seconds until very smooth. If the batter is too thick to blend, gradually add up to 2 tablespoons of water until it moves easily through the blender. Let it sit in blender for 30 minutes to allow to thicken.

Add cinnamon and erythritol with 1 teaspoon of water to a small bowl and stir well to a paste consistency and set aside.

Transfer some of the batter to cover the bottom of the loaf pan.

Add ⅓ of the cinnamon paste together with about ⅓ of the craisins, layering as you incorporate the paste and craisins.

Layer with a bit more of the batter. Layer another third of the craisins and cinnamon paste with batter. Layer the remaining third of the cinnamon paste and craisins until all are in the loaf pan.

Bake for 55 minutes or until a toothpick inserted in the center returns clean.

Allow the bread to cool in the pan for 30 minutes, then gently remove the loaf, using the parchment overhangs, and allow to cool on a wire rack before serving or slicing.

Store the loaf tightly wrapped in foil or food wrap in the refrigerator for up to 5 days. Freezing also works well.

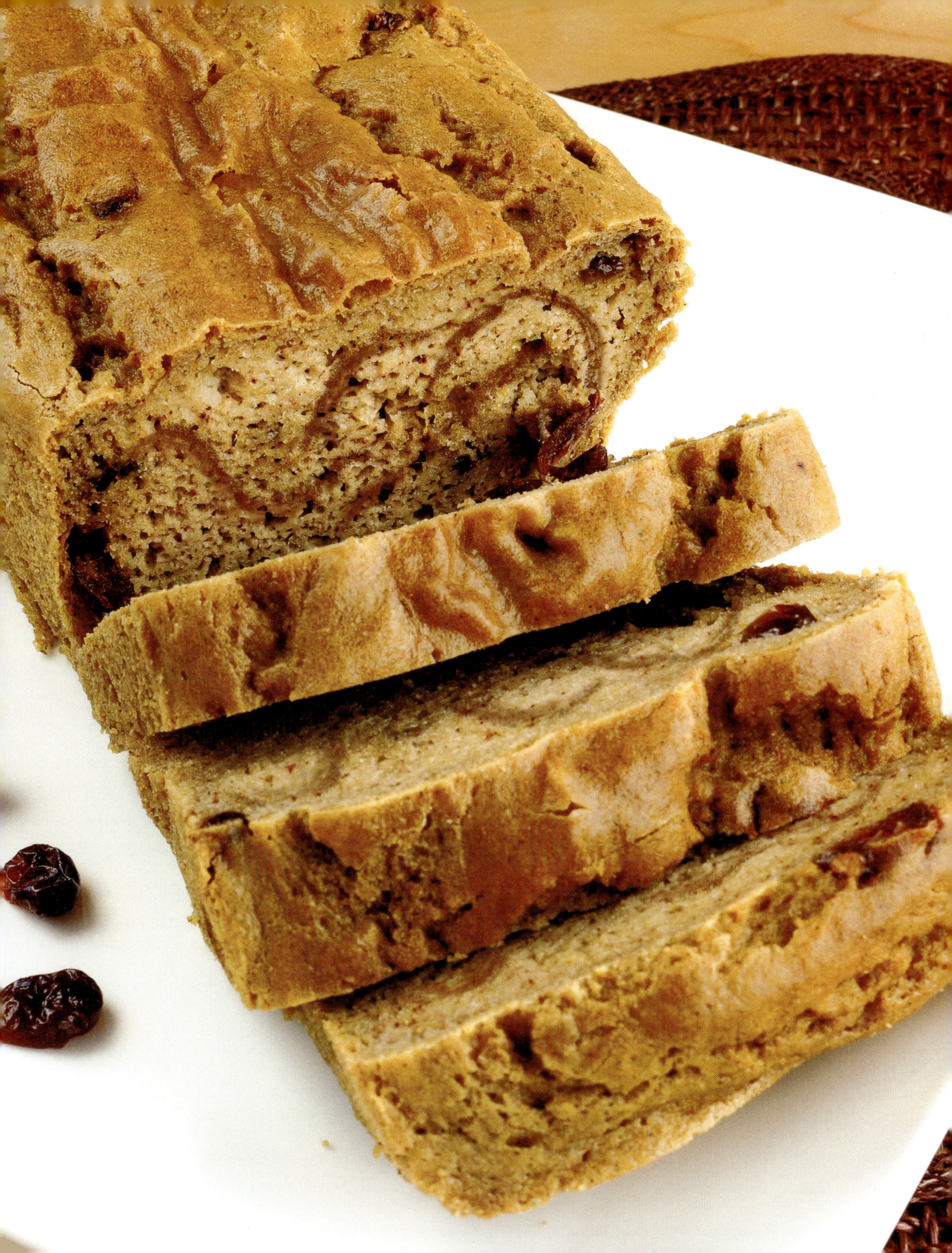

coconut flour pancakes

serves 4–6

6 eggs

6 tablespoons almond or coconut milk, unsweetened

Splash vanilla extract

2 tablespoons maple syrup or honey (optional)

½ teaspoon sea salt

1 teaspoon baking powder

6 tablespoons coconut flour

¼ cup coconut oil, melted

Coconut flakes, unsweetened

Fluffy, indulgent pancakes that are sure to satisfy your sweet tooth and keep you healthy.

Mix all of the ingredients, except the coconut oil, in a medium mixing bowl to combine well. It is easier adding the oil after everything else is combined to get the right texture. I highly recommend using a high-speed blender if you have one.

Let the batter stand about 5 minutes to allow the coconut flour to absorb everything.

Mix one more time.

Over a medium-low flame, place a cast-iron griddle or a skillet brushed with just a little more coconut oil.

Cook the pancakes until you notice bubbles beginning to pop up. They take a little longer than regular flour pancakes do, but don't be tempted to turn up the temperature—you'll just end up burning them! Slow and low heat is better for coconut flour.

Once you see the bubbles, flip the pancake to cook the other side.

Finish cooking when the pancakes are fluffy and set.

Serve with your favorite berries, butter, or garnish with coconut flakes.

banana and egg pancakes

This is a quick, easy on-the-go breakfast recipe for those busy days when you need a quick dose of protein and potassium. My friend, Barbara Kastner, shared a version of this, and I made it my own here. So delicious!

Put all ingredients (except the coconut oil for greasing and the butter) in a blender and mix until smooth. It's okay if it's a little lumpy.

Grease your frying pan with coconut oil or cooking spray. Make sure the frying pan is on medium heat and is hot. Make a 4-inch round pancake in the pan.

Wait about 3 minutes and flip over. These do not bubble-up like regular pancakes, so you really need to cook by the time indicated. Cook for about another minute. Take out and place on a dish. This should make about 2–3 pancakes!

Serve with butter or maple syrup!

serves 1–2

1 banana

2 eggs

4 tablespoons arrowroot flour or almond flour

Pinch sea salt

Coconut oil or cooking spray for greasing

4 tablespoons butter

Maple syrup (optional)

tip: You may have to play with this a few times as they cook differently. The texture should be firm, but not hard. Keep your pancakes about 4-inches in diameter because if they are too big, they may become flimsy and break when you slide your spatula underneath to flip.

country hash brown mock potatoes

serves 2–3

1 head cauliflower or a package of already-riced cauliflower

1 egg

½ cup Parmesan cheese, shredded

½ cup onion, diced

½ cup green bell pepper, diced

2 tablespoons almond flour

Pinch lemon pepper

Pinch garlic salt

Sea salt and pepper to taste

Olive oil for cooking

KF *I think potato farmers may start to complain that these hash browns are so good that people may stop buying potatoes. Just kidding, but you will like this dish.*

In a small sauté pan, grease with olive oil and sauté the onions and bell pepper, seasoning them with lemon pepper and garlic salt, until done to your liking; set aside.

Cook the riced cauliflower as directed on the package. If you are working with a head of cauliflower, then follow these directions. Peel green leaves off the head and chop cauliflower into small pieces, resembling the size of rice. You will find it easier to use a blender. Rice the cauliflower as best you can. Place in a microwaveable bowl, cover with a paper towel and microwave for 5 ½ minutes. When done, let it cool before the next step.

Place riced cauliflower into a tea towel or a large paper towel and squeeze out as much water as possible. Keep squeezing until hardly any water comes out.

Place in a bowl and add the cheese, egg, salt, almond flour, and pepper and mix well.

Add the onion and bell pepper mixture to the cauliflower mixture. Combine well.

Grease a sauté pan with olive oil and place the mixture into the pan, forming a 2 x 3-inch rectangle. The smaller the rectangle, the less likely the rectangle will break.

Brown for 3–4 minutes on one side and then turn over and brown for another 3–4 minutes.

Serve with eggs and my Homemade Breakfast Sausage, recipe on page 50, or just by itself!

tip: These hash browns are very delicate and tend to want to separate. It's okay; the taste will make up for it.

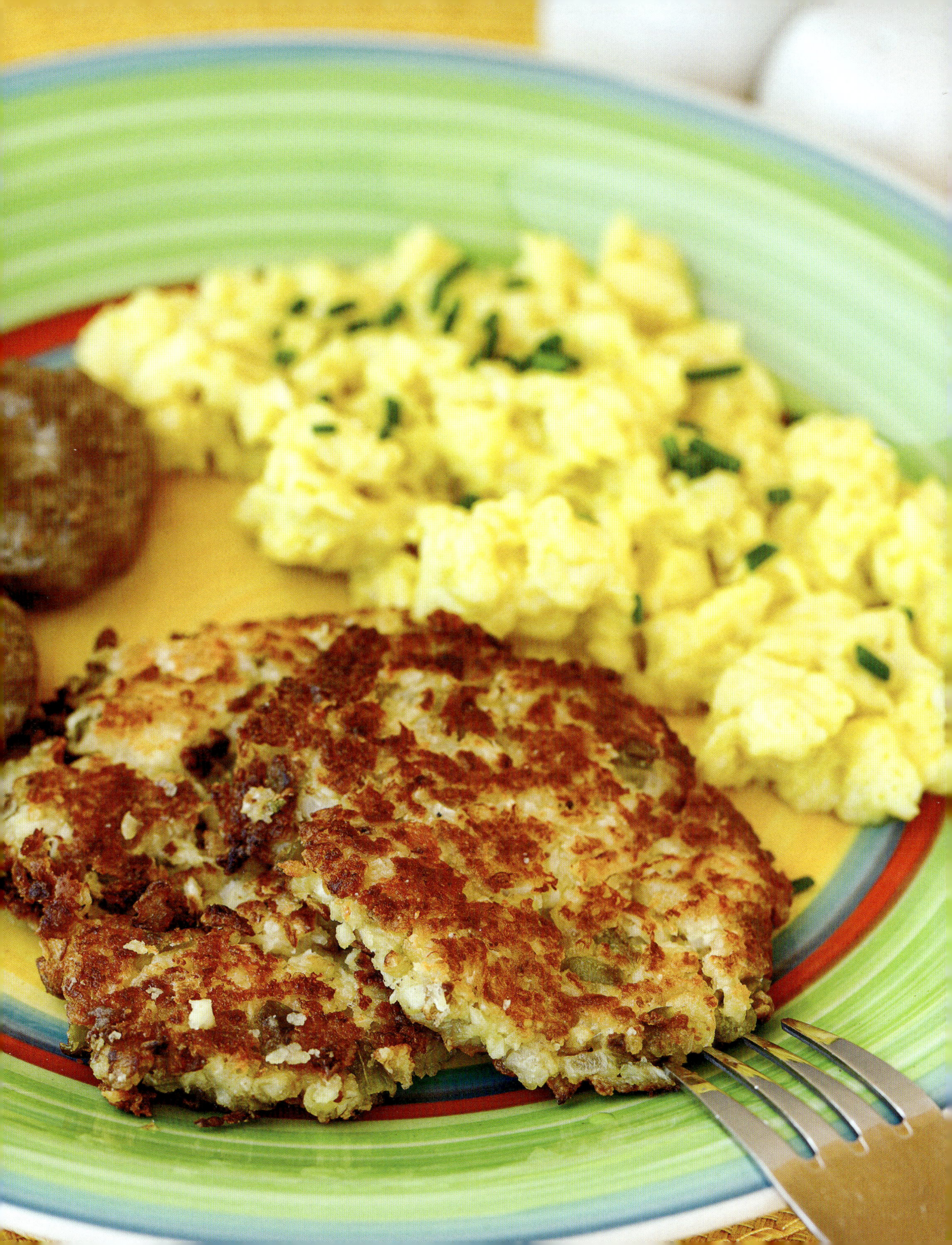

fig and strawberry jam

Here's a healthy alternative to other jams and spreads without all the sugar that the processed ones tend to have.

- 12 black mission figs, stems removed
- 1 cup strawberries, stems removed
- Juice of 1 lemon
- 1 teaspoon lemon zest
- ¼ cup raw honey

tip: Store your jam in the refrigerator. It should last a week or maybe two.

Add your figs, strawberries, lemon juice, and lemon zest to a blender or food processor and process until the mixture is well combined.

Add your fruit mixture to a saucepan and add in your honey. Bring the mixture to a boil, stirring occasionally. Once it has reduced, lower the heat and allow your mixture to simmer for 20 minutes or so. Turn off the heat and allow the jam to come to room temperature before storing in an airtight container.

green chile and egg casserole

KF *I remember when my friend, Rosie Barnes, brought over a similar recipe that had eggs, some veggies, and cheese, but there was white flour in it, so I decided to change it over to making it grain free. You can make a big batch the night before, which is what I do, and then in the morning, it's ready to eat after reheating. All I need to do is fry up some bacon or whatever side I'm serving, and breakfast is ready! I know you'll get a kick out of this dish, and it can be served for lunch too—or even dinner.*

Preheat oven to 400°F (204°C).

Sauté the meat first (until almost done) crumble, let cool, then add to the ingredients before baking. If using bacon, cook crispy.

Grease a 6 x 10-inch pan with the ½ cup melted butter.

Mix cottage cheese, Jack cheese, green chiles, eggs, baking powder, salt, crumbled meat of choice, and coconut flour together in a bowl.

Then pour mixture into the greased 6 x 10-inch pan.

Bake in the preheated oven for 15 minutes, then reduce heat to 350°F (177°C) and bake until middle of casserole is set, about 50 more minutes.

Allow to stand for 10 minutes before serving.

makes 8–10 servings

- ½ cup butter
- 2 cups cottage cheese
- 1 pound Monterey Jack cheese, shredded
- 2 4-ounce cans diced green chiles
- 1 teaspoon baking powder
- 10 eggs
- ¼ cup coconut flour
- ½ teaspoon sea salt
- ¾ cup either bacon, grass-fed ground beef, turkey, or Italian sausage (optional)

tips: This dish freezes exceptionally well.

Unprocessed ground Italian sausage (without the casing), ham, and turkey can be found at Sprouts and Whole Foods Market.

homemade breakfast sausage

serves 4–6

1 pound ground pork

1 teaspoon sage, crushed

¾ teaspoon sea salt

¾ teaspoon pepper

½ teaspoon dried thyme, crushed

½ teaspoon garlic powder

½ teaspoon onion powder

KF *Bacon is the most common food served with breakfast, but a great homemade sausage takes the cake. I love banger sausage from England but I only have that if I'm in the United Kingdom, which is not often, to say the least. Breakfast sausage is always a family treat. This is a healthy and clean recipe that will make your breakfast more complete.*

In a large bowl, combine the crushed sage, sea salt, pepper, crushed thyme, garlic powder, and onion powder. Add ground pork and mix well.

Create your patties by shaping six 3½-inch diameter patties.

Heat a large skillet over medium-high heat.

Add patties and cook 8 minutes or until done (at 160°F / 71°C in center), turning once.

maple candied bacon

Bacon! For those who just love that sweet and salty taste of bacon and maple syrup, you will be screaming in joyous ecstasy with this wonderful combination.

serves 6–8

¾-pound thick-cut smoked bacon, uncured (16 slices)

½ cup maple syrup

1 teaspoon Dijon mustard

Freshly ground pepper

Preheat oven to 400°F (204°C).

Mix the mustard, pepper, and maple syrup.

Place a baking rack on an aluminum-foil-lined baking sheet and arrange the bacon in a single layer on the baking rack without overlapping.

Brush the maple syrup mixture on the bacon generously.

Bake for 15–20 minutes or until the bacon begins to brown.

Remove the pan carefully from the oven as there will be hot grease on the baking sheet.

Carefully lift and place the baking rack to one side, discarding the excess bacon grease and removing the aluminum foil as well.

Replace the baking rack onto the freshly aluminum-lined baking sheet, turn the bacon over, and brush the bacon slices with the remaining maple syrup mix.

Bake for another 3–5 minutes, until the bacon is a warm golden brown.

Transfer the bacon to a plate and serve warm.

tips: Sometimes the bacon flares up due to the fat content. After turning the bacon over, make sure to keep an eye out for any flare ups. This is why I toss the grease after cooking the bacon the first time. Never leave your oven unattended. If the bacon grease ignites, throw baking soda or coconut flour on the flare up and start all over again.

breakfast

waffles

KF OPTIONAL *I almost never have waffles, and it's not because I don't love them but because of what they do to my body and stomach! We love to entertain, and every once in a while, we take our guests to a wonderful breakfast place at the lake. The restaurant is called The Waffle House, and I sit there and order my healthy food while they have the real deal! It's difficult watching them eat those golden waffles, but it's easier now that I decided to make a grain-free waffle, and this is a close second to the real thing. I hope you enjoy it. To make Keto-friendly, use 3-4 teaspoons erythritol syrup in place of honey or maple syrup (recipe on page 15) in your batter. Also, top with my maple syrup substitute, recipe below.*

serves 4

- 3 large eggs at room temperature
- ½ cup coconut milk, unsweetened
- 2–3 teaspoons honey or maple syrup (To make keto-friendly, use erythritol syrup, recipe on page 15.)
- 3 tablespoons coconut oil, melted
- ½ teaspoon pure vanilla extract
- 1 cup raw cashews
- 3 tablespoons coconut flour
- ¾ tablespoon baking soda
- ¼ teaspoon sea salt
- Cooking spray
- 1 teaspoon maple extract (optional, especially if replacing maple syrup)

Maple Syrup Substitute

- 2 tablespoons butter, melted
- ½ teaspoon maple extract
- 1 teaspoon erythritol or Swerve

Preheat your waffle iron.

Place eggs, coconut milk, honey or maple syrup (or replacement sweetener), coconut oil, vanilla extract, cashews, coconut flour, baking soda, and salt in a high-speed blender.

Blend on low, then increase to high, making sure the batter is completely smooth, about another 30 seconds or so.

Grease waffle iron with cooking spray on lid and bottom.

Spoon the batter into the waffle iron, filling halfway.

Close the lid and cook for 45 seconds to a minute until the steam stops rising from the machine and the waffles easily release with a fork.

Some waffle irons will give you a green light signaling that the waffles are done.

Serve immediately.

maple syrup substitute

Blend all ingredients in a small bowl until well combined. Top your waffles and enjoy!

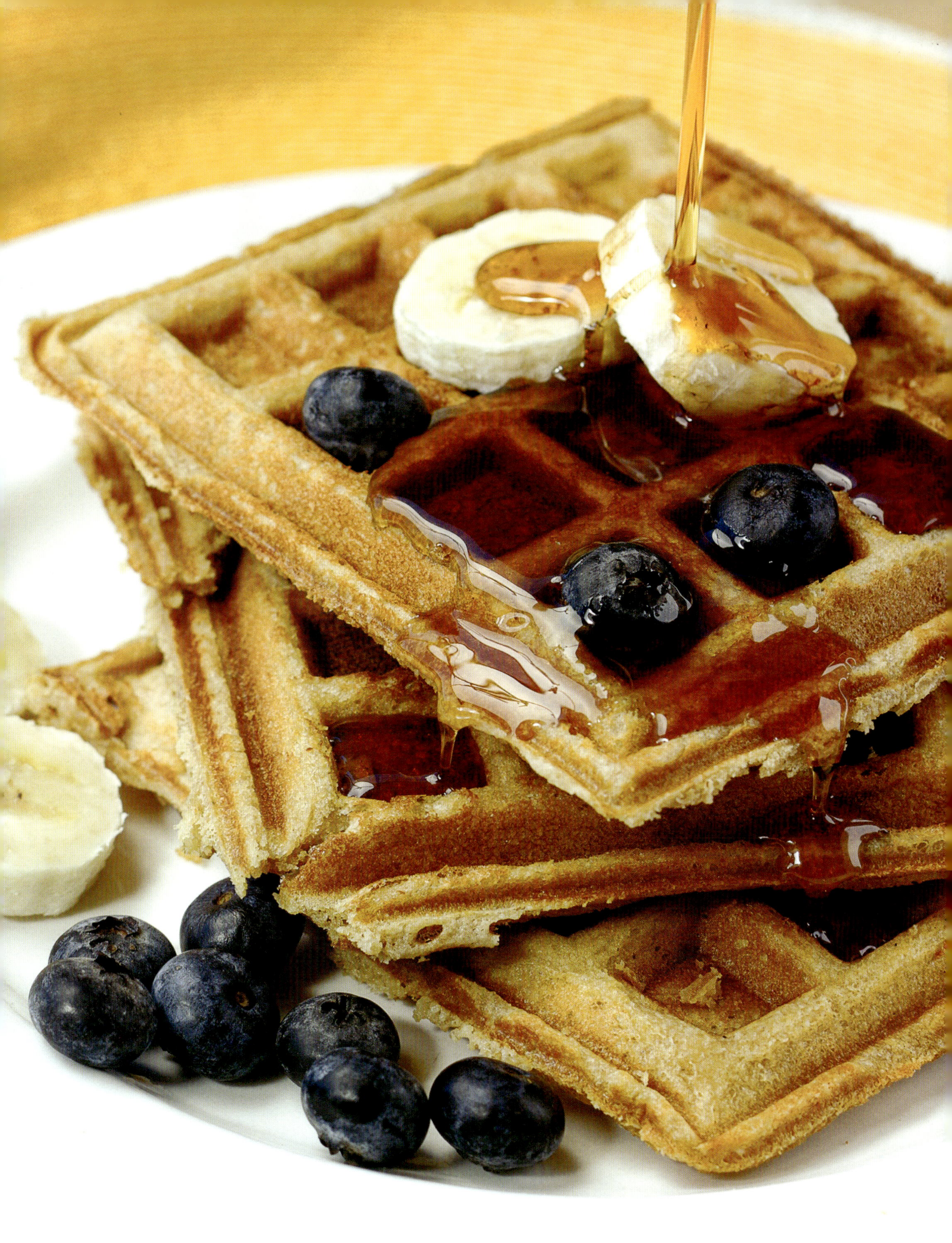

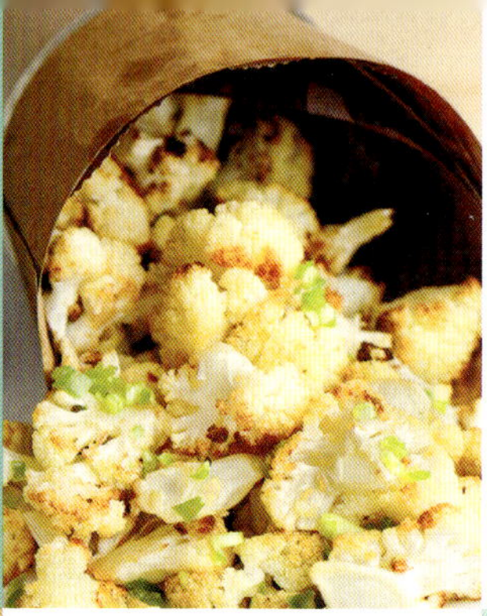
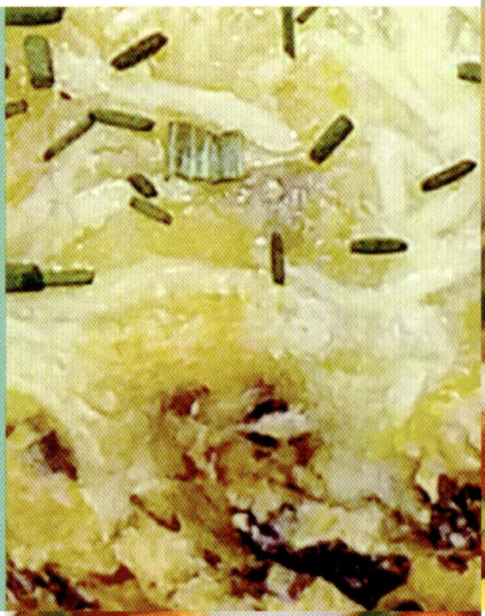
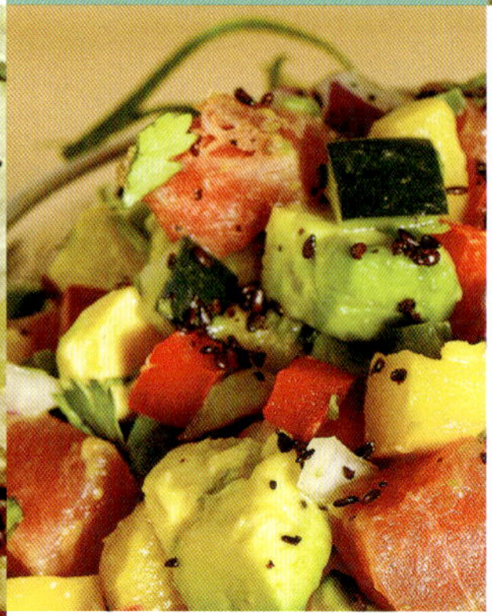
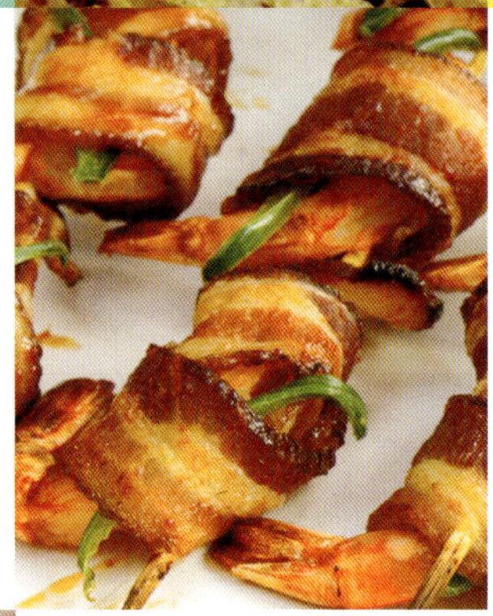
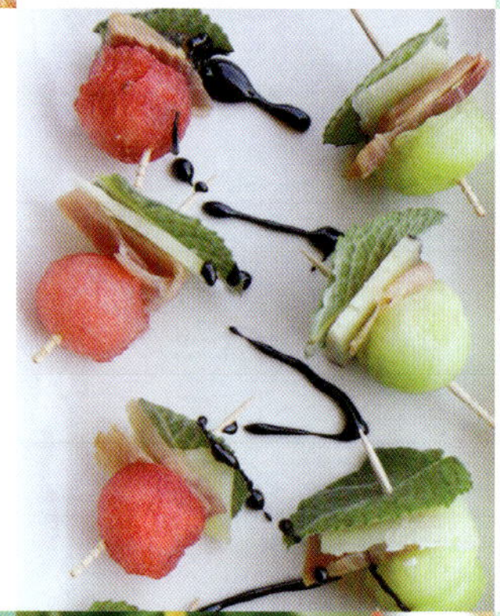
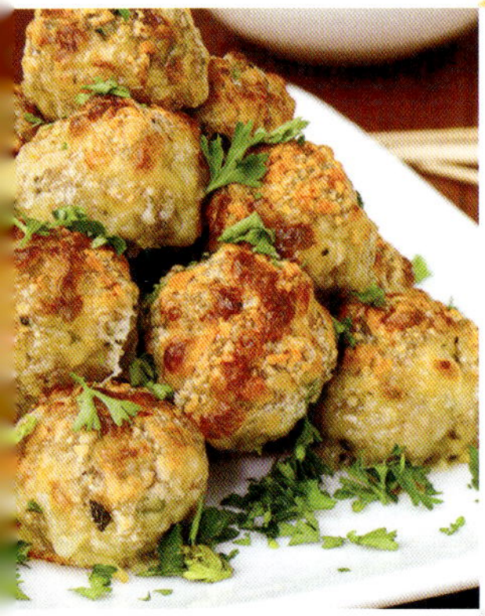
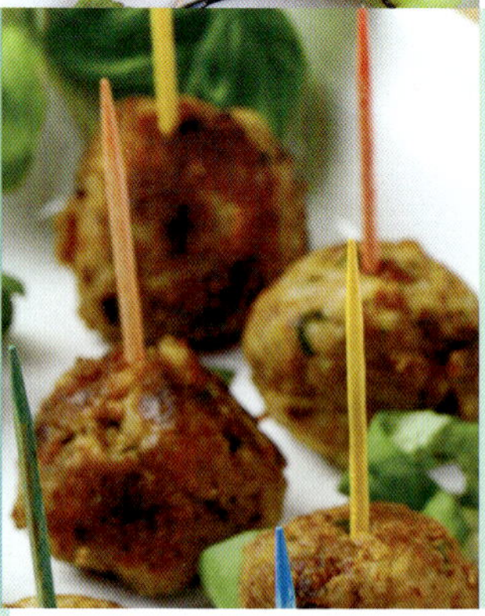
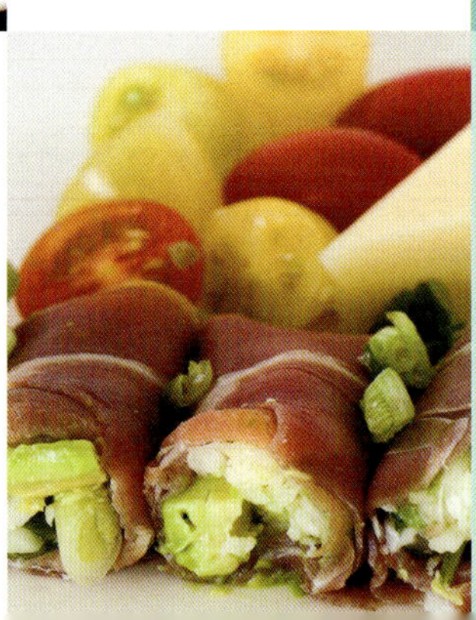

appetizers + beverages

Appetizers are so much fun to experiment with when you are entertaining or just treating yourself to something yummy before dinner, lunch, or a special occasion. It has been a joy trying many flavors while developing these recipes. I know we're focused on being grain free, but I also want every recipe to be delicious! The start of a great time with family and friends begins with opening up the conversation with refreshments and small bites. I have included many favorite recipes that I found while sampling foods at places I visited in my travels.

The intent with these recipes is to expand your experience and have you try something you may not have obtained before, in taste or in preparation. Most appetizers are simple and easy to make. Starting out with something hassle-free is the best way to enjoy spending time and creating in the kitchen.

KF Denotes that recipe can be made or is keto-friendly.

Ahi Poke Twist 56
Avocado, Mango, and Shrimp Cocktail 58
Bacon Cheddar Chips 59
Bacon-wrapped Artichoke Hearts 60
Bacon-wrapped Brussels Sprouts 61
Bacon-wrapped Pears 64
Baked Parmesan Zucchini Chips 65
BBQ Bacon-wrapped Meatballs 62
Bruschetta with French Bread 66
Caprese Meatballs 68
Cauliflower Popcorn 70
Chicken Meatballs 71
Crustless Mini-Quiche 82
Excellent Artichoke Dip 72
Maple Bacon Shrimp 76
Melon, Manchego, and Prosciutto di Parma Skewers 74
Mock Tortilla Chips 77
Prosciutto Rollups 75
Roasted Candied Nuts 79
Sautéed Sweet Peppers with Toasted Garlic and Capers 78
Season Jicama, Pineapple, and Watermelon 81
Spicy Lime Chicken Wings 80
Spicy Sriracha Chicken Wings 85
Spicy Turkey Patty with Mango Salsa 84
Thin Lizzy Cosmo 87
Guiltless Margarita 87
Sugarless Train Wreck Mojito 87

ahi poke twist

serves 2–4

1 pound ahi tuna

1 pineapple
(or ½ a cucumber if doing keto)

1 avocado

½ cup coconut nectar (liquid aminos)

1 tablespoon black sesame seeds

1 tablespoon chives, finely chopped

2 tablespoons red onion, finely chopped

2 shishito peppers (optional)

KF OPTIONAL *This twist on poke offers a fresh combination of pineapple and avocado that will surely please the palate. To make keto-friendly, you can replace the pineapple with ½ cucumber, peeled and diced.*

Wash and clean the pineapple.

Cut the top and bottom. Cut the outer skin of the pineapple and discard. Slice the pineapple into ½-inch thick slices and cut out the centers. Cut the slices into cubes and set aside in a small bowl.

Cut up the ahi tuna into ½-inch cubes. Set it aside in a separate bowl.

Take your avocado and cut from top, going against the pit around the bottom and back to top on opposite side. Separate into two halves and discard the pit.

With a tablespoon, take out the halves from the shells in one piece each. Place face down on cutting board and cube each into ¼- to ½-inch cubes and set that aside.

Boil ½ cup of coconut nectar over low heat for 10–15 minutes to reduce it. Pour into cup or bowl and place in freezer to chill and thicken for 10–15 minutes.

Chop the chives fine and set aside. Now, take out the coconut nectar reduction from freezer.

In a medium mixing bowl, add the cut-up ingredients. Drizzle the coconut nectar reduction over ingredients and add the black sesame seeds. Mix lightly with a wooden spoon so you maintain your cubes and get a nice consistent coverage of the reduction and the sesame seeds.

Serve in a small bowl, sprinkle with chopped chives, and enjoy with toasted grain-free tortilla chips.

tip: If you like it spicy, get 2 shishito peppers, cut the stems and slice them lengthwise. With the tip of a butter knife, scrape out the seeds and discard them. Slice cleaned peppers and chop them fine. Mix into your poke instead of the chives and use the chives as garnish.

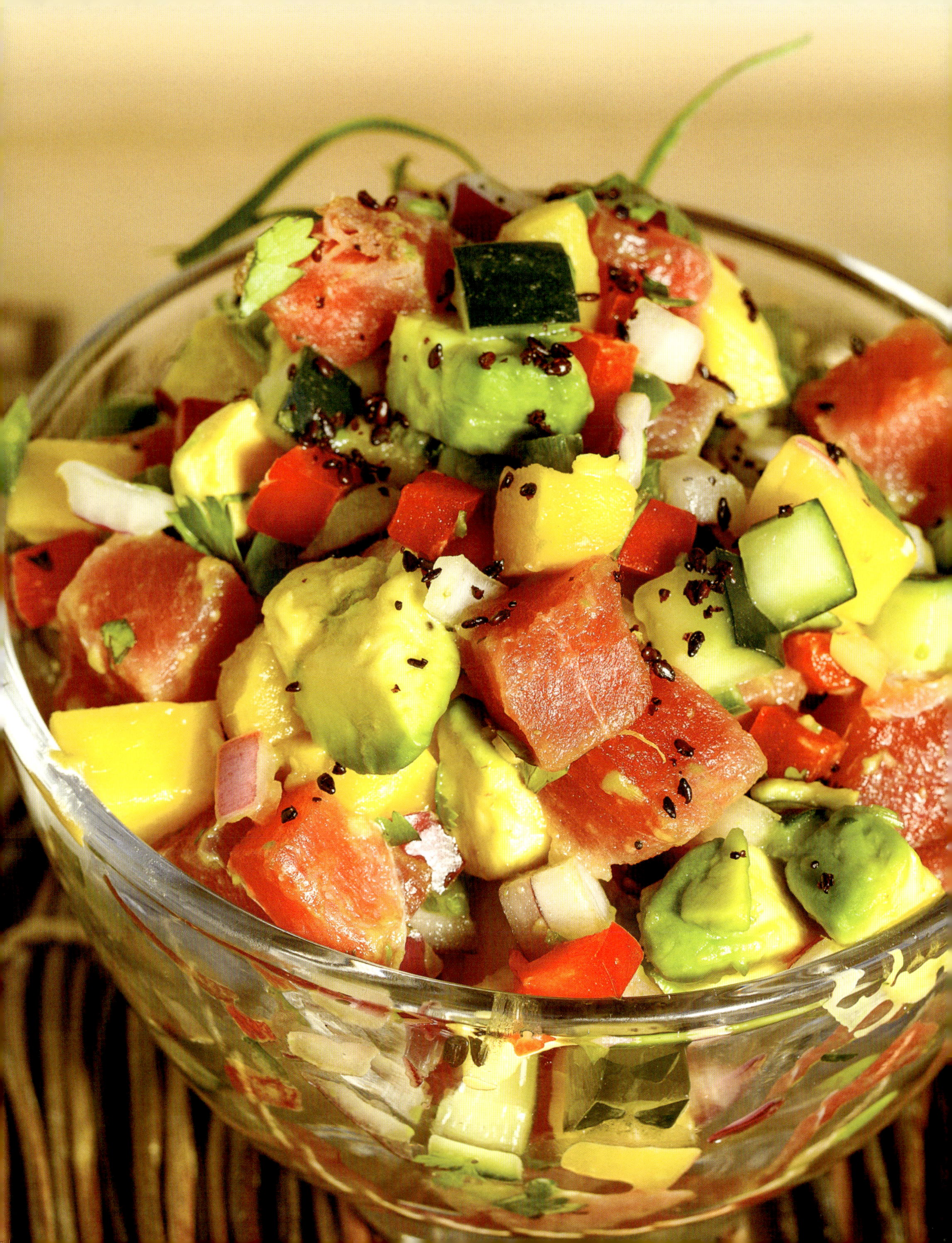

avocado, mango, and shrimp cocktail

serves 1–2

KF OPTIONAL *This is so versatile. It can be served as an appetizer, a salad, or a light, late-night meal, especially during a holiday weekend! If doing keto, just eliminate the mango.*

- 1 mango, pitted and diced (eliminate if doing keto)
- 8–10 shrimp, deveined and peeled or bought in the market already cooked
- ½ cup red bell pepper, corded and diced
- ¼–½ cup jalapeño, seeded and finely chopped
- ½ cup red onion, diced
- ½ cup bunch fresh cilantro, finely chopped
- 1 teaspoon sea salt
- 1 tablespoon lime juice
- ½ cup cucumber, diced
- 1 small avocado, cubed

You may buy shrimp already cooked or cook it yourself by putting it in boiling water and taking it out when they start to turn pink and orange, about 2–3 minutes.

Chop the shrimp into chunks however you like, leaving two shrimp for each serving to put as garnish.

Mix diced mango, diced red bell pepper, finely chopped jalapeño, diced red onion, finely chopped cilantro, sea salt (to taste), lime juice, diced cucumber, and cubed avocado together.

Serve in a martini or margarita glass, adding more salt or lime juice, if necessary.

Garnish by hanging shrimp on the edge of the cocktail glass.

appetizers + beverages

bacon cheddar chips

KF *Here we go with my favorite—bacon! These types of chips are a great way to entertain your family and friends.*

serves 18–20

6 strips bacon, uncured, cooked and crumbled

2 cups cheddar cheese, shredded

½ cup green onions, finely chopped

Sea salt and pepper to taste

Cooking spray

Preheat oven to 350°F (177°C).

Cook the bacon until crisp and place on a paper towel to soak up the grease. Let it sit awhile, about 10 minutes, then crumble.

Chop the green onions until very fine.

Mix the cheddar cheese with the crumbled bacon, green onions and add salt and pepper. Stir all ingredients together.

Take out a mini-muffin pan and grease with cooking spray.

Fill each with the mixture, pressing down so that all ingredients are firmly pressed and are about ¾ to the top of the muffin pan.

Bake for 8–10 minutes.

Let them cool in muffin pan for 5 minutes, then remove.

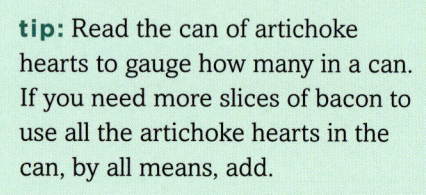

bacon-wrapped artichoke hearts

makes 12–16

KF *I just love my bacon! This bomb appetizer has a nice blend of flavors and is a sure hit when entertaining or just as a special dinner.*

Cooking spray

2 cans Vigo Baby Artichoke Hearts, drained

6–8 slices bacon, uncured, halved crosswise

½ cup Parmesan cheese, grated (I use ¾ of a cup)

Ground pepper

Preheat oven to 400°F (204°C).

Line a baking sheet with aluminum foil and spray with cooking spray.

Wrap each artichoke heart with a ½ slice of bacon along with Parmesan cheese. You may sprinkle it on the bacon as you roll it up. Try to add as much as possible because it certainly enhances the taste!

Secure with a toothpick.

Place on the baking sheet then sprinkle with the Parmesan and pepper.

Bake for 20–25 minutes until bacon is crispy.

Serve on a small tray and sprinkle more Parmesan to your liking.

tip: Read the can of artichoke hearts to gauge how many in a can. If you need more slices of bacon to use all the artichoke hearts in the can, by all means, add.

bacon-wrapped brussels sprouts

KF Here's a fun, delicious and nutritious appetizer to make for those fun afternoon get-togethers or special dinners.

makes approximately 20

2 pounds Brussels sprouts
1 pound bacon, uncured
1 cup Parmesan cheese, shredded
Sea salt and pepper to taste
3 tablespoons olive oil

Preheat oven to 375°F (191°C).

Trim off the ends of the Brussels sprouts. Make a slit in the brussels sprout ¾-inch through, doesn't matter if you cut through.

Add Parmesan cheese and close the Brussels sprout.

Take one piece of bacon and stretch on the cutting board.

Cut into three pieces…two if you want more bacon wrapped around.

Add a little bit of salt (optional) and add as much pepper as you like to the sprout and bacon.

Wrap the sprout with the piece of bacon and secure with a toothpick.

Line a baking pan with aluminum foil and drizzle some olive oil.

Add your bacon wrapped sprouts.

Bake for 30 minutes and serve.

tip: To get a crispy bacon wrap, try broiling for 2–3 minutes after baking. Do not leave unattended in the broiler. Watch for burning the oil with bacon grease if you try this step.

bbq bacon-wrapped meatballs

serves 8–10

KF OPTIONAL *For all the bacon lovers of the world, this recipe will create a unique appetizer that you'll enjoy sharing. The combination of crunchy bacon around a savory meatball will make you swoon for more. If you'd like to make this keto, eliminate the BBQ sauce.*

Cooking spray

1 pound ground beef

½ yellow onion, diced

¼ cup fresh parsley, chopped

¼ cup almond flour

1 egg

2 garlic cloves, minced

½ teaspoon dried oregano

1 teaspoon sea salt

½ teaspoon pepper

18 slices bacon, uncured

¼ cup sharp cheddar cheese, shredded

Pinch red pepper flakes for heat

¼ cup Apple BBQ Sauce found on page 159 (if doing keto, eliminate the BBQ sauce)

Preheat oven to 375°F (191°C).

In a medium-sized bowl, mix the ground beef, onion, parsley, almond flour, egg, garlic, oregano, salt, cheddar cheese, pepper, and red pepper flakes (if desired) until combined. Set aside.

Line a baking sheet with aluminum foil and grease with cooking spray, set aside.

Line two empty ice trays with bacon, overlapping each piece to cover the tray completely going across the tray, not lengthwise. Press the bacon down into each round with two fingers.

Spoon some of the meatball mixture into each round and press down to smooth. Make sure to pack the meat down to touch the bottom of the ice tray.

Fold the edges of the bacon on top of the ice tray going across the width, not lengthwise. Trim off the ends of the bacon.

Flip the ice tray over onto the baking sheet and carefully lift the ice cube tray off of the meatballs.

Bake for 15 minutes or until bacon is just brown.

Brush the bacon-wrapped meatballs with Apple BBQ sauce and bake for 6–7 minutes or until the bacon is crispy and meatballs are cooked through.

After they are done, cut the bacon to create single meatballs.

Place a toothpick in each meatball.

Place on a serving tray and serve.

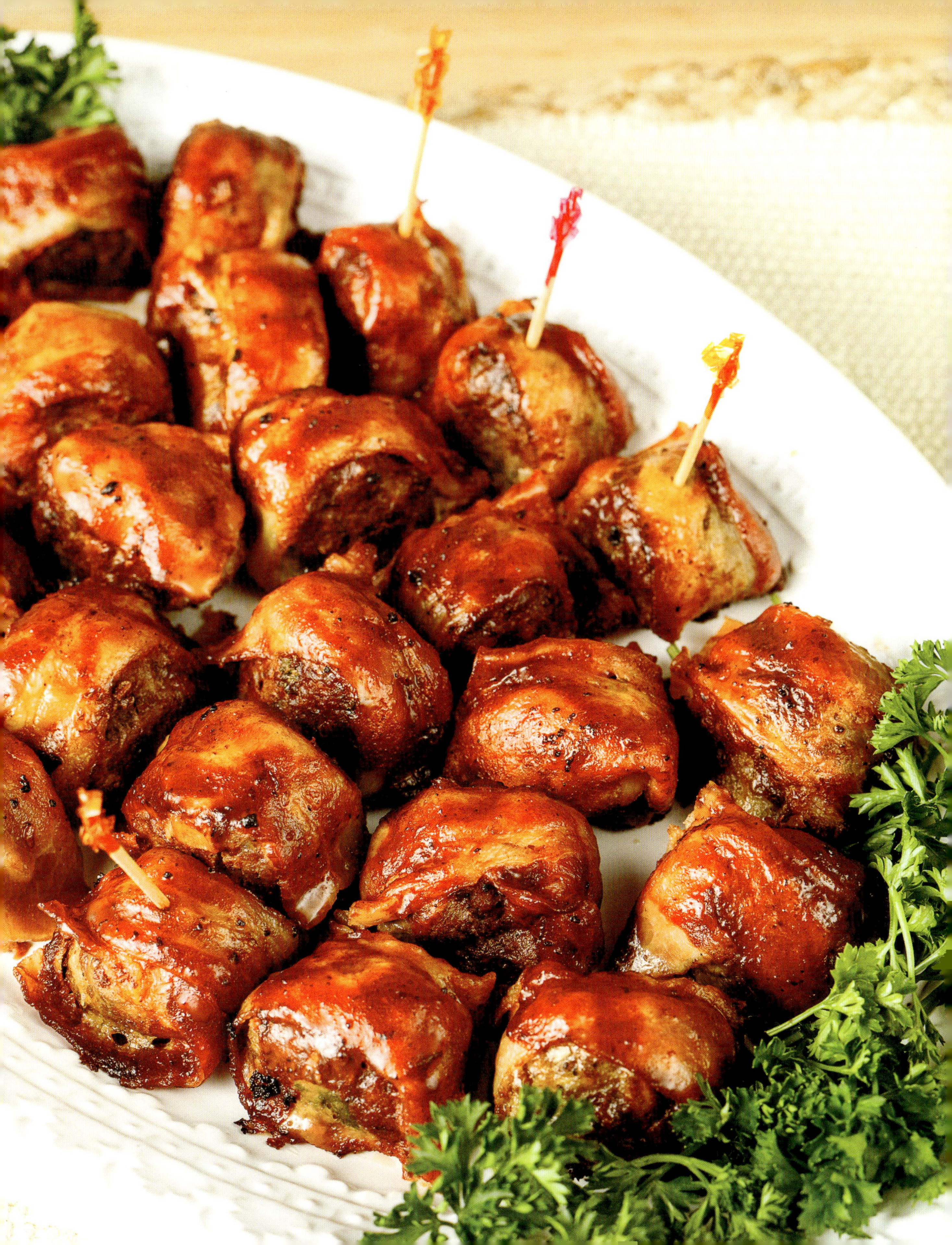

bacon-wrapped pears

makes 4–6 servings

Bacon! Yes, I believe I have your attention now! Who doesn't love bacon? And who doesn't love juicy pears? Now let's go one step further—how about if we wrap bacon around pears? Yes, and yummy!

Cooking spray

2 pears, cut into spears, lengthwise

Toothpicks

Ground cinnamon

6 slices bacon, uncured, cut in half lengthwise

Preheat oven to 350°F (177°C).

Wash pears, cut off the stem, slice in half lengthwise and remove and discard the core.

Cut pear halves into spears lengthwise, about 3–4 pieces.

Cut bacon lengthwise, making ribbon-like, and wrap each pear spear with sliced bacon making a figure 8. Secure the loose ends of bacon with a toothpick.

Sprinkle with cinnamon, lightly.

Place pear spears on prepared baking sheet.

Bake for 35–40 minutes or until the bacon browns and the pears are cooked through.

Let cool for 5 minutes and serve warm.

tip: To get a crispy bacon wrap, try broiling for 2–3 minutes after baking. Do not leave unattended in the broiler. Beware of burning bacon grease if you try this step.

baked parmesan zucchini chips

KF OPTIONAL *Who would have thought that zucchini could be so versatile? This tasty appetizer travels well and is perfect for road trips. Forget the bag of high calorie greasy chips! You can make this keto-friendly by replacing tapioca flour with almond flour.*

Preheat oven to 450°F (232°C).

Line a baking sheet with aluminum foil and coat with cooking spray.

Slice zucchini into ¼-inch thick rounds and place individually on a paper towel.

Press down on the zucchini rounds with another paper towel to eliminate as much moisture as possible.

Toss the zucchini with the oil in a plastic bag together with tapioca flour, Parmesan, smoked paprika, salt and pepper, and place in a single layer on the prepared baking sheet.

Bake the zucchini rounds until browned and crisp, 25–30 minutes.

Remove with spatula.

Serve immediately.

serves 4–6

Cooking spray

2 medium zucchini (about 1 pound total)

1 tablespoon olive oil

½ cup Parmesan cheese, grated

¼ cup tapioca flour or if doing keto, replace with almond flour

½ teaspoon smoked paprika

⅛ teaspoon sea salt

Freshly ground black pepper

appetizers + beverages

bruschetta with french bread

You'll enjoy this delicious Italian appetizer made with my grain and gluten-free French bread.

servings 4–6

- 4-6 slices grain-free French bread (recipe on opposite page)
- 2–3 teaspoons garlic, minced
- 4 tablespoons extra-virgin olive oil
- ¼ cup crumbled feta, shredded Parmesan, or Brie cheese (I use feta cheese.)
- 2 ½ cups Roma tomatoes, chopped fine
- ⅓ cup fresh basil leaf, thinly sliced
- 2 tablespoons balsamic vinegar
- ½ teaspoon sea salt
- 1 teaspoon fresh ground pepper

Preheat oven to 425°F (218°C).

In a medium mixing bowl, add the finely chopped tomatoes, garlic, basil, vinegar, olive oil, cheese, salt, and pepper. Mix thoroughly and let it sit for at least 15 minutes at room temperature to let the flavors marinate.

Slice the French bread into ¼–½-inch slices and lay slices flat on a baking sheet.

Toast the slices in the preheated oven for about 8–10 minutes.

Remove the slices and place on a serving dish, turning the bread over as you lay them on your dish.

Add the mixture to each slice and enjoy!

I think this is an excellent recipe to make you feel like you are experiencing the real deal!

french bread

makes 8–10 slices

Preheat oven to 400°F (204°C). Grease baking sheet with cooking spray or coconut oil,

Mix warm water, maple syrup and 1 package of active yeast in a bowl and set aside. Wait 10–15 minutes until it's frothy and doubles in size.

In a mixing bowl, add the 2 flours, the salt, and stir to combine.

Add the butter into the flour mixture and blend with hand mixer on medium until the butter crumbles.

Add the beaten eggs, yeast mixture and blend. The mixture will be very sticky.

Take out of mixing bowl, using some cassava flour on your hands, and shape it into a French loaf of bread on greased baking sheet.

Let the loaf rise for 40 minutes before baking.

After rising, bake for 25–30 minutes.

Remove from oven and let cool a little.

Slice as you like; then, wow, delicious!

Cooking spray or coconut oil for greasing
½ cup warm water
2 tablespoons maple syrup
1 package active dry yeast
4 eggs, beaten
1⅓ cups cassava flour
1⅓ cups arrowroot flour
1 teaspoon sea salt
4 teaspoons butter, sliced

tip: If the bottom seems a bit moist, then put the loaf on the rack without the pan for 5 minutes to harden the bottom.

appetizers + beverages

caprese meatballs

makes 16 meatballs

1 pound ground turkey

1 egg

¼ cup almond flour

½ teaspoon sea salt

¼ teaspoon ground black pepper

½ teaspoon garlic powder

½ cup mozzarella, shredded

2 tablespoons sun-dried tomatoes, chopped

2 tablespoons fresh basil, chopped

2 tablespoons olive oil for frying

Basic Marinara Sauce (recipe on page 258)

KF I love Italian food! One of my all-time favorite salads is a caprese salad. The fresh buffalo mozzarella cheese along with organic heirloom tomatoes and fresh basil picked right out of my garden is heavenly! Because I love those flavors, I thought of making a meatball that would encompass some of those ingredients or at least a hint of them. This tasty appetizer will have your friends and family asking for more. Mangiare!

Combine all ingredients except the olive oil in a medium bowl and mix thoroughly with your hands.

Form mixture into 16 meatballs.

Heat the olive oil in a large sauté pan.

Add the meatballs to the hot oil, about 1 inch apart, and cook over low/medium heat for about 3–5 minutes per side or until cooked through.

Serve with marinara sauce. They're delicious!

tips: If your sauté pan cannot accommodate 12 meatballs, cook them in two batches.

Because the cheese melts out a bit, be careful that they don't burn. If they appear to be getting dark quickly, then turn down the heat and cook them at a lower temperature.

appetizers + beverages

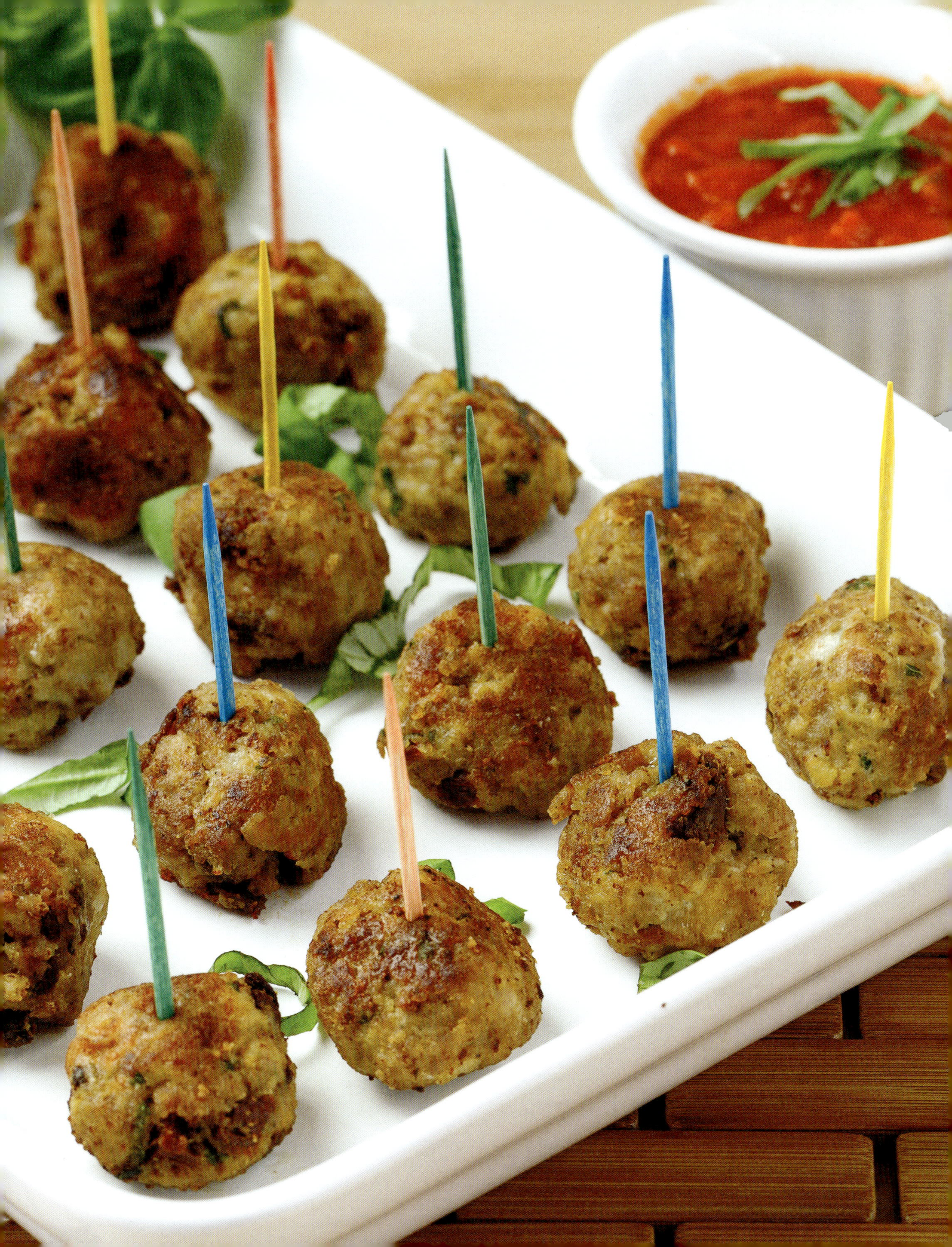

cauliflower popcorn

makes 2 cups

1 head cauliflower

4–5 tablespoons olive oil or coconut oil

Sea salt to taste

2 fresh jalapeños, chopped fine or crushed red chile pepper, after baking or while baking (optional)

KF *Popcorn is my all-time favorite snack and one that was difficult trading in, especially going to the movie theater. This is a healthier version without the corn or butter, and you can spice it up with anything. I enjoy spicing it with finely chopped jalapeño.*

Preheat oven to 375°F (191°C).

Trim the leaves off the head of the cauliflower discarding the core and thick stems. Cut florets into approximately two-inch pieces.

In a large bowl, combine the olive or coconut oil, salt, and jalapeños, if you are spicing it up, then whisk and add the cauliflower pieces to toss thoroughly.

Line a baking sheet with parchment paper or aluminum foil for easy cleanup (you can skip that if you don't have any).

Spread the cauliflower pieces evenly on the baking sheet and roast 30–40 minutes, turning 2 or 3 times, until most of each piece has turned golden brown.

The browner the cauliflower pieces become, the more caramelization occurs, making them sweeter to taste.

tip: Once cooked, you can sprinkle grated Parmesan cheese for a nice twist to the flavor.

appetizers + beverages

chicken meatballs

KF *Here's a great appetizer that's easy to make and you can dip the meatballs in just about any sauce.*

Preheat oven to 400°F (204°C).

If you haven't cooked your bacon, add your 2 strips to an aluminum-lined baking sheet and bake in oven for 10-15 minutes until crispy.

Decrease oven temperature to 350°F (177°C).

Line another baking sheet with aluminum foil. Grease the foil with 2 tablespoons of coconut oil.

Crumble your crispy bacon or chop fine and mix with all ingredients together with ¾ cup of Parmesan cheese.

Form meatballs with about 1–1½ tablespoons each of meat mixture.

Take the remainder ¼ cup of the Parmesan cheese and place it on a small dish.

One by one, roll your meatballs in the Parmesan cheese and place them in even rows on cooking sheet. Leave some room in between each row to let them breathe.

Bake for about 15–20 minutes. The cheese will ooze out a bit, but that's what makes them sooooo good!

makes approximately 18–20 one-inch meatballs

- 2 strips crispy bacon, uncured, finely chopped
- 2 cups ground chicken (16 oz)
- 1 large egg, beaten
- 1 cup mozzarella cheese, grated
- 1 cup Parmesan cheese, grated
- 1 teaspoon dried parsley
- 1 teaspoon dried basil
- 1 cup almond meal
- 2 tablespoons coconut oil for greasing

tip: Make sure the chicken doesn't overcook. Some ovens may cook in 15 minutes while others may take a few minutes longer, up to 20 minutes. It doesn't matter how much cheese oozes out. What matters is the doneness of the chicken.

appetizers + beverages

excellent artichoke dip

serves —10

KF *This is cheesy goodness that's great for entertaining guests. Try them with your favorite grain-free chip or vegetables.*

8 ounces cream cheese

⅓ cup sour cream

1 cup mozzarella cheese, shredded

¼ cup mayonnaise or Basic Paleo Mayo (recipe on page 206)

1 cup spinach, chopped (fresh, cooked, or frozen, thawed)

2 cans or jars of artichoke hearts (in water, not marinated), drained and roughly chopped

Garlic salt to taste

Chili powder to taste

Preheat oven to 350°F (177°C).

Warm the cream cheese in the microwave for 2 minutes on 50% heat to soften it. Pre-microwaving the cream cheese will help you mix it with the other ingredients, so I recommend not skipping this step.

Mix ½ cup mozzarella with all the other ingredients in a baking dish.

Be generous with the chili powder! The cream cheese and sour cream will act to "cool" the dip, so you can sprinkle away with the chili powder!

Bake 30–45 minutes until heated through.

Sprinkle the other ½ cup of the mozzarella on top, then broil until the cheese is browned.

tip: If you want to skip the preservatives in regular mayo, try my Basic Paleo Mayo recipe on page 206.

appetizers + beverages

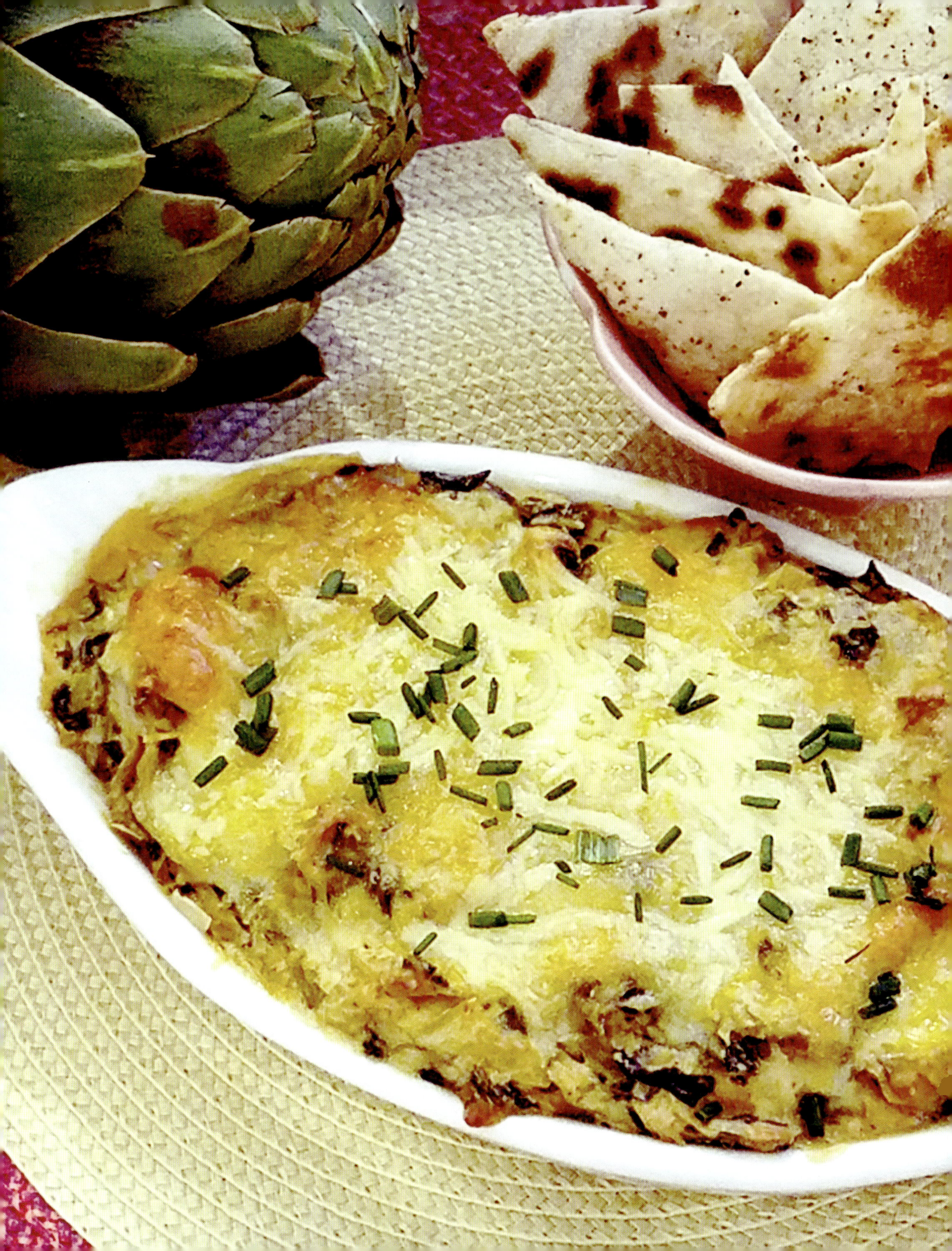

melon, manchego, and prosciutto di parma skewers

makes 10–12 Servings

Fresh taste at your fingertips. These delightfully yummy finger foods are small but large in flavor.

- 1¼ pounds watermelon
- 1¼ pounds honeydew melon
- ½ pound prosciutto, uncured
- 1 package Manchego cheese (about 10 oz.)
- Sea salt and freshly ground pepper
- 2 tablespoons Extra-virgin olive oil
- Dash balsamic vinegar
- 10–12 basil leaves

Cut flesh away from the rind of the watermelon and honeydew. Discard the rind.

Using a melon baller, scoop melon balls from the flesh of the watermelon and honeydew, or you may cut the flesh into one-inch cubes.

Cut prosciutto into one-inch squares to fit three on top of the watermelon.

Cut cheese into thin squares so that they fit the top of the watermelon squares and add on top of the prosciutto.

Top with a basil leaf.

You may add these ingredients in any order you prefer.

Secure with a skewer or toothpick.

To serve, arrange the skewers on a platter, add freshly ground pepper and salt as desired.

Mix olive oil and balsamic vinegar in small cup and drizzle to your liking.

Serve immediately.

appetizers + beverages

prosciutto rollups

Prosciutto rollups are great for entertaining family and friends. The combination of sweet and salty is perfect in this appetizer.

Take a piece of the prosciutto laid flat on a plate. Lightly drizzle olive oil along the whole prosciutto.

Take a pinch of the lettuce of your choice between your thumb and forefinger and put it at the beginning of the prosciutto.

Add a slice of avocado and a slice of the scallion and sprinkle on some cheese, roll up, and insert a toothpick. I didn't need the toothpick; they all stayed together perfectly! Actually, there's no right way to do this. It all depends on what you prefer.

This is a wonderful appetizer or even dinner.

serves about 8 people

- ½ pound prosciutto, uncured
- 2 cups arugula or your favorite lettuce
- 2 tablespoons olive oil or to taste
- 2 avocados, sliced into ½-inch thick pieces
- 4 scallions, cut on the diagonal
- 1 cup mozzarella cheese, shredded (optional)

tip: Uncured prosciutto can be found at a Whole Foods or an Italian market. Make sure it's not prepackaged; there's a huge difference in taste.

maple bacon shrimp

Another favorite! I especially like the jalapeño strip on the shrimp and the tasty bacon wrap combination.

makes –6 servings

- 10 strips thin-cut bacon, uncured
- 20 extra-large shrimp, shelled, deveined but with tails left on (about 1 pound)
- pinch kosher salt
- ½ cup maple syrup
- ¼ cup sriracha sauce or Frank's Red Hot Sauce Original
- 4 fresh jalapeños, cut into thin strips
- Wooden skewers soaked in water for 30 minutes (use metal skewers if desired; then you don't need to soak them)
- Cooking spray

Preheat oven to 400°F (204°C).

Soak wooden skewers in water for 30 minutes, if using.

Cut the jalapeños into thin strips after removing the seeds.

Line a large baking sheet with aluminum foil.

Place bacon slices in one layer onto the baking sheet.

Place into the oven, then bake about 10 minutes or until the bacon has rendered some of its fat and is starting to brown on the edges but is still floppy.

Take the bacon out of the oven and transfer to paper towels to drain excess fat.

Discard the aluminum foil with the bacon fat and re-line baking sheet with foil and grease with cooking spray.

Mix the maple syrup and kosher salt with your choice of hot sauce, and glaze the shrimp and cooked bacon with the mixture.

Now take a shrimp and a strip of a jalapeño and wrap with a piece of bacon. Sometimes it's tricky to wrap successfully, but don't give up; just keep at it. Once wrapped, place wrapped shrimp onto skewer.

Brush or spoon leftover maple syrup over skewered shrimp.

Bake the shrimp for 4 minutes. Set oven to broil and broil shrimp about 2-3 minutes until the bacon is crispy but not too long because the shrimp will be overdone.

tips: I like to stretch the bacon, then cut it in half, so I don't use too much of it.

It is almost impossible to make each shrimp have the exact crispy bacon. Just make sure the shrimp aren't overdone.

mock tortilla chips

Quite simply, the best grain free tortilla chips you can make at home.

Preheat oven to 400°F (204°C).

Preheat a 9.5 inch (or larger) pan over medium heat.

Mix the coconut milk, almond flour, tapioca flour, ½ teaspoon of salt, and turmeric together in a bowl.

Spray your pan with cooking spray.

Add ¼ cup of batter onto the pan to make a tortilla.

After about a minute, flip the tortilla and cook for another minute or until both sides are mostly firm.

Once done, place the tortilla onto a parchment-lined baking sheet. Repeat until the batter is gone.

Using scissors, cut the tortillas into small triangles and spread them out on the baking sheet.

Sprinkle salt to taste.

Bake for 10–12 minutes or until the chips are crispy.

Enjoy with your favorite salsa or guacamole.

makes 2–4 servings

1 cup canned coconut milk, full-fat

½ cup almond flour

½ cup tapioca flour

½ teaspoon sea salt, adjust to taste

¼ teaspoon turmeric

Cooking spray

Sea salt to taste

appetizers + beverages

sautéed sweet peppers with toasted garlic and capers

makes 6 servings

Exotic flavors and colors collide in an explosion of taste. This healthy vegetarian dish is sure to satisfy anyone's hunger.

- 5 tablespoons extra-virgin olive oil
- 2 large red bell peppers, sliced lengthwise, and widthwise, 1-inch thick
- 2 large yellow bell peppers, sliced lengthwise and widthwise, 1-inch thick
- Sea salt to taste
- 8 large garlic cloves
- 1 tablespoon capers

In a large deep skillet, heat 3 tablespoons of olive oil.

Add the peppers and season with salt.

Cover and cook over moderate heat about 18 minutes, stirring occasionally, until softened.

Transfer the peppers to a bowl.

Heat the remaining 2 tablespoons of olive oil in the skillet.

Add the garlic and cook over moderate heat, about 3 minutes, until golden.

Then add the capers and peppers. Toss to combine and season with salt.

Serve warm or at room temperature.

roasted candied nuts

KF *Here's a great snack or dessert that you can make ahead of going out to the movies. Best of all, it is keto-friendly.*

serves 18–20

1 large egg white
½ cup erythritol
1 teaspoon cinnamon
½ teaspoon coriander
½ teaspoon freshly ground black pepper
¼ teaspoon nutmeg, freshly grated, preferable to powdered
¾ teaspoon kosher salt
2 cups pecans
2 cups walnuts

Preheat oven to 300°F (149°C). Line a baking sheet with aluminum foil.

In a medium bowl, beat egg white until frothy, about 3 minutes.

Add erythritol, cinnamon, coriander, pepper, nutmeg, and salt and mix together.

Add the pecans and walnuts into the egg white mixture.

Stir until all the nuts are coated evenly.

Spread the coated nuts onto baking sheet so they are distributed in a single layer. Bake for 20–30 minutes or until the coating starts to look dry and the nuts smell fragrant and begin to darken.

Be sure not to overcook the nuts. Let the nuts sit a while on the baking sheet, then break apart and store in an airtight container.

Makes 4 cups of roasted nuts.

tip: I tried this with stevia, and it had that aftertaste. This would work well with coconut sugar, but I try not to use sugar whenever I can.

spicy lime chicken wings

makes 6–8 servings

Cooking spray

3 pounds chicken wings

⅔ cup Frank's Red Hot Sauce Original

¼ cup lime juice, freshly squeezed

Zest of 2 limes

3 tablespoons maple syrup or raw honey (If doing keto, eliminate or replace with erythritol syrup, recipe on page 15.)

¼ cup butter, melted

2 cloves garlic, crushed

Sea salt and freshly ground black pepper

KF OPTIONAL *A wonderfully healthy and fun recipe that is perfect for all occasions, including tailgating, football weekends, or entertaining the masses! I chose to make this KF Optional as I found out that the amount of maple syrup or honey is so little it could pass for keto-friendly. If following keto strictly, replace maple syrup or honey with erythritol syrup recipe on page 15.*

Preheat oven to 400°F (204°C).

Line a baking sheet with aluminum foil and coat with cooking spray.

Season the chicken wings to taste with sea salt and freshly ground black pepper.

Bake the wings on the greased baking sheet for about 45 minutes until cooked through, turning them over once.

In a bowl, combine the lime juice, lime zest, hot sauce, maple syrup, melted butter, garlic and mix well.

Remove the wings from the oven and transfer to a large bowl.

Pour the sauce over the wings and toss well to coat.

seasoned jicama, pineapple, and watermelon

KF OPTIONAL *I've enjoyed many wonderful trips to Los Cabos, Mexico, where I found this delicious dish, so refreshing and healthy! If you want this keto-friendly, replace the pineapple with cucumber.*

Core the pineapple and cut it in half, then cut it into spears. Store the other half to enjoy at another time.

Cut the watermelon in ½ and cut into spears with seeds removed. Store the other half to enjoy at another time.

Cut the two ends of each celery stalk, rinse, and cut in half. You can slice stalks lengthwise to create four equal pieces from each stalk.

Arrange all of these pieces on a lovely dish, then squeeze the limes onto the vegetables and fruit, making sure they're pretty saturated with the juice.

Then take Tajín and sprinkle them generously.

makes 4–6 servings

½ watermelon, sliced into spears with seeds removed

½ pineapple, sliced into spears (replace with 2 cucumbers if doing keto)

4 stalks celery, cut in ½ and cleaned

1 jicama peeled and cut into spears

3–4 limes

Tajín (wonderful Mexican spice)

tip: This works well with cucumbers and red bell peppers.

appetizers + beverages

crustless mini-quiche

makes 12 mini quiches

KF *Ever wonder how to make quiche even healthier? I've wondered the same—no crust!*

Butter or coconut oil for coating muffin pans

2 cups cauliflower, crumbled or already-riced

Pinch sea salt

3 eggs, whisked

1 cup cheddar cheese, grated

1 tablespoon coconut flour

½ teaspoon sea salt

1 cup spinach, chopped

½–¾ cup mushrooms, chopped

½ cup onion, diced

2 tablespoons olive oil

Preheat oven to 400°F (204°C).

Grease 12-cup muffin pan with butter or coconut oil.

Grind your crumbled cauliflower in a food processor into a rice consistency or if using already riced cauliflower, follow the directions on the package.

Place 2 cups of the riced cauliflower into a medium pot with 2 tablespoons of water and sprinkle with a pinch of sea salt.

Cover and steam on medium heat for 8–10 minutes, until soft, a little al dente. Stir occasionally.

Remove from heat and uncover to allow to cool. Once cooled, put into a bowl and cover with a moist paper towel. Microwave on high for thirty seconds.

In a large bowl, combine eggs, cheese, coconut flour, salt and spinach. Lightly mix and set aside.

Sauté the mushrooms and onions in a skillet with olive oil for about 3 minutes. Onions should be translucent, but not browned. Mushrooms should be lightly cooked for a nice consistency.

Add this to your cauliflower rice along with the egg mixture. Mix together well.

With a spoon, fill the muffin pan evenly across all cups. Gently flatten down the mix in the pan with the back of your spoon into the muffin pan, about halfway down the muffin cup.

Bake for 25–30 minutes or until golden brown on top.

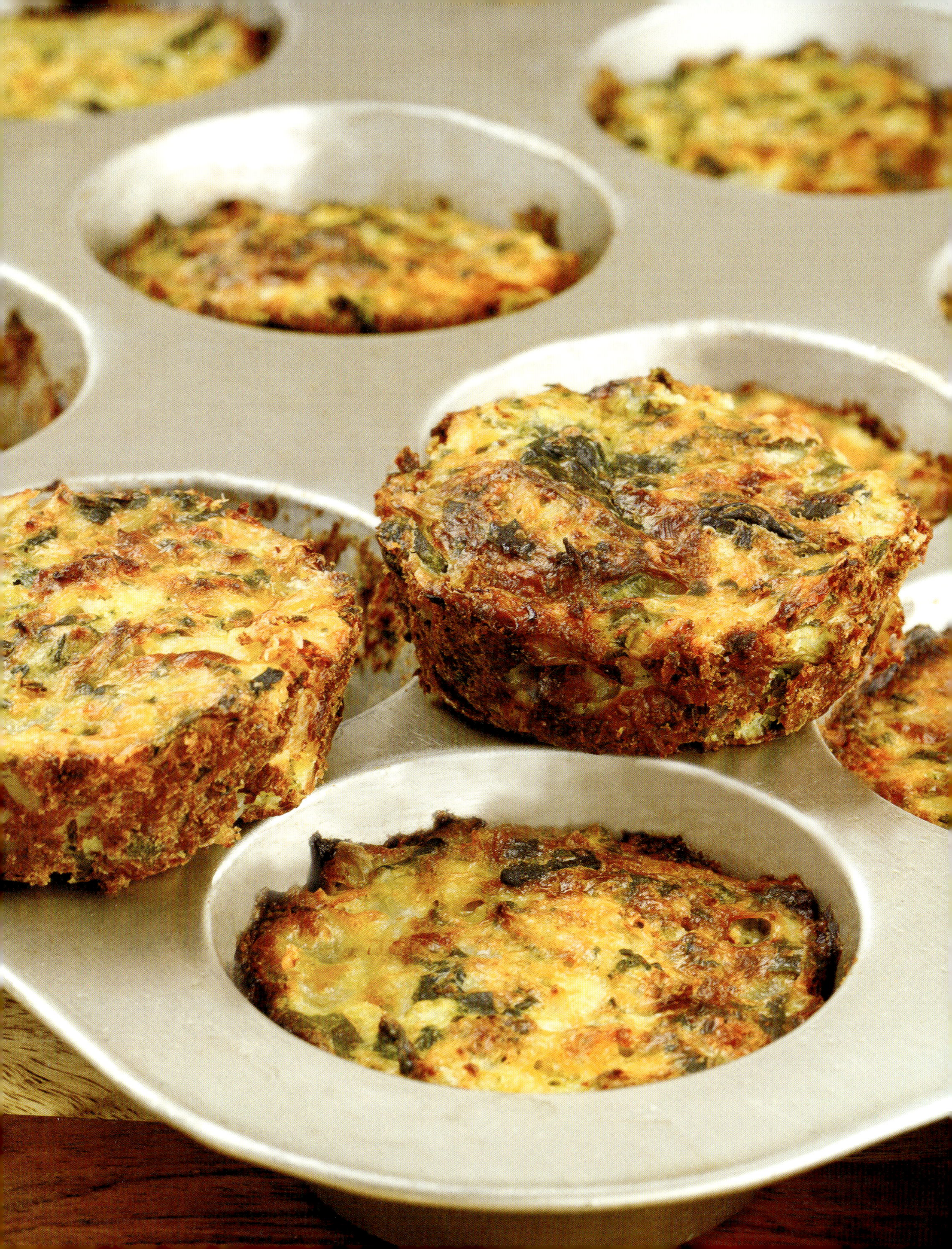

spicy turkey patty with mango salsa

makes 4–6 servings

KF OPTIONAL *This delightfully delicious combination will have your taste buds smiling with every bite. If doing keto, just replace the mango salsa with regular salsa.*

---

spicy turkey patty

- 1 pound ground turkey
- ½ medium-sized onion, peeled and finely chopped
- ½ jalapeño pepper, finely chopped
- 1 teaspoon paprika
- ½ teaspoon sea salt
- 1 teaspoon black pepper
- 1 avocado, sliced
- 2 tablespoons cilantro, finely chopped

mango salsa

- ½ cup cucumber, diced
- 2 semi-ripe mangos, cubed (If doing keto, replace with tomatoes.)
- 1 bunch cilantro, finely chopped
- ¾ cup red onion, diced (about ½ of an onion)
- 1 red bell pepper, cored and diced
- Juice of 1 lemon or lime

Place turkey, onion, jalapeño, herb and spices in a bowl, and use hands to mix well.

Form into 4–6 patties.

Place skillet over medium heat.

Add olive oil to skillet.

When skillet is hot, add patties and cook each side for about 5 minutes.

Top with mango salsa, sliced avocado, and garnish with cilantro.

For your mango salsa, put all the salsa ingredients in a bowl and mix together.

appetizers + beverages

spicy sriracha chicken wings

Zesty and spicy chicken wings are always a hit whether you are snacking or entertaining. My Spicy Sriracha Chicken Wings will have you or your guests wanting more.

makes 2–4 servings

Cooking spray

2 pounds chicken wings

1 teaspoon garlic powder

Sea salt and freshly ground pepper to taste

5 tablespoons olive oil

½ cup raw honey

¼ cup sriracha sauce

1 tablespoon gluten-free soy sauce

Juice of 1 lemon

1 teaspoon fresh cilantro leaves

Preheat oven to 400°F (204°C).

Line a baking sheet with aluminum foil and coat with cooking spray.

In a small bowl, combine the olive oil, honey, sriracha, and gluten-free soy sauce.

In a large bowl, toss the chicken wings, garlic powder, and season with salt and pepper.

Arrange the chicken wings on baking sheet and bake for 25–30 minutes, turning them over halfway through.

Brush the wings with sriracha mixture and place them under the broiler for 3–4 minutes or until crisp and crusted.

Serve immediately, garnish with fresh cilantro.

appetizers + beverages

sugar-free cocktails

If we are working to eliminate grains and hidden sugars, I thought, "Why not see if I can have a sugar-free cocktail?" You've heard of the "skinny" cocktail, right? Well, they're not totally sugar free as they use triple sec. I found a sugar-free triple sec online made with erythritol called, Le Sirop de Monin. Did you know that there are several-grain free vodkas on the market too? Tito's, Grey Goose and Hanson's are widely available today. Tequila and rum, of course are grain free. Beware of spiced rum though. Spiced and flavored rums are not always allowed on a grain-free diet and are high in sugar. I had a ton of fun making these.

appetizers + beverages

sugarless train wreck mojito

You may well end up a train wreck after a few of these. I barely tasted the rum… which is scary.

- 10-12 mint leaves
- 1-½ ounces white rum
- 1 ounce fresh lime juice
- 2 teaspoons sugar free triple sec
- 6-8 ounces Arrowhead Sparkling Water, plain or orange flavored

In a Collins glass, add the mint leaves, lime juice and triple sec. Using a muddling stick, mash the leaves until you release the fragrance of the mint. Add ice to your glass and pour rum over the ice. Top off with sparkling water and stir. Garnish with additional mint if you like.

thin lizzy cosmo

Great for sharing with the girlfriends who love a Cosmo but are watching their waistline.

- 2 ounces vodka, cold (keep a good vodka in the freezer for martinis and cosmos
- 4 ounces Arrowhead Sparkling Water, black cherry or orange flavored
- 2 ounces cranberry juice, unsweetened
- 1-2 tablespoons sugar free triple sec

Mix altogether and serve neat or with ice.

tip: Regular cranberry juice is where the sugar is. Even though it's unsweetened cranberry juice, there is still sugar in the cranberry itself. What you can do is add less. Also, depending on your sweet tooth, you can add a bit more triple sec.

guiltless margarita

The margarita dates back to 1938 and was said to have been inspired by a Ziegfeld dancer who was allergic to spirits except for tequila. If you are watching your sugar intake, I've taken the guilt out of enjoying this classic cocktail.

- 3 ounces tequila
- 2 ounces freshly squeezed lime juice
- 1 ounce sugar free triple sec
- Dash orange extract (optional)
- 2 cups ice (7-8 cubes, if using)
- ½ lime
- Salt (optional to rim your glass)

Add the ingredients, except the salt, including ice in a blender. Blend for about 20 seconds. Pour into container with lid and let liquid set in freezer for about 8 hours or overnight (it tastes better).

To rim your glass, pour salt onto a saucer or buy a container of margarita salt from your grocery store liquor department. Take your ½ lime and drag around the rim of your glass. Place top of glass into the salt.

Remove mix from freezer and using a spoon, fill your margarita glass and enjoy. It will be slushy at first and then melt, especially if you're in the sun, but that's the beauty of it.

If you want it over "rocks", blend without ice, freeze as above, and spoon over ice into your glass.

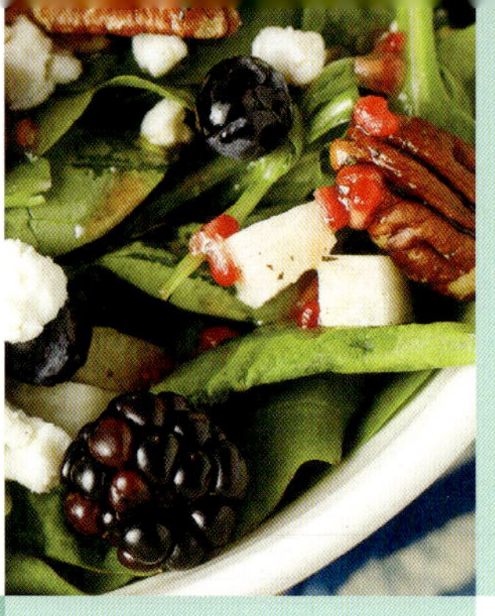
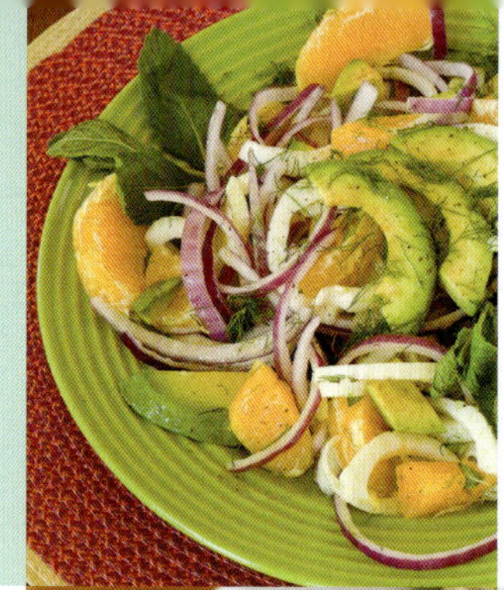
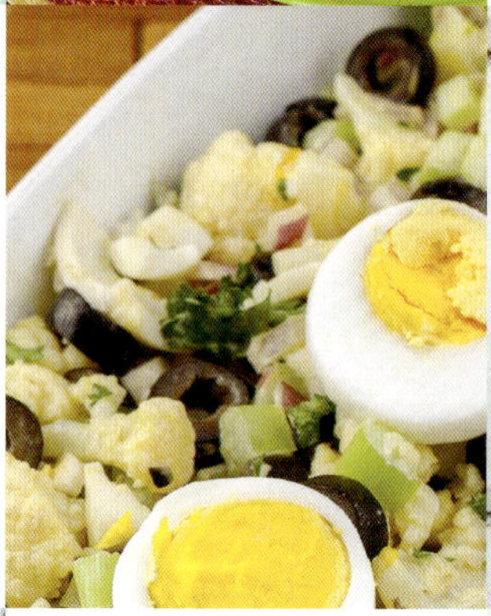
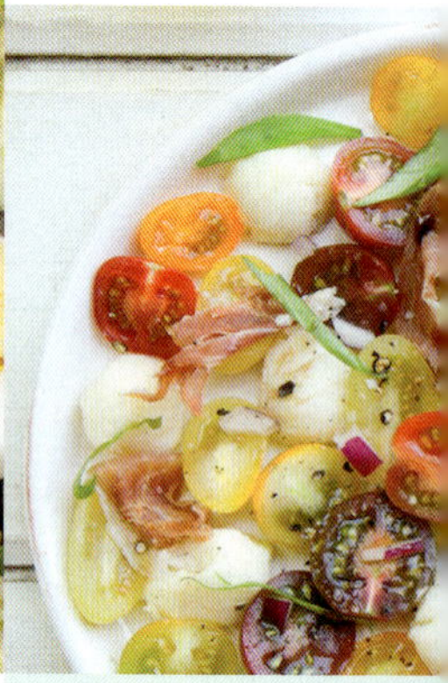
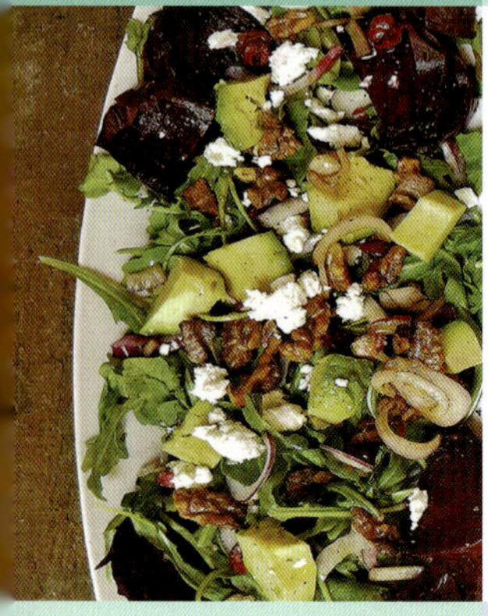
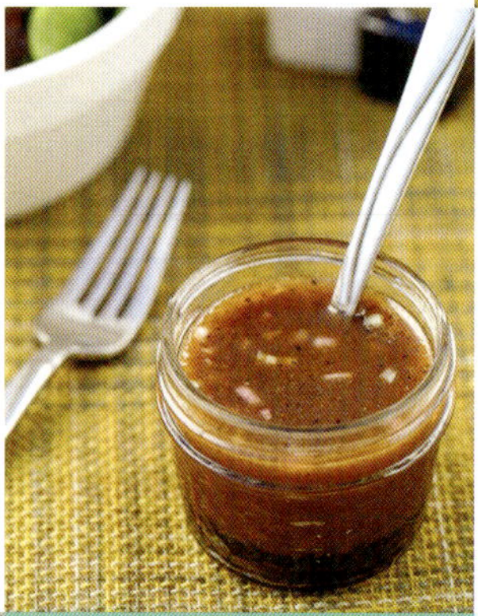
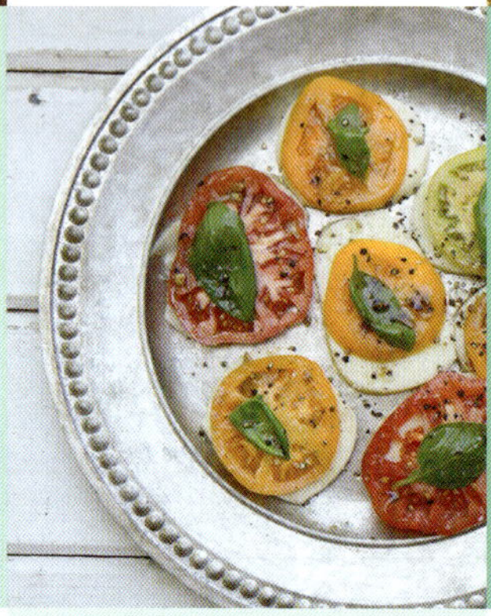
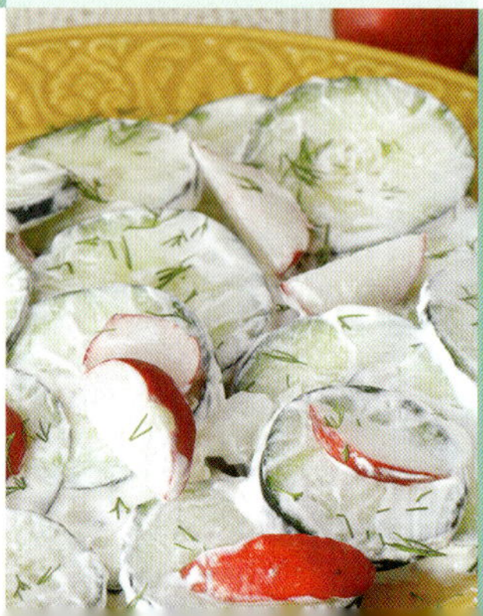

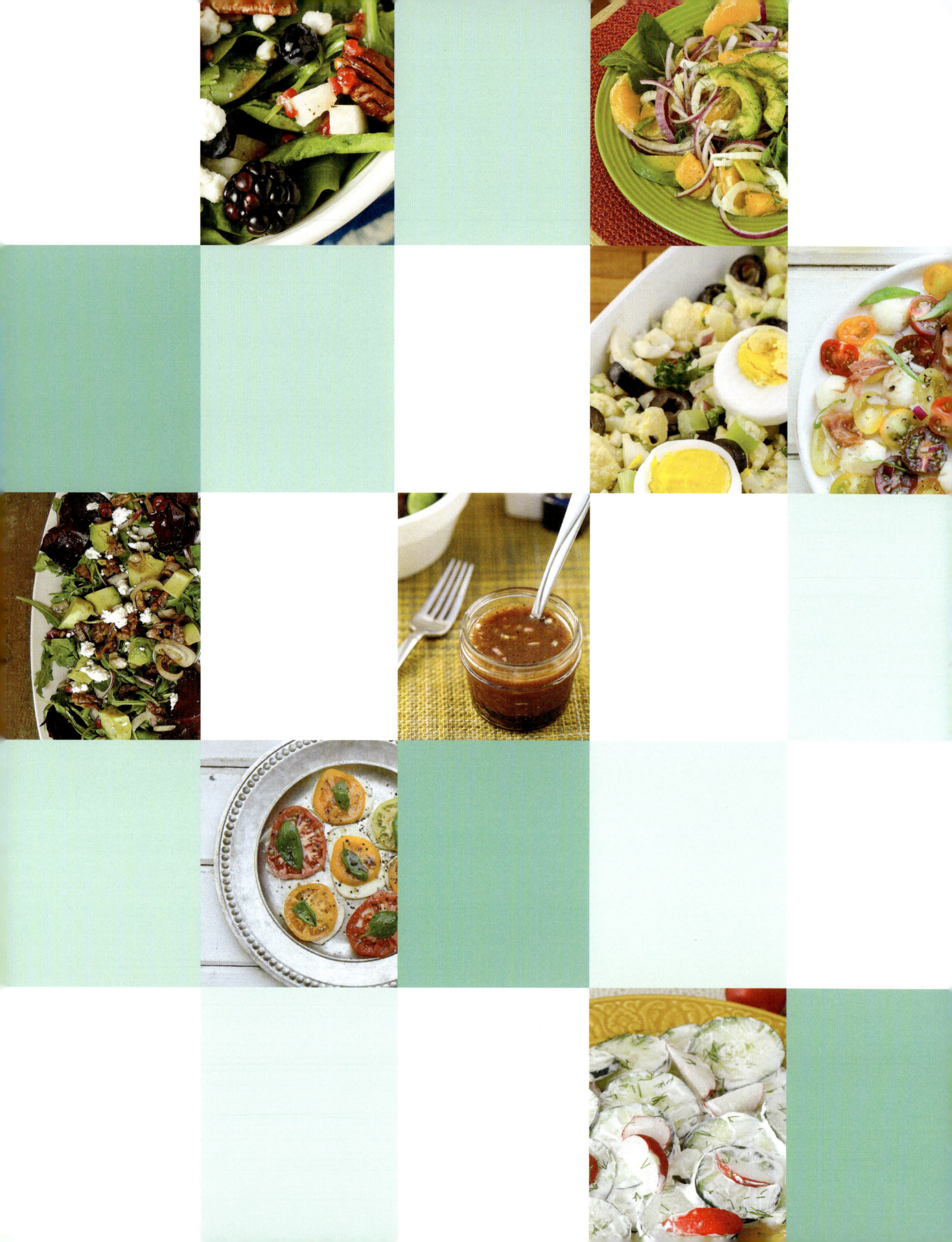

salads

Salad is a great way to tap into some of the most nutrient-dense foods on Earth. Arugula, spinach, romaine and other leafy greens are packed with some of the best nutrients we need to keep our bodies running at optimal levels.

KF Denotes that recipe can be made or is keto-friendly.

Arugula and Roasted Pear Salad 90

Avocado, Fennel, and Orange Salad 98

Baby Spinach and Arugula Salad with Berries 92

Balsamic Honey Salad Dressing 93

Beet and Arugula Salad 96

BLT Avocado Salad 100

Caesar Salad Dressing 94

Caprese Salad with Prosciutto and Mozzarella 95

Caprese Salad with Tomato and Basil 104

Cucumber Radish Salad 105

Grilled Caesar Salad 106

Iceberg Wedge Salad 102

No Potato Salad 103

Strawberry Spinach Salad 108

Warm Fig and Arugula Salad 109

Watermelon, Blueberry, and Feta Cheese Salad 110

Zucchini Noodles with Red Onion and Feta 111

arugula and roasted pear salad

serves 4–6

Arugula and pears flourish during the cooler late-autumn weather. Put them together for a great balance of sweet and piquant. The arugula is lightly dressed with a maple-sweetened vinaigrette to accentuate the natural flavor of the pears.

- 4 firm almost-ripe Bartlett or Bosc pears, peeled, cored, and thinly sliced lengthwise; stem and seeds removed
- 2 tablespoons maple syrup
- 1 teaspoon butter, melted
- 2 tablespoons pine nuts
- 3 tablespoons olive oil
- 1 tablespoon balsamic vinegar
- 1 clove garlic, minced
- Sea salt and pepper to taste
- ½ teaspoon Dijon mustard
- 2 tablespoons dried cranberries
- 3–4 tablespoons blue cheese, crumbled
- 6 cups arugula or spring mix

Preheat oven to 400°F (204°C).

In a medium bowl, toss the pears, syrup, and butter.

Arrange the pears in a single layer on an aluminum lined baking sheet.

Bake, turning once, until the pairs are barely tender, about 10–15 minutes.

Put the pine nuts in a skillet and pan roast for five minutes until toasty brown and remove from the heat. Set aside.

In a large salad bowl, prepare the salad dressing by whisking together the olive oil, vinegar, garlic, salt, pepper, mustard, and maple syrup.

Add the arugula or salad greens and toss to coat.

Divide the salad onto 4–6 chilled plates.

Sprinkle with cranberries, blue cheese, and pine nuts evenly over the salad.

Arrange the roasted pear slices attractively over the salad.

Garnish with more cheese and nuts to your liking.

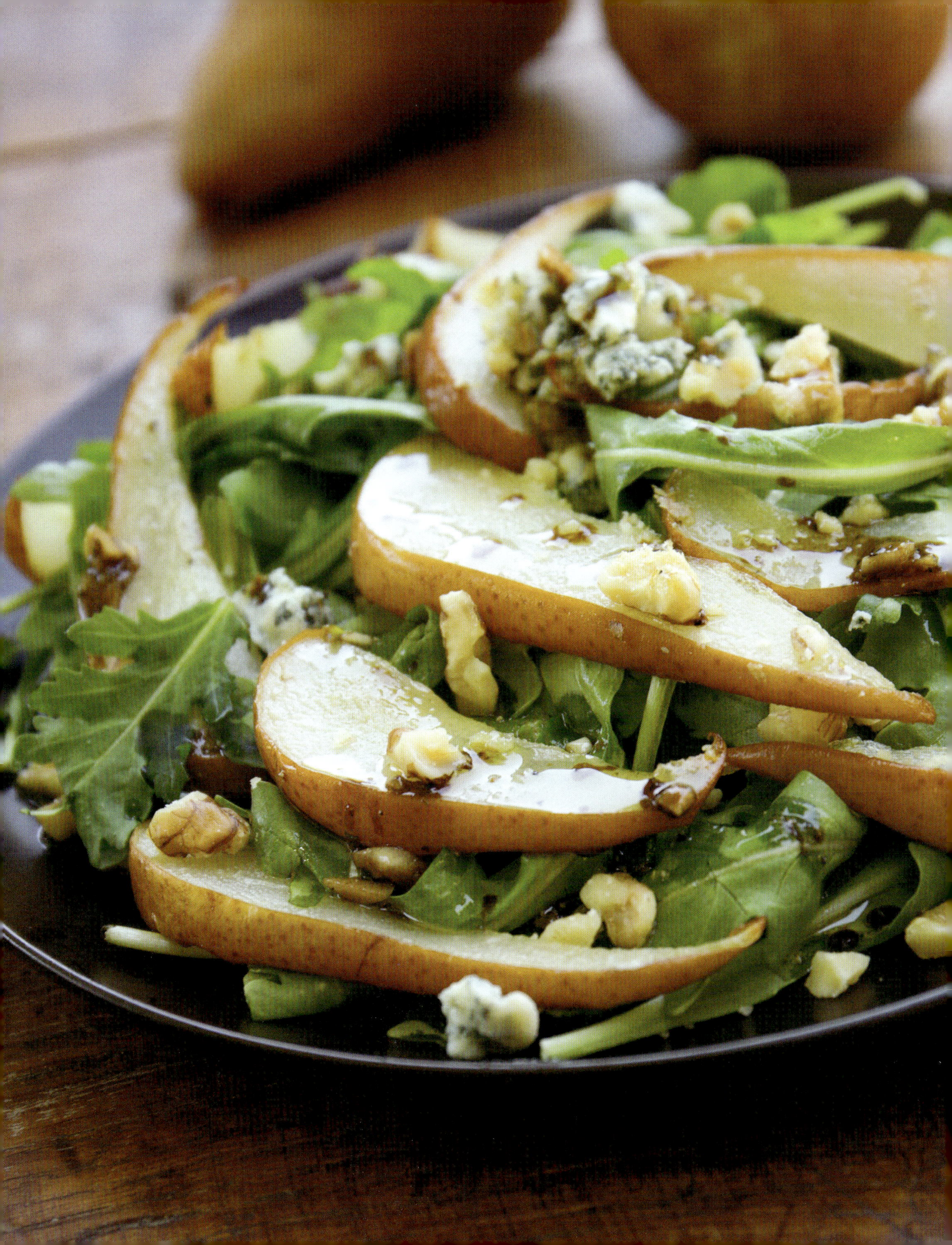

baby spinach and arugula salad with berries

serves 4–6

OPTIONAL *You just can't go wrong with these two powerhouse greens, spinach and arugula, combined with the antioxidant power of berries. If doing keto, replace the honey in the dressing with erythritol.*

6–7 cups **baby spinach**, equal to one 6–7-ounce bag

4 cups **arugula**

2 cups (1 pint) stemmed, **sliced strawberries**

1 cup (½ pint) **blueberries**

½ cup **pecans**, toasted

4 ounces **goat cheese**

¾ cup **jicama**, chopped

Raspberry vinaigrette

¾ cup **olive oil**

¼ cup **apple cider vinegar**

1 teaspoon **sea salt**

3 tablespoons **honey**; if doing keto, use 3 tablespoons of **erythritol**

1 teaspoon **dried basil**

½ cup fresh or frozen **red raspberries**

¼ cup **water**

Peel jicama and cut small square shapes for the salad. It's a hassle peeling a jicama. Today many markets offer it already peeled.

In a large bowl, combine baby spinach, arugula, strawberries, blueberries, pecans, and jicama. (You can add other berries of your choice.)

Combine all dressing ingredients together in a blender and blend.

Add the dressing, little by little, and toss until greens are well-coated.

Taste and adjust seasoning with salt and pepper.

Sprinkle crumbled goat cheese over top and serve.

tip: The salad dressing can keep for up to 2 weeks in a sealed container in the refrigerator.

salads

balsamic honey salad dressing

KF OPTIONAL *This is my go-to salad dressing. It is tastier than any bottled dressing I have tried. It adds a tangy sweetness to the salad of your choice. If doing keto, replace the honey in the dressing with erythritol.*

¼ cup balsamic vinegar

3 tablespoons shallots, chopped fine

1 tablespoon honey (to make keto, use 1 tablespoon of erythritol)

⅓ cup extra-virgin olive oil

Garlic salt

Lemon pepper

In a medium bowl, whisk the vinegar, shallots, and honey to blend.

Gradually whisk in the oil.

Season the vinaigrette with garlic salt and lemon pepper to taste.

caesar salad dressing

This zesty variation uses ingredients that make your Caesar salad flavorful and healthy.

- 2 egg yolks
- 1 cup olive oil
- 2 teaspoons Dijon mustard
- 6 teaspoons fresh lemon juice
- 2 small garlic cloves, minced
- 1 teaspoon anchovy paste
- 1 teaspoon Worcestershire sauce
- 1 cup mayonnaise or Basic Paleo Mayo (recipe on page 206)
- ½ cup Parmigiano Reggiano cheese, freshly grated
- ¼ teaspoon sea salt
- ¼ teaspoon freshly ground black pepper

Place the egg yolks, 1 teaspoon of Dijon mustard, 4 teaspoons of lemon juice and a pinch of salt to your blender and blend on medium high with the lid on. Keep blending while you slowly add the olive oil.

Empty the contents of the blender into a medium bowl, whisk the minced garlic, anchovy paste, 2 teaspoons of lemon juice, a teaspoon of Dijon mustard, and the Worcestershire sauce until well combined.

Now add the freshly grated Parmigiano Reggiano, salt and pepper.

Taste and adjust to your liking.

tip: Keep the leftover dressing in the fridge in a sealable container of your choice. Should last about a week.

caprese salad with prosciutto and mozzarella

Mama Mia! This Italian-inspired caprese salad will make your Italian grandmother blush with joy!

Add mozzarella balls together with the cherry tomatoes to a bowl. If using whole mozzarella, use a melon baller to scoop balls from the mozzarella and add to bowl.

Add shredded prosciutto.

Add diced red onion and sprinkle with mint and basil leaves.

In a small bowl, whisk the olive oil, honey/maple syrup, and white balsamic together.

Season with salt, freshly ground pepper, and garlic salt, to taste.

Drizzle dressing over salad and toss to coat.

Season with additional salt and pepper and herbs, if needed.

serves 4

½ pound cherry tomatoes, cut in half

1 8-ounce container buffalo mozzarella balls

8–10 slices prosciutto, shredded into large pieces

¼ cup fresh basil leaves, julienned

¼ cup mint leaves, julienned

3–4 tablespoons extra-virgin olive oil

1½ teaspoons maple syrup or honey

1 tablespoon white balsamic vinegar

Kosher salt and freshly ground black pepper to taste

1 small red onion, diced (I use the whole onion, but some only prefer to use a half of the onion)

Garlic salt to taste

beet and arugula salad

serves 4

¼ cup balsamic vinegar

3 tablespoons shallots, thinly sliced

1 tablespoon honey or maple syrup

⅓ cup extra-virgin olive oil

Sea salt and freshly ground black pepper

6 medium beets, rinsed and quartered

6 cups fresh arugula

½ cup walnuts, toasted, coarsely chopped

¼ cup dried cranberries

½ avocado, peeled, pitted, and cubed

3 ounces soft fresh goat cheese, coarsely crumbled

Did you know that arugula is one of the most nutritious greens on the planet? Arugula offers an herbaceous, peppery flavor with nuances of nuts and mustard. Coupled with beets, this makes for a healthy way to get immune boosting vitamin C, fiber, and essential minerals like potassium and manganese.

Preheat oven to 450°F (232°C).

Line a baking sheet with foil.

Whisk the vinegar, shallots, and honey in a medium bowl; blend to make a vinaigrette. Gradually whisk in the oil. Season with salt and pepper to taste.

Toss the beets in a small bowl with enough dressing to coat. Place the beets on the prepared baking sheet and roast until the beets are slightly caramelized, stirring occasionally, about 12 minutes. Set aside and cool.

Toss the arugula, walnuts, and cranberries in a large bowl with enough vinaigrette to coat. Season the salad to taste with salt and pepper.

Distribute the salad atop 4–6 plates.

Arrange the beets around the salad.

Add the avocado and goat cheese, and serve.

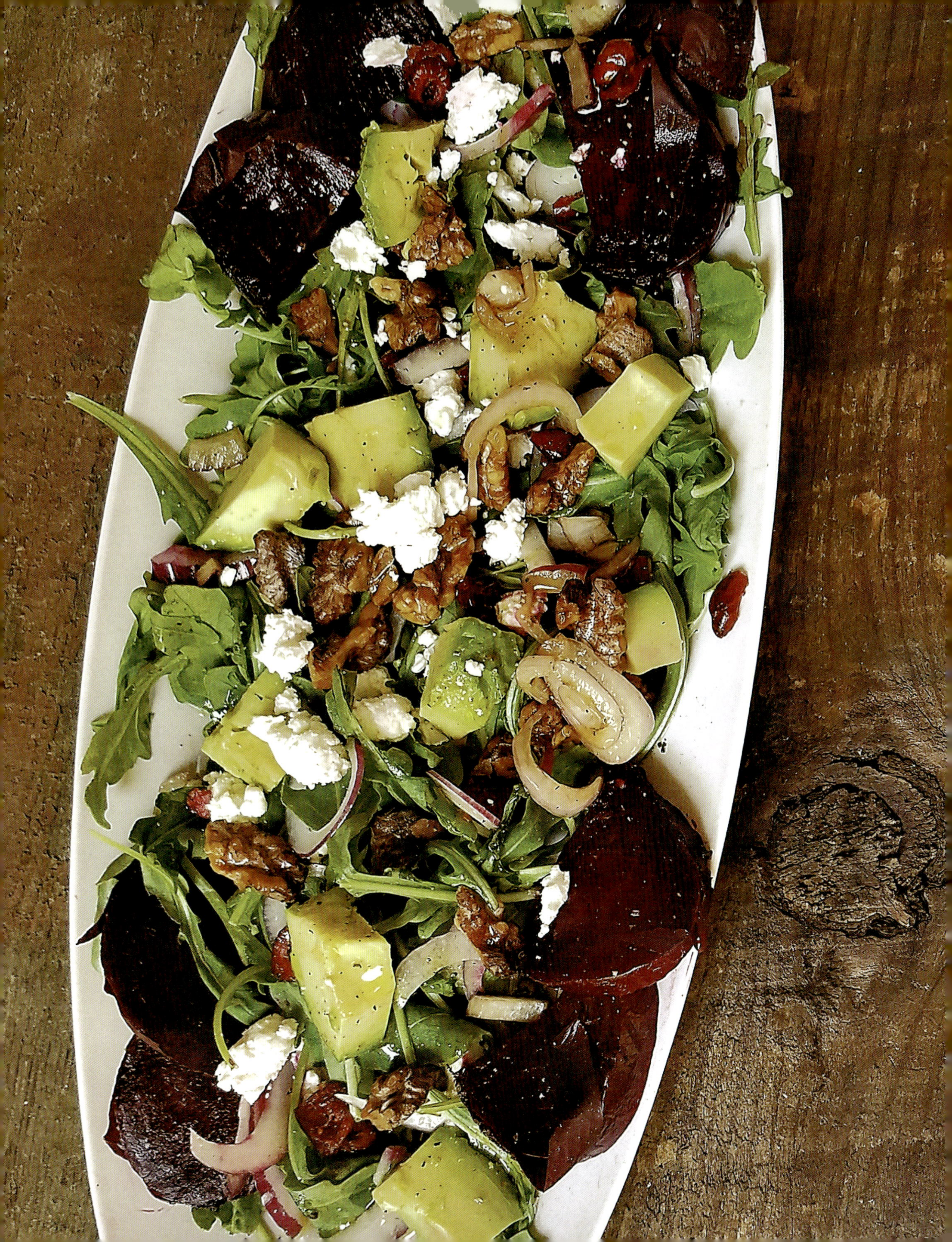

avocado, fennel, and orange salad

serves 4

This is one of the healthiest and most refreshing salads, especially over the spring and summer.

2 large fennel bulbs

2 tablespoons of the fronds from the fennel

4 Cara Cara or Valencia oranges, or 6 Cuties if you don't have the oranges—peeled, segmented, and cut in half

1 medium red onion, thinly sliced into rings and halved

3 large avocados or 4–5 small ones, sliced

1–2 tablespoons fresh mint, chopped

Dressing

2 tablespoons lime juice

3 tablespoons orange juice concentrate

¼ cup extra-virgin olive oil

Pinch cumin

¼ teaspoon sea salt

Freshly ground black pepper to taste

Peel and segment the oranges or Cuties. Remove as much pith, the white stuff holding the orange together, as possible.

Cut each segment in half and place in a bowl.

Finely chop 2 tablespoons of fennel fronds. Add about half to the bowl and save the rest for garnish.

Slice the fennel bulbs into quarters, removing outer leaves.

Core and slice the fennel thinly and add to the bowl, along with the sliced onion.

Toss the fennel, orange segments, red onion, and some sliced avocado gently.

Take some sliced avocado and set aside for topping the salad servings.

Dish the orange fennel salad onto a serving platter and garnish with the avocado slices on top.

Sprinkle salad with reserved chopped fennel fronds and chopped mint.

Make the easy salad dressing by mixing all dressing ingredients listed and drizzle over the salad.

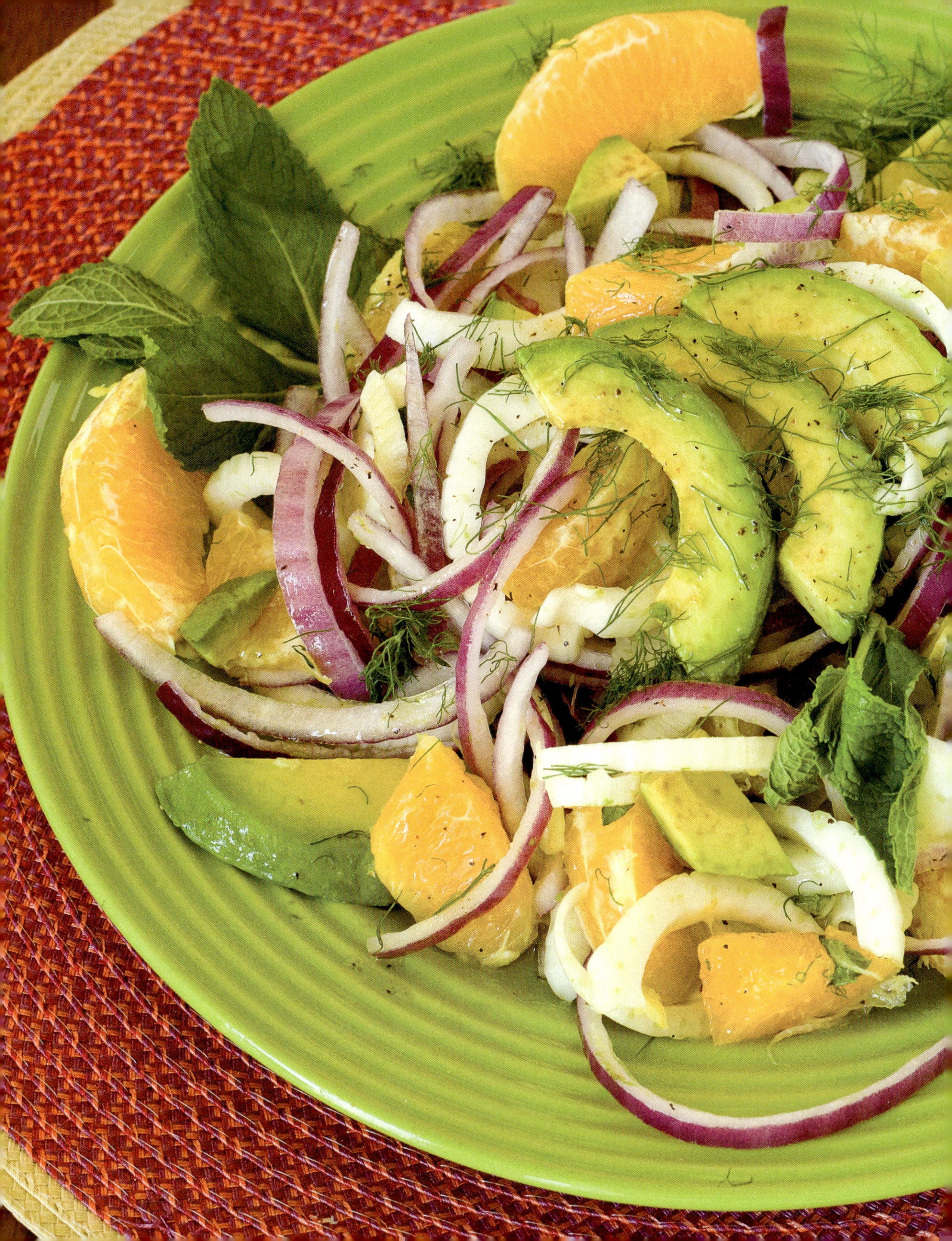

blt avocado salad

servings: 1–2

- 1 avocado
- ¾ cup grape tomatoes, cut into halves
- 2 strips bacon, uncured, cooked until crispy
- ½ cup scallions, chopped
- ½ cup spring lettuce cut fine or lettuce of your choice
- 2 teaspoons Basic Paleo Mayonnaise (recipe below)
- ½ teaspoon sea salt, more to taste

Basic Paleo Mayo
- 2 egg yolks
- 1 cup olive oil
- 1 teaspoon Dijon mustard
- 4 teaspoons fresh lemon juice
- Pinch sea salt

KF We all love the BLT sandwich, but the bread is the problem. I created this salad and you won't miss the bread. It provides great nutrients for a light snack or as an appetizer.

Cook bacon, using your desired method, and cook until crispy. The easiest way to cook bacon is to place each slice on a baking sheet lined with aluminum foil, bake (never having to turn the bacon over) for 15-20 minutes at 400°F (204°C). If there are more pieces, it will take longer, so check after 15 minutes.

While bacon is cooking, cut avocado in half and remove the pit. Take a tablespoon and scoop the avocado all around and out of its shell.

To cube your avocado, turn the scooped avocado on its back and cut lengthwise and then across making square cubes. Repeat with the other half.

Take your lettuce and tear or cut into small thin strips. Use a small bunch of the cut lettuce and start to fill small salad bowls.

Add avocado and then your bacon pieces, tomatoes, scallions, and add a teaspoon of mayo on top, if you wish.

Taste and add additional salt if needed. Toss well and serve.

basic paleo mayo

Place egg yolks, mustard, lemon juice, and a pinch of salt in a blender and blend at medium speed.

Slowly add olive oil until you get a smooth, well-mixed consistency.

Pour into Mason jar to store in refrigerator for about a week.

> **tip:** For a bit more protein, top with one sliced hard-boiled egg. While there are some good prepared mayos available at most health food markets, making your own is both easy and delicious.

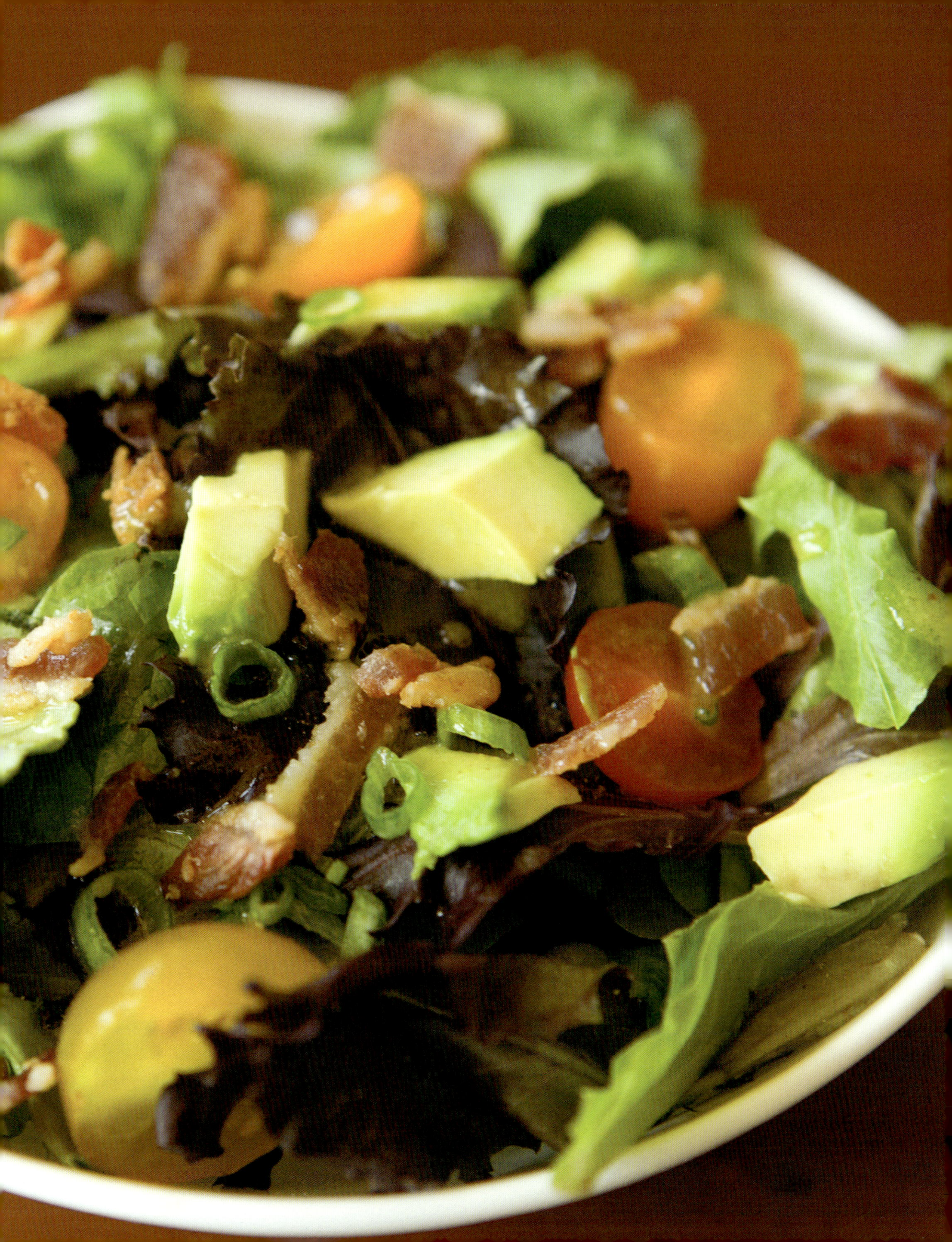

iceberg wedge salad

Refreshing and oh so good. This classic salad is a must have for entertaining or just enjoying a nice lunch with friends.

serves 4

- 1 head iceberg lettuce (cut into 4 wedges)
- 2 cups homemade blue cheese dressing (recipe follows)
- 6 ounces blue cheese, crumbled
- 2 tomatoes, diced
- 3 green onions, chopped
- Ground pepper to taste
- 8 slices bacon, uncured, cooked crispy and chopped

Blue Cheese Dressing

- 5 ounces blue cheese
- ¾ cup Greek yogurt
- ½ cup mayonnaise or my Basic Paleo Mayo, recipe on page 206
- ½ cup heavy whipping cream
- Sea salt and pepper (generous amount)
- 2 tablespoons fresh parsley, finely chopped
- 2 pinches Spike Seasoning (herb spice found in most health stores)

Place iceberg lettuce wedge on serving plate.

Top with homemade blue cheese dressing.

Garnish with diced tomatoes, chopped green onions, and chopped cooked bacon.

Pepper to taste.

Blue Cheese Dressing

Place the cheese into a small bowl and use a fork to break it into coarse chunks.

Add yogurt, mayonnaise and heavy whipping cream, mixing until well combined.

Let it sit for a few minutes to allow the flavors to develop.

Add a generous amount of salt and pepper and two pinches of Spike Seasoning.

Sprinkle with parsley and mix well.

tip: If serving for more people, double lettuce to 2 heads.

no potato salad

KF *Here is a low-carb alternative to traditional potato salads. This salad will become one of your favorites.*

Chop cauliflower into small florets, about ½ inch in size.

Place water into a steaming pot and steam cauliflower on the stove until fork-tender about 15 minutes.

Allow cauliflower to cool, then place in a large bowl.

Add celery, onion, parsley, black olives and sliced egg, saving 3–4 slices to garnish at the end.

Add mayonnaise, mustard, salt, and pepper, and stir to combine.

Serve as desired.

serves 6–8

1 head cauliflower

2 stalks celery, diced

½ small red onion, finely chopped (about 2–3 tablespoons) or green onions, sliced

1 tablespoon parsley, finely chopped

2 large eggs, hard-boiled and sliced

2 tablespoons Basic Paleo Mayo (recipe on page 206) or mayonnaise (I just use regular mayo because it's such a small amount)

1 tablespoon Dijon mustard

¼ cup sliced black olives

½ teaspoon sea salt

½ teaspoon black pepper

½ cup water

tip: Do not overcook the cauliflower because a stronger "cauliflower" smell develops. Red onions tend to have a very strong taste, so you may want to use green onions instead.

caprese salad with tomato and basil

serves 4

Here's a different version of the caprese salad for a vegetarian delight.

- 1 pound heirloom tomatoes
- 2 balls burrata cheese
- ¼ cup fresh basil leaves
- 3 tablespoons extra-virgin olive oil
- 1 teaspoon balsamic vinegar
- ⅛ teaspoon kosher salt
- ⅛ teaspoon cracked black pepper
- 3 cups arugula (optional)

Remove burrata from water and pat dry with paper towel.

Using fingers, pull burrata apart or slice with knife and arrange on a platter.

Slice and arrange medium-to-large tomato slices on top of cheese.

Arrange rinsed basil leaves and arugula (if using) on top.

Drizzle with olive oil and sprinkle with salt and pepper.

tip: Feel free to substitute mozzarella for burrata if you're unable to easily obtain it.

cucumber radish salad

This refreshing and easy salad is a cool starter for any summertime meal. The dill really brings out the flavor of the cucumber.

6–8 servings

2 cucumbers

6 radishes, thinly sliced

1 medium red onion, thinly sliced, or 4 green onions, thinly sliced

10 ounces sour cream

2 tablespoons kosher salt

1 tablespoon white vinegar

Pepper to taste

Fresh dill to taste

You may peel the cucumbers or leave unpeeled. It is your choice. Slice each cucumber very thin.

On a baking sheet, lay cucumbers in one layer and sprinkle liberally with kosher salt. Let rest for 30 minutes. Then take paper towels and blot moisture from cucumbers. Get them as dry as possible.

In a medium mixing bowl, mix sour cream and vinegar.

Add cucumbers to sour cream sauce in the bowl.

Thinly slice red or green onions (your choice).

Thinly slice the radishes and combine with the sliced onions and cucumbers, tossing to cover them in the cream sauce.

Cover and chill at least 6 hours, preferably overnight, stirring occasionally to ensure the onions, radishes, and cucumbers are covered in the cream sauce.

Dust sea salt and pepper to taste and sprinkle with finely chopped dill to your liking.

tip: I prefer using the green onions with the radishes as they are not as strong as the red onions.

salads

grilled caesar salad

serves 2 for a meal, 4–6 for a side

1 small package romaine hearts

Olive oil

Sea salt and pepper to taste

Refer to page 94 for our Caesar Salad Dressing

KF *The original Caesar salad was created in 1924 in Tijuana, Mexico, and was intended to be finger food, rather than a salad. My version uses paleo mayo for the dressing.*

Set grill to high.

Drizzle olive oil on the romaine hearts and season with salt and pepper to taste.

Place the romaine, cut side down, on the heated grill and grill 2–3 minutes until nicely marked.

Plate the romaine, cut side up and add your dressing.

Garnish with grain-free croutons

grain-free croutons

Preheat oven to 350°F (176°C).

In a small heatproof dish, add almond flour, baking powder, thyme, salt, coconut oil, and eggs.

Mix really well until smooth.

Place the heatproof dish in the microwave and heat for 3 minutes.

After 3 minutes, if the center is still raw, add another 30 seconds until the center is completely cooked.

Take out of the microwave and let it cool down a bit.

Flip the dish over and ease the bread out of the dish.

With a bread knife, make a horizontal cut across the square.

Cut the horizontal halves into cubes of your desired size.

Place cubes in a medium bowl.

Mince the garlic cloves and finely chop the parsley, and set aside.

In a small bowl, add the butter and heat in microwave until melted, 20–30 seconds.

Remove melted butter from microwave and add the parsley, garlic, and salt, and stir to combine.

Pour the mixture over the croutons and carefully mix with a spoon. You want to try and coat all of the croutons with the melted butter and seasonings.

Place the croutons on an aluminum-lined baking sheet, in a single layer.

Bake for 12–15 minutes, until golden brown.

Take the baking sheet out of the oven and let the croutons cool down completely before serving them or adding to your salad.

Grain-free Croutons

6 tablespoons almond flour

1 teaspoon baking powder

1 teaspoon thyme

¼ teaspoon sea salt

2 tablespoons coconut oil, melted

2 eggs

Crouton Seasoning

2 cloves garlic, minced or ½ teaspoon garlic powder

1 sprig parsley, finely chopped or a pinch dried parsley

½ teaspoon sea salt

¼ teaspoon Spike Seasoning (optional)

4 tablespoons butter or olive oil

strawberry spinach salad

serves 4–6

- 2 cups strawberries, sliced
- ¼ cup olive oil
- 4 ounces spinach
- 2 tablespoons balsamic vinegar
- 3 tablespoons feta cheese, crumbled
- ¼ cup roasted pecans, chopped
- ¼ cup dried cranberries (optional) (if doing keto, eliminate.)
- 2 tablespoons maple syrup or honey (If doing keto, replace with erythritol syrup, recipe on page 15.)
- 2 teaspoons poppy seeds
- Sea salt and pepper to taste

tip: Substitute spinach with arugula or kale, or your greens of choice.

KF OPTIONAL *I have seen more and more fruit in salads. Try this one with a grilled salmon fillet or chicken. To make this keto-friendly, replace the honey or maple syrup with erythritol syrup and remove dried cranberries. (Recipe for syrup on page 15.)*

Preheat oven to 400°F (204°C).

Line a baking sheet with aluminum foil then place pecans in a single layer.

Sprinkle the pecans with coconut oil and salt and roast for about 8 minutes. Set aside.

Combine the ¼ cup of olive oil and the 2 tablespoons of balsamic vinegar in a large bowl.

Add the honey or maple syrup and the poppy seeds and whisk all of these ingredients together adding salt and pepper to taste.

Then add spinach, strawberries, roasted nuts, dried cranberries, and the feta cheese and combine.

So yummy!

warm fig and arugula salad

If you like fig chutney, you'll love this salad! The flavors of the fig, walnuts, and Roquefort are out of this world.

Preheat oven to 375°F (191°C).

In a small bowl, whisk together the vinegar, mustard, honey, 1 teaspoon salt and ½ teaspoon of pepper.

While whisking, slowly add olive oil and set aside.

Cut the figs into quarters without going all the way through.

Place the figs and walnuts together on a baking sheet lined with parchment paper.

Depending on the ripeness of the figs, roast them for 8–10 minutes (if using dried figs, it takes about 8 minutes) and be careful not to overcook the walnuts. The figs need to begin to release some of their juices.

Meanwhile, place the arugula in a large bowl, add the vinaigrette, and toss well.

Distribute the arugula among six salad plates, add the Roquefort or blue cheese crumbles and then place the warm figs and walnuts on top.

Serve immediately, enjoy!

serves 4–6

- 8–12 ripe fresh figs, depending on their size, or dried figs will work
- 8–10 cups baby arugula
- 1 cup whole walnut halves (4 ounces), chopped
- 8 ounces Roquefort cheese, crumbled (blue cheese will do)
- ¼ cup aged sherry vinegar or balsamic
- 1-½ teaspoons Dijon mustard
- ½ teaspoon honey or maple syrup
- 1 teaspoon kosher salt
- ½ teaspoon freshly ground black pepper
- ½ cup olive oil

salads

watermelon, blueberry, and feta cheese salad

serves 2

- 3 cups watermelon, cut into balls
- 1 cup blueberries
- 2 tablespoons fresh mint, finely chopped
- 3 tablespoons fresh basil, finely chopped
- ½ teaspoon ground black pepper
- ¼ teaspoon sea salt
- 3 tablespoons balsamic vinegar
- ¾ cup feta cheese, crumbled
- ¼ cup olive oil

KF Here is one of the most refreshing, colorful, and appetizing recipes in this book, and so quick and easy to prepare.

Use a melon ball scooper to make watermelon balls. Set aside in a bowl.

Add the black pepper, salt, balsamic vinegar, crumbled feta cheese, and oil to a large mixing bowl and stir until well mixed.

Add in watermelon balls and blueberries and mix with your hands to cover them with the mixture.

Place in the refrigerator and let sit for 10–15 minutes for the flavors to blend.

Divide watermelon balls and blueberries into bowls and garnish with fresh basil leaves, mint leaves, and lightly mix all together.

zucchini noodles with red onion and feta

KF *This colorful dish can be a salad or main dish, you can eat it hot or cold. Yummy!*

serves 2–4

2 zucchini

½ red onion

¼ cup Parmesan cheese, shaved, or feta cheese, crumbled

6 cherry tomatoes

¼ cup black olives, sliced

1 bunch basil, julienned

3 cloves garlic, minced

¼ cup olive oil or coconut oil

Pinch red pepper flakes for heat

Sea salt and pepper to taste

Spiralize the zucchini, using a manual spiralizer or an electrical one.

Slice the onion into rings and mince the garlic and set aside. Julienne the basil and set aside. Cut cherry tomatoes in half and slice black olives, and set aside.

In a frying pan, add the olive or coconut oil and heat over medium-high heat.

Once the oil is hot, sauté onion for about 3 minutes, then add the garlic. Add the rest of the seasonings and sauté for another 2 minutes.

Add the zucchini, tossing it in the frying pan to make sure the noodles are coated with all the ingredients for about 3–4 minutes. I like mine almost overdone and crispy.

Add the basil, toss and cook for about ½ minute more.

Put all ingredients in a bowl or on a plate and crumble the Parmesan or feta cheese.

Top with sliced cherry tomatoes and black olives.

salads

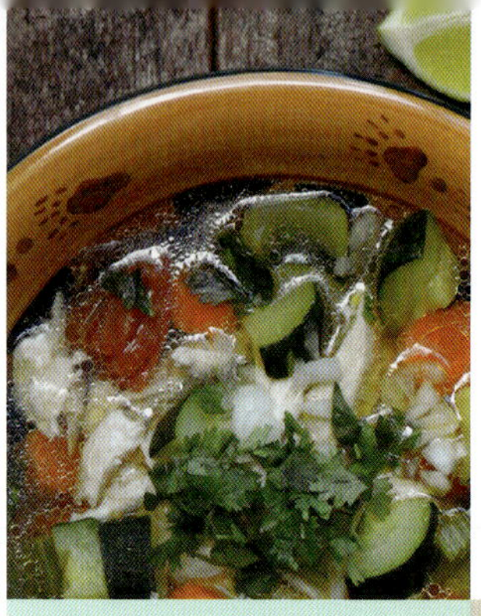

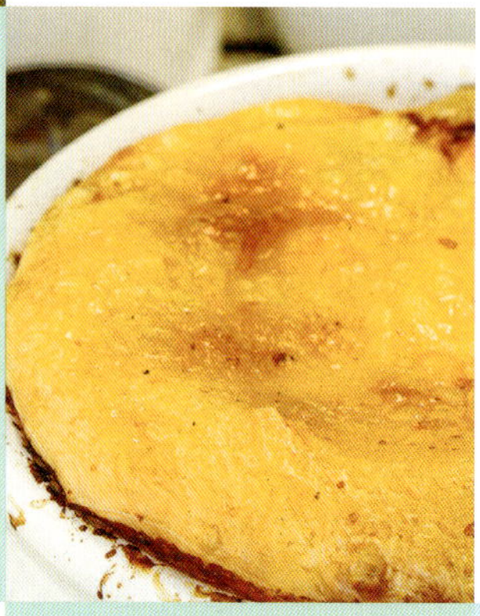

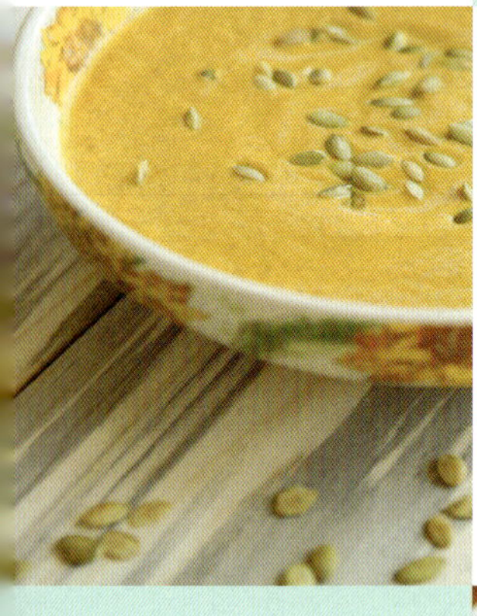

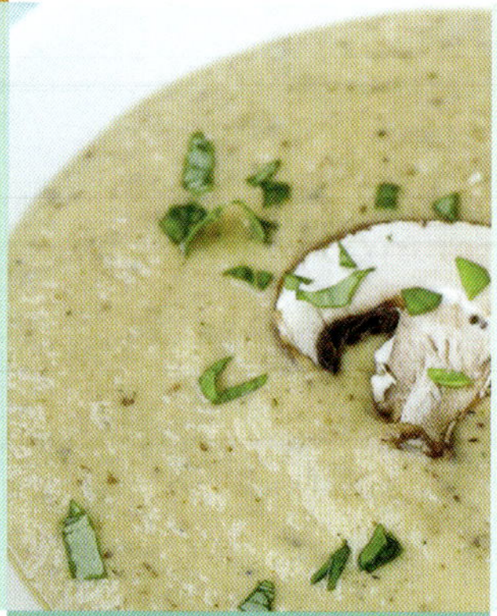

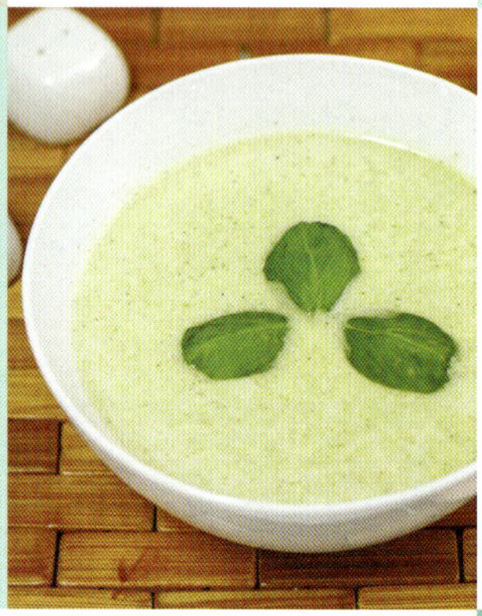

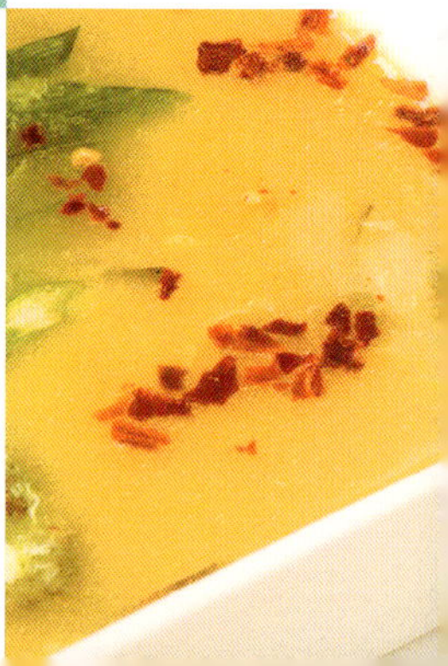

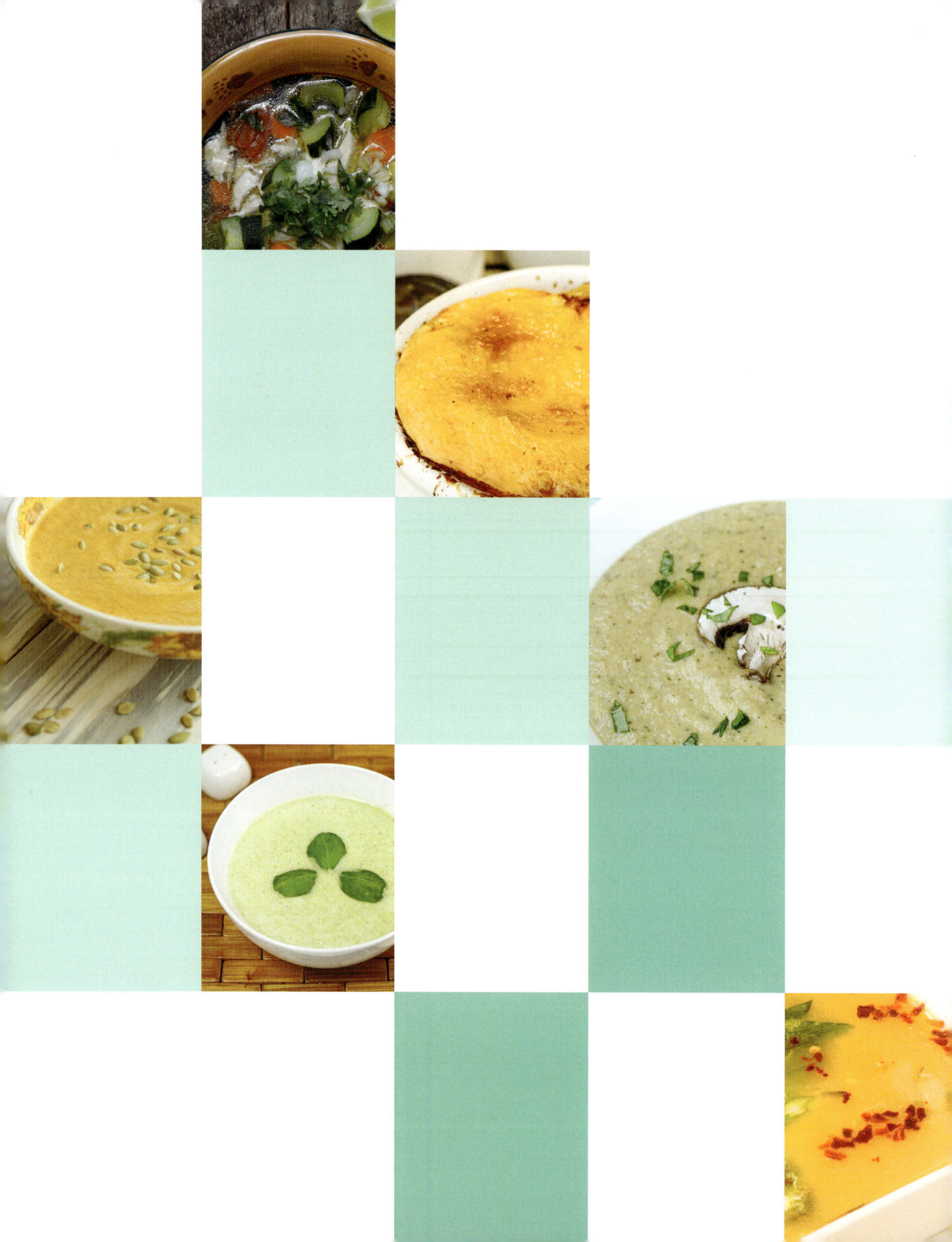

soups

Soups are a great way to blend flavors and can be used as a meal starter, main dish, or side dish. In traditional cooking, common ingredients used for thickening soups have included grains and flours. I have taken out the grains and replaced them with vegetables or seeds. These changes actually make your soups much more nutritious. Enjoy!

KF Denotes that recipe can be made or is keto-friendly.

Creamy Mushroom Soup 117

Egg Drop Soup 120

French Onion Soup 124

Hearty Mexican Chicken Soup 122

Pumpkin Ginger Soup with Toasted Pepitas 123

Roasted Butternut Squash Soup 116

Sopa de Albondigas (Mexican Meatball Soup) 114

Zucchini Cauliflower Soup 118

sopa de albondigas (mexican meatball soup)

makes 4–6 servings

KF *This is a healthy, delicious soup to make for those cool evenings. It has meat, vegetables, and no grains.*

Meatball Ingredients

2 pounds ground beef

2 eggs

¼ cup cilantro, chopped

¼ cup parsley, chopped

1 sprig mint, chopped

½ cup onion, chopped

1 clove garlic, chopped

½ cup almond flour

1 teaspoon sea salt

¼ teaspoon black pepper

½ cup raw shelled sunflower seeds (unsalted), good replacement for rice

Dash thyme

½ teaspoon oregano

Soup Ingredients

4 quarts boiling water

1 teaspoon sea salt

2 tablespoons olive oil

¼ cup onions, chopped

1 cup tomatoes, cooked and chopped (you may use canned tomatoes)

2 zucchini, cubed

2 cups cauliflower, diced

Chop all your fresh meatball ingredients to a small but not fine consistency.

To make your meatballs, mix all meatball ingredients in a large mixing bowl with your hands.

Form meatballs about the size of golf balls and place on a waxed paper-lined cooking sheet and set aside.

Bring water and salt to a boil.

Place meatballs in water and lower your flame to medium low to simmer for one hour.

This will become your soup as the meatballs cook.

In a saucepan, heat oil and sauté onions until tender; add tomatoes.

Bring saucepan to a simmer, then add into soup pot.

Add zucchini and cauliflower and cook for 15 minutes more.

Serve with fresh lemon or lime to add flavor.

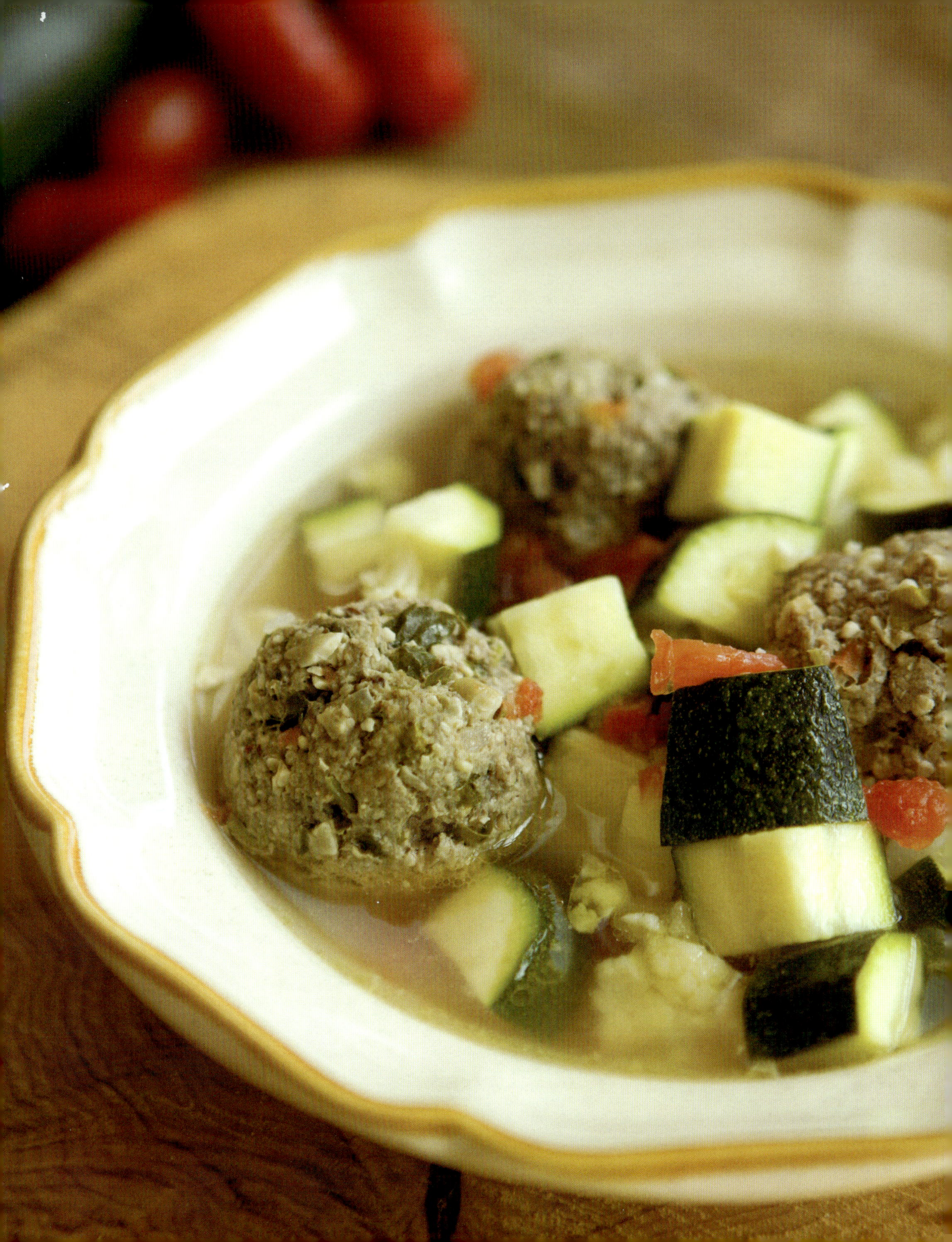

roasted butternut squash soup

serves 8–10

Butternut squash provides high amounts of potassium, vitamin A, and vitamin C. It can also be part of a low-carb diet, depending on your carb management.

- 1 large butternut squash (about 5 pounds) peeled and cut into cubes, all about the same size. It's so much easier to buy the squash already cut up for you.
- 1 green apple, cored and sliced
- 1 medium yellow onion, chopped
- 2 carrots, chopped
- 4 tablespoons olive oil
- 2 teaspoons ground cinnamon
- 1½ teaspoons sea salt
- ½ teaspoon ground cumin
- 1 teaspoon chili powder
- 2 tablespoons butter
- 3 cups chicken broth
- ½ cup canned coconut milk, full-fat

Preheat oven to 400°F (204°C).

In a large bowl, combine the butternut squash, olive oil, 1 teaspoon cinnamon, ½ teaspoon salt, and cumin. Mix together, coating the squash well. Spread out on a rimmed baking sheet.

In the same bowl that the butternut squash was in, toss the apple slices, onion, and carrots to coat with the residue of oil and seasonings.

Place on a second aluminum-lined baking sheet and add both baking sheets to the oven. Roast for 35–40 minutes until soft, stirring once.

Heat up butter over medium heat in a large pot on the stove. Add the roasted ingredients and then the chicken broth. Add 1 teaspoon each of salt, cinnamon, and chili powder. Bring to a boil, then reduce heat to low and simmer, covered, for 20 minutes.

Using an immersion blender, combine the ingredients until smooth, or transfer to a blender to purée.

Add the full-fat coconut milk at the end and blend until mixed through.

Serve warm.

creamy mushroom soup

KF *Creamy deliciousness and warm wholesomeness, this keto-friendly soup is the ultimate comfort soup.*

Add oil to a Dutch oven or heavy soup pot.

Place pot over medium heat and add onions, mushrooms and a pinch of salt.

Sauté for 10–12 minutes or until onions are translucent and mushrooms are soft.

Add garlic and serrano pepper and cook for a minute, then add the spices.

After another minute or so, add wine to deglaze the pot.

Cook for 5 minutes, stirring occasionally, then add chicken broth and coconut milk.

Let the mixture simmer for about 10 minutes or until it thickens to your liking.

Blend the creamy mixture in a blender or use an immersion blender.

Serve as a starter, main course, or as an ingredient to a cream sauce or casserole.

serves 4–6

- 1 tablespoon olive oil
- 1 white onion, diced
- 1 8-ounce package mixed wild mushrooms
- 6 cloves garlic, minced
- ¼–½ serrano pepper, roughly chopped (remove pith and seeds if you don't like spicy food)
- 1 teaspoon fresh thyme, chopped
- 1 teaspoon sea salt
- ¼–1 teaspoon Spike Seasoning (adjust to taste); I prefer 1 teaspoon.
- ½ teaspoon crushed black pepper
- ¼ cup white wine
- 1 cup chicken or vegetable broth
- 1 cup canned coconut milk, full-fat (mix well after opening)

tip: If you're eating this as a starter or main dish and don't like spicy food, you can remove the serrano entirely.

zucchini cauliflower soup

serves 6–8

The blend of zucchini and cauliflower make for a light and zesty soup to satisfy anyone's appetite.

- 3 small zucchini, trimmed and shredded
- 1 head cauliflower, stem and leaves removed, and broken into medium-sized pieces for cooking
- 1 teaspoon sea salt
- 1 teaspoon pepper
- 3 tablespoons olive oil or coconut oil
- 4 tablespoons salted butter
- 2 medium onions, finely minced
- 3 garlic cloves, minced
- 5½ cups chicken stock or broth
- 3 tablespoons lemon juice
- ½ teaspoon white pepper
- 1 tablespoon dried basil
- 1 tablespoon dried Italian seasoning
- 1 tablespoon dried parsley
- ⅓ cup almond or coconut milk, unsweetened
- 4 tablespoons heavy cream (optional)

Shred zucchini after removing stems with a cheese shredder or a mandolin.

Place the shredded zucchini in a colander over a bowl and sprinkle with salt and allow to drain for about 30 minutes.

In the meantime, cook cauliflower in a saucepan with water for 15 minutes or until tender.

Transfer cauliflower to a blender and add coconut or almond milk and the butter. Purée and set aside.

In another saucepan, add olive or coconut oil, and cook onion and garlic over medium heat, for about 5 minutes, stirring occasionally.

Dry zucchini on paper towels and add to the onion mixture.

Cook over low heat for about 5 minutes and add the stock.

Simmer for 15 minutes, then add the coconut mixture, salt, herbs, and lemon juice.

Using an immersion blender, purée the soup in the pot or add all of the ingredients into a blender, and pulse until desired consistency.

Adjust seasonings to your liking. So delicious and healthy!

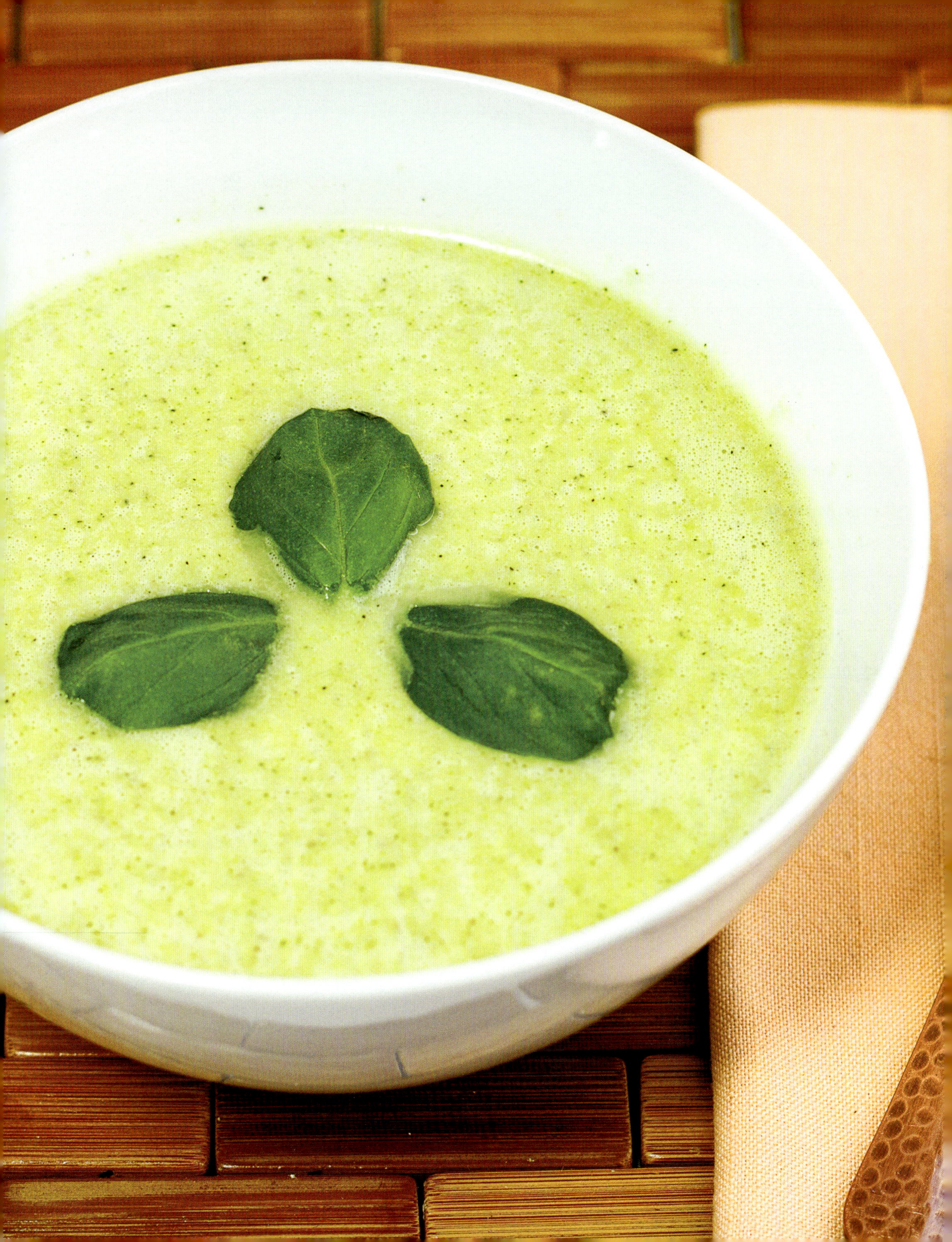

egg drop soup

serves 6–8

2 large eggs

8 ounces button mushrooms (regular mushrooms)

3 green onions

1 tablespoon ginger, freshly grated

1 tablespoon sesame oil

4 cups chicken broth

2 cups water

1 tablespoon gluten-free soy sauce

1 tablespoon almond flour

Crushed red chili flakes for heat, if desired

KF I love Chinese food! I always loved Chinatown in LA. I really miss that wonderful egg drop soup. It's really quite delightful, takes no time at all to make, and has hardly any calories or carbs!

Wash and slice the mushrooms. Thinly slice the green onions on the diagonal. Use a vegetable peeler or the side of a spoon to scrape the skin from the ginger, then use a cheese grater to grate about 1 tablespoon.

Add the mushrooms, green onions, and ginger to a large soup pot along with the sesame oil. Sauté the vegetables over medium heat or just until the mushrooms begin to soften.

Add 4 cups chicken broth, 2 cups water, and 1 tablespoon of gluten-free soy sauce to the pot.

In a small bowl, stir the almond flour together with 1 tablespoon of water until the flour is completely dissolved. Pour into the soup pot and stir to combine.

Bring the soup to a boil over medium-high heat.

While waiting for the soup to boil, whisk two eggs in a bowl.

Once the soup is boiling, turn the heat down to low and wait until the soup stops boiling.

Use a large wooden spoon to stir the pot and make the broth swirl in one direction. While the soup is swirling, slowly pour the whisked eggs into the soup in a thin stream. Let the eggs sit in the hot liquid, undisturbed, for 1–2 minutes to fully set.

Taste and adjust the salt by adding more soy sauce, if needed. Serve hot.

To spice it up a bit, sprinkle red chili flakes upon serving.

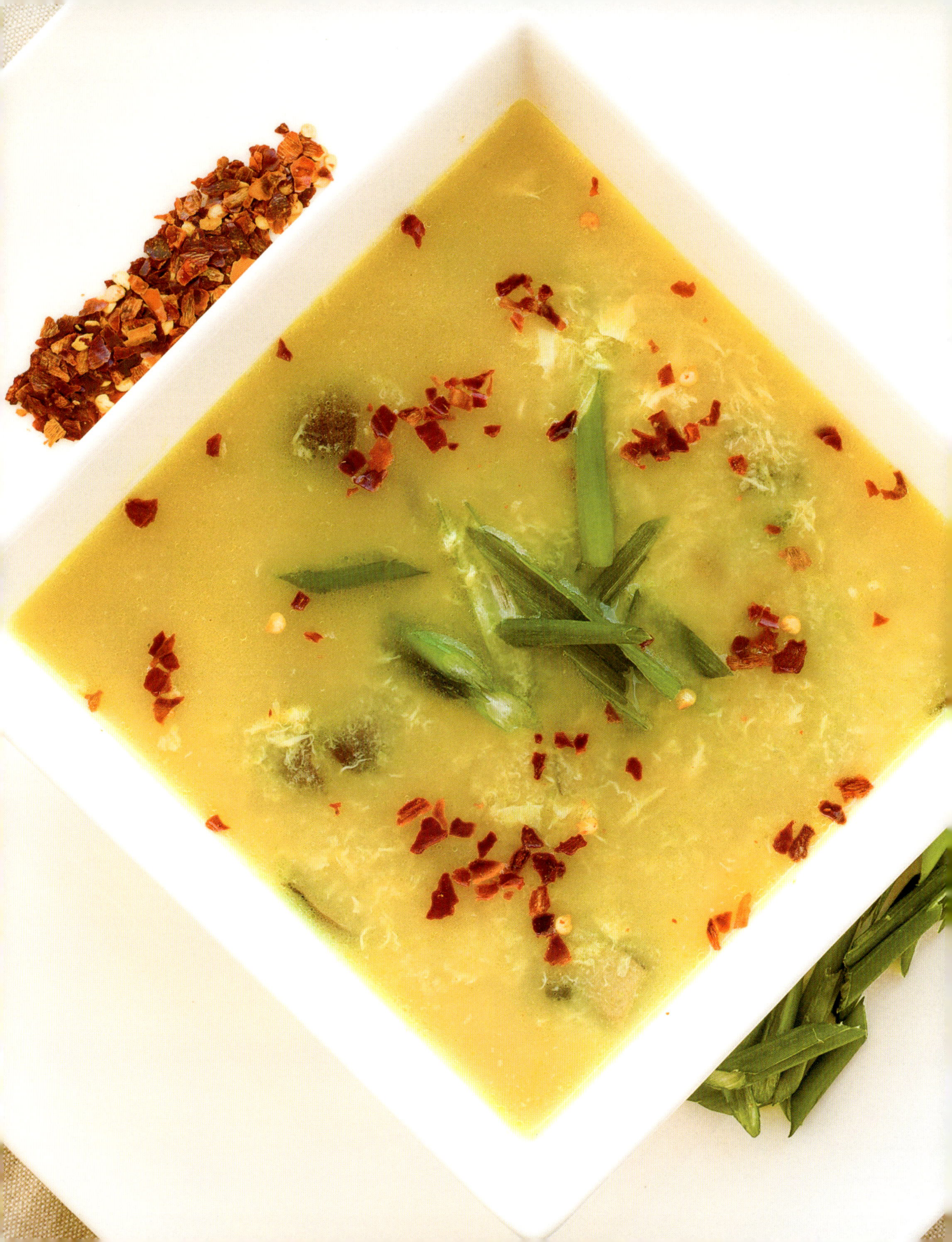

hearty mexican chicken soup

serves 4–6

KF *This hearty traditional Mexican soup, or caldo, has been served to generations of families. This is sure to revive your energy and warm your heart.*

- 1 whole chicken (cut up, if possible)
- 3 quarts water
- 1½ medium onions
- 1 tablespoon sea salt
- 3 carrots, sliced about ⅛-inch thick round
- 4 celery stalks, sliced about ⅛-inch thick
- 3 zucchini, cubed
- ½ large tomato, diced
- Cilantro

Place water, salt, and a whole onion in a large pot to boil.

If not cut up already, carefully cut the chicken into pieces: breast, thighs, legs, wings.

Once water is boiling, add the chicken pieces into the water and lower your heat to medium low to simmer for 15 minutes.

Remove the chicken, the onion, and set aside to cool.

Meanwhile, you can slice the carrots, celery, zucchini, and dice the tomato, and place vegetables into the chicken stock.

Bring to boil for 10 minutes. Reduce heat to medium low again and let simmer for 5 minutes.

While the stock is simmering, use a big serving spoon to remove some of the fat floating in the pot.

Place chicken parts into bowls and ladle soup and vegetables over the chicken.

Save unused cups of chicken stock to use in other recipes.

Serve the soup with chopped cilantro, chopped half onion, and tomatoes on the side as a nice garnish and flavor enhancer.

tip: You can use skinless chicken in this soup if you wish. Traditionally, the soup is made with the skin on, as it enhances the flavor. You can remove whatever fat you don't want.

pumpkin ginger soup with toasted pepitas

This creamy and zesty soup will warm the belly as much as the soul.

serves 8–10

1 tablespoon butter

1 tablespoon fresh ginger, peeled and diced

¼ cup carrot, diced

¼ cup celery, diced

½ cup onion, diced

1½ cups pumpkin purée, either fresh or canned

3½ cups vegetable stock

Kosher salt and freshly ground pepper to taste

¼ teaspoon ground cinnamon

⅛ teaspoon cayenne pepper

½ cup heavy cream (optional)

¼ cup raw hulled pepitas (pumpkin seeds)

In a medium saucepan, heat butter over medium-high heat, add ginger, carrot, celery, and onion, and sauté until vegetables begin to soften, stirring frequently about 3–5 minutes.

Add pumpkin and stir well. Add vegetable stock and bring to a boil.

Add salt, pepper, cinnamon, and cayenne pepper, reducing heat to simmer uncovered until vegetables are soft, about 20 minutes.

Transfer to a blender or food processor and purée mixture until smooth.

Strain the soup back into the saucepan and add the cream. Keep warm.

Place the pepitas in a medium nonstick skillet and toast over medium-high heat, stirring, until the seeds are fragrant, light brown, and begin to pop, about three minutes.

To serve, ladle the warm soup into serving bowls and garnish with the toasted pepitas sprinkled over the top.

tip: I absolutely prefer the soup without the cream. It presents a more savory taste and is a personal choice.

french onion soup

serves 10–12

KF OPTIONAL *This version is based on a European recipe shared by my friend, Vallorie Belcore-Przybylowicz. The secret is the cheese.*

4 onions, sliced very thin

1 stick butter

Sea salt and pepper to taste

3 10½-ounce cans beef broth or consommé

1 8-ounce package Gouda cheese (or more based on how many people you are serving)

French bread (recipe follows) If doing keto, eliminate the bread.

Preheat oven to 400°F (204°C).

Melt one stick of butter in a sauté pan. Sauté onion in butter over low heat, approximately 20 minutes. Do not brown. Heavily salt and pepper to your liking.

When done, pour off the butter.

Add beef consommé over the onion mixture. Bring to a boil.

Meanwhile brown 1-inch slices of French bread on both sides in oven.

Place bread in oven-safe soup bowl, add soup mixture, then top with large slice of Gouda cheese.

Increase oven to 425°F (218°C) and bake until it boils over and cheese browns.

tip: Depending on how many people you serve, you can use less Gouda and make this for fewer servings.

french bread

Preheat oven to 400°F (204°C).

Mix warm water, maple syrup and 1 package of active yeast in a bowl and set aside. Wait 10–15 minutes until it's frothy and doubled in size. It took me about 10 minutes.

In a mixing bowl, add the 2 flours and the salt, and stir to combine.

Add the butter into the flour mixture and mix on medium until the butter crumbles.

Add the beaten eggs and yeast mixture, and blend. The mixture will be very sticky.

Grease a baking pan with cooking spray.

Take out your bread dough, using some cassava flour on your hands and shape it into a French bread loaf on the greased baking pan. Let the loaf rise for about 40 minutes before baking.

After rising, bake for 25–30 minutes.

Remove from oven and let cool for 10 minutes.

½ cup warm water

2 tablespoons maple syrup

1 package active dry yeast

4 eggs, beaten

1⅓ cups cassava flour

1⅓ cups arrowroot flour

1 teaspoon sea salt

4 teaspoons butter, sliced

Cooking spray

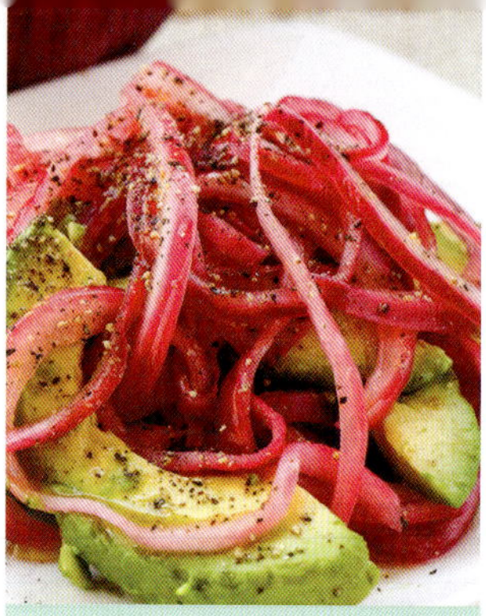
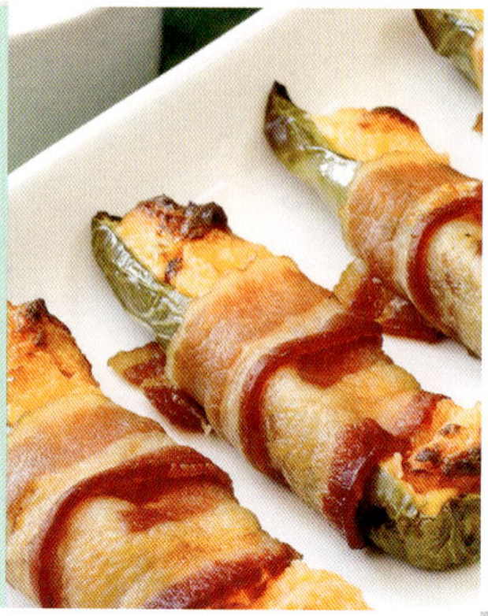
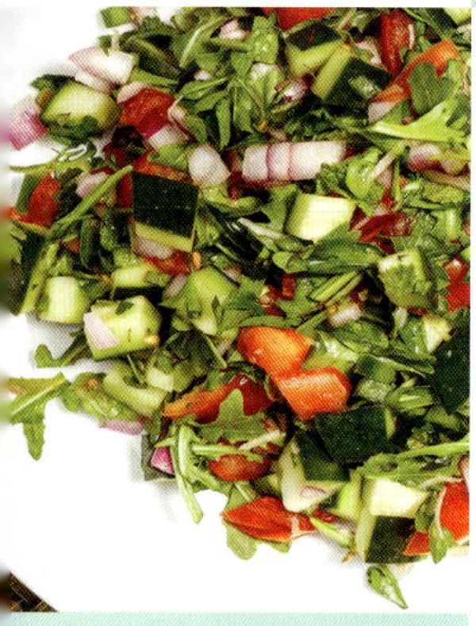
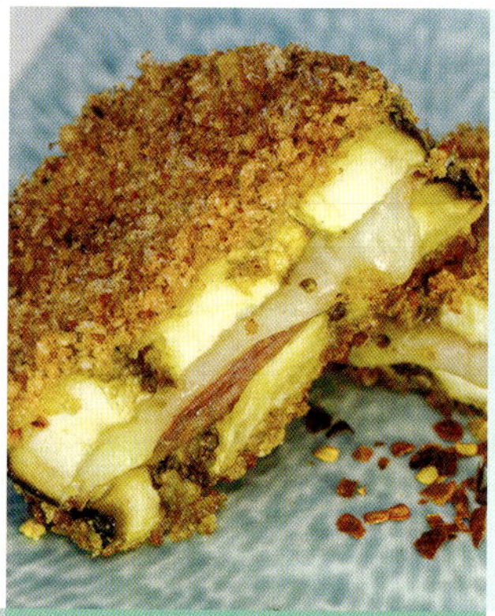
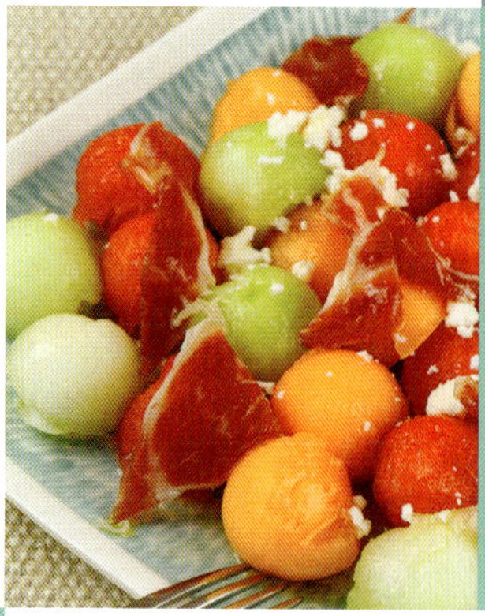

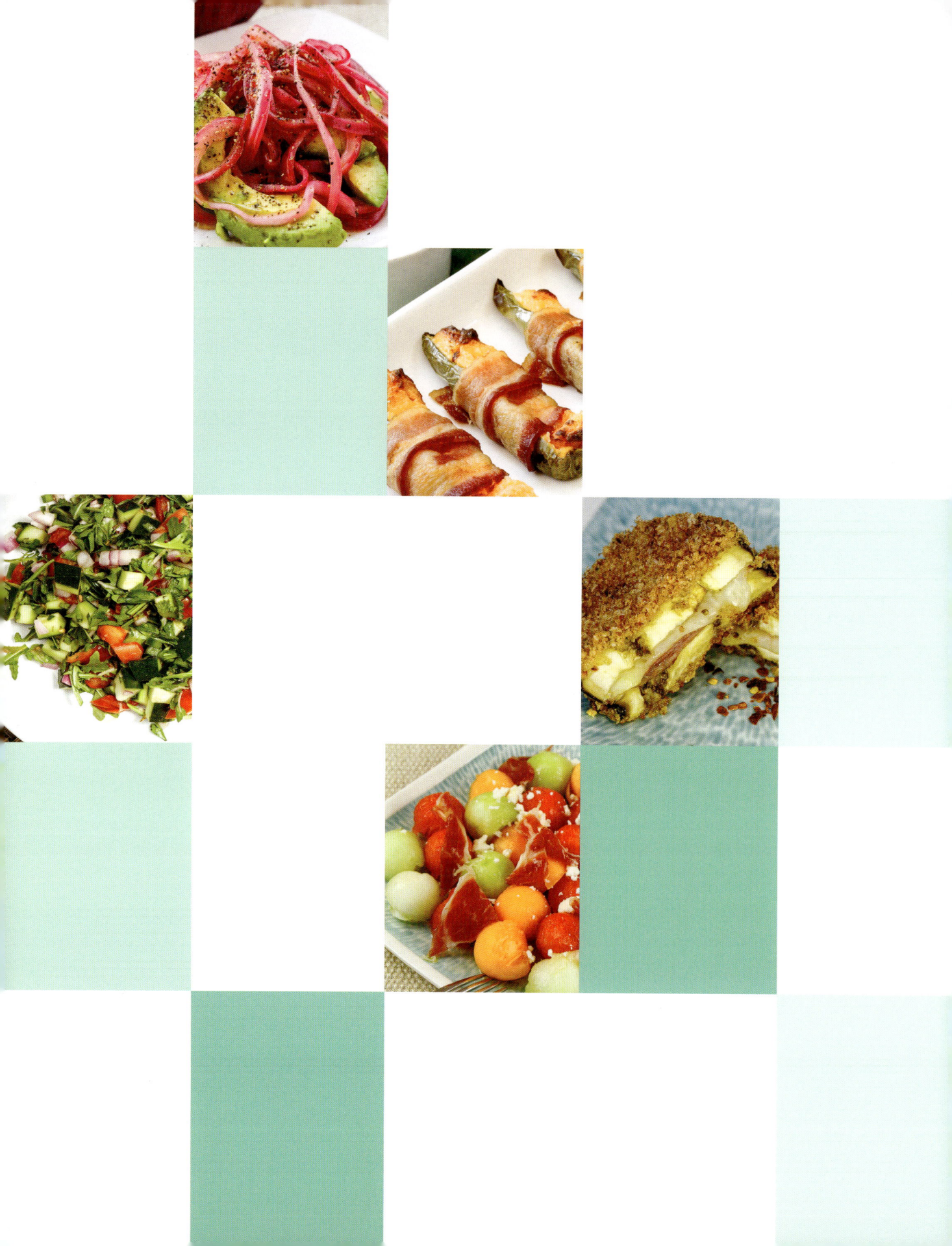

small plates

Small plates are so popular today and make a delightful contribution to a get together or happy hour. One benefit of small plates is that you can enjoy a variety of dishes. They're shareable and delicious.

KF Denotes that recipe can be made or is keto-friendly.

Avocado and Sweet Red Onion **128**

Eggplant Sandwich **136**

Jalapeño Bacon Cheese Poppers **130**

Jean's Tabbouleh **132**

Roasted Mushroom Medley **135**

Shrimp-Stuffed Yellow Chile Peppers **140**

Three Melon Salad with Feta and Prosciutto **134**

Zucchini Grilled Cheese Melt **138**

avocado and sweet red onion

serves 4–6

2 ripe avocados

½ medium-sized red onion, thinly sliced rings

2 tablespoons vinegar (red wine or apple cider vinegar)

1 tablespoon lemon juice

1 tablespoon extra-virgin olive oil

Coarse ground black pepper

Sea salt

KF *This dish is widely consumed in the Caribbean, especially in Cuba where both ingredients are abundant.*

Place the sliced red onion in a covered container.

Add 2 tablespoons of vinegar and lemon juice to the onion. Mix and store in refrigerator to marinate a few minutes.

In the meantime, cut avocados in half and take the pit out. Slice the halves lengthwise to get 6–8 slices and remove the peel. Place on a serving dish.

Place the red onion over the sliced avocado.

Drizzle olive oil and the marinade from the onions.

Sprinkle salt and pepper to taste.

tip: You can pickle the red onion overnight with the vinegar and lemon juice.

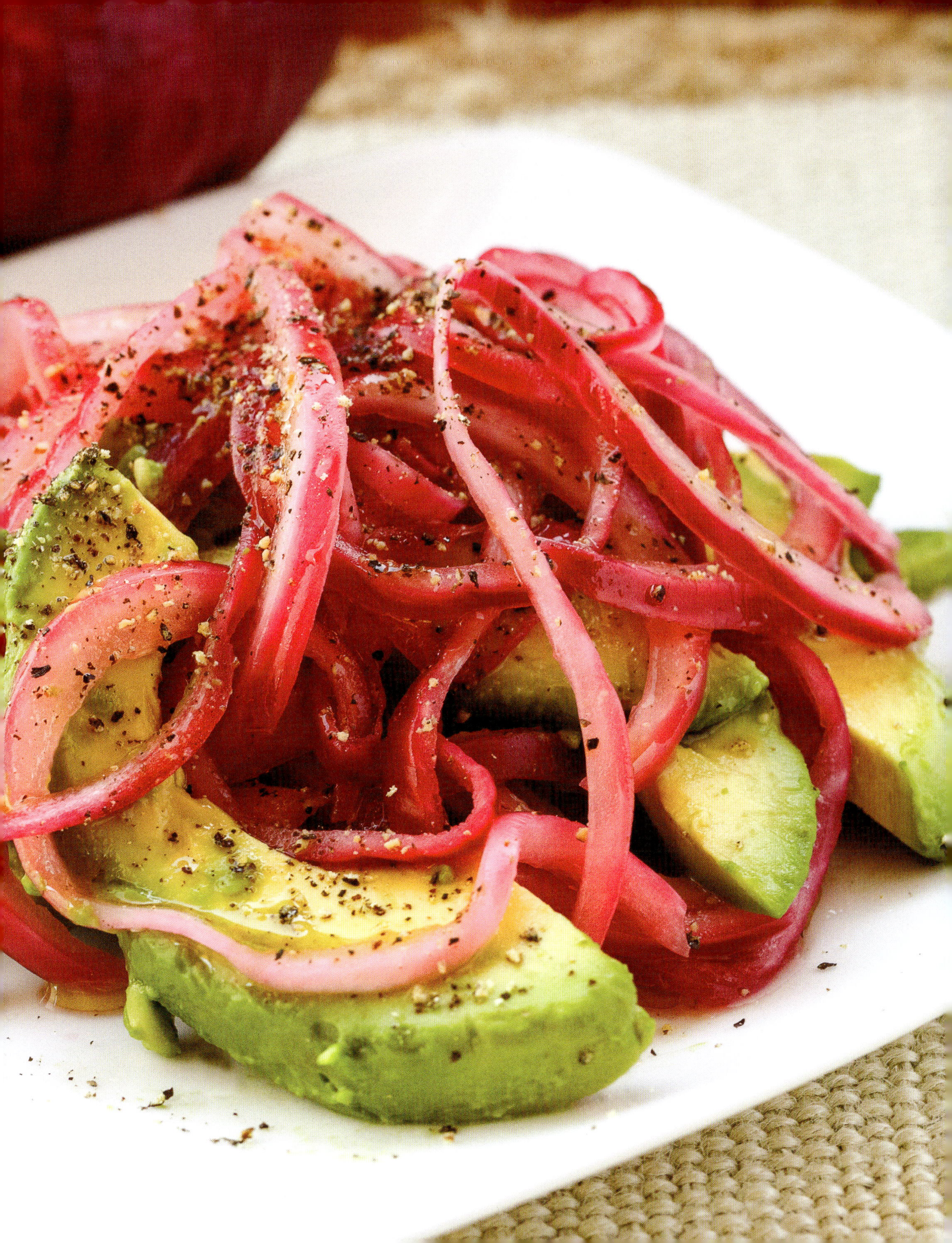

jalapeño bacon cheese poppers

serves 10–12

- 12 fresh jalapeño peppers
- 8 ounces cream cheese, softened to room temperature
- 1 cup cheddar cheese, shredded
- 1 clove garlic, chopped
- ½ teaspoon smoked paprika
- 12 slices bacon, uncured, cut in half
- 24 toothpicks
- Sea salt to taste

Here is my absolute favorite appetizer! Every time I am asked to bring a side dish, I think of this recipe. It's out of this world. Jalapeños are spicier than other peppers, just make sure to let people know. One time, I bought a batch, and they were so spicy, the whole dish was ruined, but that's very rare. Make sure to clean them well and remove all the seeds and the pith. The seeds are what make them spicy. Also wash your hands after working with jalapeños. I forgot once, and when I took my contacts out, the next time I put them back in my eye, the juice from the jalapeño was still on them. My eyes burned so badly I had to throw my contacts away.

Preheat oven to 400°F (204°C).

Line a large baking sheet with parchment paper (best for clean-up). Place a baking rack on top of the baking sheet. Set aside.

Cut the jalapeño peppers in half lengthwise. Remove seeds and center membrane. Set aside.

Mix the cream cheese, cheddar cheese, garlic, and paprika together until combined. Salt to taste. I add just a pinch.

Spoon-fill equally among all 24 jalapeño halves.

Wrap each stuffed jalapeño with a half slice of bacon and stick a toothpick through the center to ensure the bacon stays in place.

Place each on the baking rack and bake for 20–30 minutes or until the bacon is crisp to your liking. I like to turn the oven to broil for the last minute or two to get the bacon extra crispy.

Serve immediately.

Cover leftovers and keep in the refrigerator for up to 4 days.

Make ahead tip: Jalapeño peppers can be stuffed and wrapped 1 day in advance. Refrigerate until ready to bake. You can also assemble and freeze up to 2 months. Thaw overnight in the refrigerator and bake as directed.

tips: Instead of jalapeño peppers, try using those mini sweet peppers often sold in the produce section. They are a great option if you don't like spicy.

I like to cook the bacon halfway through and then wrap the pepper because oftentimes the bacon isn't crisp when the rest is done!

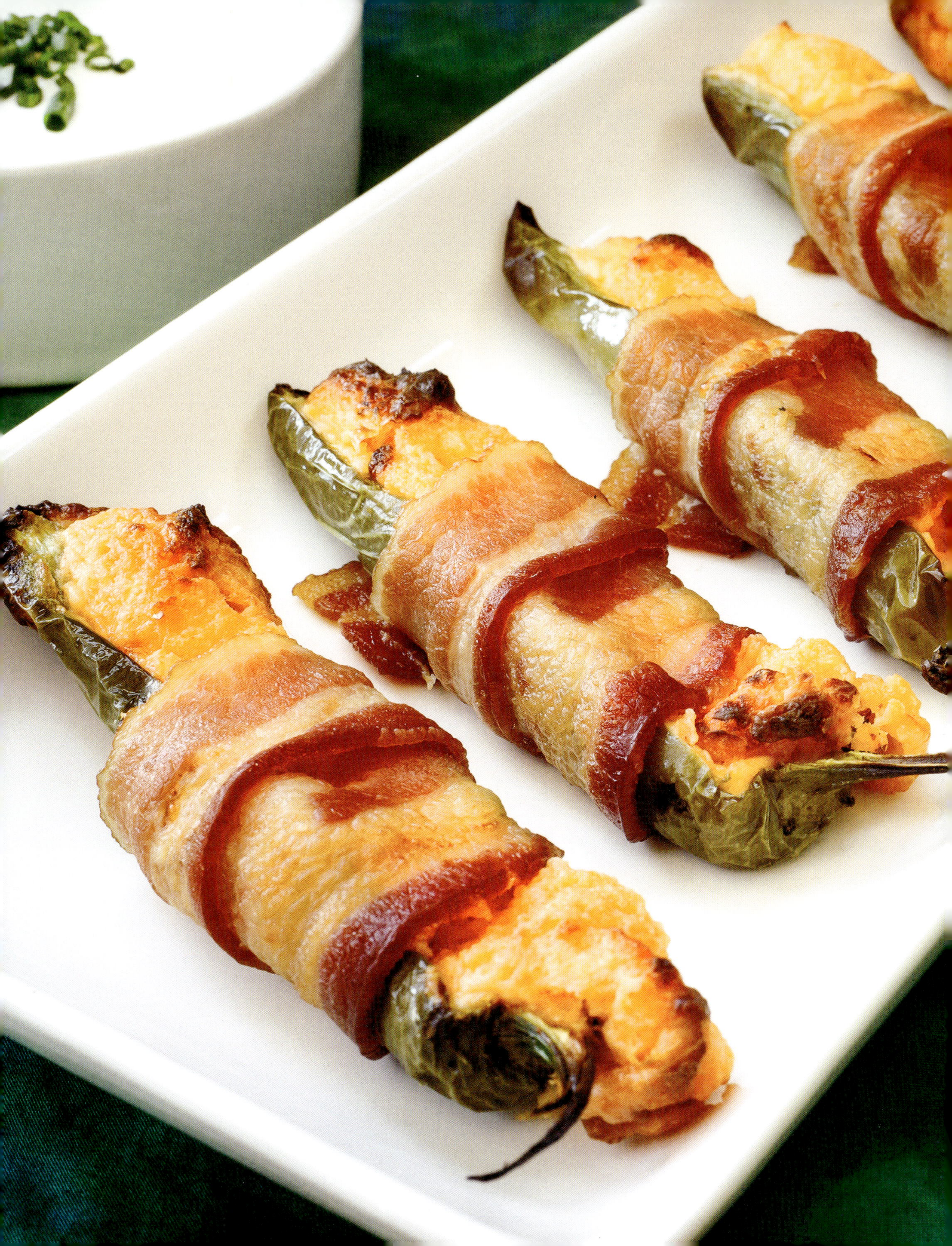

jean's tabbouleh

serves 6–8

KF *I had a dear friend, Jean Nelson, who was part Lebanese. She would always make tabbouleh. When I realized how healthy it was, I wanted to include this recipe in remembrance of Jean.*

---

1 cup arugula, finely chopped

2 seedless cucumbers, peeled and diced

4 ripe tomatoes, diced

3 cups parsley leaves, about 2 bunches, diced

1 cup fresh mint leaves or basil, chopped

6 scallions or 1 small red onion, diced

4 cloves fresh garlic, finely chopped

1 jalapeño, chopped fine for some heat, if desired

Dressing

⅓ cup lemon juice (about 3 lemons)

¾ teaspoon sea salt

½ teaspoon ground black pepper

Zest of 1 lemon

½ cup extra-virgin olive oil

Cut the cucumber and tomatoes into ¼-inch cubes, place in a colander, sprinkle generously with salt, and let the vegetables "sweat" out their excess moisture for about 15–20 minutes.

Wash the parsley, then pat dry with paper towels, a clean dish towel, or spin in a salad spinner.

Repeat with the mint and or basil. When the herbs are clean and dry, use a sharp knife to dice them. Place herbs in a large mixing bowl together with the finely chopped arugula.

Trim scallions or red onion and dice into very small pieces and add into mixing bowl. Now add chopped jalapeño, if desired.

Drain cucumbers and tomatoes of the released liquid and then add vegetables to the herbs. Toss to combine.

In a small bowl, use a fork to mix lemon juice, salt, pepper, and lemon zest.

Slowly drizzle in olive oil while you continue to mix with a fork. Then pour dressing over the vegetables and toss gently until all the ingredients are coated.

Cover and refrigerate for at least an hour so the flavors can blend.

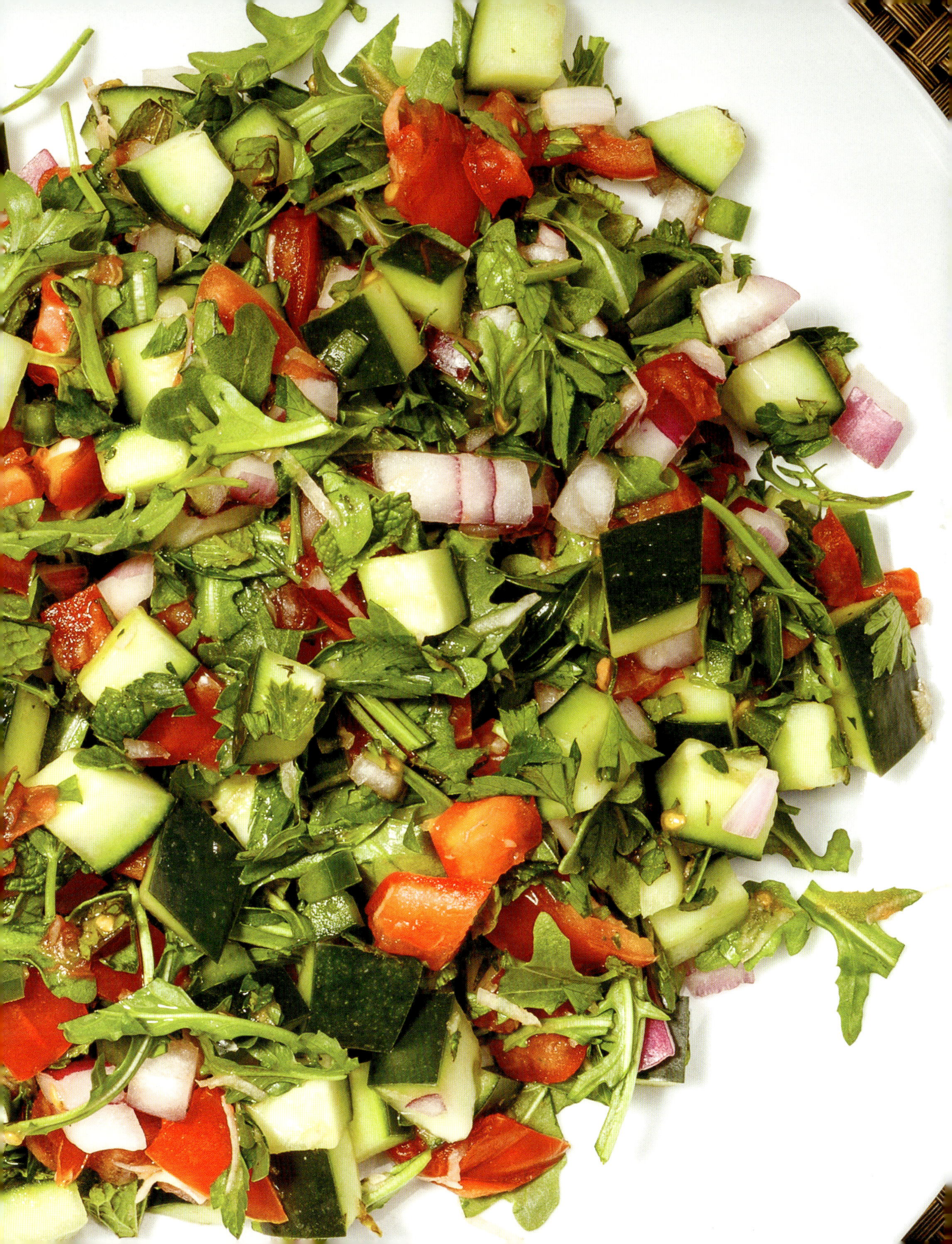

three melon salad with feta and prosciutto

serves 2 - 4

Have your taste buds yelled "OMG!"? My Three Melon Salad with Feta and Prosciutto just might do that at every bite!

3 slices prosciutto, uncured

½ honeydew melon, cubed or in balls

½ cantaloupe, cubed or in balls

¼ watermelon, cubed or in balls

½ cup feta cheese, crumbled

3 leaves fresh basil or mint leaves, julienned

Dressing
Juice of 3 lemons

3 tablespoons Tajín (a Mexican spice)

2 tablespoons smoked paprika

4 tablespoons olive oil

½ teaspoon maple syrup

Sea salt and pepper to taste

tip: Tastes really good garnished with mint leaves.

Arrange the slices of prosciutto in a single layer on a cutting board and cut into one-inch length strips.

Use a melon baller to create balls of honeydew, cantaloupe, and watermelon. If you don't have a melon baller, cut melons into ½-inch cubes. Place in a serving bowl and refrigerate.

Dressing
Mix all dressing ingredients together and set aside.

When ready to serve, sprinkle feta and prosciutto strips over balled or cubed melons. Sprinkle the julienned basil on top.

Drizzle dressing over melon. Serve and enjoy.

small plates

roasted mushroom medley

KF *Did you know that mushrooms are a great source of potassium? This is a great replacement for grain and potato-based chips that go a long way in pleasing your taste buds.*

Preheat oven to 300°F (149°C).

Wash and slice mushrooms very thin, using a mandolin if possible. The mushrooms shrink so much that I prefer to buy large ones.

Place mushrooms and olive oil in a bowl.

Using your hands, mix the mushrooms with the oil to coat as best as you can.

Line a cookie sheet with parchment paper and place a single layer of mushroom slices.

Pour the butter over the mushrooms and sprinkle the seasonings to your liking.

Bake in the oven for 20–30 minutes until golden brown and semi-crispy.

Check to see if they are the right crispness. Ovens vary, so make sure you check them at 20 minutes so that they don't overcook.

serves 8–10

1 box cremini mushrooms
1 box button mushrooms
6 large shiitake mushrooms
½ cup butter, melted
¼ cup olive oil
Lemon pepper
Garlic salt
Smoked paprika

tip: Crispiness will depend on how much butter you prefer. The more you use, the less crispy they will be. Either way, they are very delicious.

small plates

eggplant sandwich

This has become a favorite of mine because it's so amazing and can be served as an appetizer or lunch. You can experiment with so many different fillings as long as you don't load too much filling between the slices. It just doesn't work well if it's overly stuffed. I hope you'll find it as tasty as I do!

serves 4

- 1 eggplant
- 2 eggs, beaten
- ¾ cup almond flour, or more as needed
- Sea salt and ground black pepper to taste
- Pinch red pepper flakes or more if you like heat
- 1 cup pork rinds
- 4 slices provolone cheese, cut into quarters or any cheese you prefer
- 4 thin slices cooked ham or turkey, uncured
- Olive oil
- ½ cup Parmigiano Reggiano cheese, finely grated

Preheat oven to 450°F (232°C).

Cut the eggplant into 8 slices, ⅛-inch thick or (as thin as you can), which will make 4 sandwiches. Make sure the slices are not too thick.

Beat eggs in a small, shallow bowl. Set aside.

Mix flour, salt, black pepper, and cayenne pepper in a large shallow dish, set aside.

Put the cup of pork rinds in a blender and blend until they look like breadcrumbs and pour into another large shallow dish.

Line a baking sheet with aluminum foil. Drizzle 1 teaspoon of olive oil in circles about 3 inches in diameter onto the foil, where the sandwiches will be placed.

Top one slice of eggplant with 1 slice provolone cheese or any cheese of choice, and 1 slice of cooked ham or turkey.

Place an equally sized slice of eggplant on top and set aside on a flat dish.

Repeat with remaining eggplant slices. Be very careful not to overstuff with ingredients.

Gently press each eggplant sandwich into the seasoned flour to coat; shake off excess.

Dip both sides of each sandwich into beaten egg, then press into pork rind crumbs.

Place on the prepared baking sheet onto the oiled areas while you work the remaining eggplant sandwiches.

Sprinkle about 2 teaspoons of Parmigiano Reggiano cheese over the sandwich. Repeat with remaining 3 sandwiches.

Drizzle tops of each sandwich with 1 teaspoon of olive oil.

Bake in the preheated oven for 10 minutes.

Turn over sandwiches and sprinkle 1 teaspoon Parmigiano Reggiano cheese onto the top.

Bake until browned and a paring knife inserts easily into the eggplant, 8–10 minutes more.

Serve warm or at room temperature.

zucchini grilled cheese melt

serves 2–4

- 2 zucchini, grated (about two cups)
- 2 cups cheddar cheese, shredded
- 1 large egg
- ½ cup Parmesan cheese, freshly grated
- 2 green onions, thinly sliced
- ¼ cup arrowroot flour (if doing keto, use almond flour)
- Sea salt and pepper to taste
- Cooking spray or coconut oil
- Waxed paper

KF OPTIONAL *This is a healthy and tasty alternative to using bread for your grilled cheese sandwich. Great for a meal or cut them up as appetizers.*

Squeeze excess moisture out of zucchini with a clean kitchen towel. Repeat the process until liquid is almost gone.

In a medium bowl, combine zucchini with egg, Parmesan, green onions, and arrowroot flour. Season with salt and pepper.

In a large skillet, apply cooking spray to layer the bottom of the pan away from any open flame. Place sprayed skillet over medium heat.

Scoop about ¼ cup of the zucchini mixture onto one side of the waxed paper and shape into small squares

Add a square to heated skillet. Add another formed patty on the other side.

Cook until lightly golden brown on both sides, about 4 minutes per side.

Remove from heat to drain on paper towels and repeat with remaining zucchini mixture patties.

Wipe skillet clean. Place two cooked zucchini patties in the same skillet over medium heat.

Top both with shredded cheese, then place two more cooked zucchini patties on top to form two sandwiches.

Cook until the cheese has melted, about 2 minutes per side.

Repeat with remaining ingredients. Serve immediately.

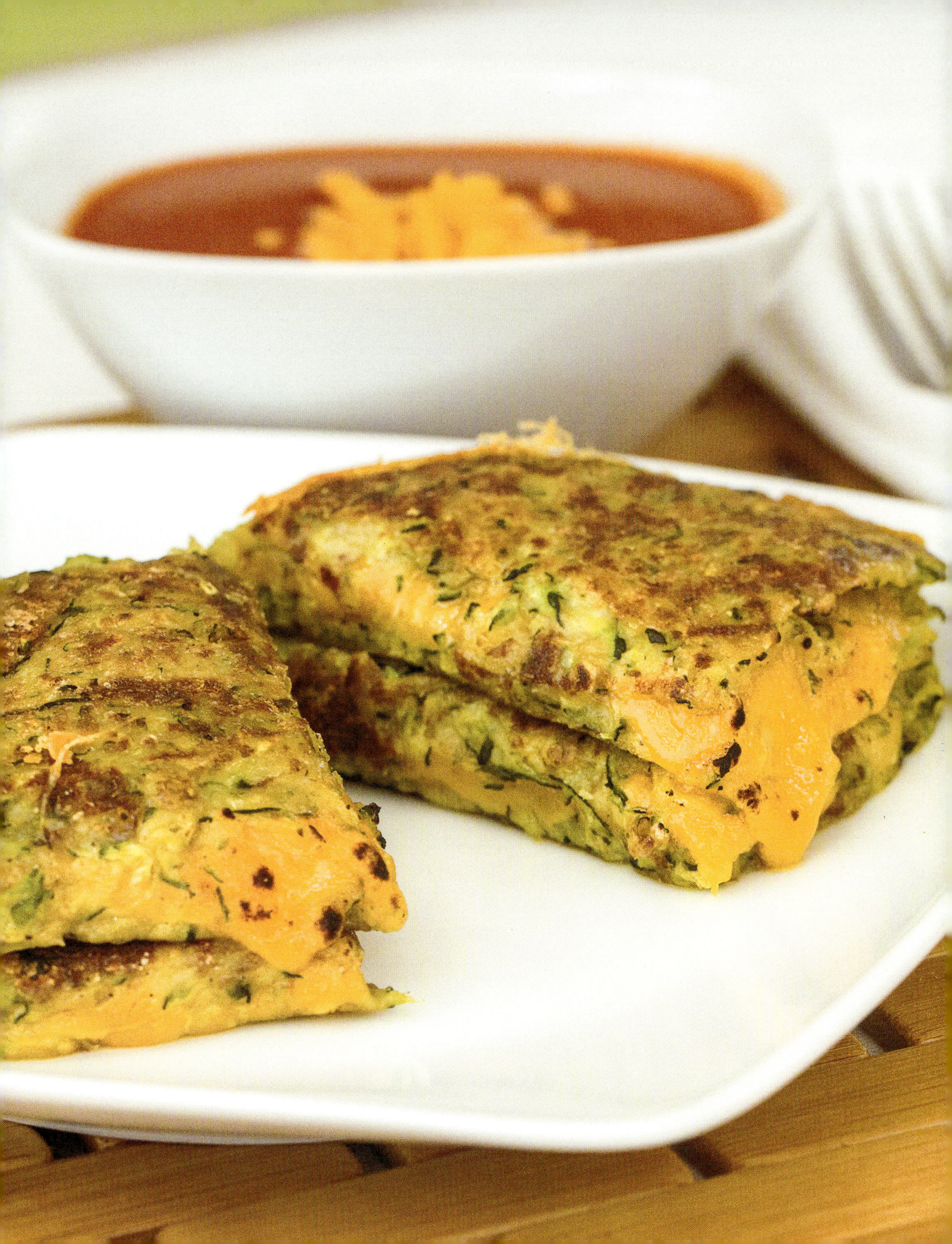

shrimp-stuffed yellow chile peppers

serves 2–4

KF *Influenced by Mexican cuisine, these peppers stuffed with shrimp are the perfect treat for weekend get-togethers.*

6 yellow chile peppers

6–8 raw medium shrimp, peeled, deveined, and chopped

1 cup onion, chopped

½ cup red bell pepper, chopped

2–4 garlic cloves, chopped fine

1 tablespoon lemon juice

Gluten-free soy sauce

Mayonnaise or my Basic Paleo Mayo (recipe on page 206)

Spike Seasoning—a blend of 39 different herbs, spices, and vegetables (optional)

Lemon pepper

Olive oil

Preheat oven to 450°F (232°C).

Make a slit on one side of each yellow chile pepper, lengthwise. With the blunt tip of a butter knife or a teaspoon, remove the seeds and pith (the white stuff seeds are attached to) to make room to stuff with shrimp. Be careful not to cut all the way through the pepper.

Bake at 450°F for 10 minutes until slightly cooked and softened.

If you haven't done so, chop onion, red pepper, and garlic. Chop the shrimp into small pieces, about ¼ inch.

In a 10-inch skillet, heat 1 tablespoon of olive oil over medium heat.

Add onion and cook for 3 minutes, then add the red pepper and garlic and cook for another 3 minutes.

Add the shrimp and sprinkle Spike spice (if using) liberally and add lemon pepper to your liking for added flavor. Stir and cook for about a minute or less until shrimp is done, like a stir-fry.

Once shrimp is not translucent, add lemon juice. Remove from heat, cover, and let stand for a couple of minutes.

Once the peppers are done, remove from oven and while still warm, stuff with the shrimp mixture. Drizzle with soy sauce.

To add the mayonnaise, take a small plastic sandwich bag and add 2–3 tablespoons of mayonnaise inside a lower corner and seal the bag.

With a pair of scissors, cut the tip of the opposite corner to make a small, ¼-inch hole. You can squeeze the mayo toward the hole to "stripe" your stuffed pepper.

Or, you can just put a dollop of mayo on top, using a teaspoon. Use extra soy sauce and mayo if desired.

tip: I've tasted many variations of this dish. Some recipes call for cream cheese or Pepper Jack cheese instead of the mayo. I prefer using mayonnaise. Also, some recipes wrap the chiles in bacon, but I find that bacon overwhelms that wonderful shrimp flavor. I know you will love this!

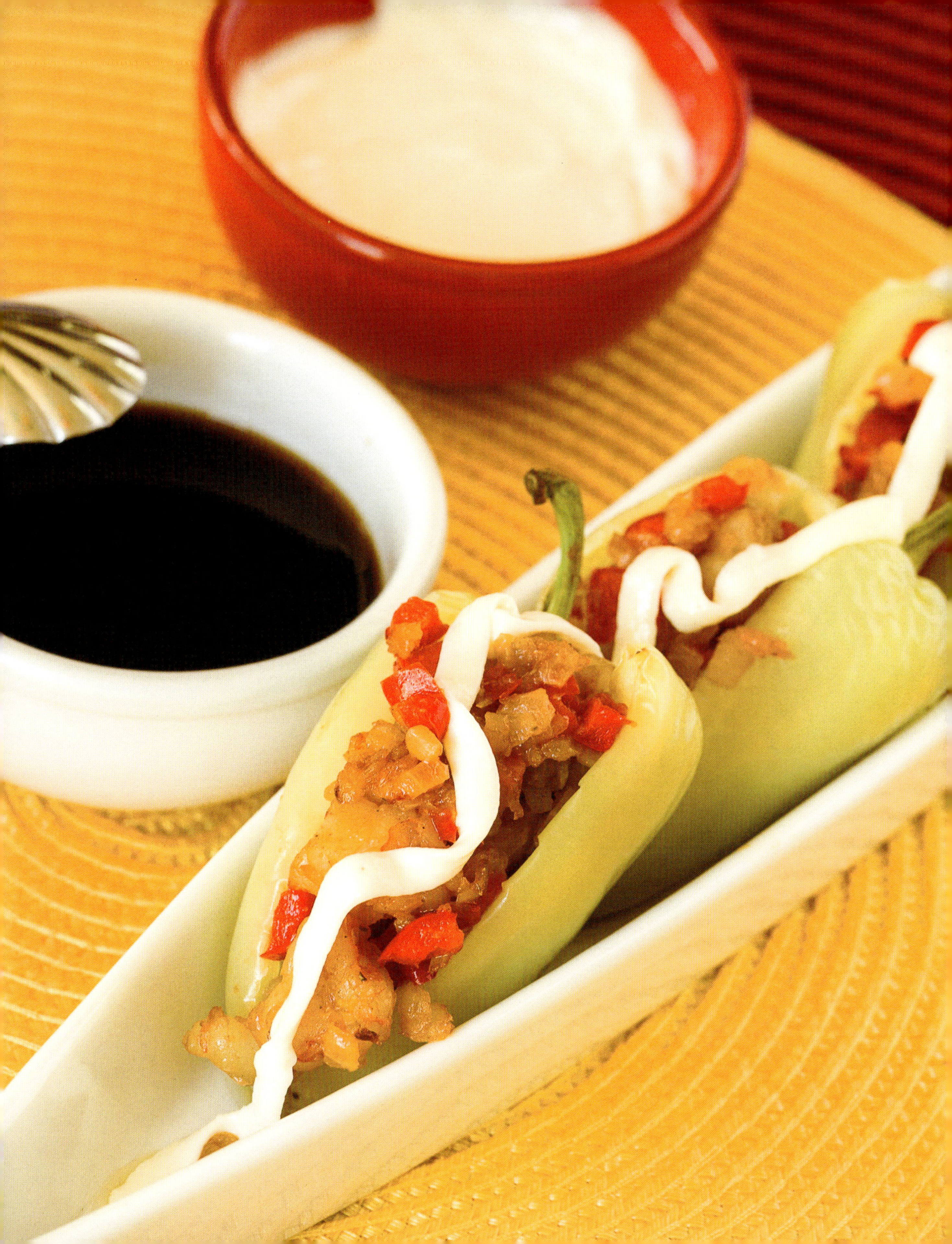

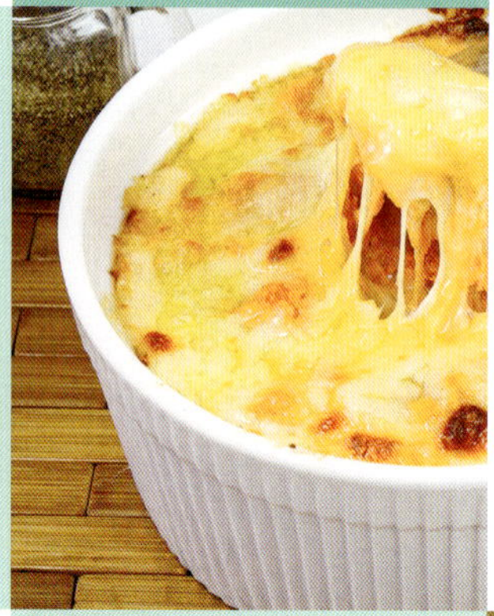
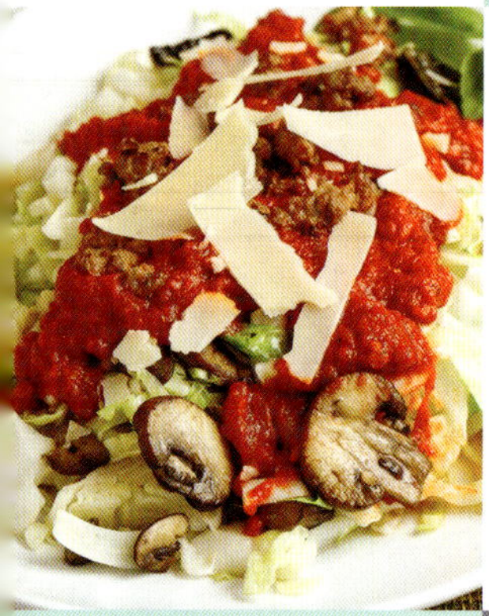
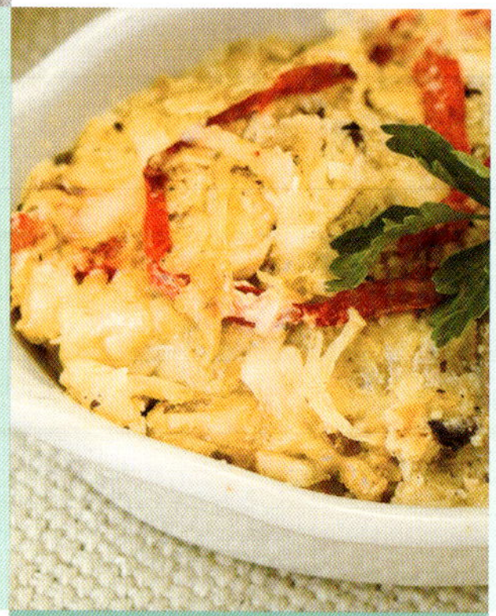
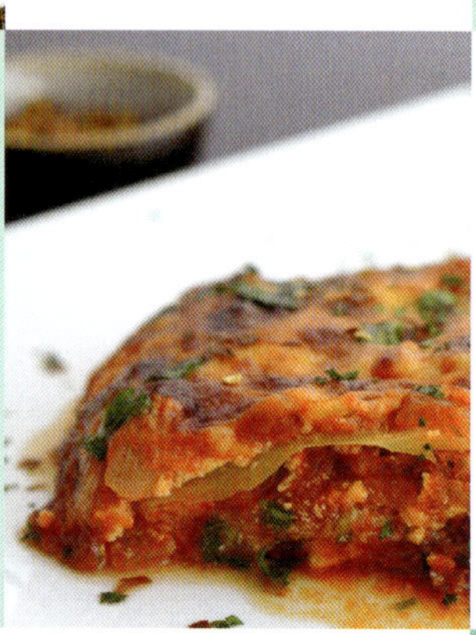
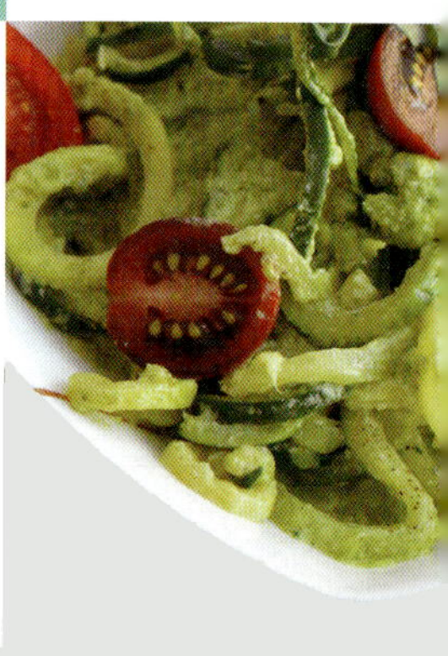

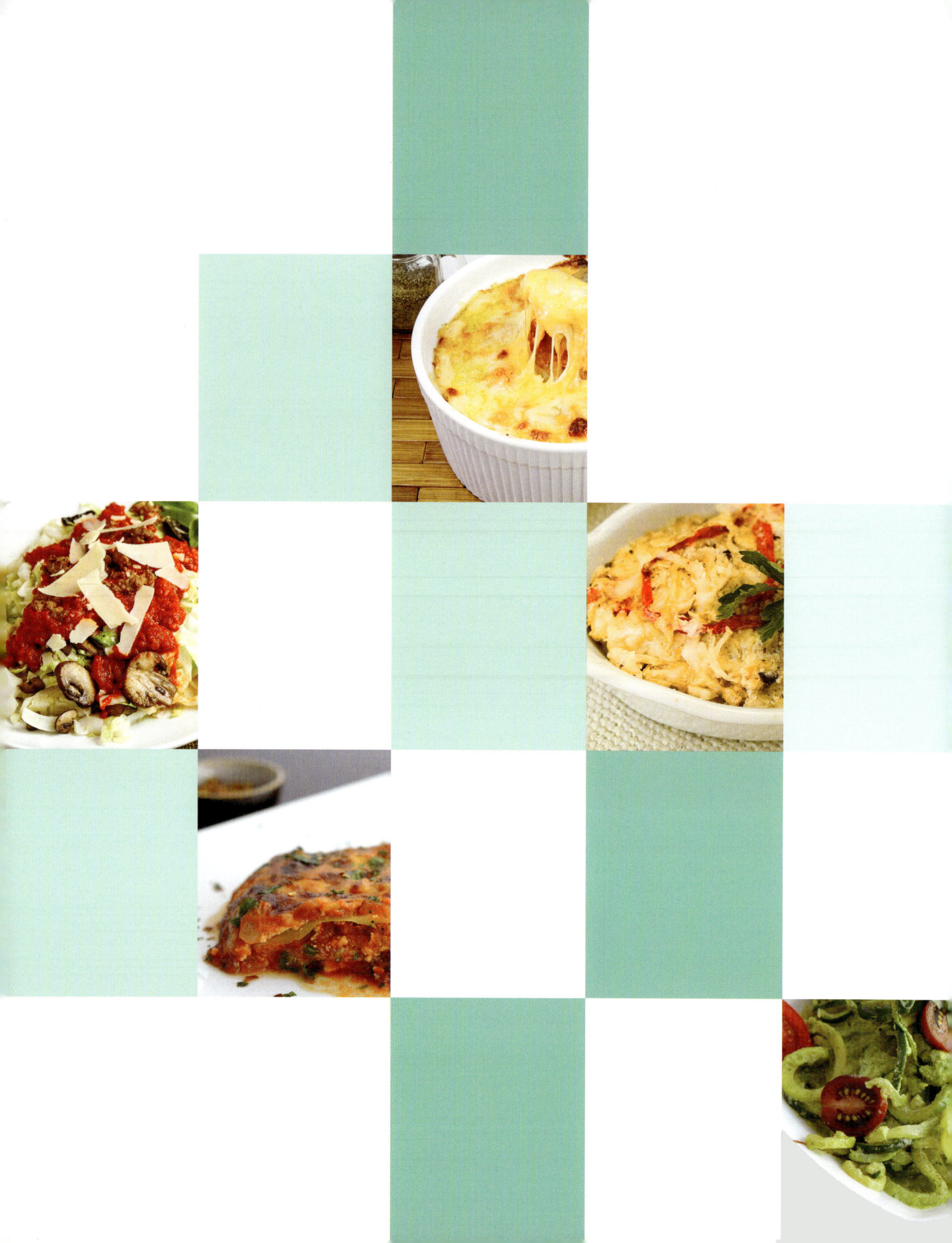

pasta dishes

On my journey to replace grain-based foods, I discovered plant-based alternatives to make creative and healthier choices. Spaghetti squash, butternut squash, zucchini, cabbage, and carrots can be enjoyed instead of pasta and they're tasty too!

KF **Denotes that recipe can be made or is keto-friendly.**

Butternut Squash Mac and Cheese 144

Cabbage Lasagna 145

Cabbage or Zucchini Pasta Bolognese 148

Cheesy Spaghetti Squash Casserole 146

Chicken Tetrazzini 150

Zucchini Pesto Pasta 147

Zucchini Ravioli 152

butternut squash mac and cheese

serves 8

1 whole butternut squash

2 tablespoons olive oil

3 tablespoons butter, unsalted

¼ cup arrowroot flour (if doing keto, use almond flour)

1 cup coconut or almond milk, unsweetened

½ cup cream

⅛ teaspoon nutmeg, freshly grated

¾ cup Gruyère cheese, shredded (save ¼ cup for end of recipe)

¾ cup white cheddar cheese, shredded (save ¼ cup for end of recipe)

¼ cup Parmesan cheese, grated

Sea salt and pepper to taste

KF OPTIONAL *Cheesy! Here's a really fun and healthy alternative to traditional mac and cheese for you to enjoy! I discovered how well the sweet and nutty taste of butternut squash can be substituted for pasta. If doing keto, replace arrowroot with almond flour.*

Preheat oven to 375°F (191°C).

Cut the squash in half lengthwise. Place on baking pan for preparation.

Scoop out the seeds. Drizzle the olive oil on the two halves, salt and pepper to taste.

Place both halves skin side up on the baking sheet and bake for 30–40 minutes or until done or almost done since you will bake again.

In the meantime, sauté butter over medium-high heat with arrowroot flour and cook stirring well with a wooden spoon until no visible flour remains, 1–3 minutes.

Whisk in the milk, cream, nutmeg, and a generous pinch of salt and bring to a boil. Simmer, whisking frequently to smooth out any lumps until the sauce is thickened, about 4–5 minutes.

Remove from heat and add a pinch of pepper and ½ cup each of the Gruyère and cheddar cheese. Stir until smooth.

When the squash is done, scoop out meat from both halves and chop into small pieces. Add squash to the cheese sauce and mix well.

Sprinkle the top with remaining ¼ cup of the Gruyère and cheddar cheeses, including the Parmesan cheese.

Pour into a 9 x 13-inch casserole dish and bake for 25–30 minutes until lightly browned and bubbly.

cabbage lasagna

I had to give up all pasta because they are grains. When I figured out you could use cabbage as the noodle for lasagna, I was thrilled! You can also use it for regular pasta; just slice it thinly. Just be sure to soften the cabbage. This actually works very well substituting for a wide noodle. Of course, the other option that works well are zucchini noodles sliced wide. I think you'll really get a kick out of this recipe.

Preheat oven to 350°F (177°C).

Wash and peel cabbage leaves off head. Boil for 1½–2 minutes so they are pliable to use in this dish. Drain well.

In a saucepan, sauté onion and garlic in olive oil until soft, but not brown. Add Basic Marinara Sauce; bring to boil.

Meanwhile, combine ricotta, half of the mozzarella, eggs, parsley, basil, and pepper in a large bowl and blend.

Coat an 11 x 9-inch baking pan with cooking spray. Spread a thin layer of sauce in bottom of pan.

Cover with a layer of cabbage leaves. Spread ½ cup of sauce over the cabbage and top with half of the ricotta cheese mixture.

Repeat with another layer of cabbage, sauce, and cheese mixture. Finish with a layer of cabbage and remaining sauce. Sprinkle remaining mozzarella cheese on top.

Bake for 40–45 minutes until cheese is melted and golden brown.

Let it stand 10 minutes before serving.

Garnish with fresh, chopped basil leaves.

tip: May add browned ground turkey or beef.

serves 4–6

- 1 head cabbage
- 1 cup onion, chopped
- 1 teaspoon garlic, minced
- 3 tablespoons olive oil
- 2 cups Basic Marinara Sauce (see recipe page 258)
- 15 ounces ricotta cheese
- 8 ounces mozzarella cheese, grated
- 2 eggs
- ¼ cup fresh parsley, chopped
- 1 teaspoon dried basil
- ½ teaspoon ground black pepper
- Basil leaves for garnish
- Cooking spray

cheesy spaghetti squash casserole

serves 10–12

KF *If you and your family enjoy cheesy goodness, my Cheesy Spaghetti Squash Casserole will bring smiles and become a favorite for all to enjoy without the usual pasta. Great for a potluck and a delicious vegetarian dish.*

Olive oil

2½ cups spaghetti squash, cooked

½ cup sour cream

1 large egg, lightly beaten

1 tablespoon garlic, minced

1 teaspoon sea salt

½ teaspoon dried thyme

1 cup sharp cheddar cheese, shredded

Ground black pepper to taste

Preheat oven to 350°F (177°C).

Lightly coat 1.5-quart baking dish with olive oil and set aside.

Cut the squash in half, clean out the seeds from each half, and generously sprinkle with olive oil, sea salt, and pepper. Place on a baking sheet skin side up and bake for 45 minutes at 350°F (177°C).

When done, let squash cool before removing the flesh. Once cooled, take out all squash "strings" with spoon or fork and place in a bowl.

Add sour cream, egg, minced garlic, thyme, and cheddar cheese and mix well.

Pour mixture into the prepared baking dish, add the cheese as liberally as you would like and bake at 350°F (177°C) for 40–45 minutes.

Allow to stand 10 minutes and serve.

zucchini pesto pasta

Making your own zucchini pasta is always fun, and this tasty recipe has a bit of a different slant on the pesto sauce. I think you will love this one.

Put the nuts and the next five ingredients in a blender and purée until mixture is smooth but with a little grainy texture.

Add sea salt and pepper to taste. Set aside.

Using a vegetable peeler or vegetable spiralizer, make thin zucchini ribbons.

Add zucchini ribbons to a 3-quart pot with 2 cups of water and boil for 3 minutes or sauté in a pan with a little olive oil. I prefer to sauté them, but both methods work well.

Pour the pesto mixture over the zucchini and serve.

makes 2–4 servings

2 zucchini, trimmed and cut in half, widthwise

½ cup raw cashew nuts (soak the cashews in a bowl of water overnight, preferably, then drain and discard the liquid. If time is an issue, soak for 4 hours, then drain.)

½ cup olive oil

1 garlic clove, peeled

Handful fresh basil

Handful fresh parsley

1 lemon, juiced and zested

Sea salt and freshly ground black pepper

Water

cabbage or zucchini pasta bolognese

serves 4—6

KF *Here's a versatile meal that you can have with or without meat. Best of all, you avoid the noodles. Have fun with this one!*

2 zucchini (if using cabbage, take 1 cabbage head, remove leaves and boil 1½ minutes to soften)

Water

Bolognese Sauce

8 ounces sausage, uncured, chicken, or pork (optional)

3–4 tablespoons olive oil

8–10 baby bella or cremini mushrooms, sliced

2–3 garlic cloves, minced

1 cup Basic Marinara Sauce (see page 258 for recipe.)

2 tablespoons fresh basil, chopped

Sea salt and ground black pepper to taste

¼ cup Parmesan cheese, grated

For Cabbage
Peel cabbage head taking off leaves from head.

Fill a 3-quart pot half way and set on medium-high heat and bring to a boil.

Add cabbage leaves and let them boil for 1–1½ minutes. Try not to over boil. A bit al dente will work best.

Strain leaves in colander and run cool water over them.

Place cooked cabbage leaves on cutting board and slice thin to make your noodles. Set aside while you prepare your sauce.

For Zucchini
Using a vegetable peeler, peel the zucchini. Cut the zucchini lengthwise into ribbons, using the vegetable peeler, until you reach the seed core. (Reserve the seed core and peel for another use, such as a salad). Set aside while you prepare your sauce.

Bolognese Sauce
In a saucepan, heat your Basic Marinara Sauce. Set aside.

If using meat in your sauce:
Simmer 1 tablespoon olive oil in a large skillet.

Cook the meat, breaking it up with a spoon, until cooked through. Drain off the fat.

Add to the Basic Marinara Sauce and continue simmering over low heat.

Cooking Your Noodles
Heat 2 tablespoons of the oil in a large skillet over medium heat.

Add the mushrooms to cook for 2–3 minutes. Then add garlic to continue cooking without toasting the garlic and until the mushrooms soften.

pasta dishes

If using zucchini noodles, add the noodles to the skillet and cook no more than 5 minutes. If using cabbage, 1–2 minutes would suffice.

Add the chopped basil and salt and pepper to taste.

Serve on a dish topped with sauce and sprinkle with Parmesan.

tips: I personally like the taste with the cabbage better.

If you don't want to make the Basic Marinara Sauce, you can use a cup of Rao's Spaghetti Sauce.

chicken tetrazzini

serves 4–6

½ spaghetti squash (approximately 4 cups)

2 cups cooked chicken, shredded (leftover rotisserie chicken works well for this)

4 teaspoons coconut oil or olive oil

2 cups mushrooms, sliced

1 small onion, diced

½ cup red bell pepper, sliced

1 cup raw cashews

1 cup chicken stock

1 teaspoon garlic salt

3 eggs, beaten

1 teaspoon dried basil

1 ¼ teaspoons lemon pepper

½ teaspoon onion powder

¼ teaspoon Spike Seasoning (you can find that almost anywhere or any seasoning of your choice will do)

½ teaspoon dried basil

1 ⅓ cups Parmesan cheese, grated or shredded

Sea salt and ground black pepper to taste

KF *My Chicken Tetrazzini is cheesy, rich, comfort food without the grain-based pasta. Tastes so good, you won't even miss the pasta.*

Directions to Cook Spaghetti Squash

Preheat oven to 375°F (191°C).

Cut squash down the middle lengthwise and pull apart. Remove the seeds and string bits from the middle of each half with a spoon.

Prepare a baking sheet with aluminum foil and grease with 1 teaspoon of coconut oil or olive oil. Place spaghetti squash on baking sheet skin side up. Place in oven for 35–40 minutes or until you can easily pierce the flesh with a fork.

Remove from oven and let cool until you can pick up the squash by hand or with an oven mitt on.

Take a fork and run it lengthwise along the squash's flesh to create "noodles" and place in bowl. Set aside.

Directions to Cook Casserole

While spaghetti squash is baking, add 3 cups of water to a saucepan and bring to boil. Add raw cashews and boil for 30 minutes.

In a large skillet, sauté onion, bell pepper, and mushrooms in 2 teaspoons of coconut or olive oil until mushrooms have cooked down, about 10 minutes.

Reduce oven temperature to 350°F (177°C).

Once cashews are done, strain the cashews and reserve the liquid.

Add cashews to the blender, add ¾ cup of reserved cashew cooking water, chicken stock, all seasonings, and blend until smooth and creamy. If not creamy enough, add a tablespoon of the reserved cashew water.

pasta dishes

In a large bowl, mix chicken, mushrooms, bell pepper, onion, cashew mixture, eggs, and 1 cup of Parmesan cheese.

Grease a 9 x 13-inch casserole dish with 1 teaspoon of coconut or olive oil.

Pour everything into dish and top with the ⅓ cup of Parmesan cheese before cooking.

Bake for 55 minutes to an hour; let cool slightly and serve.

zucchini ravioli

serves 4–6

4 medium zucchini

2 cups ricotta cheese

½ cup Parmesan cheese, finely grated, plus more for garnish

1 clove garlic, minced

1 egg, lightly beaten

½ cup basil, thinly sliced

Olive oil

1½ cups Basic Marinara Sauce, recipe on page 258

½ cup mozzarella, shredded

Sea salt and freshly ground pepper

KF *There's just some foods you miss having when you ditch the grains, and ravioli is one of them. I was happy to find an ingredient to substitute for wide noodles, and zucchini is the perfect alternative. You may add spicy sausage, grass-fed beef, or just keep it vegetarian.*

Preheat oven to 375° F (191° C).

Grease a large baking dish with olive oil.

To make the noodles, slice two sides of each zucchini lengthwise to create two flat sides using a vegetable peeler.

Using a vegetable peeler, slice each zucchini into thin flat strips peeling until you reach the center (these are your noodles).

To make the filling, combine ricotta, Parmesan, egg, and 2 tablespoons of basil in a medium bowl and season with salt and pepper.

Lay two strips of zucchini noodles on a cutting board so that they overlap lengthwise, then lay two more noodles perpendicular to the first strips, making a t-shape.

Spoon about 1 tablespoon of filling into the center of the zucchini.

Bring the ends of the strips together to fold over the center working one-side at a time.

Turn the ravioli over and place in the baking dish, seam side down.

Pour marinara sauce around the zucchini.

Top ravioli with mozzarella cheese and some Parmesan cheese.

Bake until al dente and the melted cheese is starting to brown on top, 30 minutes.

Top with more basil, add salt and pepper to taste, and serve.

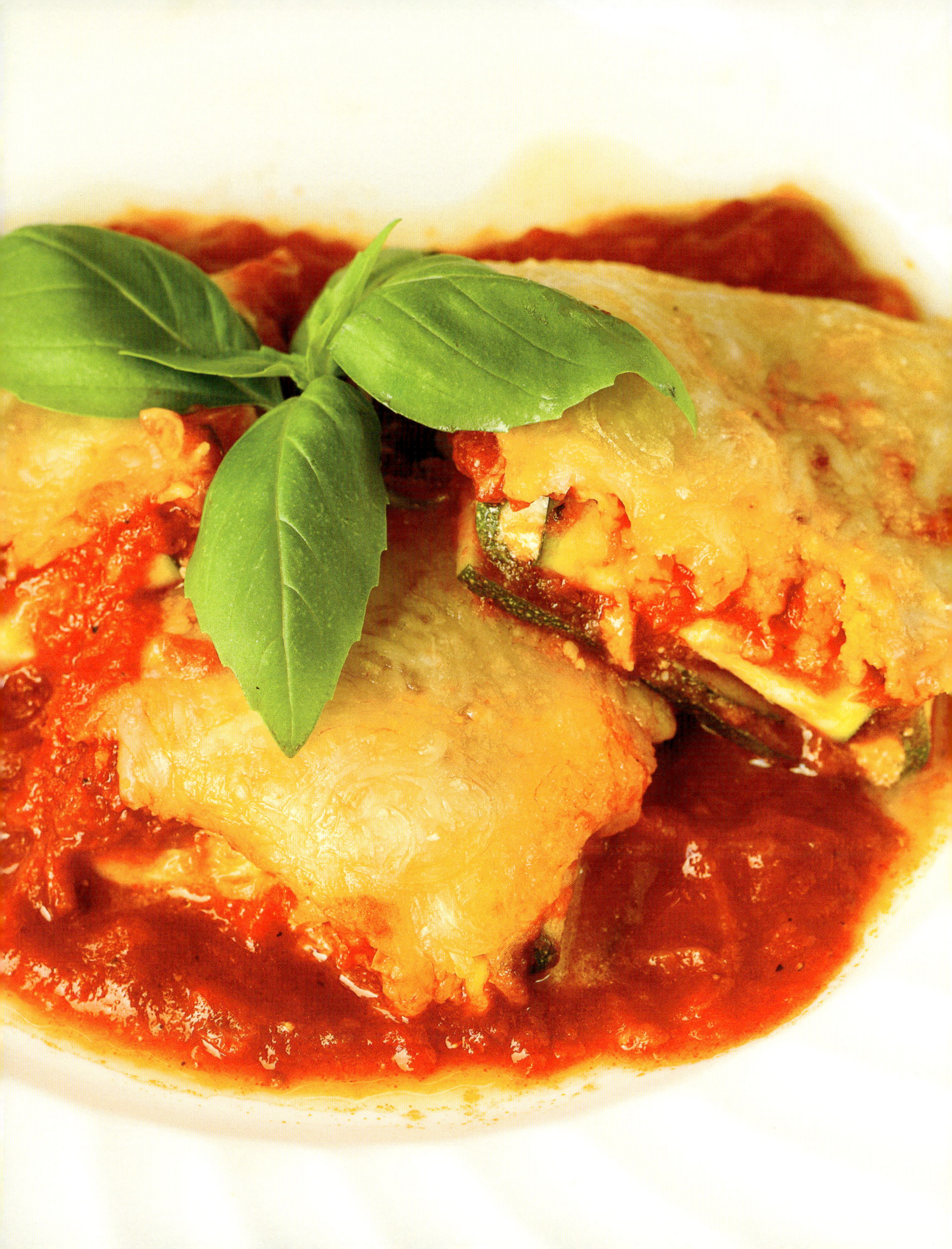

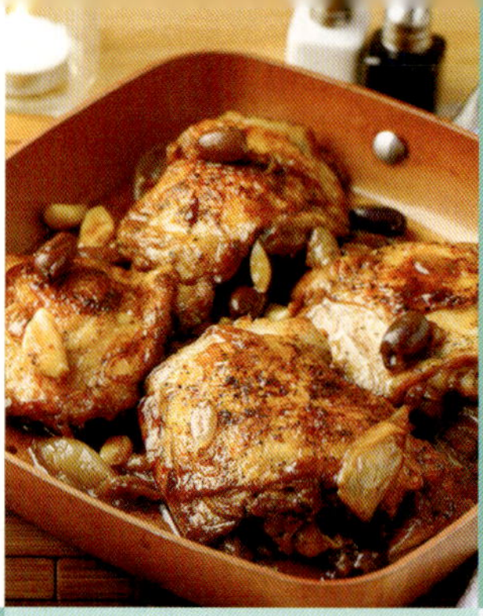
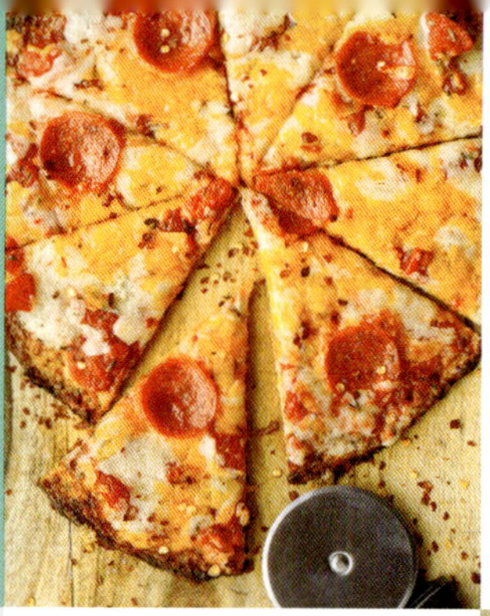
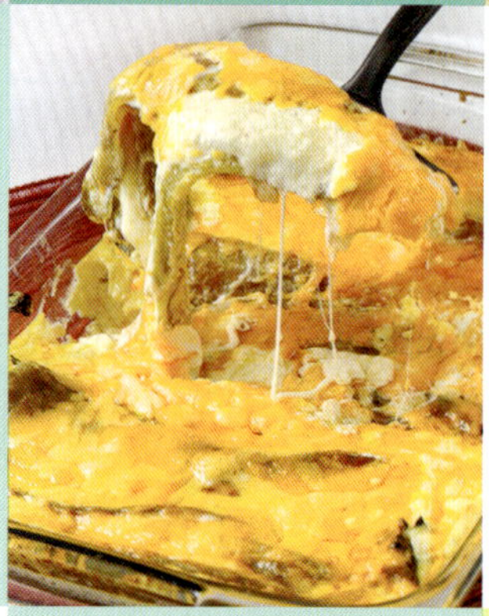
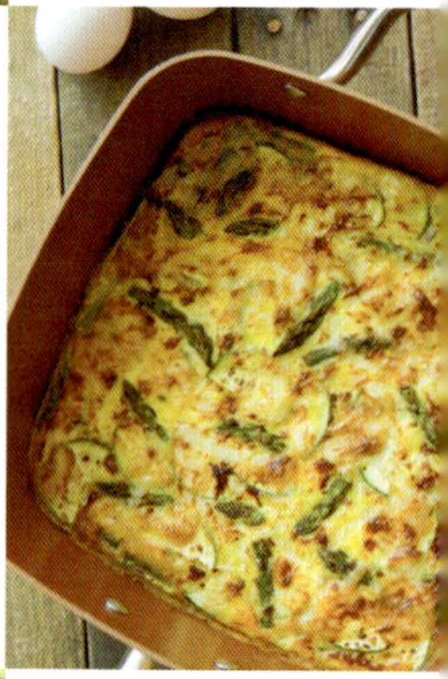
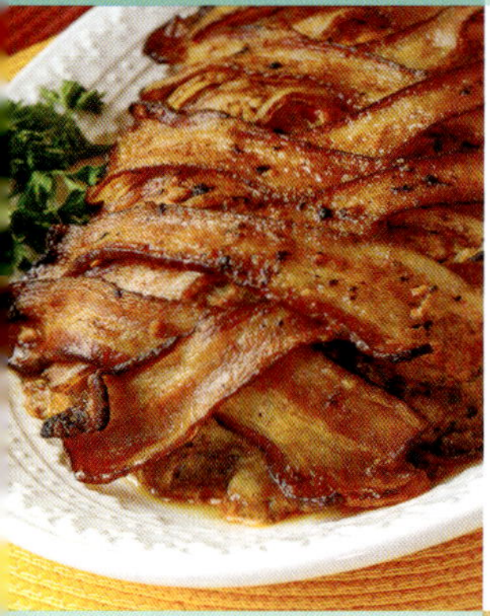
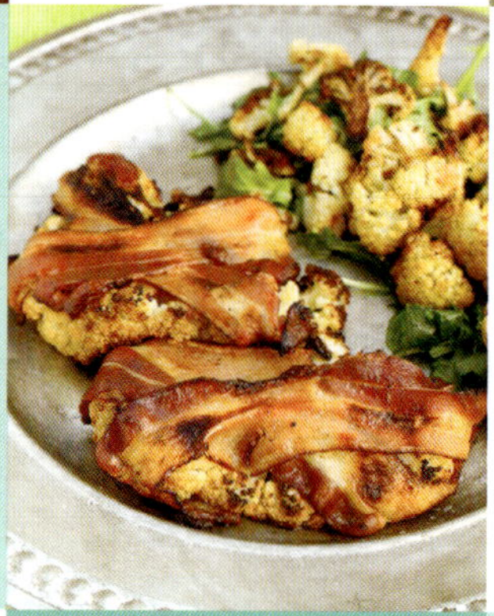
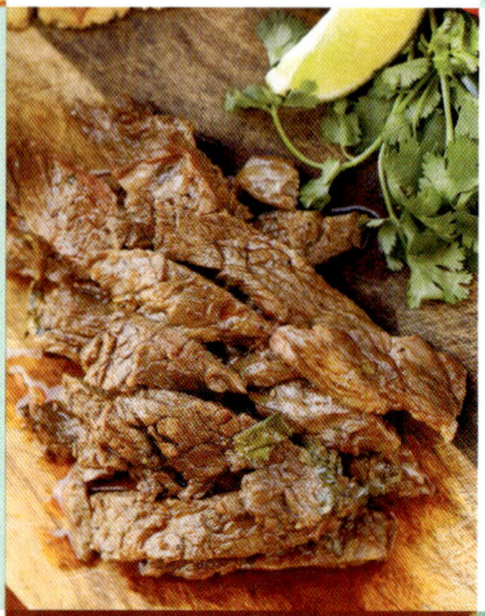
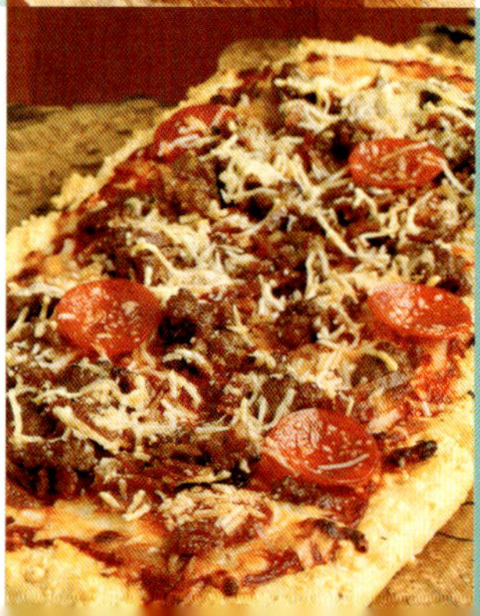
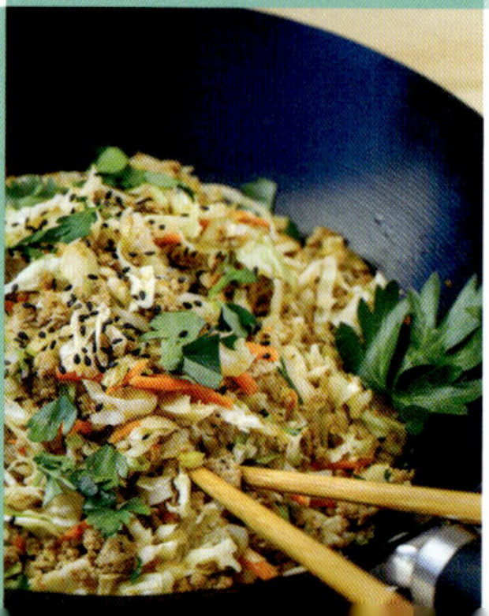

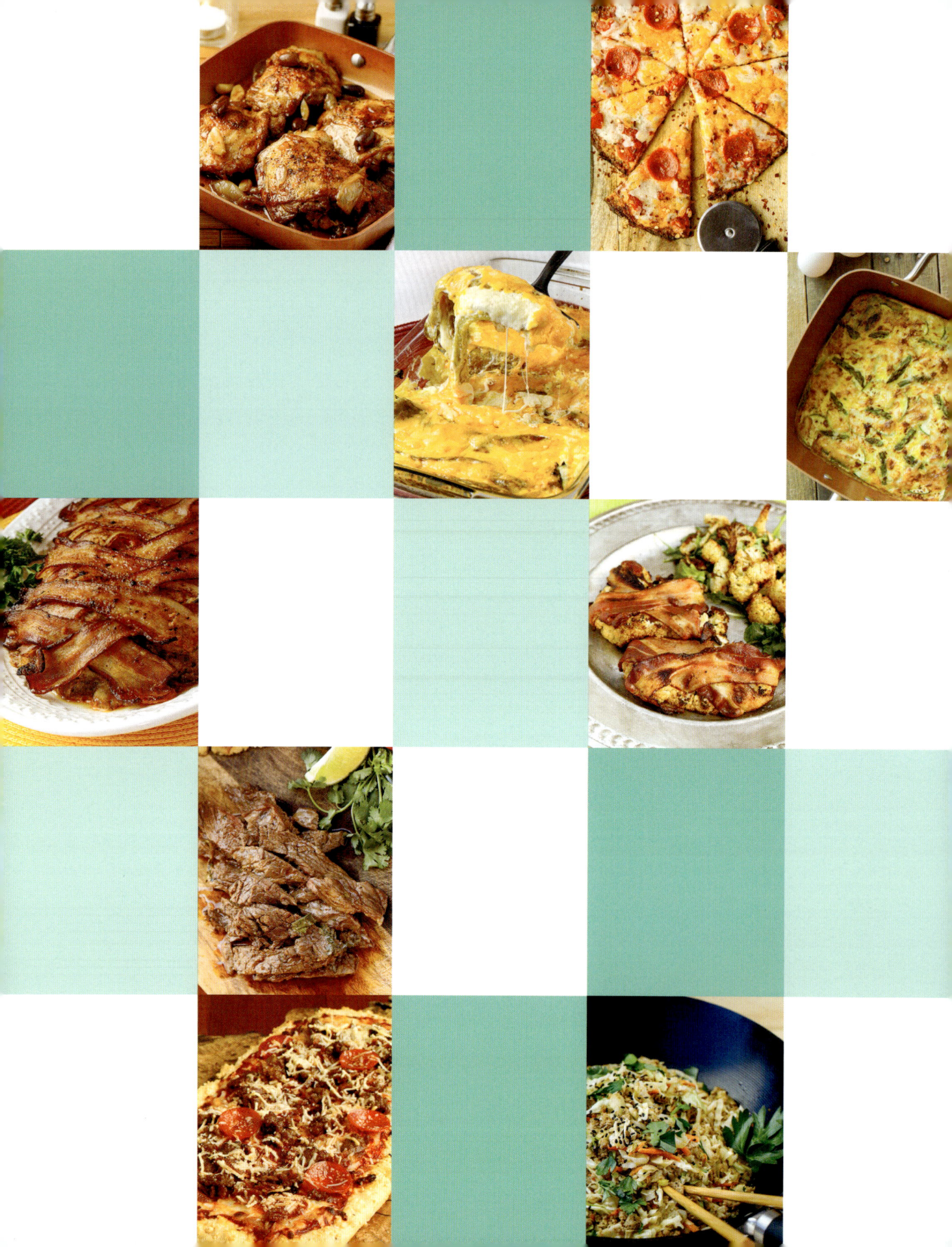

main dishes

Whether for lunch, dinner, or a special occasion, home chefs take pride in making the main dish stand out and delight the taste buds. I have curated so many dishes from my travels and from friends who shared their recipes. I've also added my own creations to compile some really tasty meals. Hopefully, you will enjoy these as much as I have. You can find some great side dishes to accompany them later in the book.

KF Denotes that recipe can be made or is keto-friendly.

Asian Turkey Stir Fry 156

Baby Back Ribs with Apple BBQ Sauce 158

Bacon-wrapped Cauliflower Steak 160

Bacon-wrapped Meatloaf 162

Butternut Squash Pizza Rounds 183

Brisket of Beef 165

Cabbage Enchiladas 166

Carne Asada 168

Carnitas 164

Cauliflower Crust Pepperoni Pizza 190

Cauliflower Dreaming 172

Chicken Marsala 170

Chicken-Stuffed Poblano Peppers 174

Chicken with Sautéed Fennel 175

Chile Relleno Casserole 176

Citrus Rotisserie Chicken 180

Date Night Chicken 178

Eggplant Parmesan 177

Flatbread, Heirloom Tomato, and Basil Pizza 193

Flatbread, Meat Lover's Pizza 192

Fried Chicken 181

Herb-Roasted Lamb Chops 182

Oven-Roasted Crispy Chicken 186

Parmigiano-Reggiano Chicken 188

Salt-Encrusted Prime Rib 184

Smoked Pork Roast 194

Spinach and Mushroom Crustless Quiche 196

Vegetable Frittata 198

asian turkey stir fry

Here's a new twist for ground turkey.

makes 4–6 servings

- 1 pound ground turkey
- 2 tablespoons toasted sesame oil
- 1 medium onion, diced, about ½ cup
- 3 cloves garlic, minced
- 3 green onions, cut on the bias, white and green separated
- 1 teaspoon sea salt
- ½ teaspoon dried ginger powder
- ¼ teaspoon ground black pepper
- ½ teaspoon Spike Seasoning (can be found in most health markets), optional
- ¼ teaspoon lemon pepper
- 1 tablespoon sriracha sauce
- 1 14-ounce bag of coleslaw mix
- 3 tablespoons coconut aminos or gluten-free soy sauce
- 1 tablespoon apple cider vinegar
- 2 tablespoons toasted sesame seeds for garnish
- Cilantro or Italian parsley for garnish

Heat the sesame oil in a large skillet over medium-high heat.

Add the onion, garlic, and the white portions of the green onions to the skillet.

Sauté until the onions are translucent and the garlic is fragrant.

Add the ground turkey, ginger, lemon pepper, sriracha sauce, salt, pepper, Spike Seasoning (if using) to the skillet and cook while stirring until the meat is cooked thoroughly.

Add the coleslaw mix, the coconut aminos or gluten-free soy sauce and vinegar, sauté until the coleslaw is tender.

Serve in small bowls, drizzle sriracha over the bowl and garnish with green onions and sesame seeds. You can also top with fresh cilantro or Italian parsley.

tip: You can replace the ground turkey with ground chicken or pork. If using pork, once cooked, drain any excess fat, if desired. The fat from pork blends well with the flavors in this dish.

main dishes

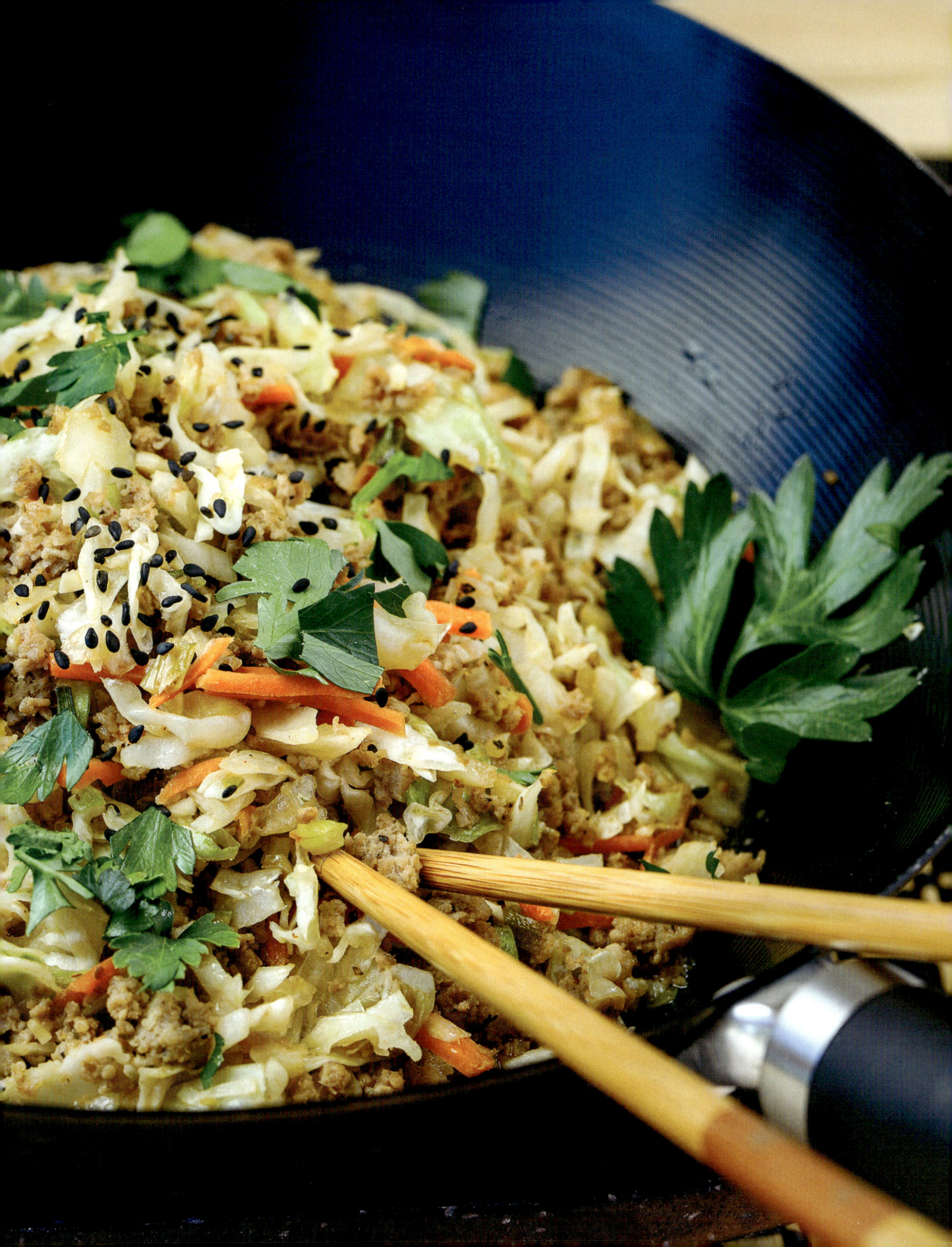

baby back ribs with apple bbq sauce

serves 6–8

KF OPTIONAL *These are deliciously both sweet and savory. So tender, the meat falls off the bone. If you want to make this keto-friendly, simply eliminate the BBQ sauce.*

2 baby back rib racks (typical rack has 10–13 ribs)

Garlic salt

Lemon pepper

Smoked paprika

½ cup apple juice (If doing keto, use ½ cup of light beer)

Apple BBQ Sauce (Recipe follows)

Peel the membrane off the back of each rack of ribs.

Generously rub the spices all over the ribs.

Set the smoker to 225° F (107° C) and use your wood of choice. If you don't have a smoker, use your gas grill. To do this place a metal pan or tray under the grill where the ribs will cook. Fill the pan ¾ full of water. Set the grill to medium-high heat. The water helps the ribs 'slow cook' and keeps the heat indirect.

Place the ribs in the smoker and smoke for 3 hours.

After the ribs have been in the smoker or gas grill for 3 hours, take them out and wrap each rack with aluminum foil making a pouch by folding the edges to hold the liquid you will add.

Pour a ¼ cup apple juice into the wrapping for each rack.

Fold over the foil and pinch all the edges to ensure it is sealed well to allow steaming.

Place the wrapped ribs in the smoker or gas grill and continue baking another 2 hours. You can also bake them in the oven, set at 225° F (107° C), for 2 hours.

After these 2 hours, remove the ribs carefully from the foil.

Generously coat the ribs in my BBQ sauce. Put them back in the smoker or the oven for 1 final hour.

They are so delicious without the BBQ sauce. Maybe, leave some without the sauce so you can try them after the final hour.

Apple BBQ Sauce

If you are making your own ketchup, see the recipe below. Otherwise, add ketchup, applesauce, chili powder, paprika, ground cinnamon, sea salt and freshly ground black pepper.

As racks typically have 10–13 ribs, you may want to cut them after they have been baked, as instructed above, into twos or threes so that the sauce adheres better to the ribs.

Homemade Ketchup

Place all ingredients in a mixing bowl and blend well. Store in jar or squeeze bottle for up to 10 days.

Apple BBQ Sauce

1½ cups homemade ketchup, recipe below

1 cup applesauce

½ onion, minced

3 cloves garlic, minced

3 tablespoons clarified butter

3 tablespoons apple cider vinegar

2 tablespoons chili powder

1 tablespoon paprika

½ teaspoon ground cinnamon

Sea salt and freshly ground black pepper to taste

Homemade Ketchup

1 6–7 ounce can or jar tomato paste

¼ cup water

3 tablespoons apple cider vinegar

1 tablespoon maple syrup, or more to taste

1 teaspoon garlic powder

1 teaspoon onion powder

½ teaspoon sea salt

bacon-wrapped cauliflower steak

serves 2

1 head cauliflower

4 strips bacon, uncured

⅛–¼ cup olive oil; I tend to use more oil

Lemon pepper

Garlic salt

Sea salt and pepper to taste

KF *I love my bacon—just not every day. For that special occasion, my Bacon-Wrapped Cauliflower Steak will sure please your family and friends.*

Preheat oven to 350°F (177°C).

Take the extra green leaves off the cauliflower.

Cut the cauliflower into two steaks, about 1- to 1½-inch thick; season with plenty of olive oil, lemon pepper, garlic salt, and salt and pepper.

Bake on an aluminum-lined baking sheet for 15 minutes at 350°F (177°C).

Take out and increase temperature to 375°F (191°C).

Let the two steaks cool slightly so you can wrap each with 2 slices of bacon. I would say about five minutes to cool. When slightly cooled, wrap the bacon pieces crisscross across the cauliflower steaks.

Bake for 25 minutes more at 375°F (191°C).

Check the steaks, the bacon may need a little crispness. If so, increase the oven to broil and broil for five minutes or until bacon is crisp.

Take out and enjoy!

tip: I tend to broil the bacon at the end but it's a personal choice.

main dishes   160

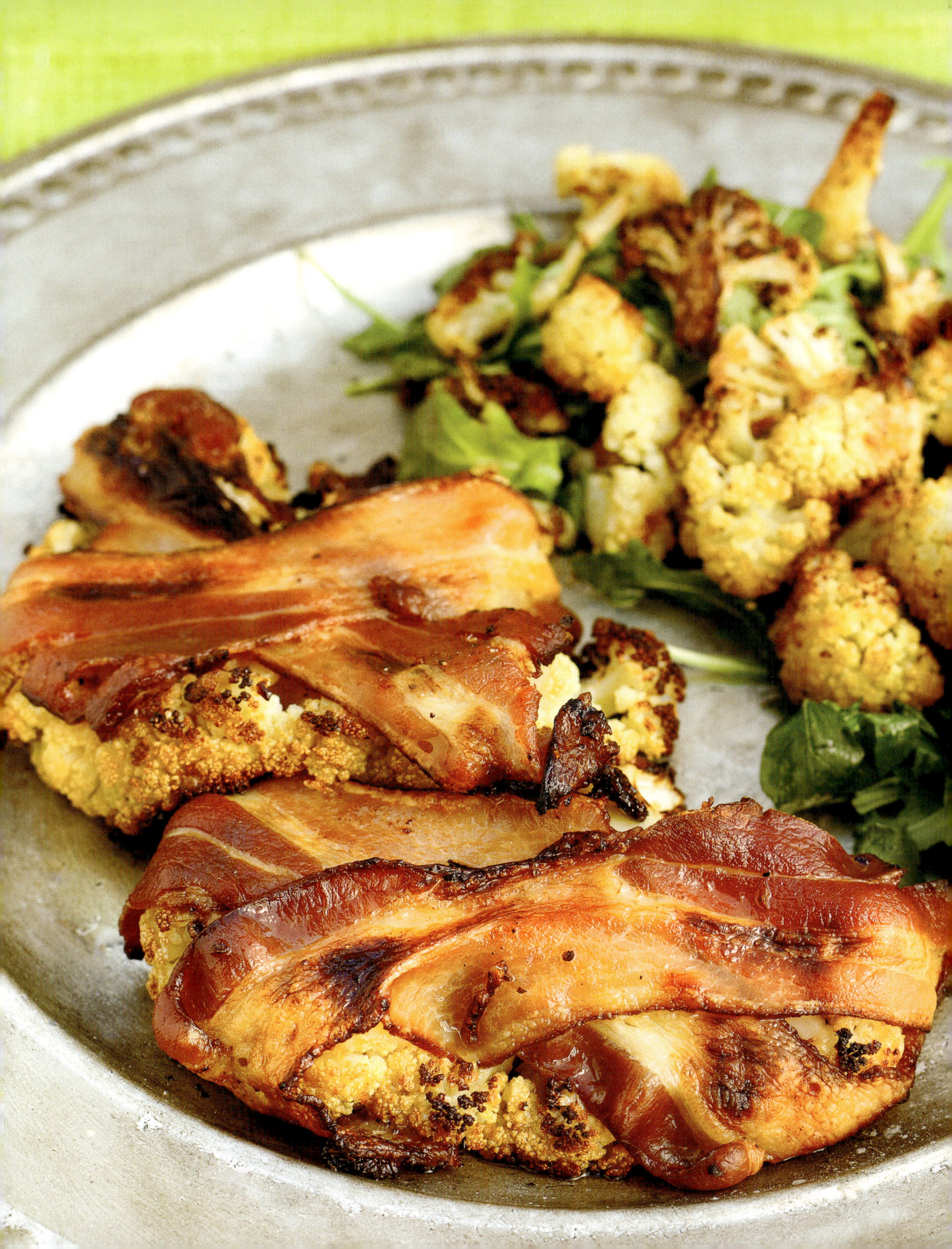

bacon-wrapped meatloaf

serves 4–6

1 pound grass-fed ground beef or ½ pound of grass-fed ground beef and ½ pound of ground pork

2 tablespoons olive oil

1 yellow onion, diced

¼ cup celery, diced

½ cup carrot, diced

1 red bell pepper, diced

1 egg, whisked

½–¾ cup almond flour

1 teaspoon dried basil

1 teaspoon dried thyme

1 teaspoon dried parsley

½ cup tomato sauce

½ teaspoon garlic salt

12 pieces bacon, uncured

Sea salt and pepper to taste

KF *Meatloaf is one of my favorite comfort foods. This recipe demonstrates that grains are not necessary when making meatloaf. The bacon adds more flavor into the meat. I discard the bacon after the meatloaf is cooked, but you may choose to indulge in it. Adding pork does make the meatloaf juicier. I've never stopped loving meatloaf. Now it's even more wonderful, knowing I've eliminated breadcrumbs, white flour, and rice.*

Preheat oven to 400°F (204°C).

Place a medium skillet over medium heat and add a tablespoon or two of olive oil.

Then add your onion, red pepper, celery, and carrots to the skillet.

Cook until all have become soft and translucent.

Once cooked, add them to a bowl along with the rest of the ingredients (except the bacon) for your meatloaf. Use your hands to mix it all together.

Place meatloaf mixture on a aluminum-lined baking sheet. Layer bacon crisscross-wise across the top of the loaf, stretching the bacon so that you can tuck it underneath the loaf.

Bake for 30 minutes at 400°F (204°C), then take out and increase oven to 500°F (260°C) to get bacon crispy, about another 5 minutes.

So good!

tips: This is really tasty, even if you don't feel like adding the bacon. Just enjoy it!

You can add more bacon if you'd like, or less depending on your preference.

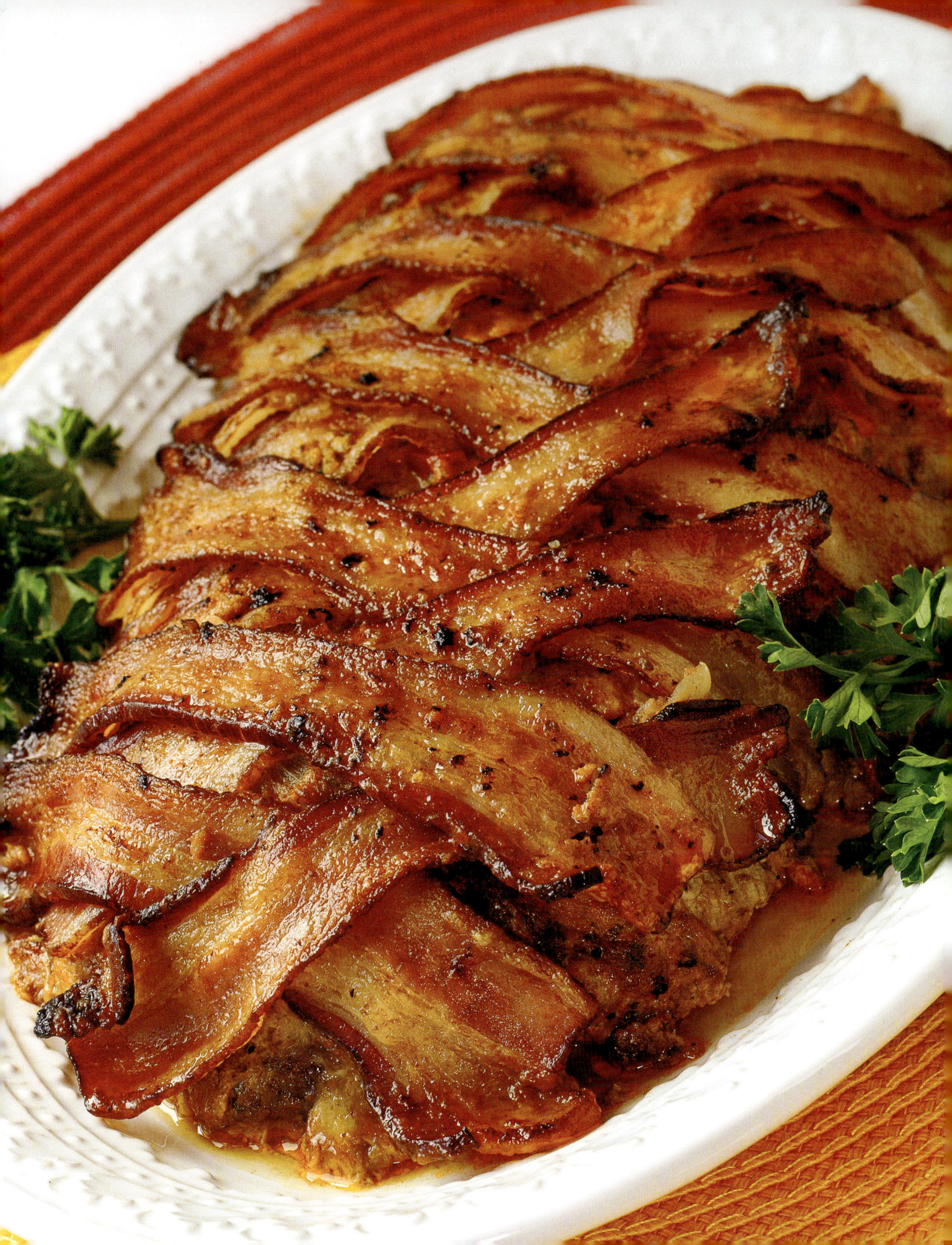

carnitas

If you love pulled pork, the other white meat, you'll love my carnitas. This south-of-the-border dish is tender and flavorful.

serves 6–8

5 pounds pork shoulder

1 cup olive oil

1 tablespoon sea salt

1 head garlic, unpeeled

½ cup orange juice

½ tablespoon monk fruit sweetener

Cut meat into chunks the size of baseballs.

In a 10- or 12-quart cast iron pot (Dutch oven), heat the oil, and add the meat, salt, and garlic.

Brown over high flame for about 10 minutes.

Once browned, let simmer over medium heat uncovered for 60 minutes. Stir a couple of times to even out cooking.

Cover and let simmer another 45 minutes.

Once the meat has cooked and you can see clear juices from the meat, add sweetener and orange juice and let simmer for 10–15 minutes or when you can pull the meat apart.

Slow Cook Method

Add all ingredients except oil in slow cooker.

Cover and cook on low for 8–10 hours or on high 4 hours.

Once the meat is tender, remove from slow cooker and let cool slightly before pulling apart with a fork.

Serve with vegetables and Tomatillo Salsa, recipe on page 262.

brisket of beef

KF *Slow cooking wins the race with tender and delicious brisket of beef. It tastes great, and the juices mix well with my side dishes too!*

Preheat oven to 350°F (177°C).

First, we make a dry rub by combining chili powder, sea salt, garlic and onion powders, together with black pepper, dry mustard, and bay leaf. Mix really well with your hands or a spoon.

Next, place the uncooked brisket over wax paper on a cutting board. At this point, you may trim excess fat down to about ⅛ th-inch thickness if you prefer. Then season the raw brisket by massaging in the dry rub you made. With your hands, spread on the top side. Flip it over and do the same on the other side.

Once covered with rub, place brisket in a roasting pan and roast uncovered for 1 hour.

After the first hour, add beef stock and enough water to yield about ½-inch of liquid in the roasting pan.

Cover the roasting pan with its lid and reduce heat to 300°F (149°C). Continue cooking for 3 hours or until fork-tender.

Trim the fat and slice meat thinly against the grain.

Top with juice from the pan.

tip: If you have a technique for slicing very thin, this makes great sandwiches or wraps. If you would like to try this in a slow cooker, follow the instructions of use for your cooker. Try it with my Mock Garlic Mashed Potatoes or other side dishes.

serves 6–10

2 tablespoons chili powder

2 tablespoons sea salt

1 tablespoon garlic powder

1 tablespoon onion powder

1 tablespoon ground black pepper

2 teaspoons dry mustard

1 bay leaf, crushed

4 pounds beef brisket, trimmed

1½ cups beef stock

cabbage enchiladas

KF *This is a great way to make a favorite Mexican dish—without using tortillas. The good news is you can use cooked shredded beef, pork or turkey, if desired.*

serves 6

- 1 head cabbage
- 1 teaspoon sea salt
- 2 tablespoons coconut oil
- 1 onion, chopped
- 1 28-ounce can enchilada sauce, green or red
- 2 cups cooked chicken, shredded (I used leftovers from a rotisserie chicken)
- 2 cups cheddar or jack cheese, shredded or combined
- 1 small can of black olives, sliced
- ½ cup fresh cilantro, chopped
- Sea salt and pepper to taste
- Salsa of your choice (optional)
- 1 avocado, sliced
- 1 small pint sour cream or may use a combination of ½ pint cream cheese and ½ pint Greek yogurt, a new item at your grocer premixed

Preheat oven to 350°F (177°C).

Bring a large pot of water with a teaspoon of sea salt to a boil.

Peel the cabbage leaves—make sure to peel them gently as you don't want them to tear. I run the cabbage under warm water as I am peeling. This helps a ton.

Throw the cabbage leaves into the pot of boiling water for a couple of minutes.

Remove leaves from water and set on a paper towel to dry.

Sauté the chopped onion in coconut oil until lightly browned, about 8 minutes; set aside.

Open the can of enchilada sauce and pour enough into a 9 x 13-inch baking pan to cover the bottom. Set aside for later.

Take a cabbage leaf and fill with shredded chicken, a handful of cheese, some black olives, chopped cilantro, chopped onion, and salt and pepper to taste. Also, you may add your salsa of choice in each individual cabbage leaf or add at the end. Fold or roll your filled leaf to make an enchilada and place seam side down into the baking pan. Repeat the process to make rows of enchiladas.

Pour remaining sauce over the cabbage enchilada rolls and top with the remaining cheese. Bake for 20–25 minutes.

Serve individually or two at a time and add a slice of avocado on each enchilada.

Add a dollop of sour cream atop each enchilada and ole!

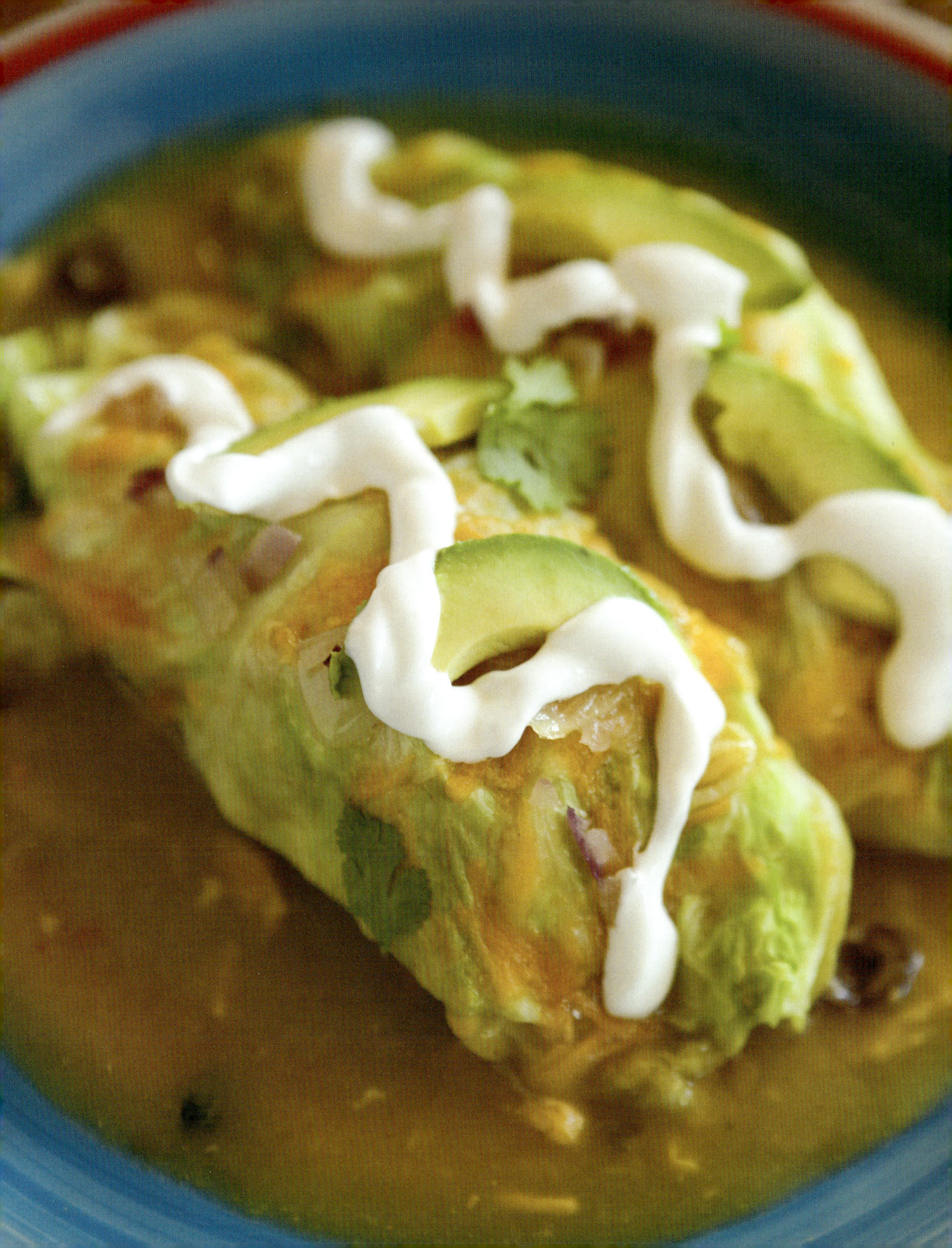

carne asada

This is a favorite for most people, and I have a great way of making it so that your meat is tender and flavorful.

serves 6—8

- 3 pounds flank steak
- ½ cup orange juice
- ¼ cup lemon juice
- ¼ cup lime juice
- 4 cloves garlic, minced
- ½ cup soy sauce, gluten free
- 1 canned chipotle pepper, finely chopped
- 1 tablespoon chili powder
- ½ teaspoon ground cumin
- 1 tablespoon paprika
- 1 teaspoon dried oregano
- 1 tablespoon black pepper
- 1 bunch fresh cilantro, chopped
- ½ cup olive oil

Combine the orange, lemon, and lime juice in a large glass or ceramic bowl along with the garlic, soy sauce, chipotle pepper, chili powder, ground cumin, paprika, dried oregano, black pepper, and cilantro.

Slowly whisk in the olive oil until marinade is well combined.

Remove one cup of the marinade and place in a small bowl, cover with plastic wrap and refrigerate for use after the meat is cooked.

Place the flank steak between two sheets of parchment paper on a solid, level surface.

Firmly pound the steak with the smooth side of a meat mallet to a thickness of ¼ inch.

After pounding, poke steak all over with a fork.

Add the meat to the marinade in the large bowl, cover, and allow to marinate in the refrigerator for 24 hours. I marinate it for two days—incredible!

Preheat an outdoor grill to medium-high heat, and lightly oil the grate.

Remove the steak from the marinade and grill to desired doneness, about 5 minutes per side for medium rare.

Discard used marinade.

Remove meat from heat and slice across the grain.

Heat reserved marinade in microwave for at least 30 seconds and pour over hot meat. Serve immediately.

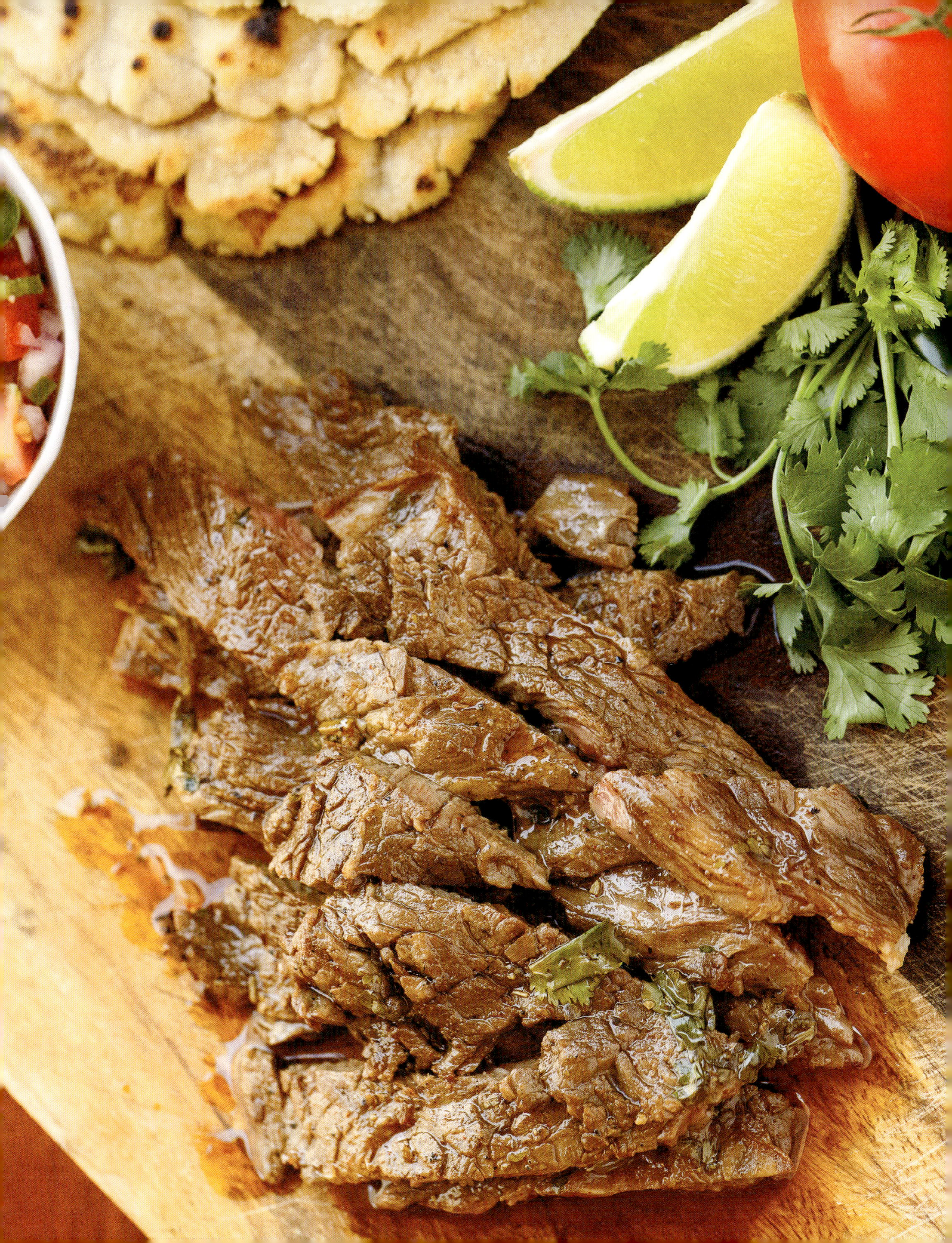

chicken marsala

serves 4

KF OPTIONAL *Oh, the savory, tender chicken combined with the mushrooms and the tanginess of the Marsala wine will leave you speechless.*

4 organic chicken breast fillets, skinless and boneless

¼ cup arrowroot flour (if doing keto, use almond flour)

½ teaspoon garlic salt

½ teaspoon lemon pepper

½ teaspoon dried oregano

¼ cup olive oil

4 ounces pancetta, diced

1 cup cremini or button mushrooms, sliced

½ cup Marsala wine

½ cup chicken stock, broth will do

4 tablespoons butter

Sea salt and pepper to taste

1 teaspoon dried parsley

Place the chicken breast fillets, side by side on a cutting board and cover with a piece of plastic wrap.

Pound the breasts with a flat meat mallet until they are ¼ inch thick.

In a bowl, mix together the arrowroot flour, garlic salt, lemon pepper, and oregano.

Dredge the chicken breasts in arrowroot flour mixture, turning a few times to coat well.

Add olive oil to a large skillet over medium-high heat.

Place the chicken breasts in the skillet and lightly brown, turning only once, about 4 minutes.

Remove chicken breasts and cover with aluminum foil to keep warm for later use.

Lower the heat to medium and add the diced pancetta to the drippings in the skillet. Sauté for 1 minute to render some of the fat.

Add mushrooms until they are nicely browned and their moisture has evaporated, about 5 minutes. Season with salt and pepper.

Gently pour Marsala wine into the pan and let it boil down to cook out the alcohol, about 5 seconds. It may flare up, but don't be afraid. It will settle down on its own.

Add the chicken stock or broth to reduce sauce slightly.

Stir in the butter and return chicken to the pan.

Simmer gently, about a minute to heat the chicken through.

Season with salt and pepper.

Garnish with parsley and enjoy!

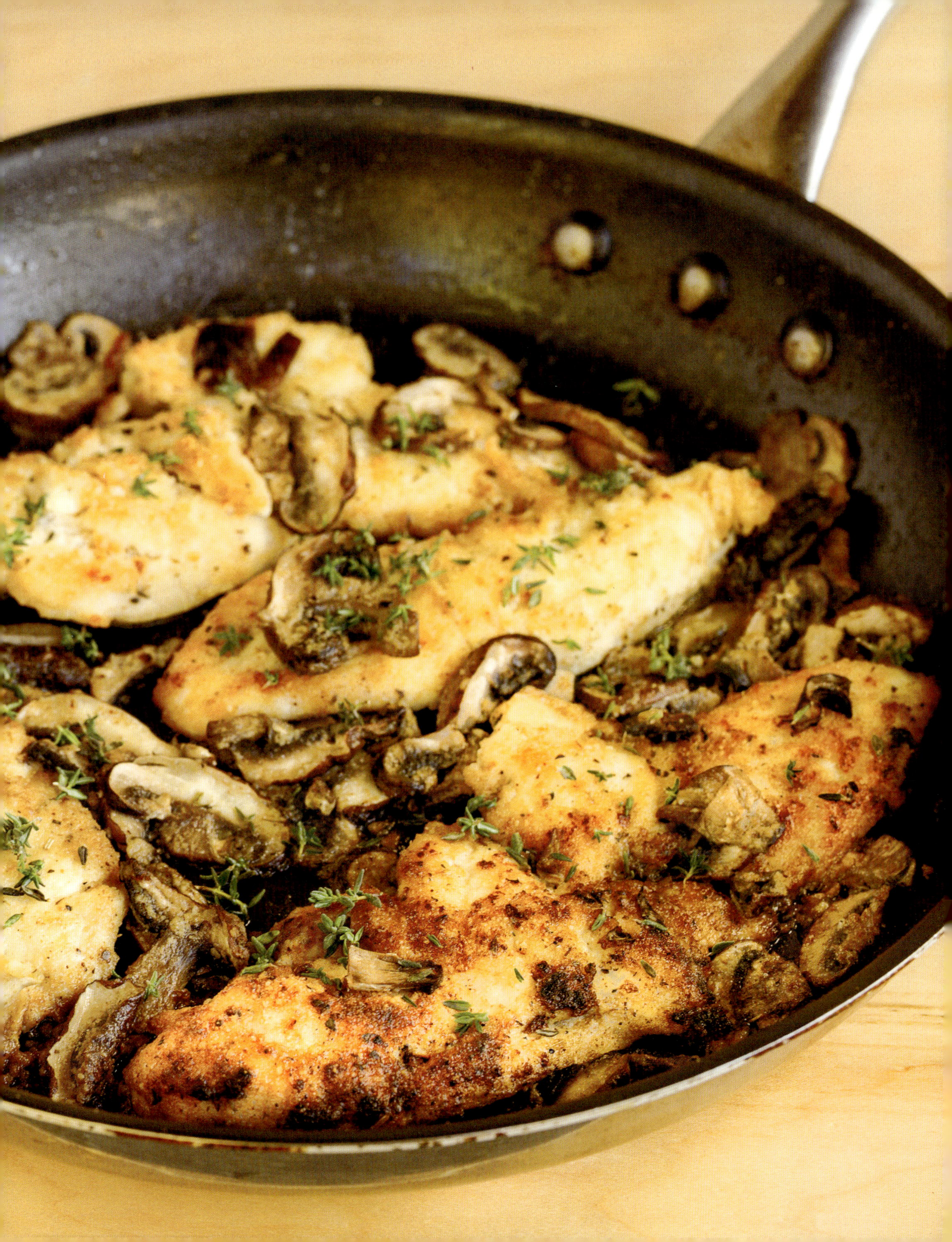

cauliflower dreaming

serves 4 as a main dish or 8 as an appetizer

2 heads cauliflower, large enough to produce 2 steaks each

½ cup olive oil

½ teaspoon garlic salt

½ teaspoon lemon pepper

¼ teaspoon sea salt

¼ teaspoon chipotle chili powder

1 stick butter, unsalted

Juice of 1 lemon

½ cup vegetable stock

2 tablespoons butter, unsalted (for the mushrooms)

4 cups mushrooms, sliced (any type will do). I use cremini mushrooms.

KF *Every time I barbeque a big juicy steak, I think about replacing it with a vegetable, only because it's easier to digest veggies than red meat. The older I get the more I realize the importance of plant food. When I started on my journey of eliminating grains, I was eating more meat, mostly because it was allowed, and of course, it tastes so good. However, throughout my research, I've come to the realization that meat should be a side dish and not eaten every day. I hope you enjoy this cauliflower steak as much as I do!*

Preheat oven to 325°F (163°C).

Peel the leaves of the cauliflower and cut their stem, leaving 1 inch or enough for the florets to stay intact.

For best results, wet the knife before cutting the steaks, make the knife slick and nonstick when cutting the cauliflower. Cut 1 inch off the left and right edges of the cauliflower leaving 2 inches of the center intact. Slice the remaining portion in half. Pour a ⅛th cup of olive oil into a glass dish that can hold the four steaks.

Season each steak on both sides with the garlic salt, lemon pepper, sea salt, chipotle chili powder and add all to the glass dish. Marinate for 30 minutes or up to two days, if desired.

Heat an oven-safe large skillet on high heat.

Add ⅛th cup of olive oil into skillet.

Add cauliflower steaks and let them sear for about two to three minutes. Then turn the steaks over gently.

Add 1 stick of butter to the skillet, melt and brown the butter to give the steaks a wonderful flavor. Baste the steaks often with the browned butter. Then add the juice of one lemon.

When the butter is frothy, pour the vegetable stock into the skillet and let it come to a boil.

Remove from the stovetop and bake for 20–25 minutes in the oven.

Meanwhile slice mushrooms and sauté them in olive oil and two tablespoons of butter until soft and caramelized for about 8–10 minutes on medium-high heat in a sauté pan.

When the steaks are done, serve them with a heaping amount of mushrooms!

If using as an appetizer, cut the steaks into four pieces and add a dollop of mushrooms on top. Yummy!

tip: This dish is so delicious even without the mushrooms. If you love mushrooms, you may want to use more of them since they shrink after sautéing.

chicken-stuffed poblano peppers

serves 2

If you like artisan foods, you will love this traditional chile relleno. Best of all, it is baked, not fried.

- 1–2 chicken breasts with skins on
- 1 tablespoon olive oil
- 2 poblano peppers
- 2 tablespoons black olives, diced
- ½ cup cheddar cheese or your choice of cheese, shredded
- ½ cup mozzarella cheese or your choice of cheese, shredded
- 2 tablespoons sour cream
- Sea salt and pepper to taste

Preheat oven to 350°F (177°C).

Line a baking sheet with aluminum foil.

Drizzle olive oil on chicken breasts liberally on the baking pan and bake for about 35 minutes.

In the meantime, wash and char the peppers on the stove top. If you can use a charring screen, even better.

After cooling a bit, place peppers in a plastic bag to steep for about 10 minutes, to allow you to peel the skin easily. This also softens the pepper.

Remove peppers from bag and peel the charred skin, slit them lengthwise, discard the seeds, and set aside.

Chop the cooked chicken into cubes or shred if you prefer.

Add the chicken and cheese along with 1 tablespoon of black olives into each pepper.

Bake the peppers in the oven for about 10 minutes or until cheese has melted.

Serve with a dollop of sour cream and enjoy.

tips: I like to buy rotisserie chicken because it saves time, and it's always so tender.

And if you like something a bit milder, replace the Poblano pepper with Anaheim pepper.

chicken with sautéed fennel

KF *I took a cooking class while visiting Tuscany, and this was one of the best dishes I learned to make. The fennel, combined with the chicken, really brings up that flavor I think you will love.*

Cover the bottom of a sauté pan with olive oil and cook the freshly sliced onion, garlic, carrot, and celery on high heat for 6–8 minutes.

Reduce heat to medium and add the chicken, salt, and pepper to taste, and brown the meat, stirring occasionally about five minutes.

Then add the wine, fennel, herbs, and cook uncovered on low heat for 45 minutes. Add water as necessary to keep the sauce liquid.

Check every 15 minutes with a timer to make sure sauce is liquid.

serves 4

2 tablespoons olive oil

1 large carrot, peeled and cut into ¼-inch slices

1 stalk celery, chopped

1 sweet onion, quartered

1–2 cloves garlic, thinly sliced

4 chicken thighs, skinless

½ cup white wine (pinot grigio, chardonnay, or sauvignon blanc)

1 fennel bulb, thinly sliced

1 teaspoon dried rosemary or thyme or ½ teaspoon each

Sea salt and pepper to taste

chile relleno casserole

KF *Some like it hot! Here's a zesty south-of-the-border inspired casserole that will have you wanting more.*

serves 6–8

- 8 fresh Anaheim peppers (if you like spicier, use poblano peppers)
- 8 ounces Monterey Jack or cheddar cheese
- 3 eggs
- 1 cup heavy cream
- 1 teaspoon sea salt
- 4 ounces sharp cheddar cheese, shredded

Preheat oven to 350°F (177°C).

Steam or char your peppers for about 10 minutes until they have softened. Broiling them works too, and it's quicker. Let them cool.

Make sure to peel the burned skin after broiling, charring, or steaming.

Slice each pepper lengthwise and remove the vein with the seeds and discard, along with the stem.

Cut Monterey Jack cheese into 8 equal lengthwise strips and stuff a strip into each pepper.

Place your cheese-stuffed peppers in a greased casserole dish or a small lasagna pan.

Beat the eggs, cream, and salt until blended and pour over the peppers.

Top generously with sharp cheddar cheese.

Bake for 35 minutes. Let stand 10 minutes before eating.

tip: If using poblano chiles, char first on the stove top as instructed above.

eggplant parmesan

KF *A meatless wonder! This dish is wonderfully delicious and easy to prepare. This is right up your alley, vegetarians!*

makes 6–8 servings

1 eggplant

3 cups Basic Marinara Sauce, (recipe on page 258)

¼ cup olive oil

2 teaspoons oregano or Italian seasoning (optional)

Burrata mozzarella, 1 container with 2 cheese balls or 2 cups mozzarella cheese, shredded

1 cup Parmesan cheese, shredded, more if desired

Sea salt and pepper to taste

Several leaves of basil for garnish

Cooking spray

Preheat oven to 350°F (177°C).

Slice the eggplant as thin as you can to keep them from falling apart, about ⅛-inch. Make sure the slices are similar in size. Salt the eggplant and leave for 30 minutes in a colander or longer, up to two hours.

Pat the eggplant dry and then either pan fry or grill. I pan fried with a small amount of cooking spray for about 4 minutes each side. You do not need any flour.

In an ovenproof dish, layer the tomato sauce, add a layer of eggplant, and then the mozzarella, and then sprinkle Parmesan on top liberally. Repeat for next layer. You may add slices of basil on top if desired.

Bake for 20–25 minutes until golden brown

date night chicken

serves 4

4 chicken thighs, skins on
Smoked paprika to taste
Sea salt and pepper to taste
Lemon pepper to taste
4 tablespoons butter
3 tablespoons avocado oil
1 medium onion cut into quarters
4–5 cloves garlic, peeled whole
8–10 Kalamata olives, pitted
¾ cup white wine

KF *This chicken will fall apart with every scrumptious bite. Of all the chicken recipes, this one is my favorite. The savory flavors complement the simplicity, and the tenderness of the chicken is beyond description.*

Preheat oven to 375°F (191°C).

Pat the chicken dry.

Combine the salt, pepper, lemon pepper, and smoked paprika in a small bowl. Mix well.

Season the chicken on both sides, rubbing the spice mixture on the skin. Set aside.

In an ovenproof sauté pan, add 3 tablespoons of avocado oil and 4 tablespoons of butter.

Heat on high and sear the chicken thighs skin side down for 3–5 minutes to brown the skin.

Turn heat off.

Turn the chicken over with the skin facing up.

Add the onion, garlic, and pitted olives to your pan.

Pour the wine and turn heat back on to bring to a boil.

Cover with oven-safe glass top and bake covered for 90 minutes.

The flavors blend so beautifully!

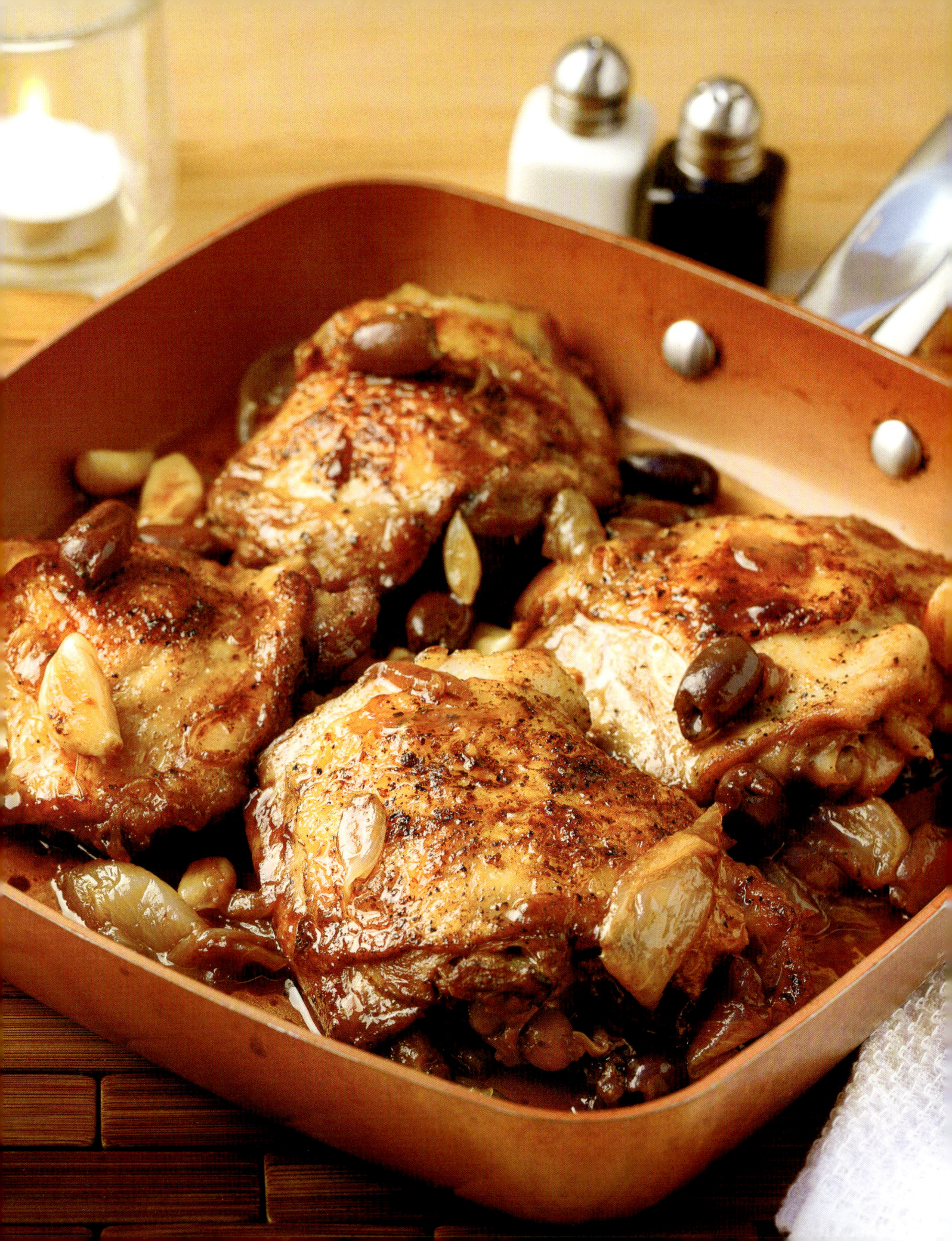

citrus rotisserie chicken

serves 4–6

This is a really easy, healthy, and mouth-watering recipe for the whole family to enjoy. You'll say goodbye to takeout.

- 1 whole chicken
- 1 lemon
- ½ cup orange juice
- Sea salt and pepper
- Olive oil for rubbing on chicken
- 1 16-ounce spray bottle

Fill spray bottle with orange juice. Cut lemon into quarters. After removing the guts of the chicken, stuff cavity with the lemon quarters.

Secure the chicken with the rotisserie spit forks and insert the spit rod.

Take a pie pan filled with water and place on the grill, off to the side, away from the heat.

Place the chicken into the grill housing.

Rub olive oil all over the chicken and season with salt and pepper while turning it over to equally rub on all sides, making it easier to season completely.

Set burner furthest away from the water to high and close the lid.

Spray the chicken with the orange juice every 15 minutes.

Let it cook slowly for approximately for 1½ to 2 hours or until thermometer says it's done. It's done when internal temperature reaches 165 degrees in the thickest part of the chicken breast.

This is so simple but oh so tender and easy!

tip: Check the amount of water in the pie pan to ensure you don't run out. The steam generated helps in the cooking process.

main dishes   180

fried chicken

If I was given a choice for my last meal, it would be fried chicken. The delicious crunchy coating on fried chicken can be hard to give up, but this alternative creates something special with this flourless fried chicken. Growing up, this was one of my favorite comfort foods and with this recipe, I eliminated the grains and made it taste as close to the real thing as possible.

Preheat oven to 350°F (177°C).

Line a baking sheet with aluminum foil and grease with cooking spray.

Put the pork rinds and seasonings in a food processor and pulse until crumbly and combined and pour onto a dinner plate. Set aside.

Crack the eggs into a small bowl and add the cream. Combine using a whisk.

Pat the chicken thighs dry. Dredge them one at a time in the egg wash, then coat each side in the seasoned pork rinds.

Once coated, lay them on the lined baking sheet in a single layer. If using thighs, bake them for 30 minutes, then turn the oven to broil and broil for about 3–4 minutes. Keep checking the chicken constantly, adding a few more minutes if chicken hasn't browned.

If using chicken breasts, cook for 40 minutes, then turn your oven to broil for about 3–4 minutes, since chicken breasts are a little bit thicker.

serves 2–4

Cooking spray

4 thighs, skinless or 4 breasts, skinless

8 ounces pork rinds, plain (Two brands to consider are Epic or 4505. Humanely raised, no antibiotics)

2 teaspoons dried oregano (optional) or your choice of seasoning

2 teaspoons lemon pepper

½ teaspoon sea salt

½ teaspoon garlic salt

1 teaspoon onion powder

4 large eggs

4 ounces heavy whipping cream or canned coconut cream, full-fat

1 teaspoon white pepper or red pepper flakes for heat (optional)

tip: If you prefer chicken legs, bake for 25 minutes.

herb-roasted lamb chops

serves 4

KF *These are always a huge hit as an appetizer or main dish! Your skill in managing the cooking time is important as lamb chops taste better medium rare.*

1 rack of lamb, individually cut

4 large garlic cloves, pressed

1 tablespoon fresh thyme leaves, lightly crushed

1 tablespoon fresh rosemary leaves, lightly crushed

2 teaspoons coarse kosher salt

2 tablespoons olive oil, divided

Mix garlic, thyme, rosemary, and kosher salt with 1 tablespoon of olive oil in large bowl.

Add lamb chops and turn to coat.

Let marinate in the bowl at room temperature at least 30 minutes, up to 1 hour

Preheat oven to 400°F (204°C). In heavy large ovenproof skillet, heat remaining 1 tablespoon of olive oil over high heat.

Add lamb and cook until browned, about 1 minute per side.

Transfer skillet to oven and roast lamb chops to desired doneness, about 4 minutes for medium rare.

Transfer lamb to platter, cover, and let rest 5 minutes.

butternut squash pizza rounds

KF *A great replacement for flour-based mini-pizzas, my Butternut Squash Pizza Rounds are so tasty and versatile. It's pizza party time!*

serves 4–6

- 1 butternut squash, preferably wide with a long stem end
- 2 tablespoons coconut oil or butter
- 16 ounces Mozzarella cheese, shredded
- Sea salt
- Pizza toppings of your choice, including Basic Marinara Sauce on page 258 and cheese

Preheat oven to 400°F (204°C).

Line a large baking sheet with parchment paper.

After peeling the squash, slice the stem end into ¼-inch thick slices. The wider your squash, the larger the diameter of your mini pizza rounds. It's best to pick a squash with a long "stem end." Scoop out the seeds at the bottom part of the squash. Slice and roast these pieces to enjoy as a snack or side dish.

Place the pizza rounds on the prepared baking sheet. Brush lightly with the melted oil and sprinkle with sea salt.

Bake for 35–40 minutes, until tender and lightly browned. Flip the squash halfway through baking.

Add mozzarella and pizza toppings and broil to melt cheese.

Serve immediately.

tip: The crusts are not crunchy, but they provide an easy grain-free pizza crust that stands up to plenty of cheese and sauce. You can eat these with your hands or with utensils or just plain with salt and pepper. They are great!

salt-encrusted prime rib

Serves 4–6

1 5-6 pound prime rib roast
1 tablespoon ground black pepper
4 cups kosher salt
1 tablespoon garlic salt
½ cup water

My favorite red meat is prime rib. For years I struggled to make a decent one and that's exactly what it was… just decent. I did some researching and finally discovered the most delicious way to cook prime rib. Luckily, it's both paleo- and keto-friendly. It's easy and always a favorite during the holidays and special occasions.

Preheat oven to 450°F (232°C).

Line a 9 x 13-inch roasting pan with aluminum foil.

Cover the bottom of the pan with 2 cups of kosher salt.

Generously season the meat with garlic salt and pepper.

Place the meat on the lined pan on top of the salt on the meat's fat side.

In a medium sized bowl, make a paste with a ½ cup of water and the 2 remaining cups of kosher salt.

Apply salt to the fat part only, not on the meat. Make a crust as best you can. Pat the fat with the salt paste.

Bake at 450°F (232°C) for 15 minutes then reduce oven to 325°F (163°C) for about 2½ hours.

For best cooking results, insert a meat thermometer in center of meat and when the temperature reaches 130°F (54°C), it's done for medium rare.

After the meat is done to your liking, take it out and let it stand for 15 minutes.

Remove the kosher salt crust and throw away.

Slice and serve with one of my side dishes.

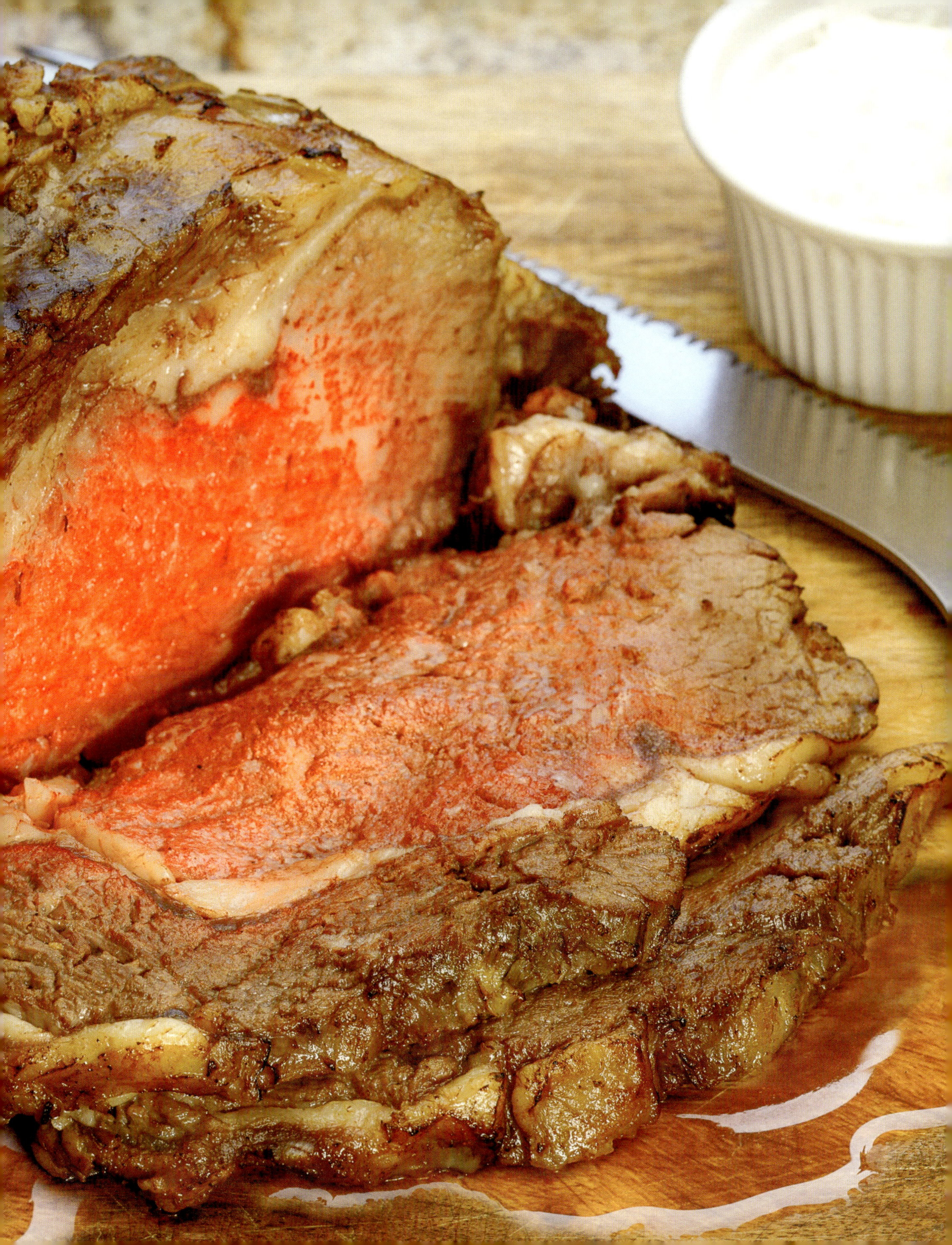

oven-roasted crispy chicken

serves 4–6

KF *This recipe is easy to make and versatile. You can stuff the chicken with fruit and vegetables or roast plain. Serve it with one of my side dishes to make a complete meal.*

1 2–3 pound organic chicken

2 teaspoons thyme, rosemary, or herb of choice, minced

2–3 tablespoons butter, unsalted, melted

Kosher salt and freshly ground black pepper

Optional Stuffing
1 each apple, pear, celery stalk, onion, quartered

Remove the chicken from the refrigerator about ½ hour before you're ready to roast.

Preheat oven to 450°F (232°C).

Rinse the chicken, then dry it very well with paper towels, inside and out. The less it steams, the drier the heat, the better.

Salt and pepper the cavity, then add your quartered stuffing and truss the chicken.

Trussing is easy, and if you roast chicken often, it's a good technique. Trussing helps the chicken to cook evenly, keeps it from drying out, and makes for a more beautiful roasted chicken.

When you truss a chicken, the wings and legs stay close to the body; the ends of the drumsticks cover the top of the breast. You can use cooking grade twine or bands.

Now, salt the outside of the chicken so that it has a nice uniform coating that will result in a crisp, salty, flavorful skin (about 1 tablespoon). When it's cooked, you should still be able to see the salt granules baked on the crispy skin. Season to taste with pepper.

Place the chicken in a sauté pan or roasting pan and put the chicken in the oven for 50–60 minutes.

Don't baste it or add butter as this may create excessive steam. Open oven door and check it every so often. Continue to roast until skin is golden brown and crisp.

Insert an instant-read thermometer into the thickest part of the breast. The optimal internal temperature on this part is 160°F (71°C). Then insert the thermometer into the thickest part of the thigh and look for 175°F (80°C).

main dishes

Remove chicken from the oven and add the thyme or herb of your choice, if using, to the pan.

Baste the chicken with the juices and thyme in the pan.

Remove from pan and place on serving dish and cover with aluminum foil. Let it rest for 15 minutes.

Remove the twine and slather the chicken with melted butter, if desired.

Remove and discard the stuffing, it's mostly to add flavor.

Enjoy!

parmigiano-reggiano chicken

KF *Parmigiana or Chicken Parmesan is a dish that normally consists of breaded chicken. Here, I offer you a grain-free twist on the recipe. Parmesan is actually the French simplification of Parmigiana. This cheese became popular among the French nobility of the 1500s.*

serves 3–4

- 3–4 chicken breasts, boneless, skinless (about 1½ pounds), pounded ¼-inch thick
- ½ cup almond flour
- 2 eggs
- ⅓ cup Parmigiano-Reggiano cheese, freshly grated
- ¼ teaspoon sea salt
- ¼ teaspoon ground black pepper
- 2 tablespoons fresh herbs, such as thyme, parsley, chives, or rosemary, finely chopped
- 1½ tablespoons butter
- 2 tablespoons olive oil
- Juice of 1 lemon
- 2 tablespoons capers
- 2 tablespoons Dijon mustard
- Fresh parsley for garnish

tip: If chicken breasts are large (8 or more ounces), you can cut them in half once they are pounded out.

First, you'll prepare your breasts by pounding them to a thinner cut. Cover the chicken breasts with parchment paper or plastic wrap and use a meat mallet or heavy-bottomed pan to pound them to about ¼-inch thickness.

If you thought that was fun, now set up three large shallow bowls in an assembly line. Place almond flour in the first bowl; beat the eggs in the second bowl; and mix the cheese, salt, pepper, and chopped fresh herbs in the third bowl.

Season chicken breasts with salt and pepper.

Dredge the first chicken breast in the flour and shake off the excess until just a light coating remains.

Next, dip the chicken in the egg mixture and turn to coat evenly, letting any excess egg drip off.

Finally, dredge the chicken in the cheese-and-herb mixture, turning a few times to coat well.

Set coated chicken on a plate and repeat until all of the chicken breasts are coated.

Add olive oil in a large sauté pan and warm over medium heat. When the oil is hot, add the chicken breasts to the pan and cook for 2–3 minutes until the first side is golden brown. Carefully flip and continue cooking until done, 2–3 minutes longer. Set chicken aside.

While the pan is still hot, add the butter to the sauté pan and cook until lightly browned (should take about a minute).

Stir in capers, mustard, and lemon juice, using a wooden spoon to scrape up any brown bits to make a nice gravy. Turn off the heat. Pour the gravy over chicken, getting good coverage, and add parsley.

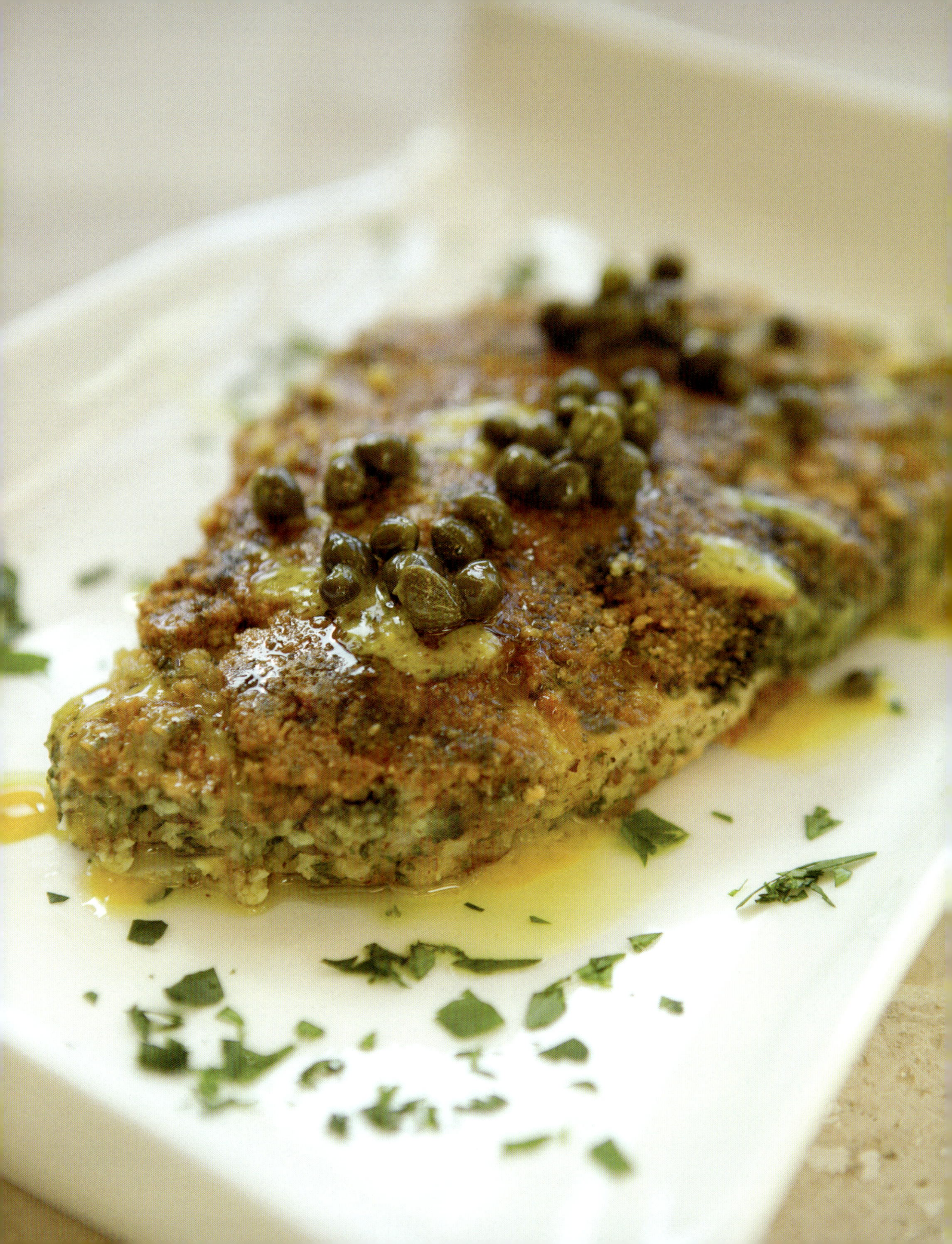

cauliflower crust pepperoni pizza

No floury dough here! This pizza is so good, you'll hardly notice it's not the real deal. If you liked my Cauliflower Cheese Bread, you'll be head over heels with this version.

tip: Of all the options, spaghetti squash crust, tapioca crust, or cauliflower crust, this one is the least fattening. If you are watching your waistline, this may become one of your favorites!

main dishes 190

Preheat oven to 375°F (191°C).

Remove the outer leaves from the cauliflower and cut it into florets. If buying the already-riced cauliflower, follow the directions on the package as to how to cook it.

Place the florets in a bowl or a food processor and pulse until finely chopped (it should look like rice).

Transfer the cauliflower to a microwave-safe dish or bowl. Cover and cook in the microwave for 10 minutes. Alternately, you can steam the cauliflower in a steamer basket or bake it in the oven at 375°F for 20 minutes.

When the cauliflower is cool, transfer it to a bowl lined with a kitchen towel or cheesecloth. Paper towels work.

Bring the ends of the cloth together and squeeze as much liquid out of the cauliflower as you can. It may take several times before almost all the water is gone. Remember the less water, the crisper the crust!

Transfer the cauliflower to a mixing bowl.

Add the eggs, ½ cup of cheese, Italian seasoning, salt, and pepper, and mix to combine.

Transfer the mixture to a baking sheet lined with parchment paper.

Form the dough into a rectangle, 8 x 12 inches and ¼-inch thick or a round pizza shape (about 7-inch round) bake for 20 minutes or until browned.

Remove the pizza crust from the oven and add the toppings.

Turn the oven to broil.

Place the pizza back into the oven on the middle rack and broil for 5 minutes until cheese melts.

serves 3–4

Cauliflower Crust

1 large head cauliflower (to make 3 cups cauliflower rice) or already-riced in many markets today

1 egg

¼ cup egg whites, about 2 large eggs

¼ teaspoon dried Italian seasonings

¼ teaspoon sea salt

⅛ teaspoon garlic powder

½ cup mozzarella cheese

Ground black pepper to taste

Toppings

¼–½ cup Basic Marinara Sauce (recipe on page 258) or I prefer to brush with olive oil only

5–7 pepperoni slices

¼ teaspoon oregano

4 slices tomatoes (optional)

Bunch basil, julienned or torn

¾–1 cup mozzarella, Parmesan, or use your choice of cheese

flatbread, meat lover's pizza

If you really like a loaded pizza, you'll need a forklift for this one.

serves 6–8

Pizza Crust
- 2 cups tapioca flour
- ¾ cup almond or coconut milk, unsweetened
- ⅓ cup butter
- 1 teaspoon sea salt
- 2 eggs, beaten
- 1 cup Parmesan cheese, finely shredded
- Garlic salt to taste
- Red pepper flakes for heat
- Cooking spray

Toppings
- 1½ cups mozzarella, shredded
- 8–10 slices pepperoni
- 1 cup Basic Marinara Sauce, (recipe on page 258)
- 2 slices crispy bacon, crumbled
- 1 link spicy Italian sausage, removed from casing and crumbled
- ¼ cup Parmesan cheese, shredded

tip: The more toppings you add, the heavier the pizza will become and may require a fork to eat it. Dig in!

Pizza Crust

Preheat oven to 425°F (218°C) and line a baking sheet with parchment paper or aluminum foil. If using foil, grease with cooking spray

Place tapioca flour into a large bowl. Set aside.

In a saucepan, bring milk, butter, and salt to a boil and turn off heat. Pour milk mixture over tapioca flour and mix until well incorporated. Allow dough to rest for 10 minutes to cool.

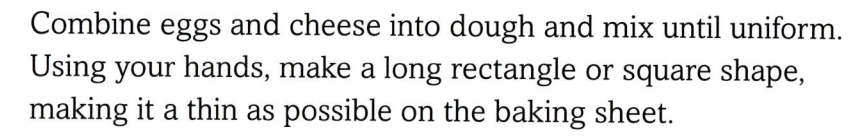

Combine eggs and cheese into dough and mix until uniform. Using your hands, make a long rectangle or square shape, making it a thin as possible on the baking sheet.

Transfer baking sheet to oven and decrease oven temperature to 375°F (190.6°C). Bake until golden on the edges about 20–25 minutes. Take out of oven.

Toppings

Preheat oven to 400°F (204°C).

In a sauté pan, place the crumbled sausage and cook until lightly browned and set aside.

Spread sauce on the flatbread. Add a layer of shredded mozzarella and top with pepperoni and sausage over the layer of sauce.

Sprinkle crumbled bacon on top. Add the Parmesan on the very top.

Bake for 8–10 minutes until cheese is melted.

flatbread, heirloom tomato, and basil pizza

Here's a flatbread pizza crust idea for you that is versatile with various toppings or styles.

Pizza Crust

Preheat oven to 425°F (218°C) and line a baking sheet with parchment paper or aluminum foil. If using foil, grease with cooking spray.

Place tapioca flour into a large bowl. Set aside.

In a saucepan, bring milk, butter, and salt to a boil and turn off heat.

Pour milk mixture over tapioca flour and mix until well incorporated. Allow dough to rest for 10 minutes to cool.

Combine eggs and cheese into dough and mix until uniform.

Using your hands, make a long rectangle or square shape, making it as thin as possible on the baking sheet.

Transfer baking sheet to oven and decrease oven temperature to 375°F (191°C).

Bake until golden on the edges about 20–25 minutes. Take out of oven.

Toppings

Preheat oven to 400°F (204°C).

Add cheese with sliced tomatoes and bake in oven for 8–10 minutes until cheese is melted. Top with torn basil leaves before serving.

---

serves 6–8

Pizza Crust

- 2 cups tapioca flour
- ¾ cup almond or coconut milk, unsweetened
- ⅓ cup butter
- 1 teaspoon sea salt
- 2 eggs, beaten
- 1 cup Parmesan cheese, finely shredded
- Garlic salt to taste
- Red pepper flakes for heat
- Cooking spray

Toppings

- 1 fresh heirloom tomato, thinly sliced (if heirlooms not available, regular tomatoes will work)
- ⅓ cup packed fresh basil leaves, torn
- 3 ounces burrata or mozzarella cheese (in liquid), sliced

main dishes

smoked pork roast

serves 8–10

1 5–7 pound bone-in pork shoulder roast

Garlic salt

Lemon pepper

2 cups apple juice, in a spray bottle

Every time we have ten or more people over for dinner, we always serve this wonderful smoked pork roast recipe. We have a Traeger Grill, but if you don't have one, you can always use a smoker. The pork comes out unbelievably tender. We always get rave reviews, and of course, it's grain free. I serve it with Mock Garlic Mashed Potatoes and veggies or my Celery Root Purée.

Generously season all sides of the pork roast with the ingredients, minus the apple juice.

When ready to cook, start the Traeger Grill on smoke with the lid open until the fire is established (about 5 minutes).

Set the temperature to 225°F (107°C) and preheat, lid closed, for 10–15 minutes.

Insert a remote thermometer into the thickest center of the meat without touching the bone.

Put the roast on the grill grate, fat-side up, and smoke for 1 hour.

Spray with apple juice every hour after the first hour.

After three hours, transfer to a disposable aluminum foil pan large enough to hold the roast.

Spray it generously with the apple juice.

Tent the pan with aluminum foil.

Increase the temperature to 250°F (121°C), and roast for 3–4 additional hours, or until the inserted thermometer registers 180°F (82°C) internal temperature.

Carefully transfer the pork roast to a cutting board and let it rest for 10 minutes.

Remove the bone if you can and slice. If you cannot remove the bone, slice around it.

So delicious!

tip: If you do not have a Traeger Grill or a smoker, use a slow cooker and follow the manufacturer's directions. The smoke in this recipe permeates the meat and is the best way to go.

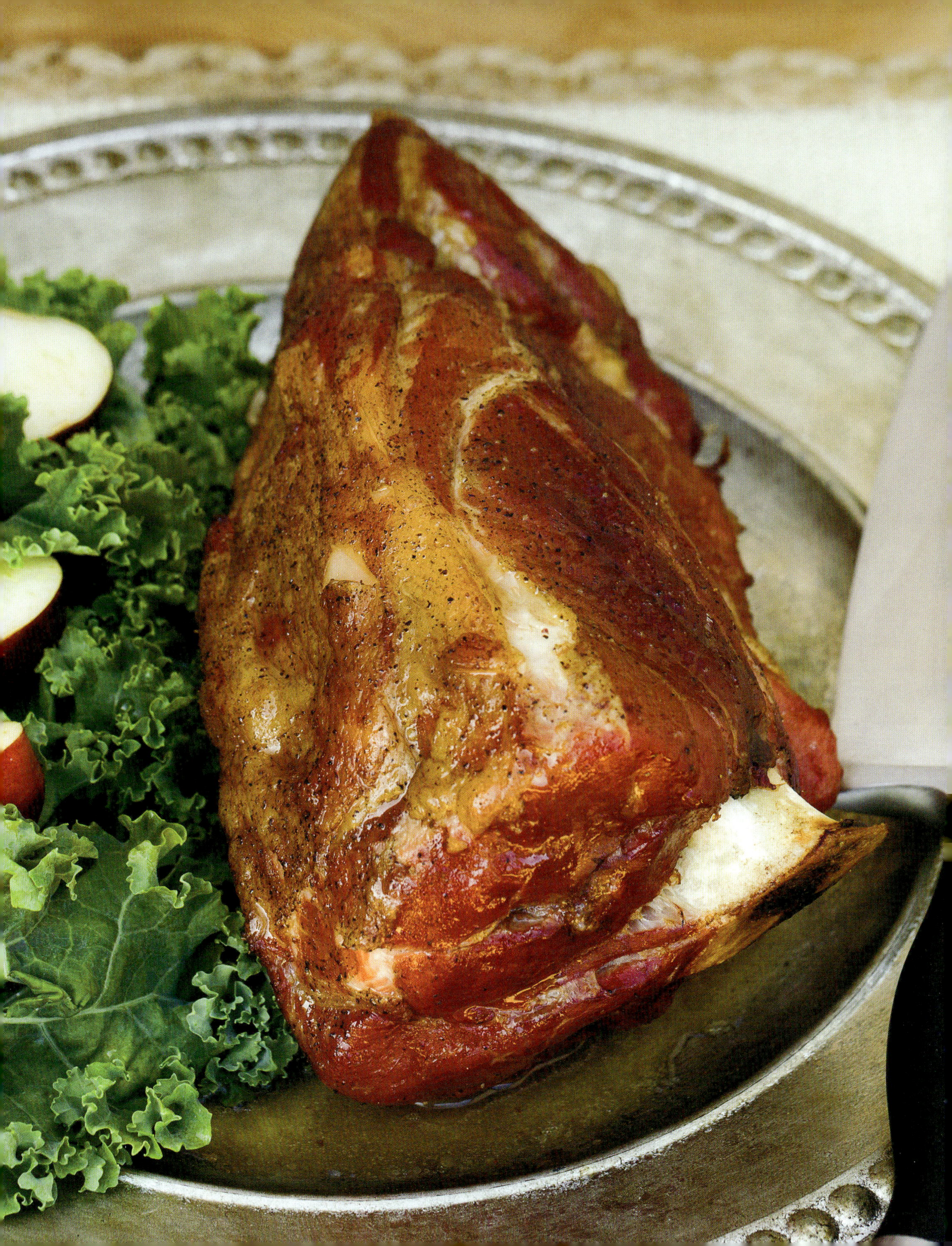

spinach and mushroom crustless quiche

serves 8–10

KF *This is a perfect Sunday brunch meal to share with your family and friends. Best of all—no grains!*

- 3 tablespoons butter or coconut oil
- ½ medium onion, chopped
- 3 cloves garlic, minced
- ¼ teaspoon sea salt
- ¼ teaspoon ground pepper
- 4 slices bacon, uncured, or 1 large Italian sausage (casing removed) or both, if desired
- 6 mushrooms, sliced
- 2 packed cups fresh spinach
- 8 large eggs
- ½ cup heavy cream
- ¾ cup white cheddar cheese, shredded, or cheese of your choice. A Mexican 4-cheese blend is very good.
- 1 fresh jalapeño, sliced (optional for heat) or red pepper flakes

Heat the butter or coconut oil in a cast-iron or oven-safe skillet over medium-high heat.

Add the onion, garlic, salt, and pepper and sauté until the onion is translucent. Then add the garlic and cook until it is fragrant, about a minute.

Chop the bacon and sausage, reserving 4 to 5 pieces for the top of the quiche. Add to the skillet and cook until crispy.

Add the mushrooms and spinach to the skillet reserving a few of each to top the quiche.

Preheat oven to 350°F (177°C).

Crack the eggs in a mixing bowl and whisk with a fork. Whisk in the cream and the cheese until all combined.

Pour the egg mixture into the skillet over the top of the sausage, bacon and vegetables.

Cook without stirring until the sides and bottom begin to set.

Take the remaining sausage slices or bacon, mushroom and spinach and add to the top of the skillet. Also add jalapeños or red pepper flakes (optional) to add heat.

Transfer the skillet to the oven and bake 20–30 minutes until the eggs are firm.

You can tell by inserting a toothpick.

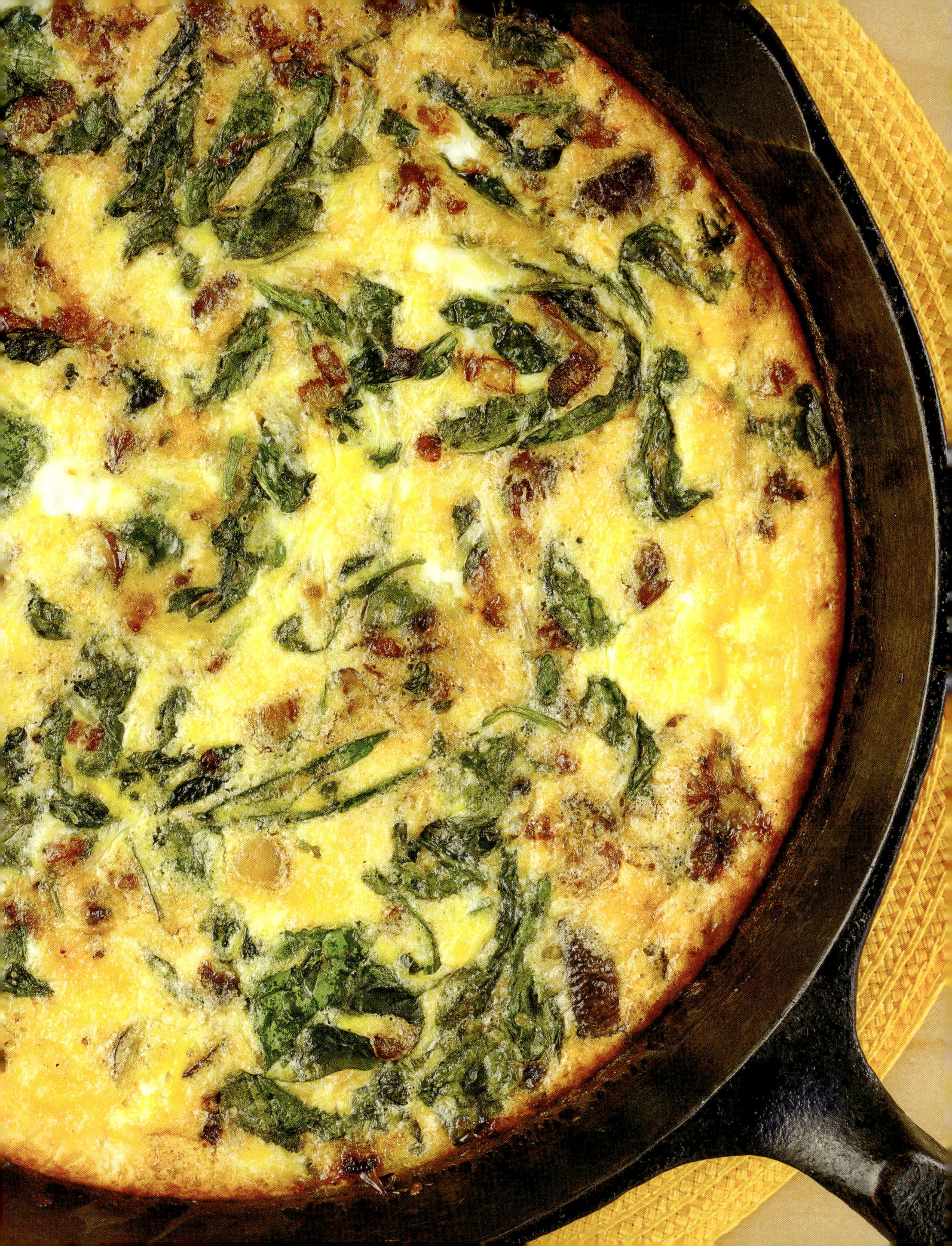

vegetable frittata

makes 8–10 servings

🆔 *Another perfect brunch or Sunday dinner dish. Nice combination of flavors and just the right amount of zest from the yellow pepper.*

Cooking spray

1½ pounds fresh asparagus or 2 10-ounce packages of frozen cut asparagus

1 medium yellow sweet pepper, stemmed, seeded, and cut into ¼-inch wide strips

⅓ cup onion, chopped

1 small zucchini, halved lengthwise and cut into ¼-inch thick slices, about a cup

10 eggs, lightly beaten

1 cup light or heavy cream, your choice

2 tablespoons Italian flat leaf parsley, chopped

1¼ teaspoons sea salt

¼ to ½ teaspoon ground black pepper

½ cup fontina cheese, shredded

Preheat oven to 350°F (177°C).

Grease a 2-quart rectangular or round baking dish with cooking spray and set aside.

If using fresh asparagus, snap off and discard woody bases; if desired scrape off scales.

Cut asparagus into ¼-inch to 1-inch pieces.

In a saucepan, bring about 1 inch of water to boiling.

Add asparagus, sweet pepper strips, and onion; return just to boiling.

Reduce heat slightly and boil covered, about a minute or until crisp tender.

Drain well set aside.

Save a few asparagus tips for garnish.

Spread the asparagus mixture evenly in the prepared baking dish.

Layer zucchini slices over asparagus.

In a large bowl combine eggs, cream, parsley, salt, and black pepper.

Pour mixture over vegetables in baking dish and sprinkle with cheese.

Bake about 35 minutes or until knife inserted near the center comes out clean.

Let stand for 10 minutes before serving.

Garnish with the reserve asparagus tips.

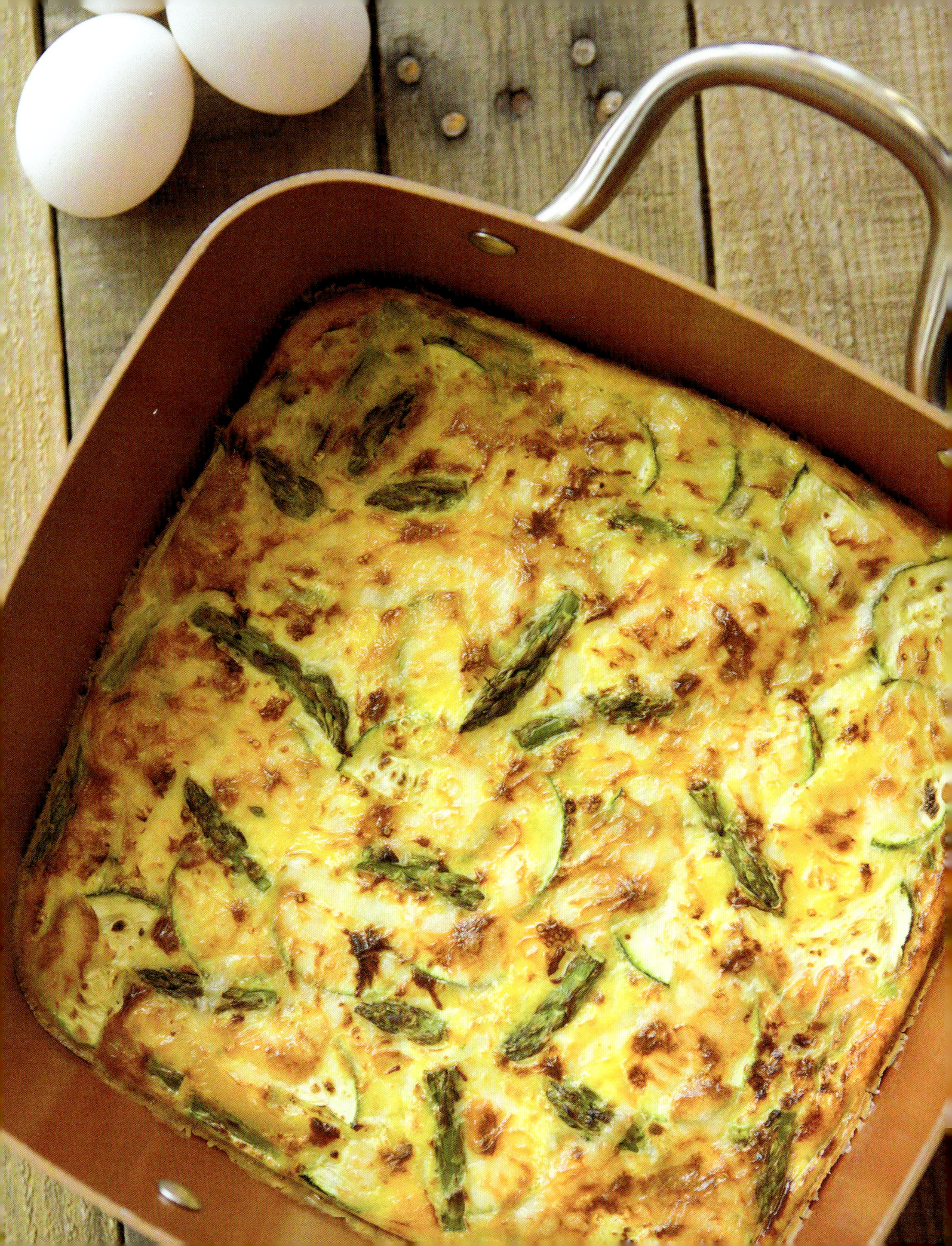

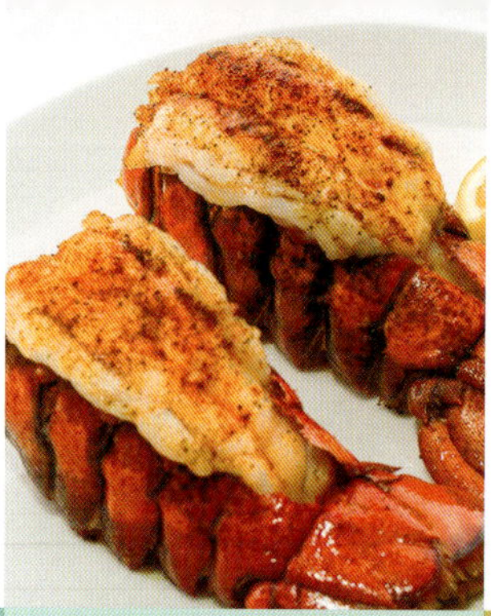
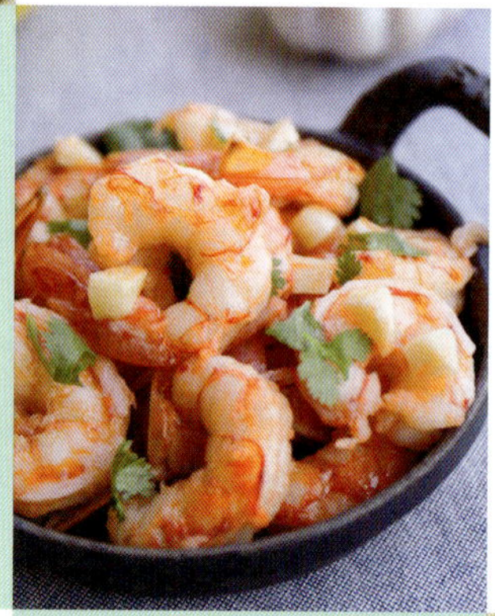
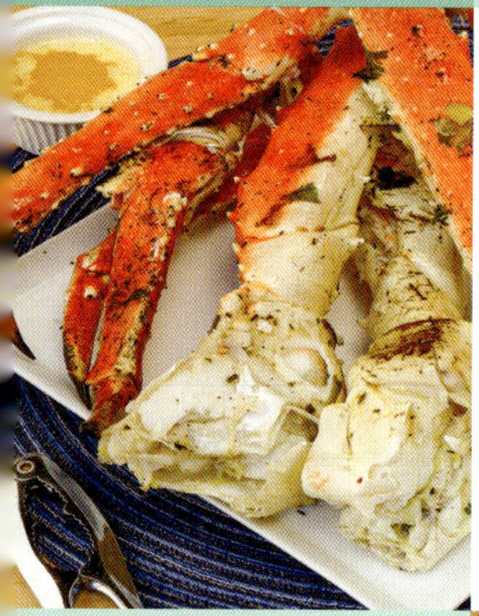
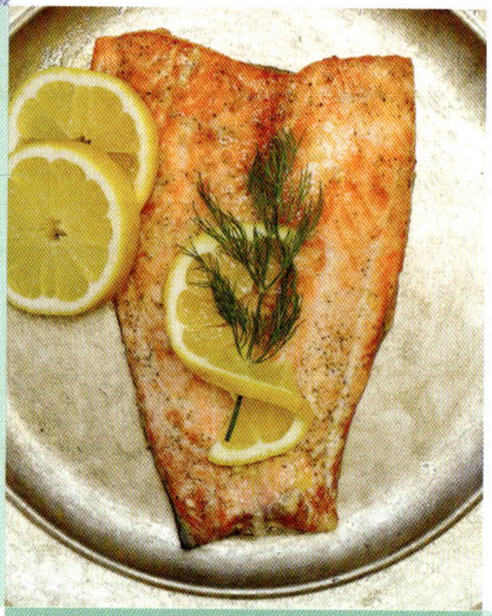
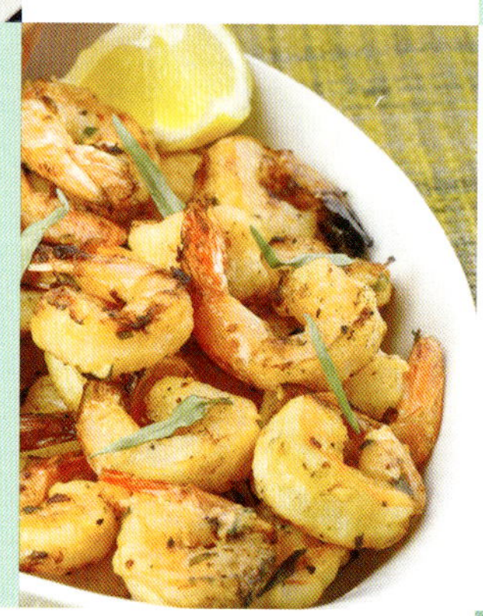
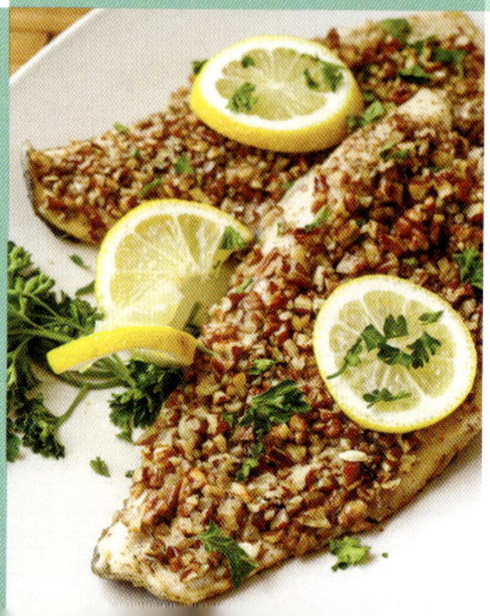

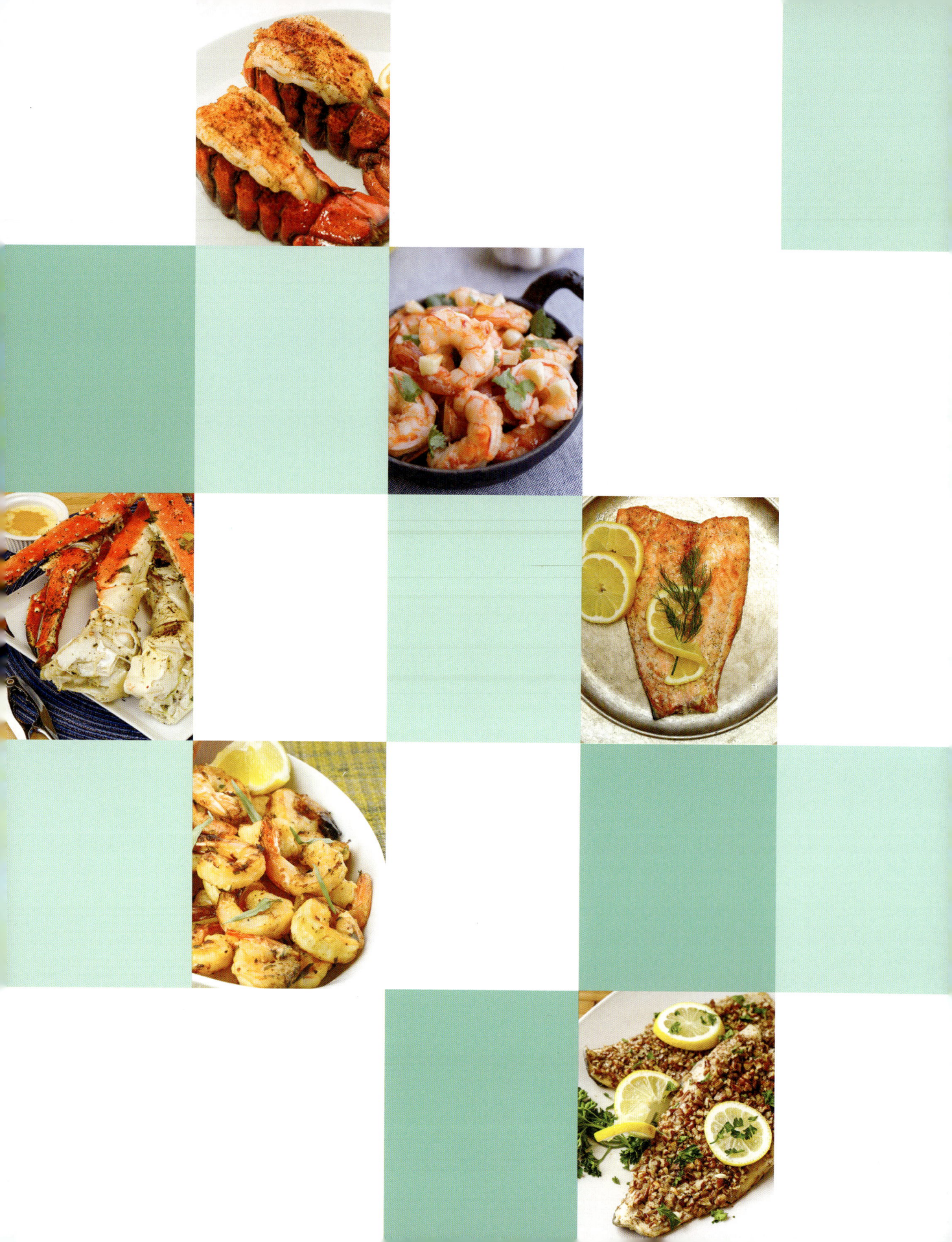

seafood + fish

Seafood and fish continue being a key part of my diet. Added to that, seafood and fish are rich in Omega-3 and other key nutrients and are the fruits of the sea and lakes, for us to enjoy.

KF Denotes that recipe can be made or is keto-friendly.

BBQ Citrus Salmon 202

BBQ Shrimp with Lemon Sauce 206

Broiled Lobster Tails 208

Broiled Salmon Fillets 209

Garlic Shrimp with Cauliflower Coconut Rice 210

Grilled Swordfish Steaks 213

Infused King Crab Legs 216

Lemon Pepper Salmon 217

Maple Sriracha Salmon 204

Pecan-Encrusted Trout 214

Pineapple Salmon 205

Salmon Rellenos with Caramelized Onions 218

Spicy California Sushi Stack 222

Steamed Manila Clams 212

Tuscan Salmon 220

bbq citrus salmon

serves 3–4

4 salmon fillets or 1 large fillet as shown in the picture, skin on

¼ cup olive oil

¼ cup orange juice

Juice of 1 lemon

Lemon pepper and ground black pepper to taste

Sea salt to taste

4 sprigs dill

Garlic powder to taste

Ah, my very favorite fish. So many wonderful cooking options and so very healthy as long as you consume the wild caught variety. Zesty and savory, salmon never tasted so good!

Heat the BBQ grill to high.

Rinse the salmon in cold water, pat dry with paper towels, and place on a platter, skin side down. Set aside.

In a bowl, combine half of the olive oil with the orange juice and the lemon juice.

Brush the juice and olive oil on all of the fillets.

Sprinkle lemon pepper and salt to taste.

Add the 4 sprigs of dill to the fillets.

Cut aluminum foil to fit the size of the salmon and grease with olive oil. Place onto grill, skin side down.

Barbeque the 4 fillets for 7 minutes or longer, depending on the thickness, on high (do not turn over).

Remove from heat and place on serving platter. Garnish with sliced lemon.

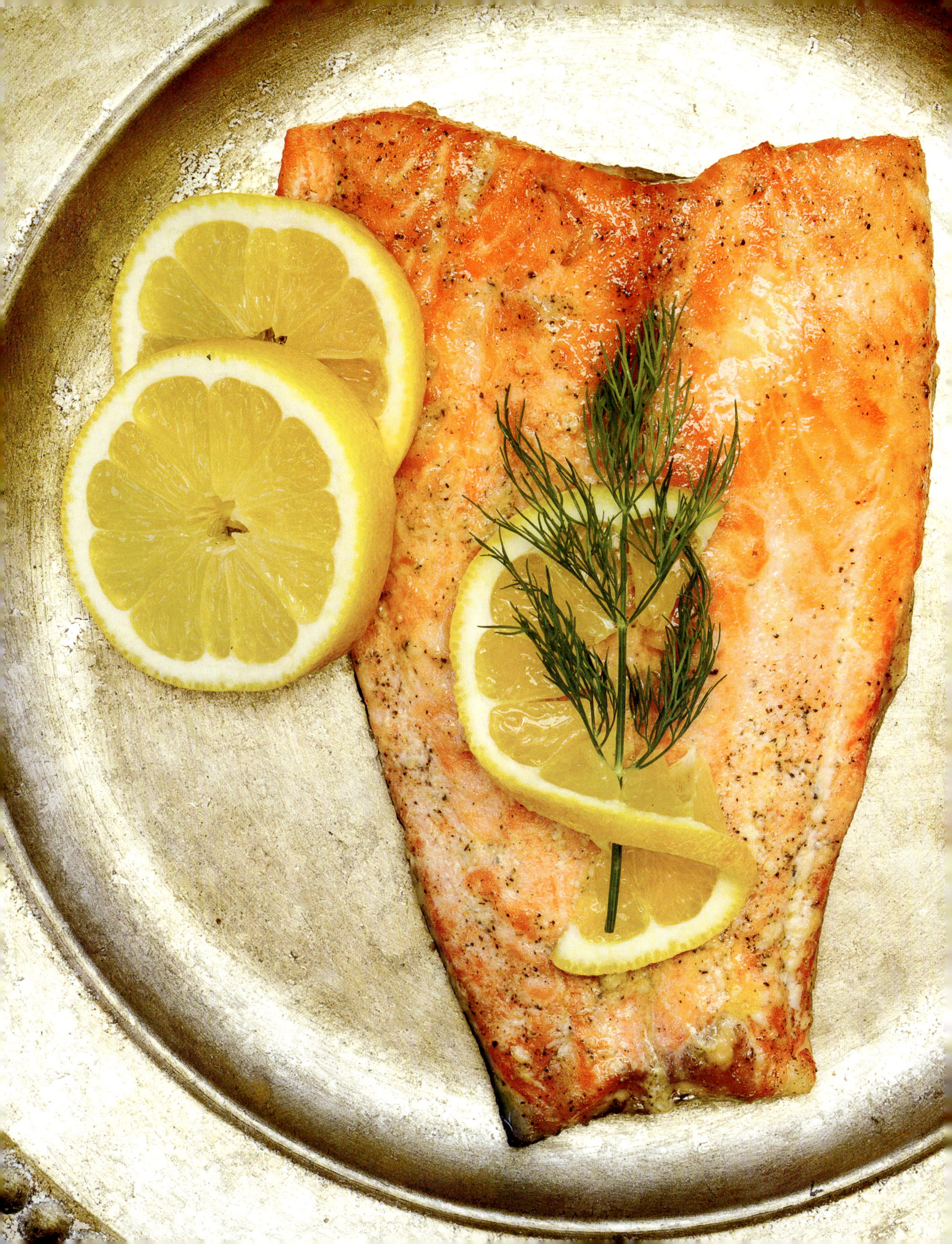

maple sriracha salmon

The spicy, tangy, and sweet flavor of this salmon dish is out of this world.

serves 3–4

- 4 fillets salmon or 1 large piece, skin on (as shown in the picture)
- ¼ cup sriracha sauce
- ¼ cup maple syrup
- Juice of 1 lemon
- Sea salt and pepper to taste
- Olive oil

Heat the BBQ grill to high.

Mix the sriracha sauce and maple syrup in a bowl.

Cut aluminum foil to fit 4 fillets or one large piece and place on grill grates.

Place your salmon on a plate and brush ½ of sauce mixture over the salmon fillets. Drizzle olive oil on aluminum foil.

Place salmon on the foil on the grill and brush on more sauce.

Barbeque on high for 8 minutes or longer, depending on how you like your salmon cooked.

Remove from grill and brush with remaining sauce before serving.

pineapple salmon

The Polynesian-Thai twist for this dish will delight your taste buds with the sweet and savory combination.

serves 4

1 large salmon fillet or 4 individual fillets

2 tablespoons fresh ginger, finely chopped

3 tablespoons sesame oil

½ cup butter, melted

3 green onions, thinly sliced

¼ cup sweet chili sauce (find sugar free at Trader Joe's)

1 bunch cilantro, chopped

3 garlic cloves, thinly sliced

½ cup pineapple juice from a can of pineapple rings, unsweetened

Sea salt and pepper to taste

Red pepper flakes to taste

Cooking spray for greasing

Preheat oven to 350°F (177°C).

Peel the ginger with a peeler and chop fine to get 2 tablespoons.

In a mixing bowl, mix together ginger, sesame oil, butter, onions, chili, cilantro, garlic, pineapple juice, salt, pepper, and red pepper.

Place salmon on a greased, aluminum foil-lined baking sheet.

Pour mixture over salmon fillet(s) and spread evenly, reserving some of the mixture for after baking.

Place the pineapple rings on top of and around the salmon, if desired.

Bake 15–20 minutes for individual fillets or 25–30 minutes for a large fillet.

bbq shrimp with lemon sauce

serves 4–6

KF *This is a very special and easy dish with an extra-zesty lemon sauce for dipping. You're gonna love it!*

1 pound jumbo shrimp, peeled and deveined

Zest of 2 lemons

1 tablespoon lemon juice

1 cup mayonnaise (or Basic Paleo Mayo recipe below)

1 tablespoon fresh tarragon, minced

½ teaspoon liquid smoke

1 tablespoon olive oil

1 teaspoon smoked paprika

½ teaspoon kosher salt

Basic Paleo Mayo

2 egg yolks

1 teaspoon Dijon mustard

4 teaspoons fresh lemon juice

Pinch sea salt

1 cup olive oil

First, to make lemon sauce, stir lemon zest, lemon juice, mayonnaise, and tarragon together in a bowl. Cover bowl with plastic wrap and chill in the refrigerator until cold, at least 15 minutes. Longer would be preferred.

Preheat an outdoor grill on high heat, and lightly oil the grate.

Put shrimp in a separate bowl. Drizzle olive oil and sprinkle paprika, liquid smoke, and salt over the shrimp. Stir to coat shrimp completely.

Cook the shrimp on the preheated grill until they are bright pink on the outside and the meat is no longer transparent in the center, about 2 minutes per side.

Transfer shrimp to a plate and serve with lemon sauce.

Basic Paleo Mayo

Mix everything together except the oil and blend in a blender.

Then pour the oil to the blender, making sure to go slowly to ensure it has the consistency of mayo.

Store in Mason jar or other covered glass container for about 10 days.

tip: If you want to skip the preservatives, try our Paleo Mayo. Store what you don't use in a Mason jar or other covered glass container for up to 10 days.

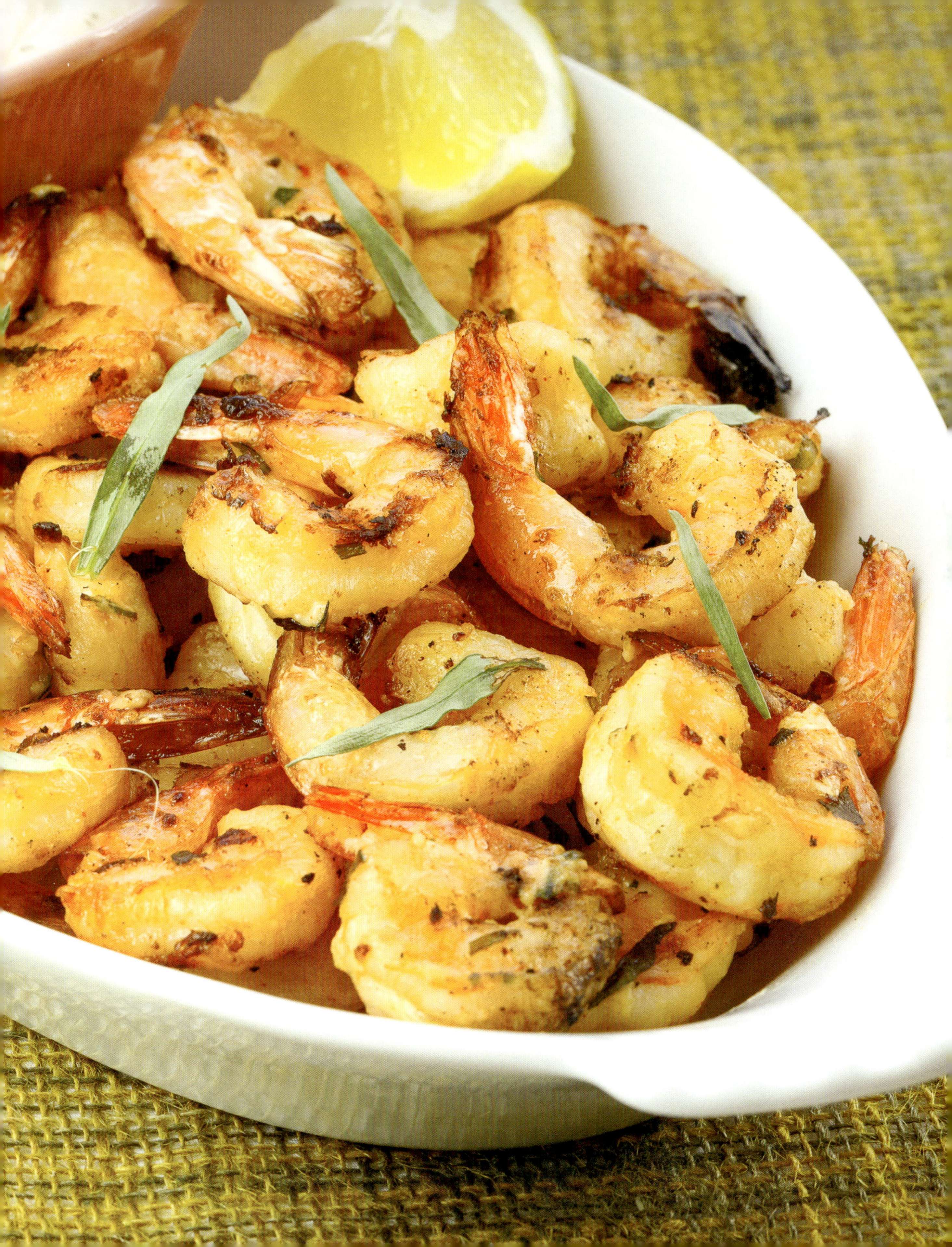

broiled lobster tails

serves 2

2 lobster tails (cold water tails are the tastiest)

¼ cup butter, melted

1 lemon cut into wedges

Pinch smoked paprika

Sea salt and pepper

For years, I was looking for the perfect way to cook lobster tails. I boiled them, barbequed them, and baked them. Every recipe was a little different than the last one. I kept looking for the most moist cooked lobster, and finally, I think I've got it covered—albeit not without perseverance and patience! I share with all of you my favorite method of cooking lobster. It's very easy and oh so delicious!

Preheat broiler for at least 15 minutes.

Place lobster tails on a baking sheet.

With a sharp knife or kitchen shears, carefully cut top side of lobster shells lengthwise. Pull out the lobster meat, keeping it intact on top of the shell.

Brush with lots of butter, smoked paprika, salt, and pepper to taste.

Broil lobster tails until lightly browned and lobster meat is opaque, about 7–10 minutes.

Garnish with lemon wedges and serve.

Since the lobster was brushed with butter, you don't need to add more butter for dipping unless you desire more.

tip: For added flavor, I like to finely chop fresh garlic and lightly coat with almond flour and pan fry until golden, about 1 minute. Then, I add the garlic to the dipping butter. Get the mouthwash ready if you want that second date.

broiled salmon fillets

KF *The biggest mistake when cooking salmon is over cooking it. I love mine cooked medium, otherwise, I find it too dry. Here's one of my favorite salmon recipes. It's so moist, it'll melt in your mouth!*

Preheat the oven's broiler and set oven rack below about 8–10 inches from the heat to broil.

Line a pan with aluminum foil with an edge that holds the fillets or an oven-safe 10-inch cast iron skillet. Grease with cooking spray.

Place garlic and oil in a bowl and microwave for 1 ½ minutes.

Melt the butter in a saucepan and stir in with the garlic.

Remove from heat, stir in Worcestershire sauce, lemon juice, white wine, black pepper, garlic salt, and chopped dill.

Place the salmon fillets skin side down in your prepared pan.

Spoon about a third of the butter sauce over the fillets.

Broil in the oven for 3 minutes.

Turn the fillets on their side so that the fillet faces up and baste fillets with about ⅓ of the butter sauce; broil for 3 minutes.

Turn fillets to the opposite side facing up, spoon on the remaining butter sauce, and broil until the fish flakes easily with a fork, about another 3 minutes.

Serve with your favorite vegetables and cauliflower rice.

serves 4–6

Cooking spray

4 cloves garlic

2 tablespoons olive oil

4 6-ounce salmon fillets

½ cup butter

2 tablespoons Worcestershire sauce

2 tablespoons lemon juice

¼ cup white wine

1 teaspoon ground black pepper

1 teaspoon garlic salt

¼ cup chopped dill

garlic shrimp with cauliflower coconut rice

serves approximately 4

KF *This is a simple way to make a meal. You'll especially enjoy the complex flavor combination of the shrimp with the cauliflower coconut rice!*

4 or more garlic cloves (I prefer to add more) sliced very thin

Red pepper flakes to your liking for a little spice

1 dozen jumbo shrimp or more depending on servings

½ cup or more olive oil to marinate the shrimp to make sure they are saturated.

Preheat oven to 350°F (177°C).

Place the shrimp in a bowl and add olive oil, the sliced garlic, and red pepper and marinate for at least ½ hour or longer up to two hours.

Spread the shrimp on a aluminum-lined baking sheet along with the olive oil from the marinade (including the sliced garlic and red pepper flakes) poured over the shrimp.

Bake for 7-10 minutes or until done.

Cauliflower Coconut Rice

1 medium cauliflower or a bag of already-riced cauliflower from Trader Joe's

⅓ cup white onion, finely diced

3 tablespoons coconut oil

½ teaspoon ground cardamom

¾ cup canned coconut milk, full-fat

A generous amount of sea salt and ground black pepper

¼ cup of cilantro chopped

Cauliflower Coconut Rice (See color photo on page 234.) Break the cauliflower into florets and either grate the florets with a cheese grater or buy it already riced from Trader Joe's. You may also rice the cauliflower slowly in a blender, pulsing it to get it into rice form.

Heat a large skillet over medium-high heat for 1–2 minutes; add the coconut oil.

Add the onion and sauté until tender, about five minutes. Then add the cardamom and stir with a wooden spoon until fragrant, about 30 seconds.

Add the cauliflower rice and coconut milk stirring to combine for about 10–12 minutes until the coconut milk is absorbed. The consistency will be a little off for a while, but it will come together as the cauliflower dries out a bit and brown specks begin to appear. Season with a generous amount of salt and pepper and add the ¼ cup chopped cilantro.

tip: I like to add the drippings from baking the shrimp into the rice.

seafood + fish

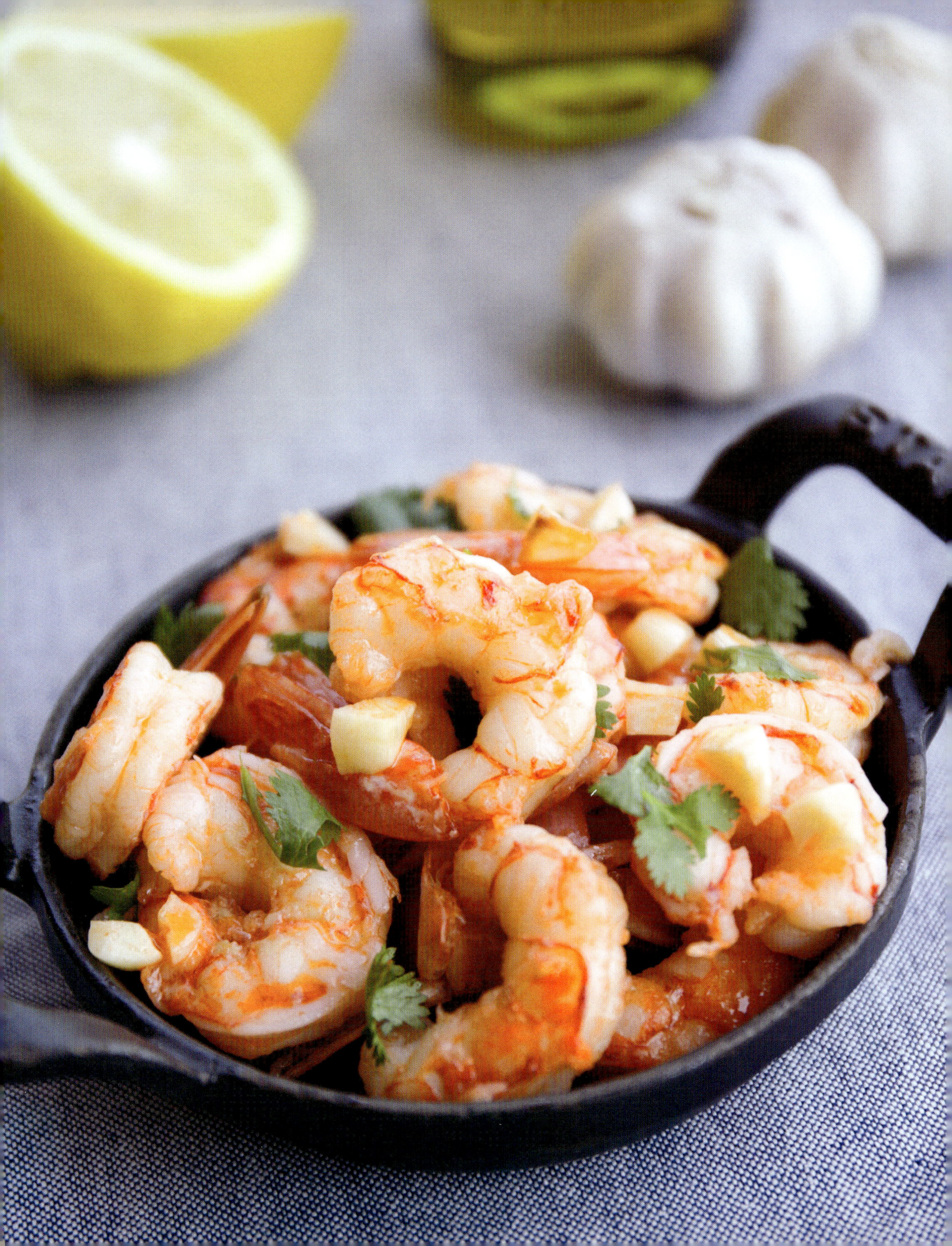

steamed manila clams

serves 2

2½ pounds Manila clams

6 tablespoons olive oil

1 mild Italian sausage, casing removed and crumbled

1 poblano pepper, de-stemmed and cut into rings

3 cloves garlic, thinly sliced

1½ cups dry white wine

1½ cups vegetable or chicken broth

6–8 basil leaves, julienned

½ cup parsley, chopped

KF *I remember the first time I tried Manila clams. I was in Hawaii, in Oahu to be exact. The distinct flavor of the Manila clams far surpasses cherry stone or little necks in my opinion. Manila clams are so tender they melt in your mouth! I thought I'd try my hand and offer you a wonderful recipe. The key is in the sauce. This new twist spices them up with poblano peppers and sausage.*

In a 10–14-inch sauté pan, heat the olive oil.

Add the crumbled sausage and heat over medium/high heat until browned, 1–2 minutes.

Add the sliced poblano pepper and cook for about five minutes.

Add the sliced garlic and cook for two minutes.

Add the wine and broth and bring to a boil.

Then add the clams and cook covered until the clams open, about ten minutes. Two minutes before they are done, lightly stir in the basil and parsley, and continue to cook covered.

Serve immediately and enjoy.

grilled swordfish steaks

KF *This is a nice change from salmon, sea bass, and halibut. It provides a rich source of selenium and protein and is loaded with niacin, vitamin B12, zinc and omega 3.*

Marinate steaks with the olive oil, lemon pepper, garlic powder, salt, and pepper for an hour or up to 4 hours in the refrigerator.

Preheat grill to high.

Meanwhile melt the butter with soy sauce in the microwave for about 40 seconds. Use this combination to baste the fish while grilling.

Place swordfish steaks on the grill.

Baste steaks with butter sauce for the first 4 minutes, then turn on the other side and baste for an additional 4 minutes.

If the steaks are thinner, cut the time to 3 minutes on each side. Save some of the sauce and pour over the steaks when done.

The fish should be a little pink in the center. By the time you serve them, the pink will disappear.

Squeeze lemon juice on each steak.

serves 4

4 swordfish steaks
4 tablespoons olive oil
Lemon pepper
Garlic powder
Sea salt and pepper to taste
¼ cup butter
½ cup gluten-free soy sauce or coconut aminos
2 lemons

seafood + fish

pecan-encrusted trout

KF *This rich and buttery fish is simply luxurious in texture and flavor. Easy to make any night of the week. You'll love this rich buttery flavor.*

serves 2

- 2 trout fillets
- Juice of 1 lemon
- 3 tablespoons olive oil
- ½ cup pecans, finely chopped
- ½ cup butter, melted
- Sea salt and pepper to taste

Preheat oven to 425°F (218°C).

Rinse fillets in cold water and pat dry.

Squeeze the juice of the lemon onto both fillets and add salt and pepper; set aside.

Add the olive oil to an ovenproof skillet on medium-high heat.

While the skillet is heating, take the pecans and press them into the fish.

Add the fillets to the heated skillet, skin side down, and cook for two minutes on stove top.

While the fish is cooking, add ¼ of the butter to the top of the fish, pouring it over the fillets.

If any pecans fall off, leave them cooking in the skillet, moving them close to the fish.

After two minutes remove from heat and roast fish in the oven for 7–10 minutes.

Take out the fish and drizzle remaining butter over top of fish.

Plate the fish.

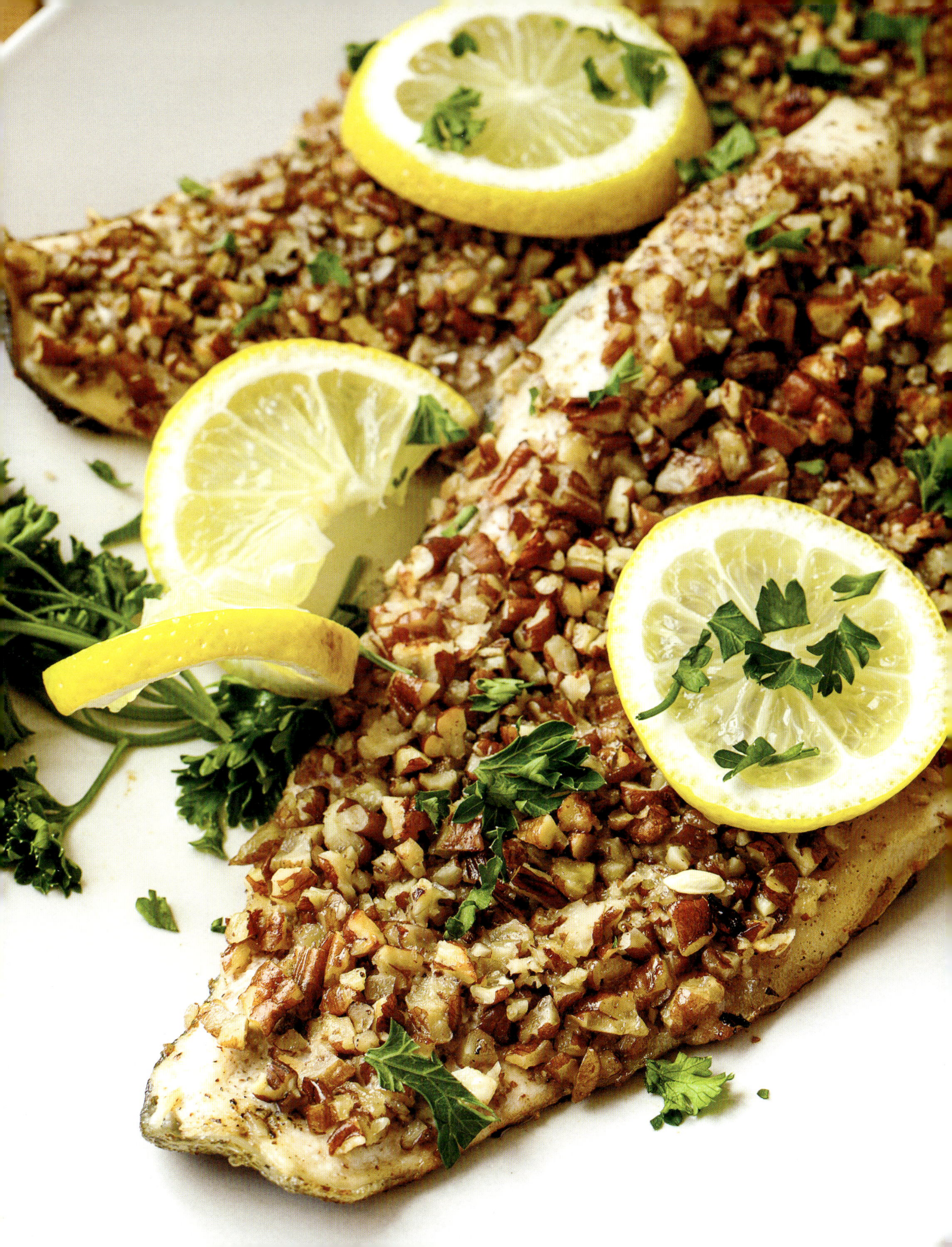

infused king crab legs

serves 3–4

KF *My friend from Lake Arrowhead, Heather Langle, made these for me and they were out of this world. I made minor changes to the recipe and the flavors are phenomenal. You're gonna love this!*

3–4 pounds king crab legs

1 cup white wine; dry is better

1 cup olive oil

1 shallot, peeled and sliced

4 cloves garlic, sliced

½ onion, finely chopped

1 teaspoon oregano

1 teaspoon thyme

1 tablespoon parsley, finely chopped

Sea salt and pepper to taste

4 tablespoons butter, melted

Add all ingredients, except the crab legs and butter, together in a bowl, cover and marinate in the refrigerator for at least 2 hours, longer if possible, even up to 6 hours.

Meanwhile, carefully cut the crab legs with kitchen shears lengthwise along the soft white side to make easy removal of the crabmeat when ready to steam.

Then, cut the legs to about 6-inch sections to better fit in the steam pot.

Put about a quarter of an inch of water at the bottom of a 3-quart pot and place a steamer in the pot.

Place the first layer of crab leg chunks and pour some of the marinade over the legs. Add the next layer of crab and repeat, adding more of the marinade. Add the marinade until all is used. The marinade will infuse through the crab meat.

Steam for about 8–10 minutes.

Serve with melted butter.

seafood + fish

lemon pepper salmon

KF *Here is a delicious way to prepare salmon to serve over my Cauliflower Coconut Rice or with my Mock Garlic Mashed Potatoes.*

serves 4–6

- 1 4-pound center-cut, wild-caught salmon fillet, skin on
- 8 tablespoons lemon juice (about three lemons)
- 4 tablespoons ground black pepper
- 6 tablespoons mayo or my Basic Paleo Mayo, recipe on page 206
- 4 tablespoons gluten-free soy sauce
- 8 teaspoons Dijon mustard
- 2 pinches cayenne pepper powder
- Sea salt to taste

Preheat oven to 450°F (230°C).

To make the lemon pepper sauce, whisk together lemon juice and black pepper in small bowl. Add mayonnaise, soy sauce, Dijon mustard, and cayenne pepper powder; whisk together and set aside.

Line a baking sheet with parchment paper and place salmon fillet on the baking sheet. Spread the lemon-pepper mixture over fillet with a spoon. Save about a tablespoon for later use.

Cover salmon with plastic wrap and refrigerate for 30 minutes.

Spread remaining lemon-pepper mixture on fillet without letting it pool around base. Sprinkle with a pinch more of black pepper and a pinch of sea salt on top.

Bake in the preheated oven until the fish flakes easily with a fork, about 10 minutes. Do not overcook.

Once baked, take out baking sheet and cut the fillet into your desired serving size.

salmon rellenos with caramelized onions

serves 4

4 oblong slices salmon, cut to fit in the poblano pepper, skinless

4 poblano peppers

3 tablespoons olive oil

Sea salt to taste

Lemon pepper to taste

Garlic salt (optional)

1 yellow onion, thinly sliced

Cooking spray

KF *I absolutely adore poblano peppers. I was experimenting one day and thought it would be great to have salmon and my Mexican pepper. So I devised a recipe from two things that I absolutely love. The result is Salmon Rellenos with Caramelized Onions.*

Preheat oven to 350°F (177°C).

Unwrap salmon and rinse in cold water. Pat salmon very dry after washing.

Season salmon to your liking, then sear the salmon (side of where skin was removed) in a skillet with 2 tablespoons of olive oil on medium-high heat for about 2 minutes. Set aside.

In the meantime, wash the peppers, then char them on the stove top over medium heat. If you can use a charring screen, even better.

After cooling to the touch (2–3 minutes), place in a plastic bag to steam for about 10 minutes. This allows for you to peel the skin easily and also softens the pepper.

Remove peppers from bag and peel the skin.

Slit the pepper lengthwise and discard the seeds; set aside. If some seeds are left in, it shouldn't be too spicy.

In a skillet, add a tablespoon of olive oil with a pinch of salt, and sauté onions on low to medium heat for 20–25 minutes to caramelize them until golden brown.

Now, put aluminum foil on a baking sheet and spray generously with cooking spray. Place your roasted peppers on the greased baking sheet.

Insert the salmon into the pepper and fold the pepper over leaving slight opening.

Bake for 7–10 minutes, depending on thickness of your fish to finish the salmon.

Top with caramelized onions and serve.

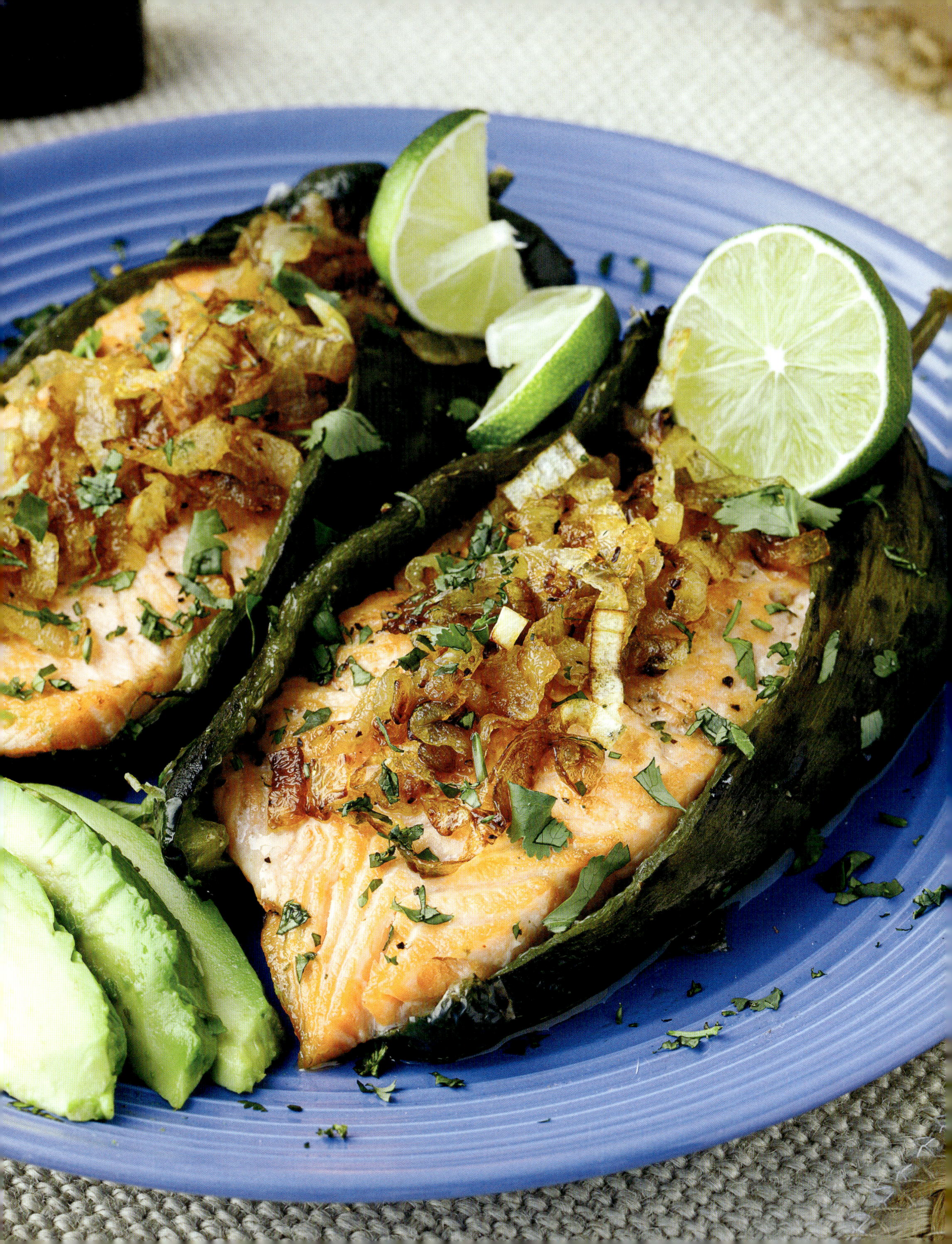

tuscan salmon

serves 4

This version of Tuscan Salmon combines a creamy sauce with tomatoes, spinach, and fresh basil.

- 4 6-ounce salmon fillets, skin off
- 2 teaspoons olive oil
- 4 tablespoons butter
- 1 small yellow onion, diced
- 6 cloves garlic, finely diced
- 1 ½ cups cherry tomatoes, sliced in half
- ½ cup heavy cream
- Sea salt and pepper to taste
- 3 cups baby spinach leaves
- 2 tablespoons fresh parsley, chopped
- Bunch fresh basil, julienned
- 1 tablespoon almond flour for thickening sauce (optional)

Heat the olive oil in a large skillet over medium-high heat.

Season the salmon fillets on both sides with salt and pepper, and sear in the hot pan, flesh-side down first, for 3 minutes on each side, or until cooked to your liking. Once cooked, remove from the pan and set aside.

Melt the butter in the remaining juices leftover in the pan. Fry the onion in the butter.

Add in the garlic and fry until fragrant (about one minute).

Add tomatoes and let cook for 2–3 minutes to release their flavors.

Reduce to low heat, add heavy cream and bring to a gentle simmer, while stirring occasionally. If your sauce is too thin or watery, add the tablespoon of almond flour.

Add the spinach; let it wilt into the sauce and season with salt and pepper to your taste.

Add the salmon back into the pan. Sprinkle with the parsley and basil and spoon the sauce over each fillet.

Serve immediately.

tip: Trout, sea bass, or any white fish will also work in this recipe for a delightful flavor.

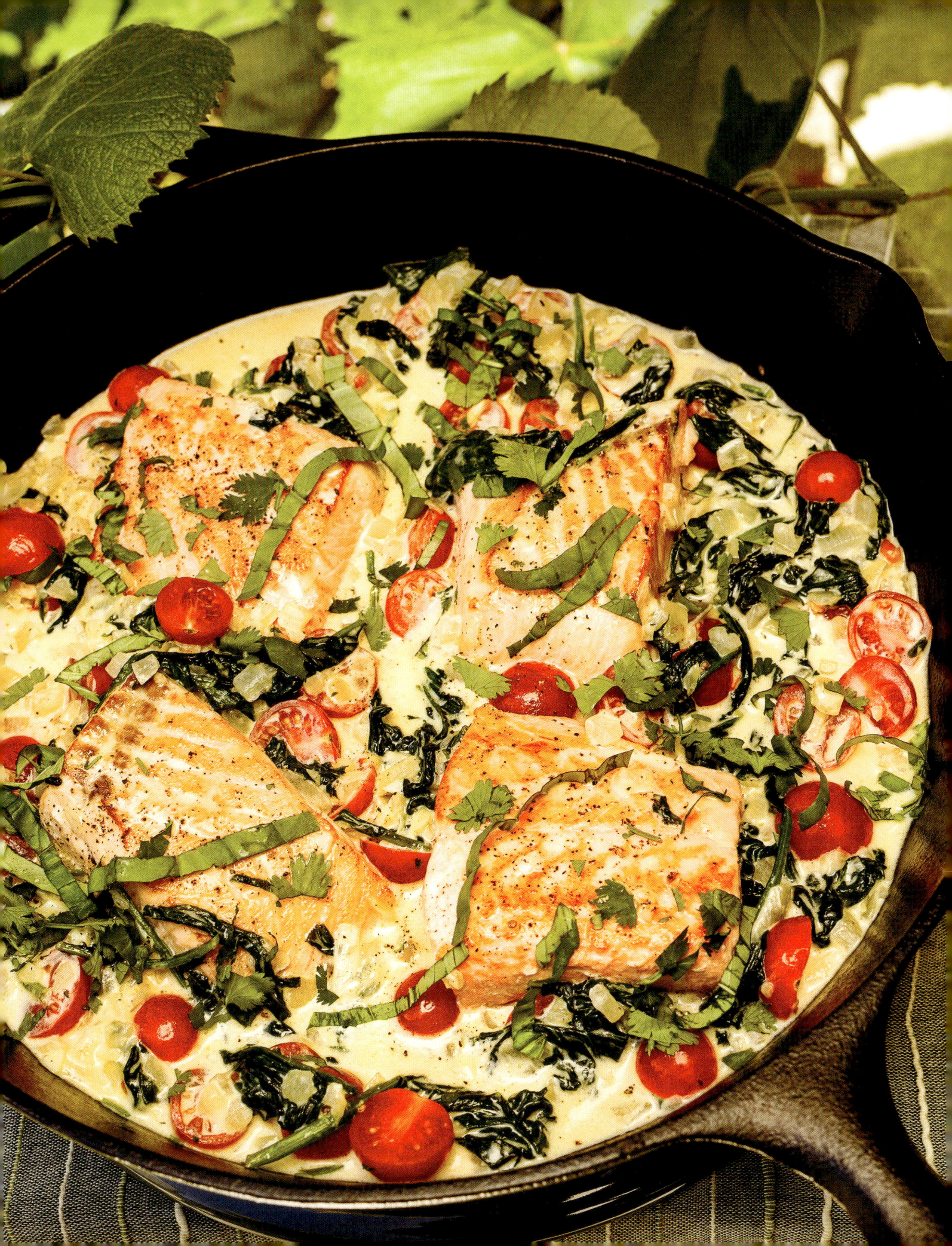

spicy california sushi stack

serves 2

1 ⅓ cups cooked already-riced cauliflower

2 tablespoons rice vinegar

8 ounces ahi tuna, cut in cubes

1 cup cucumber, diced (about 1 small)

4 teaspoons fresh chives, chopped

½ cup avocado (about 1 medium), mashed lightly with a fork

4 teaspoons black sesame seeds

4 teaspoons reduced-sodium soy sauce (gluten-free)

2 teaspoons Basic Paleo Mayo (see recipe below)

3 teaspoons creamy wasabi

Basic Paleo Mayo

2 egg yolks

1 cup olive oil

1 teaspoon Dijon mustard

4 teaspoons fresh lemon juice

Pinch sea salt

KF *I love ahi tuna, but unfortunately, it's high in mercury, so I don't have it too often. Many times, it's prepared with sticky rice, which contains too much sugar. Here's a yummy dish with a twist that I am sure you'll love. I replaced the rice with cauliflower.*

Cook cauliflower rice according to package directions, without any salt or oil. When rice is done, add rice vinegar and stir. Evenly spread rice on a sheet pan to cool.

Cut ahi into 1-inch cubes.

In a small bowl, combine cucumber and chives.

In another small bowl, combine mayonnaise, soy sauce, and wasabi to make your drizzle sauce.

Using a 1-cup food mold, layer ⅓ cup rice, then ¼ of the ahi tuna, 2 tablespoons of avocado, and then a ¼ cup cucumber.

Carefully press the stack out of the food mold onto a plate.

Sprinkle with sesame seeds and the drizzle sauce. Repeat with remaining ingredients.

Basic Paleo Mayo

Place egg yolks, mustard, lemon juice and a pinch of salt in a blender and blend at medium speed.

Slowly add olive oil until you get a smooth well mixed consistency.

tips: Riced cauliflower can be found at Trader Joe's, Whole Foods, and other fine grocery stores.

You may add more or less wasabi, depending on how spicy you want it.

I enjoy the Inglehoffer Creamy Wasabi by Beaverton Foods.

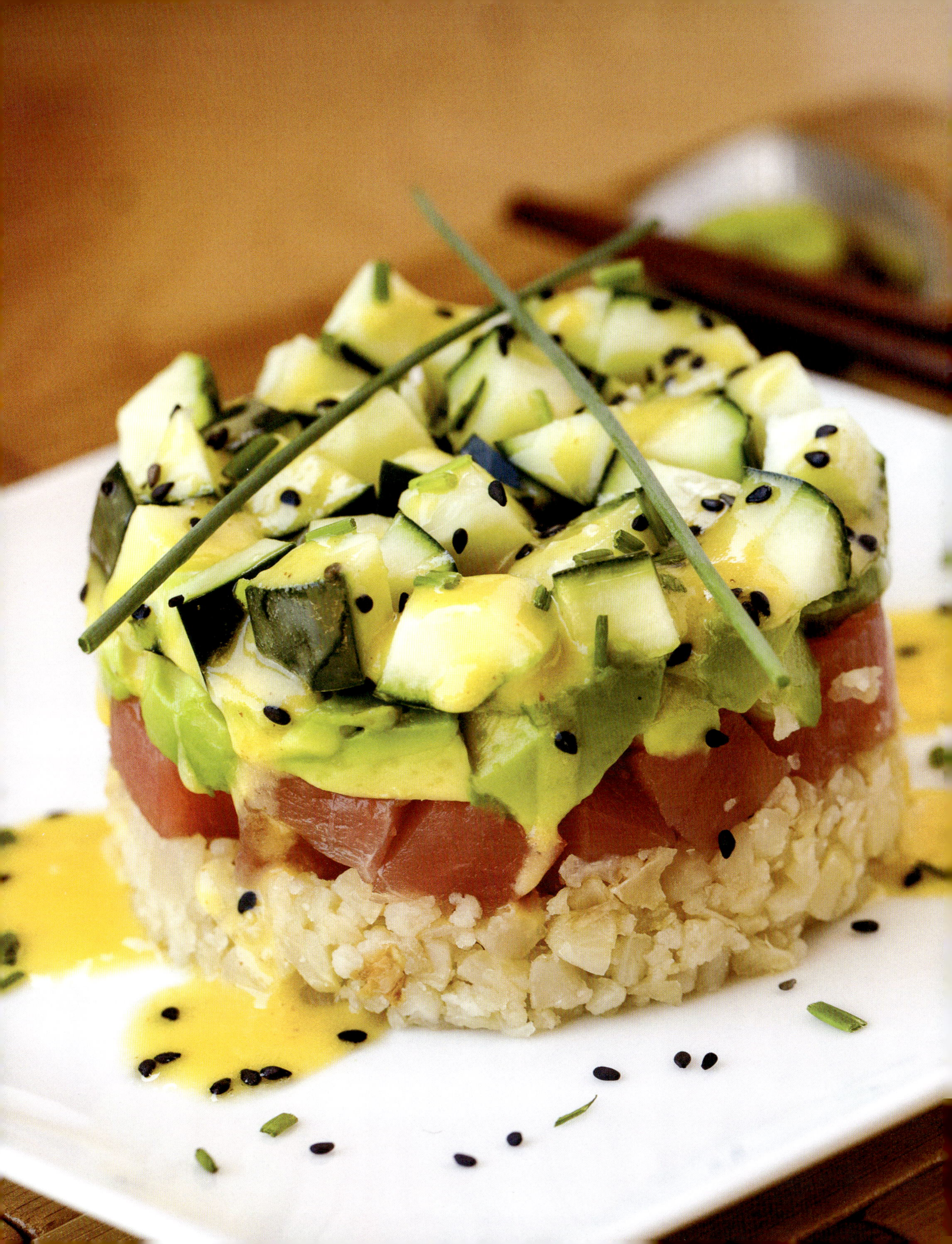

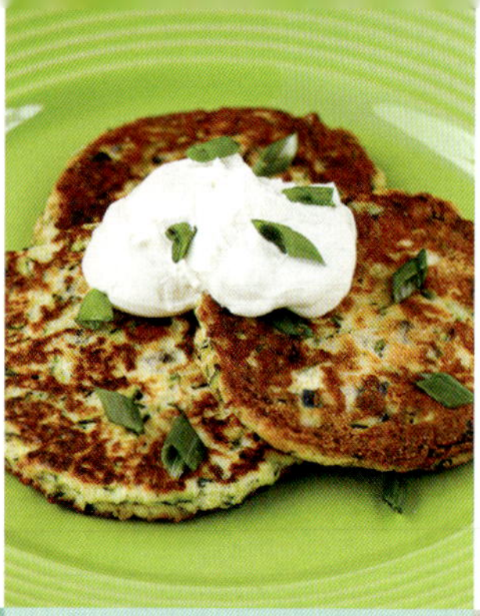

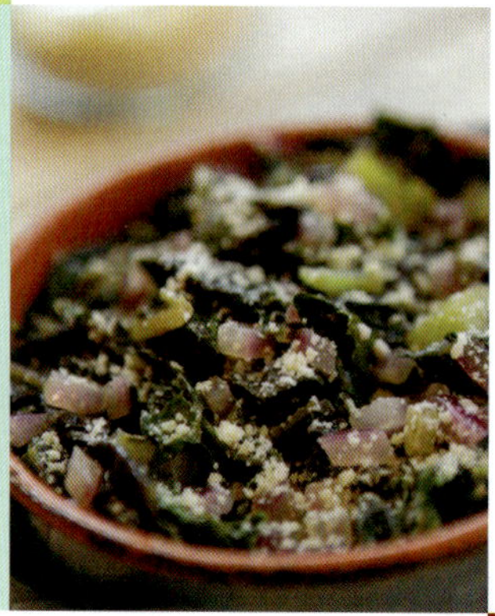

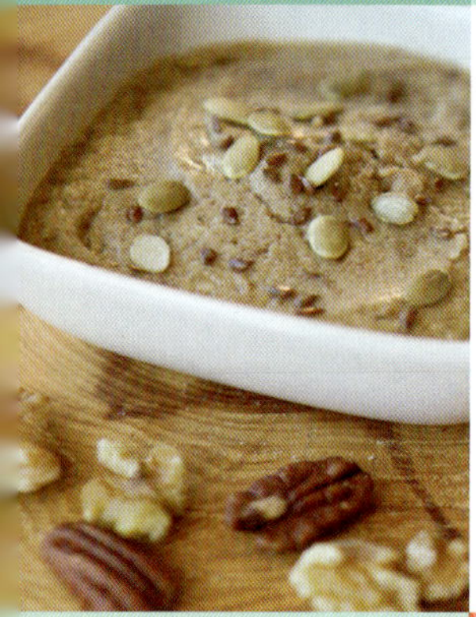

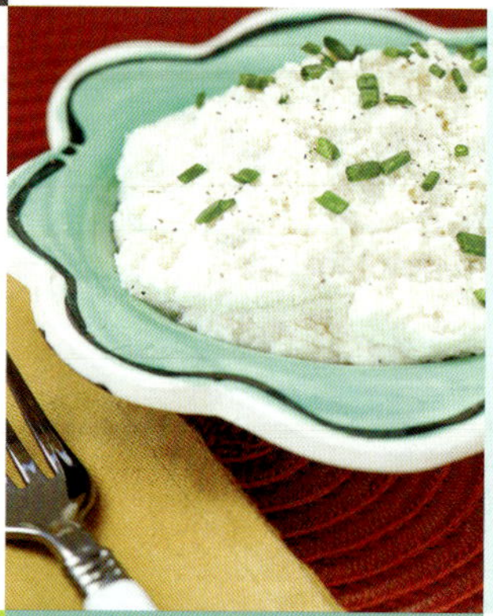

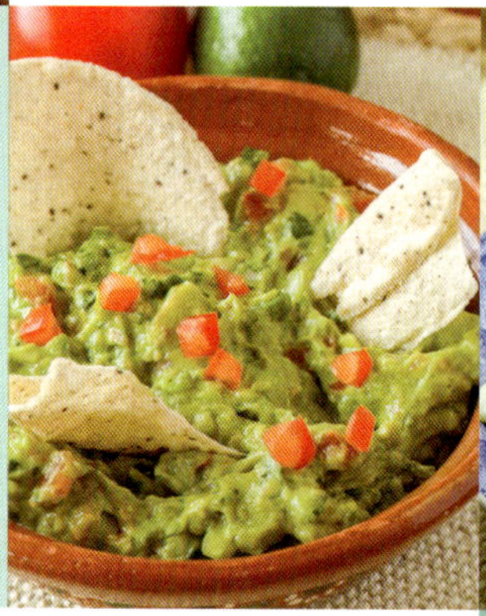

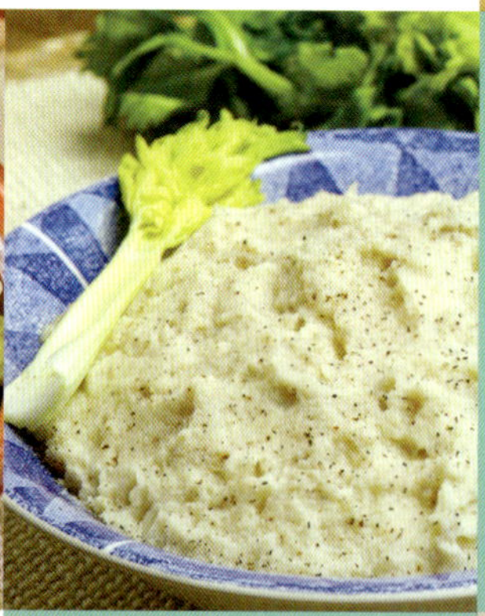

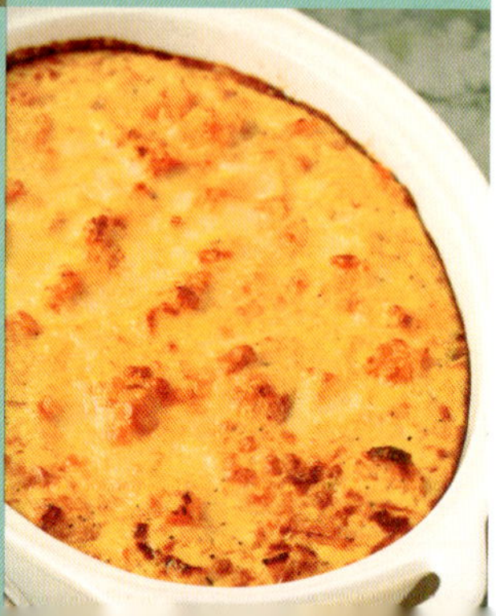

side dishes

Side dishes are commonly used with main courses throughout the western world. Many side dishes have included various forms of rice and grain combinations. Remember when we all grew up with French fries, mashed potatoes and onion rings? Here are some healthy alternatives.

KF Denotes that recipe can be made or is keto-friendly.

Baked Artichokes **226**

Butternut Squash Fries **230**

Butternut Squash Purée **233**

Cassava Flour Tortillas **228**

Cauliflower Coconut Rice **234**

Celery Root Purée **235**

Cheese Soufflé **236**

Cheesy Cheese Bread **240**

Easy Creamy Cauliflower Mash **238**

Fig Chutney **239**

Heavenly Butternut Squash Casserole **242**

Jalapeño Bacon Queso **244**

Killer Guacamole Dip **245**

Mock Garlic Mashed Potatoes **232**

Nut and Seed Butter **250**

Pico de Gallo **246**

Pumpkin Cauliflower Gratin **254**

Sautéed Swiss Chard with Parmesan Cheese **247**

Savory Breadless Stuffing **248**

Zucchini Pancakes **252**

baked artichokes

serves 4

2 artichokes (½ of an artichoke per serving)

½ lemon

½ teaspoon garlic, minced

Extra-virgin olive oil

Sea salt and pepper to taste

Parsley, finely chopped

Parmesan cheese, grated

½ cup Mayonnaise or my Basic Paleo Mayo (recipe on page 206)

tip: Just a reminder to wrap the artichokes twice with aluminum foil. It really does make a difference.

My dear friends, Rev. Arthur Hammons and his wife, Dr. Virginia Foster, Ph.D. of La Jolla have shared several culinary treats over the years that inspired this recipe. Here is a finger-licking good side dish or warm appetizer for your enjoyment.

Preheat oven to 400°F (204°C).

Remove the stem of the artichoke and cut off about one inch off the top of the artichoke.

Take a pair of kitchen scissors and snip off the thorns on the tip of the artichoke petals.

Take half a lemon and rub lemon juice over the cut portion of the artichoke to prevent it from browning.

Spread open the petals and rub minced garlic all over.

Drizzle olive oil over the top of the cut side and season with salt and pepper.

Add the parsley and Parmesan, making sure to get some in between the petals.

Wrap the artichoke twice in aluminum foil and place on baking sheet.

Bake 1 hour and 20 minutes.

When done, cool and unwrap, while saving the liquid inside. Cut the artichoke in half, lengthwise.

Remove the fibers from each half, leaving the heart and most of the leaves.

Drizzle more olive oil with any leftover liquid from baking the artichoke and sprinkle seasonings inside and out.

Transfer onto a serving plate and spoon melted butter into each and serve with my Basic Paleo Mayo or regular mayonnaise.

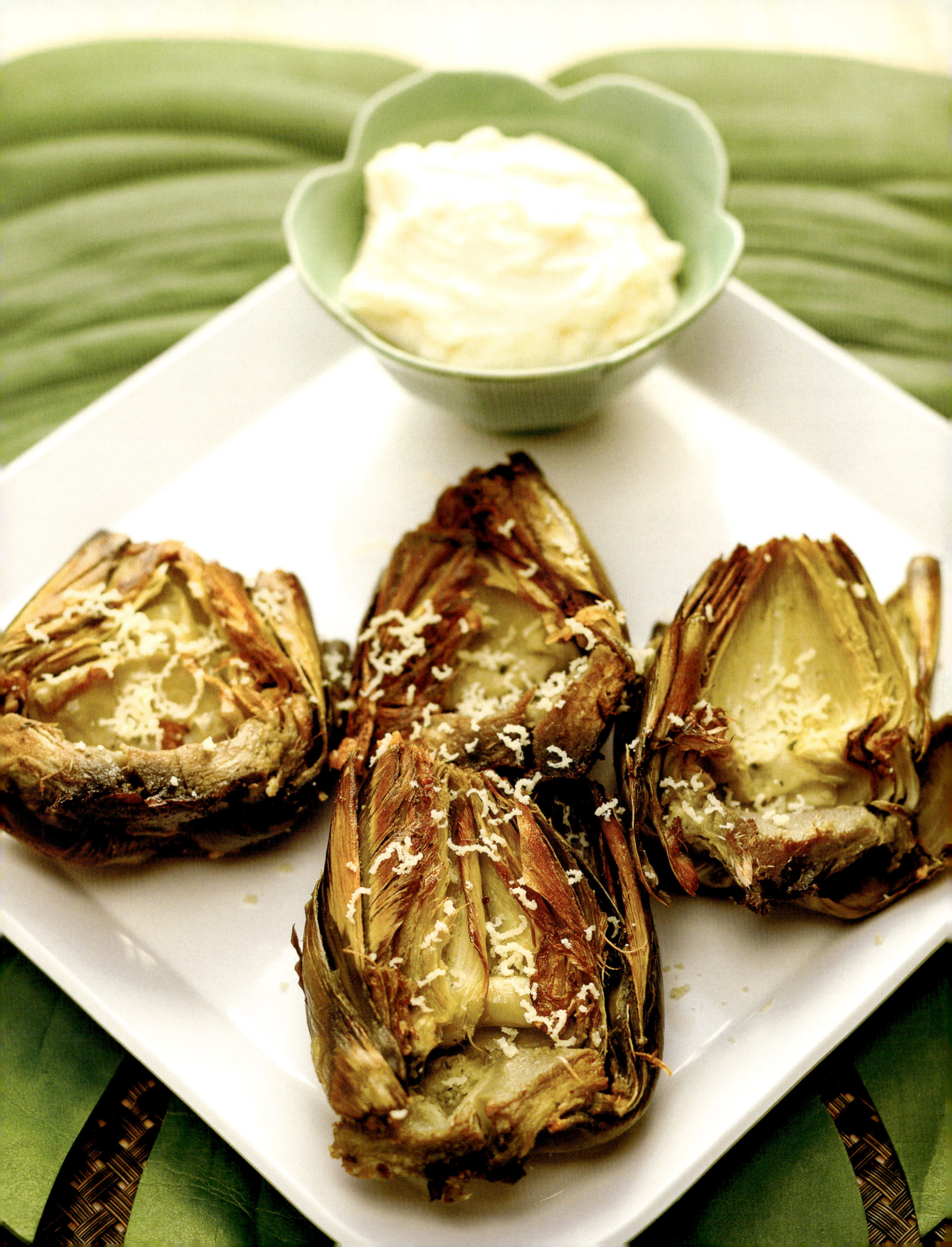

cassava flour tortillas

makes 6–8

1½ cups cassava flour

¾ teaspoon sea salt

¼ teaspoon cream of tartar

⅛ teaspoon baking soda

¾ cup warm water

6 tablespoons olive or avocado oil

I love Mexico and have really enjoyed the tortillas. It took some time experimenting with different flours to get what I think is a tasty alternative to flour tortillas. ¡Buen provecho!

Combine flour, salt, cream of tartar, and baking soda in a mixing bowl.

Add oil and water and mix with a wooden spoon or your hands until a stiff dough forms. If dough is sticky, use a bit more flour. If the dough is crumbly, add a bit more olive oil.

Divide dough in half, then in half again to create 8 fairly equal portions. Form each piece into a ball.

Place one dough ball at a time on a silicone baker's mat, parchment paper, or wax paper and flatten with the palm of your hand as much as possible.

Cover flattened dough with a sheet of parchment paper or wax paper. Roll dough into a very flat rough circle, about 8–10 inches in diameter.

Carefully remove the bottom parchment paper so the rolled-out tortilla is stuck to one piece of parchment paper or wax paper.

Set remaining dough balls aside and roll out. When they're stuck to parchment or wax paper, you can easily stack them in preparation for cooking.

Preheat a 10-inch or larger skillet (a well-seasoned cast iron or enameled cast iron pan works well over medium-high heat).

When pan is hot, peel one rolled-out raw tortilla off its parchment or wax paper and place into pan.

Cook about 1 minute or until bottom surface has a few pale brown spots. The top surface will begin to show a few little bubbles.

side dishes

Flip and cook for about 30–45 seconds. Ideally, the tortillas will be soft with a few small pale golden-brown spots on the surface. If tortilla is browning too fast, reduce heat. If it's taking longer than a minute to see a few pale golden-brown spots on underside of tortillas, increase heat.

Remove from pan with tongs and stack in a covered container until all tortillas are cooked.

Serve warm or allow to cool for later use.

To freeze, separate tortillas with parchment paper or wax paper and place in a zippered bag before placing in freezer.

butternut squash fries

serves 6–10

1 large butternut squash, peeled

2 tablespoons coconut oil

3 tablespoons fresh dill, chopped

Sea salt and pepper to taste

Parmesan cheese, grated

KF *I love French fries — heck, we all do! But sometimes we just wish we could enjoy them without the guilt. So, I went to work and created a delicious and healthy alternative. Say hello to my Butternut Squash Fries!*

Preheat oven to 400°F (204°C).

Line baking sheet with aluminum foil.

Cut the bottom off the squash so you have an easy cutting surface.

Use a sharp knife or a peeler to remove the skin of the squash. Cut the squash in half, remove seeds, and cut into fry-size strips.

Toss the fries in a bowl with oil, dill, and salt.

Place fries on the prepared baking sheet, making sure not to overlap in order to keep the fries cooking evenly.

Bake in the preheated oven until golden, tender on the inside and crunchy on the outside, for 35 minutes or longer, depending on your oven.

You may add Parmesan cheese instead of the dill or any seasoning of your choice.

Eat while warm.

This is a better option than yams, fewer carbs and calories.

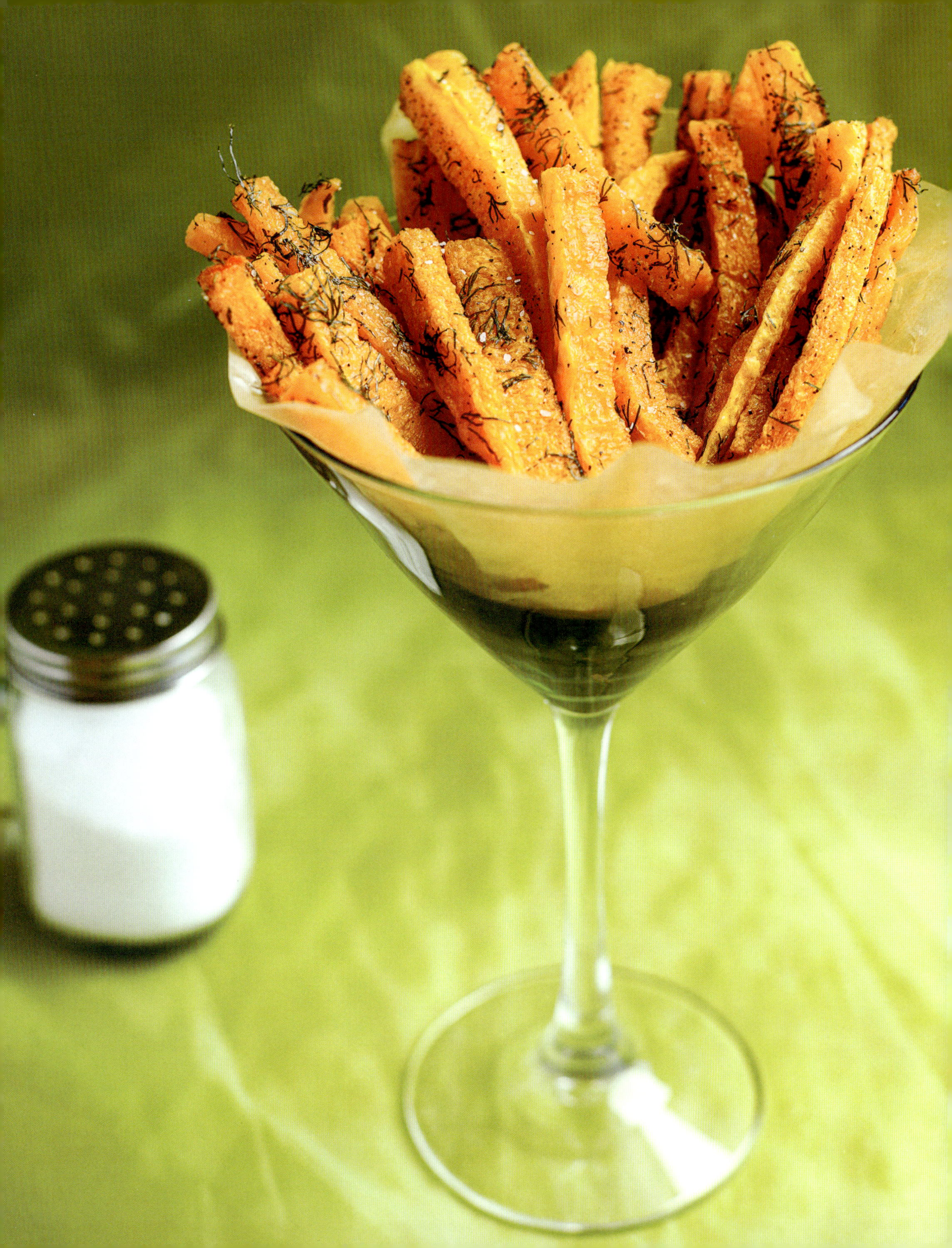

mock garlic mashed potatoes

serves 8–10

KF *This is a magical replacement for the usual mashed potatoes. My friend, Lori Bagdasarian, told me about substituting cauliflower for mashed potatoes. I loved it so much that now I don't miss the real deal. It's a great side dish for almost any meal.*

- 1 medium cauliflower or a bag of already-riced cauliflower
- ¼ cup coconut milk, unsweetened
- ½ teaspoon garlic, minced
- ⅛ teaspoon chicken base or bullion (may substitute ½ teaspoon sea salt)
- ½ teaspoon ground black pepper
- ½ teaspoon fresh or dry chives, chopped for garnish
- 3–4 tablespoons butter, unsalted

Set a stockpot of water to boil over high heat.

Clean and cut cauliflower into florets. If using already-riced cauliflower, follow directions on the package, placing the already-riced cauliflower into a microwave safe bowl covered with a wet paper towel and microwave for five minutes. Otherwise, cook florets in boiling water for about 6 minutes, or until well done.

Drain well. Do not let it cool. If using florets, pat cooked cauliflower very dry between several layers of paper towels.

Place the hot cauliflower with the garlic, chicken base, coconut milk, and pepper into a food processor or blender and purée until almost smooth.

Garnish with chives, and serve hot with pads of butter.

butternut squash purée

Here's a great low-carb alternative to yams or potatoes. My Butternut Squash Purée has half the carbs and is high in potassium and vitamin A, among other nutrients.

serves 8–10

1 butternut squash

½ teaspoon lemon-pepper seasoning

3 tablespoons chipotle sauce from a small can of chipotle peppers

⅓ cup butter

½ cup white onion, chopped

2–3 cloves garlic, chopped

¼ cup olive oil

Sea salt and pepper to taste

Preheat oven to 375°F (191°C).

Cut the butternut squash in half; take the seeds out. Season with lemon pepper, together with salt and pepper.

Evenly spread the olive oil over the open face of the squash.

Line a baking pan with aluminum foil. Bake the squash skin side up for approximately 45–50 minutes or until soft when punctured with a knife.

Remove from oven and let cool a bit. Scoop out all the squash away from its peel and put in a bowl.

Melt butter and add the rest of the ingredients to the squash and mix well.

Add all ingredients to a blender or food processor and purée. Add more seasonings if need be.

Place the puréed squash in an oven-safe casserole and bake in oven for 15 minutes uncovered.

Serve as a side dish to your favorite meal.

tip: I purposely do not add too much chipotle sauce because I don't want to overpower the taste of the squash. You may prefer to add more.

cauliflower coconut rice

serves about 4

1 medium cauliflower or a bag of already-riced cauliflower available at most grocery stores

⅓ cup white onion, finally diced

3 tablespoons coconut oil

½ teaspoon ground cardamom

¾ cup, canned coconut milk, full-fat

¼ cup cilantro, chopped

Generous amount of sea salt and pepper

tip: When I am browning meat, I like to add the meat drippings to enhance the flavor of the rice.

KF Here's a really great grain-free rice made with cauliflower. It goes great with roasted veggies, chicken breast, pork, beef and shrimp.

Break the cauliflower into florets and either grate the florets with a cheese grater or buy it already riced. You may also rice the cauliflower slowly in a blender, pulsing it into its rice form.

Heat a large skillet over medium-high heat for 1–2 minutes, add the coconut oil.

Add the onion and sauté until tender, about five minutes. Then add the cardamom and stir with a wooden spoon until fragrant, about 30 seconds.

Add the cauliflower rice and coconut milk stirring to combine for about 10–12 minutes until the coconut milk is absorbed. The consistency will be a little off for a while, but it will come together as the cauliflower dries out and brown specks begin to appear. Season with a generous amount of salt and pepper and add the ¼ cup chopped cilantro.

celery root purée

KF *Ever wonder what to do with the root of a celery? Bet you didn't know it could taste so good, and it's healthy too. If you are looking to replace potatoes, here is another tasty alternative.*

serves 3–4

1 **celery root**

2–3 cups **water**

2–4 tablespoons **butter**

½ **yellow onion, diced**

¼ cup **coconut milk, unsweetened**

Sea salt and pepper to taste

Cut off the weird-looking roots and peel the celery root. Cut into roughly 2-inch pieces.

In a saucepan, add enough water to cover celery root pieces. Add the celery root pieces and bring to a boil until tender, about 15 minutes.

Drain the water and put the cooked celery root into a blender.

In a saucepan, melt the butter and sauté the onions for a few minutes until translucent.

Add the sautéed onions and the cooked butter to the celery root.

Add the other ingredients to the blender and pulse until you reach the consistency of mashed potatoes. Add more milk or butter, if desired.

cheese soufflé

serves 4–6

Cooking spray

½ cup Parmesan cheese, grated

¼ cup coconut flour

¼ teaspoon paprika

¼ teaspoon sea salt

⅛ teaspoon cayenne pepper

⅛ teaspoon white pepper

Pinch ground nutmeg

4 tablespoons butter, unsalted

1⅓ cups coconut milk, unsweetened

1½ cups Gruyère cheese, shredded

6 large eggs, separated

2 teaspoons fresh parsley, minced

¼ teaspoon cream of tartar

KF Soufflé—the name immediately causes fear! Many years ago, I studied French cooking, and I learned how to make a good soufflé. I changed it to a healthier version. I took the white flour out, added a couple of other ingredients and voilà, it came out great! Yes, it will fall, so hurry and serve your guests immediately!

Preheat oven to 350°F (177°C). Adjust oven rack to middle position.

Spray 8-inch round (2-quart) soufflé dish with cooking spray, and then sprinkle with 2 tablespoons Parmesan.

Combine flour, paprika, salt, cayenne, white pepper, and nutmeg in a bowl and set aside.

Melt butter in small saucepan over medium heat. Stir in flour mixture and cook for 1 minute.

Slowly whisk in coconut milk and bring to a simmer. Cook, whisking constantly until mixture is thickened and smooth, about 1 minute.

Remove saucepan from heat and whisk in Gruyère cheese and 5 tablespoons Parmesan until melted and smooth. Let cool for 10 minutes, then whisk in egg yolks and 1½ teaspoons of parsley.

Using stand mixer fitted with whisk, whip egg whites and cream of tartar on medium-low speed until foamy, about 1 minute. Increase speed to medium high and whip until stiff peaks form, 3–4 minutes. Add cheese mixture and continue to whip until fully combined, about 15 seconds.

Pour mixture into prepared dish and sprinkle with remaining tablespoon of Parmesan. Bake until it rises above the rim, top is deep golden brown, and interior registers 170°F, 30–35 minutes.

Sprinkle with remaining ½ teaspoon of parsley and serve immediately.

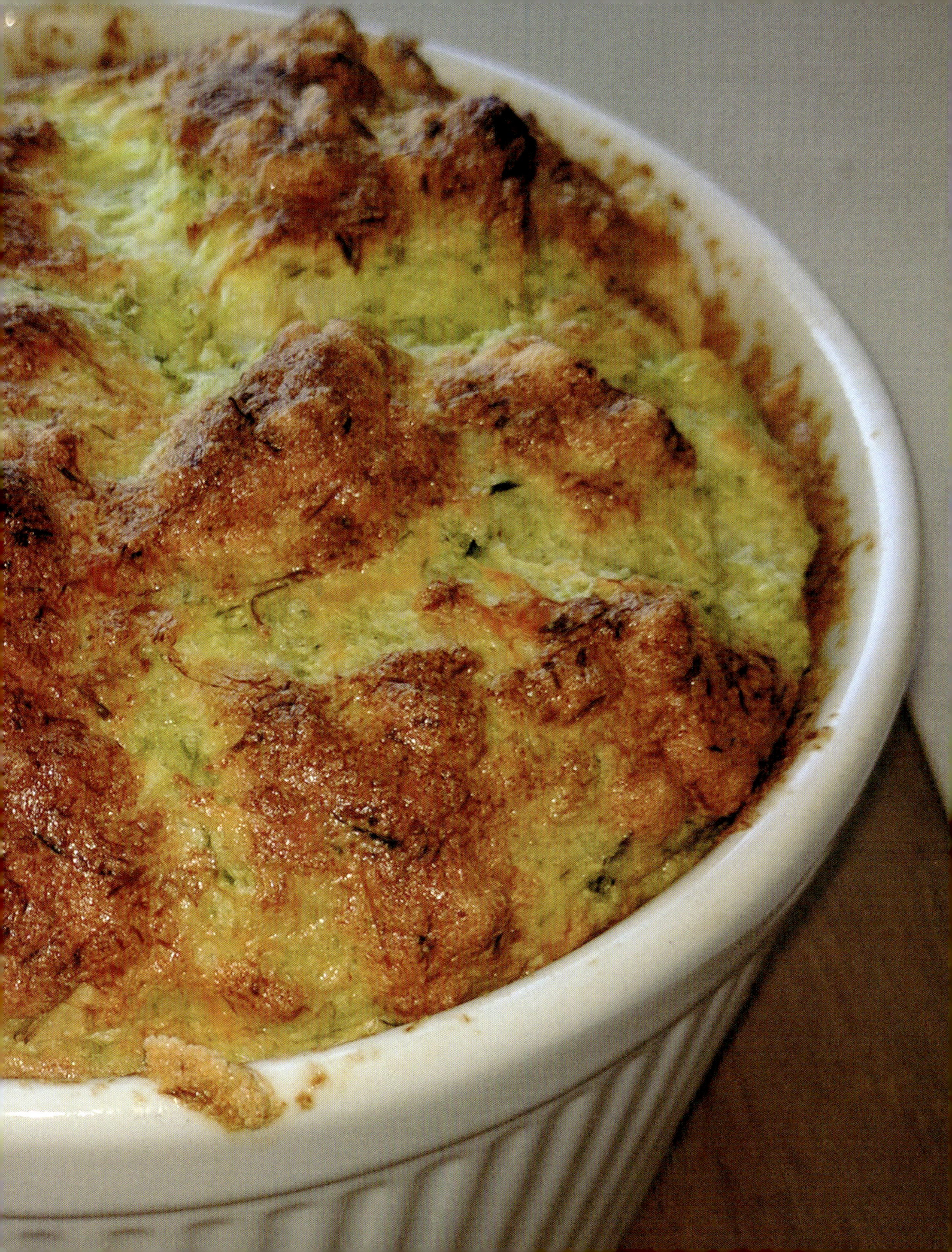

easy creamy cauliflower mash

serves 8–10

1 head cauliflower or 10 ounces already-riced cauliflower

¼ cup sour cream

3 tablespoons heavy whipping cream

3 tablespoons butter

4 tablespoons Parmesan cheese, grated

¼ teaspoon garlic powder

2 teaspoons chives, chopped

Sea salt and pepper to taste

KF *Let's make a mockery of mashed potatoes! This delectable replacement uses cauliflower that adds a new slant to an old favorite.*

If using whole cauliflower, cut into florets and rice it using a food processor. If using already-riced cauliflower, follow directions on the package.

Pour the riced cauliflower into a microwave safe bowl covered with a wet paper towel and microwave for five minutes.

In a blender, add all the other ingredients and blend. Add the cooked cauliflower and blend well.

Pour into serving dish and add 1 teaspoon or more of chopped chives, mixing together.

Add salt and pepper to taste. Garnish with remaining chives to your liking.

fig chutney

Chutney has its origins in the Indian subcontinent and can be made of fruit, vegetables, or both. This delightful variation calls for fresh figs which in California are in season twice. Gourmet shops sometimes have them in glass jars ready to use.

In a saucepan, bring all ingredients to a boil. Then reduce heat and simmer uncovered for about 30 minutes, stirring occasionally until jam like and figs have broken down.

Taste for seasoning and remove cinnamon and clove. Let it cool a little.

Put chutney into a Mason jar and seal.

Refrigerate up to three months.

makes 6–8 servings

½ pound whole fresh figs, approximately 8 figs, rinsed, stemmed, and halved

4 teaspoons white wine

4 teaspoons sherry vinegar

1 small cinnamon stick

1 whole clove

½ teaspoon cayenne pepper

2 teaspoons honey

½ teaspoon extra-virgin olive oil

½ teaspoon coarse sea salt

side dishes

cheesy cheese bread

serves 6–8

KF *Sinfully delicious, you can't go wrong with this recipe. It is not too difficult to make and can be versatile with additions and flavor combinations.*

3 cups mozzarella cheese, shredded

4 tablespoons cream cheese

1½ cups almond flour

2 teaspoons xanthan gum

2 eggs, at room temperature

2 teaspoons dried yeast, approximately 1 packet

2 tablespoons warm water

3 tablespoons butter, melted

Cooking spray for greasing

Onion flakes or dried minced onion (optional)

Preheat oven to 400°F (204°C).

Place the mozzarella cheese and cream cheese in a microwave safe dish and microwave in 30-second increments, stirring in between, until fully melted and almost liquid.

Dissolve the yeast in a small bowl of warm water and allow it to sit and activate for 2 minutes.

In a large bowl, place the almond flour and xanthan gum and mix well.

Add the eggs, yeast mixture, and 1 tablespoon of the melted butter to the bowl and mix well.

Add the hot melted cheese and knead the dough until all the ingredients are fully combined, about 5–10 minutes. I just use a large spoon and keep mixing. The dough is easiest to work with while it is warm.

Line a baking sheet with aluminum foil and grease generously.

Place 6 balls of dough on the lined baking sheet and form them into round bagel-like shapes.

Brush bread rounds with melted butter and add the dried onion flakes or minced dried onion if desired.

Bake in oven for 12–15 minutes or until golden brown.

When the breads are golden brown, remove from oven.

They are best eaten that day and they do freeze well.

They taste great with butter or cream cheese.

tips: I put them in a toaster after they have been frozen or just out of the refrigerator. They are quite yummy!

You can also add 1 teaspoon of sesame seeds, poppy seeds, or dried garlic flakes instead of onions.

side dishes

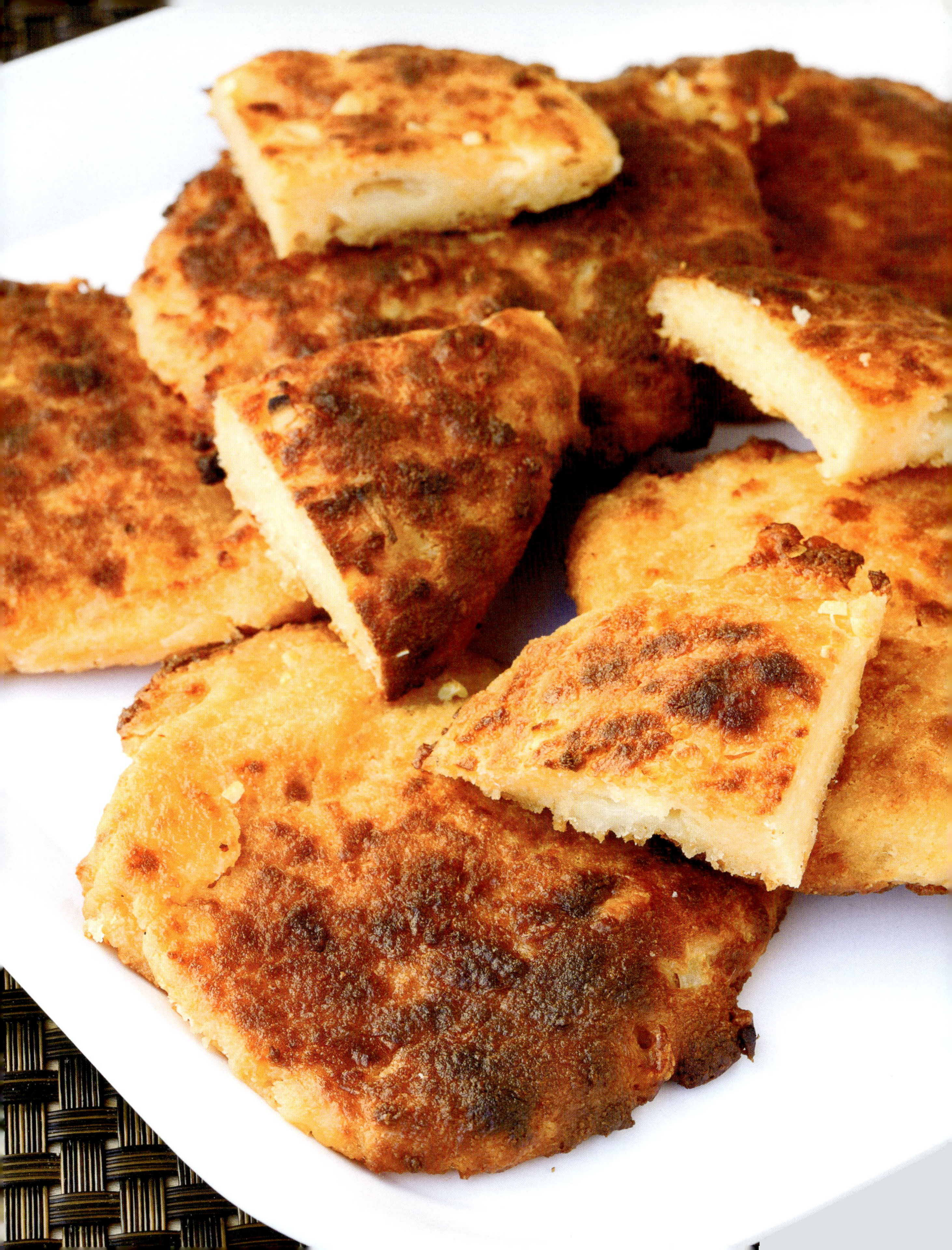

heavenly butternut squash casserole

serves 8–10

KF *Yes, heavenly it is! This is a healthy way to eat meals and side dishes.*

Cooking spray

- 1 butternut squash, seeded, peeled and cut into cubes (you can buy already cubed)
- 2 tablespoons olive oil
- 2 tablespoons butter, unsalted
- Garlic salt
- Lemon pepper
- 3 eggs
- ¾ cup sour cream
- ½ cup mozzarella cheese, shredded
- 1 cup Parmesan cheese, grated
- 1 medium onion, diced
- ¼ teaspoon sea salt
- ¼ teaspoon pepper

Preheat oven to 425°F (218°C).

Grease a 9 x13-inch casserole dish with cooking spray.

Place the squash in the dish and drizzle olive oil over the squash.

Add garlic salt and lemon pepper.

Toss with your hands to coat.

Bake for 40 minutes until squash is almost done.

Meanwhile, in a medium bowl, beat eggs.

Add the sour cream, mozzarella, and Parmesan cheese to the eggs, and mix well. Set aside.

In a skillet, add the butter and olive oil over medium-high heat and add diced onion.

Sauté until caramelized about 4 minutes and let cool.

Once cooled, add caramelized onions to the egg and cheese mixture.

When the squash is done add the mixture to the squash dish, stirring and mashing the squash.

Add your salt and pepper; stir again.

Bake for 25–30 minutes until bubbly.

tips: As stated above, you may buy a 2½-pound package of squash already peeled, seeded, and cut into cubes. This is so much easier if you can find it.

Some people like to brown the top of this dish. Set your oven to broil and let your casserole toast on top for 4–5 minutes.

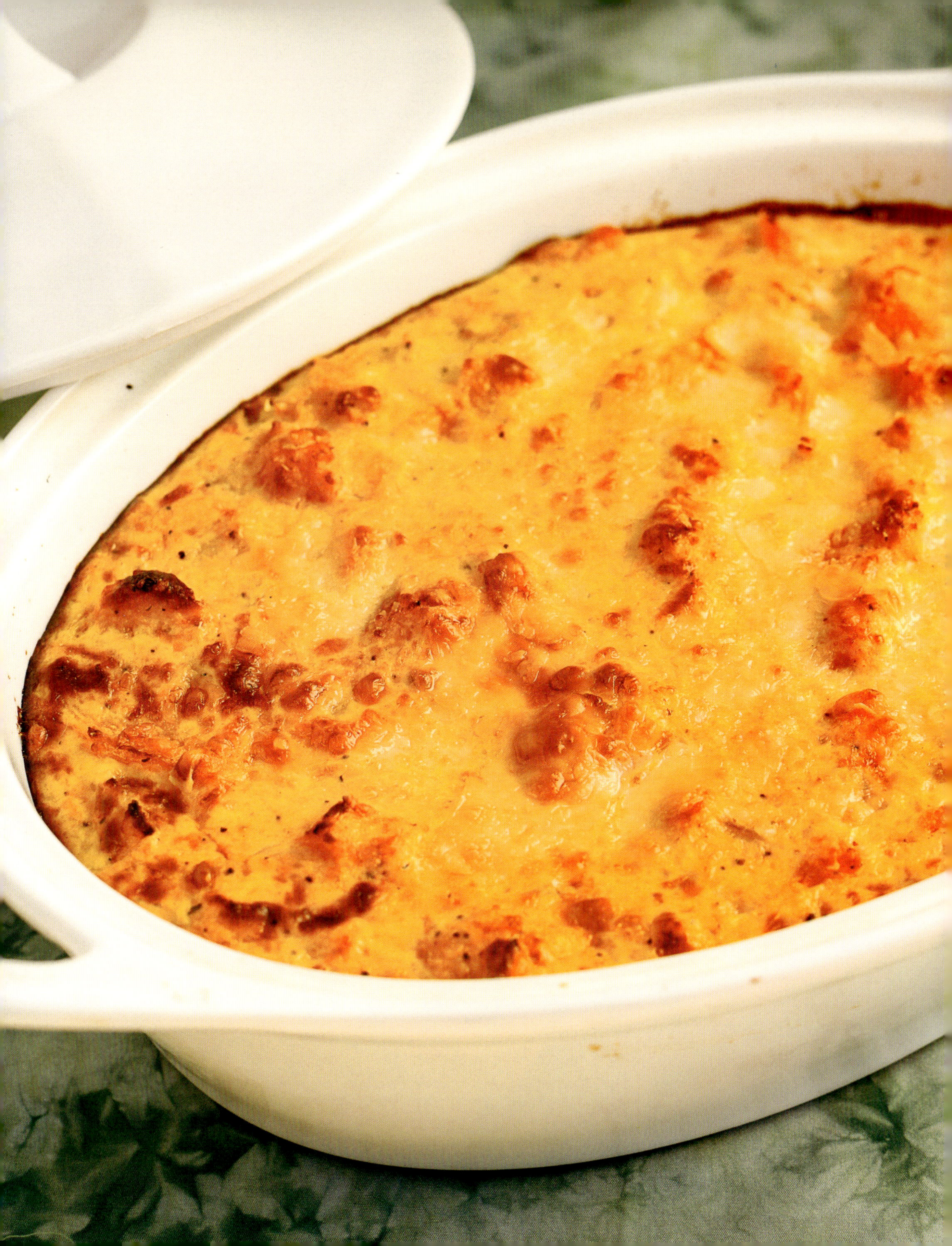

jalapeño bacon queso

serves 6–8

KF *Cheesy goodness with bacon? Yes, spicing it up with jalapeño just makes it the best cheese dip for any occasion!*

8 ounces cream cheese, softened

⅓ cup Basic Paleo Mayo (recipe on page 206)

⅓ cup sour cream

1 teaspoon garlic powder

10 slices bacon, uncured, cooked and chopped

4 ounce can pickled jalapeños or less, depending on your tolerance for heat, minced

1½ cups cheddar cheese, shredded

1½ cups Monterey Jack cheese, shredded

Sea salt and freshly ground black pepper to taste

Preheat oven to 350°F (177°C).

In a large bowl, stir together cream cheese, mayo, sour cream, garlic powder, most of the cooked bacon (reserve some for topping), most of the jalapeños (reserve some for topping), 1 cup cheddar cheese, and 1 cup Monterey Jack. Season with salt and pepper.

Transfer to a baking dish and sprinkle with remaining ½ cups of cheddar cheese and Monterey Jack, together with the rest of the bacon and jalapeños.

Bake until bubbly for 15 minutes.

side dishes

killer guacamole dip

KF *Who doesn't love guacamole? I like guacamole that's spicy. If you're not crazy about spiciness, eliminate the jalapeño in the following recipe. This can be used as a dip, a spread or in a salad. Its origins in Mexico date back to the 1500s.*

serves 4–6

4 medium avocados

¼ cup onion, finely chopped

½ cup tomato, diced

2–3 pickled jalapeños, finely chopped

2 tablespoons jalapeño juice (from the pickled jalapeño can)

½ cup cilantro, thoroughly rinsed and finely chopped

⅓ teaspoon sea salt

2 limes

After you have chopped the onions, tomato, pickled jalapeños, and cilantro, toss in a medium bowl with a fork or spoon to get a very nice mix of colors and place in the refrigerator.

Take your avocado and slice in half lengthwise. Carefully split the two pieces of each avocado. Save one of the pits for later.

Using a tablespoon, scoop out the avocados into a separate medium mixing bowl. Add the salt, the juice of your limes, plus the jalapeño juice.

With a fork, begin mashing the avocado, stirring to mix the salt and juices to a semi-chunky consistency.

Add the rest of the previously mixed ingredients and combine with a tablespoon.

tip: The saved pit can be placed in the guacamole to preserve the color and keep from spoiling too quickly. You can leave the pit in, even while you are serving and store in refrigerator to preserve your guac.

side dishes

pico de gallo

makes 3–4 cups

1 bunch cilantro, thoroughly rinsed and chopped fine

2 large fresh tomatoes, diced

1 medium onion, diced

6 serrano peppers, chopped fine

1 teaspoon lime juice (1 lime should do it)

½ teaspoon sea salt

Fresh salsa never tasted as good as this Pico de Gallo. It is a zesty and flavorful side dish for almost any meal. I also use it as a salad dressing.

Take your bunch of cilantro and thoroughly rinse in cold water. Shake off excess water.

Grab the cilantro bunch with one hand and with the other, twist off the long stems. Chop the leafy bunch as fine as you can and set aside.

Dice the tomatoes and place in a medium mixing bowl.

Dice the onions and add to tomatoes.

Take the serrano peppers and pull off the stems. Slice long-ways to reveal the seeds and the pith.

You can spoon out the seeds for a milder version if you wish, depending on how hot you like your Pico de Gallo.

Once cleaned of seeds, chop very fine. Add to mixing bowl. Add the cilantro, lime juice, and salt to taste.

tip: Whenever handling hot peppers like serrano peppers, always wash your hands thoroughly, along with your utensils. Some of us learned the hard way when we scratch an itch in an eye and bingo! For safety, you may want to use kitchen gloves.

side dishes

sautéed swiss chard with parmesan cheese

KF *Swiss chard is number three on the list of the 41 most nutrient-dense foods on the planet. It contains high levels of vitamin A and C, calcium, potassium, and magnesium.*

serves 4

2 tablespoons butter

2 tablespoons olive oil

1 tablespoon garlic, minced

½ small red onion, diced

1 bunch Swiss chard (stems and center ribs cut out and chopped together, leaves coarsely chopped separately)

½ cup dry white wine

1 tablespoon fresh lemon juice

2 tablespoons Parmesan cheese, freshly grated

Sea salt to taste (optional)

In a large skillet, melt butter and olive oil together over medium-high heat.

Stir in the garlic and onion and cook for 30 seconds until fragrant.

Add the chard stems and the white wine.

Simmer until the stems begin to soften, about 5 minutes.

Stir in the Swiss chard leaves and cook until wilted.

Finally, stir in lemon juice and Parmesan cheese.

Season to taste with salt if needed.

savory breadless stuffing

serves 7–10 people

2 packages butternut squash, cubed

2 small apples, cored and cut into small cubes

3 tablespoons coconut oil or butter

3 ½ cups onion, diced

2 ½ cups celery, diced

½ cup red bell pepper, diced

1 teaspoon sage

1 teaspoon thyme

½ teaspoon rosemary

2 eggs

¾ cup almond flour

¾ cup raisins or dried cranberries, chopped into small pieces

¼–½ pound ground mild or hot Italian sausage, casing removed

1 teaspoon sea salt

1 teaspoon pepper

Thanksgiving, my favorite holiday—why? Because of all those phenomenal dishes we indulge in and all in one night! I can't even imagine doing that today. My stomach is trained not to eat such foods. When I think back, all those carbs in one night, or I should say all weekend because of leftovers, was such an overkill. Do you remember moaning and groaning after finishing a Thanksgiving meal? It was no wonder! The next day I loved the turkey sandwiches, but the stuffing and pumpkin pie were my favorites. Here is a great substitute for the real thing. I actually love this recipe so much I don't miss the one I grew up with. I hope you enjoy it as much as I do!

Preheat oven to 350°F (177°C).

First prepare to roast the butternut squash cubes and the apple cubes in a 9" x 13" oven-safe casserole dish with 2 tablespoons of coconut oil or butter and ½ teaspoon of salt. I use coconut oil. Bake for 25 minutes until squash is tender.

While that is roasting, in a large skillet, add 1 tablespoon of coconut oil or butter and sauté the onions, celery, peppers, and herbs over medium heat for 5 minutes. Remove from heat.

In a small bowl, beat the two eggs, add almond flour and raisins or cranberries, and mix well. Set aside.

In the skillet with the herbs and vegetables, add ground sausage, using a wooden spoon to reduce the lumps by breaking and stirring as it cooks. Cook the sausage and veggies until done and add to a large bowl.

Now add the rest of the salt and pepper and stir.

Add the egg mixture and mix altogether.

Add mixture to the greased 9 x 13-inch casserole dish.

Bake for 15 minutes until browned.

Garnish with fresh parsley, if desired.

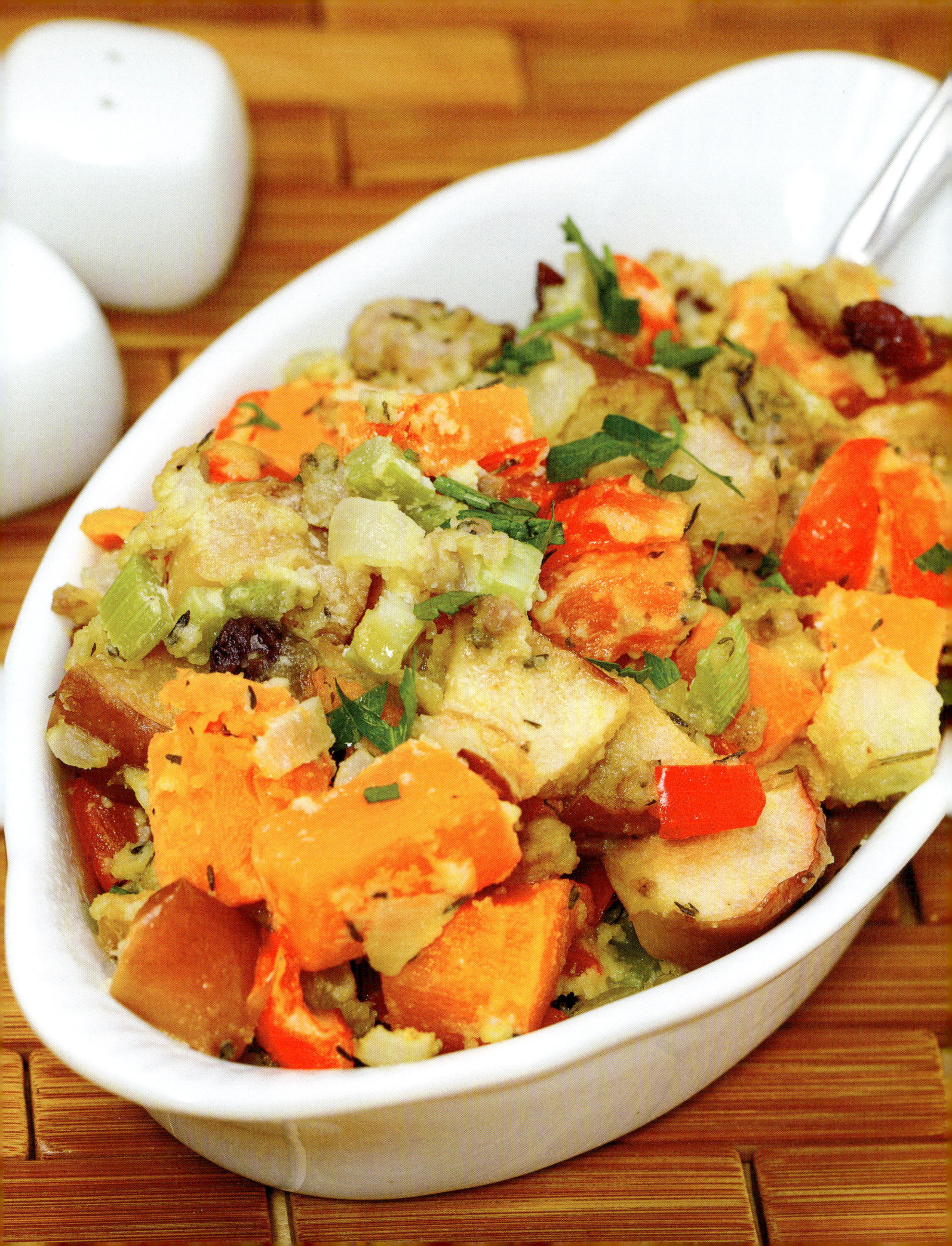

nut and seed butter

makes about 3 ½ cups of nut butter

1 cup raw cashews

1 cup raw almonds

1 cup raw pecans

I cup raw walnuts

1 cup raw macadamias

½ cup sunflower seeds

¼ cup raw pumpkin seeds

¼ cup flax seeds

1 tablespoon maple syrup (if doing keto, replace with erythritol syrup, recipe on page 15)

3 tablespoons coconut oil, melted

Sea salt to taste

KF OPTIONAL *Peanut butter isn't the only nut butter. There are so many healthier ones to try. If doing keto, replace maple syrup with erythritol syrup (recipe on page 15)*

Add all nuts and seeds, maple syrup, and coconut oil to a high-speed blender or food processor and run continuously for a short while, about 5–10 minutes.

Stop and scrape down the sides and the bottom of the bowl. At this point, the nut butter will look gritty and dry, almost like couscous. This is arduous but well worth it.

Keep at it. Be patient. Run the blender or processor continuously for another 3 minutes, then stop and scrape down the sides some more.

At this point, the seed butter will start clumping together. Run the food processor again. The nuts will start to release some of their oil, making the mass more pliable and more inclined to stay within the path of the spinning blade, so you won't have to stop as often.

Still, I recommend stopping the food processor every 3 minutes or so to give the food processor a break to scrape the sides of the bowl.

After 10 minutes, the mixture will look more like nut butter. Continue processing, it will take roughly 15–20 minutes in total to get a very smooth, creamy, and almost liquid-like butter.

Add sea salt. Transfer to Mason jars or other containers and store at room temperature or in fridge for up to 3–4 weeks.

tip: I recommend refrigerating the nut and seed butter to make it last longer. You may use any combination of nuts and seeds.

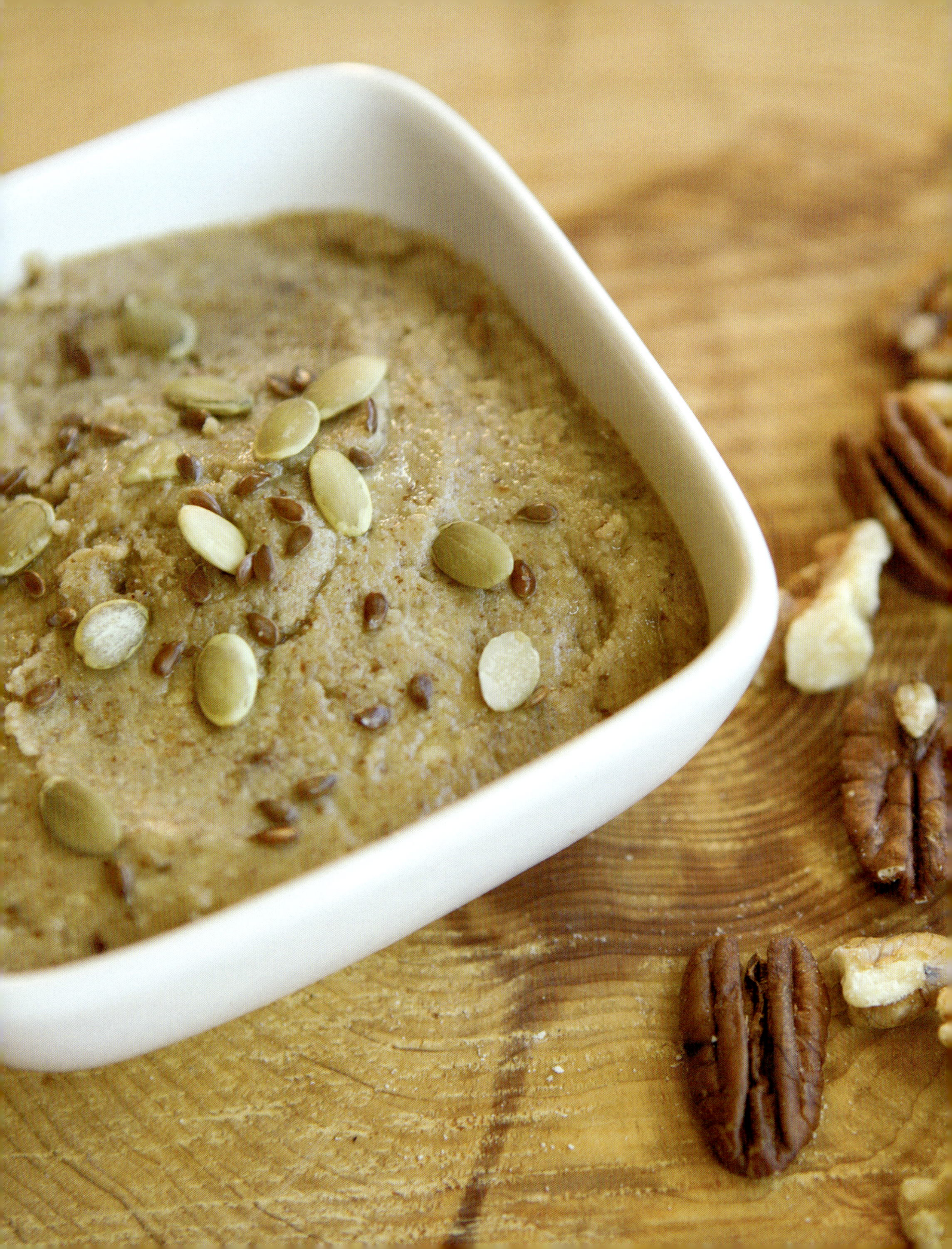

zucchini pancakes

KF *Healthy and delicious, these savory pancakes are sure to delight any foodie. Perfect anytime of the day.*

makes 10–12 three-inch round pancakes

- 2 medium zucchini
- ¼ cup red onion, chopped
- 2 extra large eggs, lightly beaten
- 6–8 tablespoons almond flour
- 1 teaspoon baking powder
- 1 teaspoon kosher salt
- ½ teaspoon freshly ground pepper
- ⅛ teaspoon garlic powder
- 2 tablespoons butter, unsalted
- 2 tablespoons coconut oil
- Sour cream
- Green onions, chopped (optional for garnish)

tip: Make sure that you have enough butter and coconut oil to regrease the sauté pan each time you cook more pancakes to keep them from sticking to the pan.

Preheat oven to 175°F (79°C).

Grate the zucchini into a medium-sized mixing bowl, using the large grating side of a box grater.

Squeeze all the moisture out of the zucchini in a tea towel or paper towel so that it's as dry as possible. Make sure to squeeze as much of the moisture as you can and put the zucchini back into the bowl.

With a spoon or fork, stir in the onion and the eggs.

Stir in 6 tablespoons of the flour, the baking powder, kosher salt, pepper and garlic powder. If the batter gets too thin from the liquid in the zucchini, then add remaining 2 tablespoons of flour.

Heat a large 10–12-inch sauté pan and melt 2 tablespoons butter and 2 tablespoons coconut oil together in the pan.

When the butter is hot but not smoking, lower the heat to medium low and drop heaping soup spoons of batter into the pan.

Shape diameter into about 3-inch round pancakes.

Cook the pancakes for about 2–3 minutes on each side until browned.

Place the pancakes on a baking sheet and keep warm in the oven. Add more butter and oil, and repeat the process until all batter is used. The pancakes can stay warm in the oven for 30 minutes.

Serve on a dish and add dollop of sour cream with green onions for garnish.

side dishes

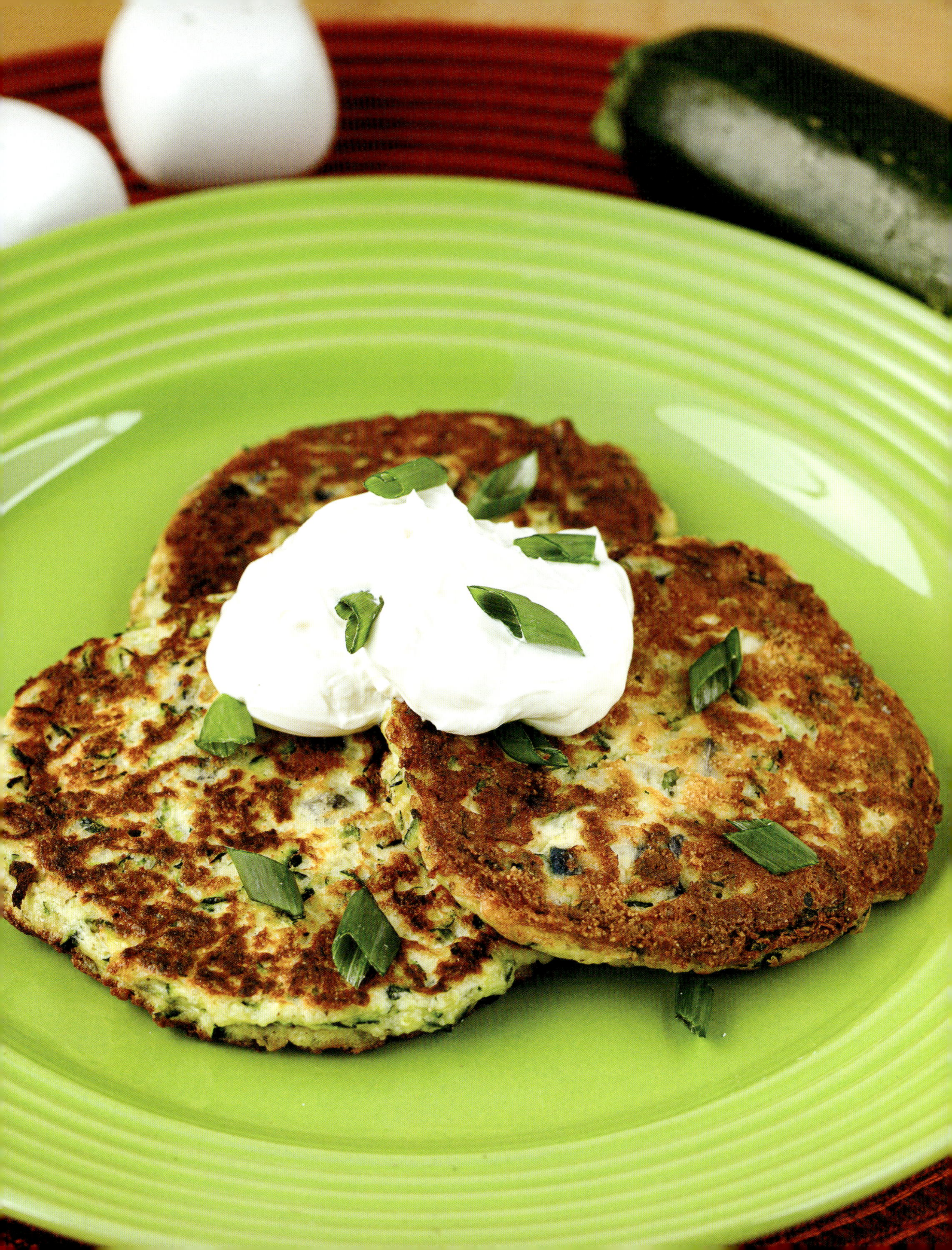

pumpkin cauliflower gratin

serves 8–12

KF OPTIONAL *This is a really good-for-you replacement for potatoes and delicious too!*

Ingredients

- 1 head cauliflower, crumbled or florets
- 2 tablespoons butter, salted
- 1 sweet onion, diced
- 3 tablespoons arrowroot flour (if doing keto, use almond flour)
- 1 cup canned pumpkin
- ¾ cup canned coconut cream, full-fat
- ¼ teaspoon smoked cayenne pepper
- 8 ounces Gruyère cheese, shredded, about 2 cups, divided
- ½ cup Parmesan cheese, grated
- 1½ teaspoons kosher salt, divided in half
- 1 teaspoon black pepper, divided in half
- 1 tablespoon olive oil
- 12 fresh sage leaves

Instructions

Preheat oven to 425°F (218°C).

Melt butter in a large, oven-safe skillet over medium heat. Then add onion and cook, stirring occasionally until caramelized, about 10–12 minutes. Stir in arrowroot flour and cook, stirring constantly for 30 seconds.

Slowly stir in pumpkin and cream. Increase the heat to high and bring to a boil. Cook, whisking constantly until thickened, about 1 minute.

Remove skillet from heat, stir in cayenne pepper and 1 cup of the Gruyère cheese, leaving the remainder for later. Sprinkle with half of the salt and pepper.

Add the crumbled cauliflower to the skillet, stir to coat with sauce, and top with remaining 1 cup of Gruyère cheese. Cover and bake for 30 minutes.

Uncover to add ½ cup of the Parmesan cheese, recover and bake until lightly golden, about 10–15 minutes more.

Meanwhile, over medium heat, add oil in a small skillet. Once hot, add sage and let cook 30 seconds. Flip over and cook until it's dark but not burnt for about 30 seconds. Sprinkle with remaining salt.

Drizzle sage-oil mixture on top of the dish to add to the wonderful flavors!

side dishes

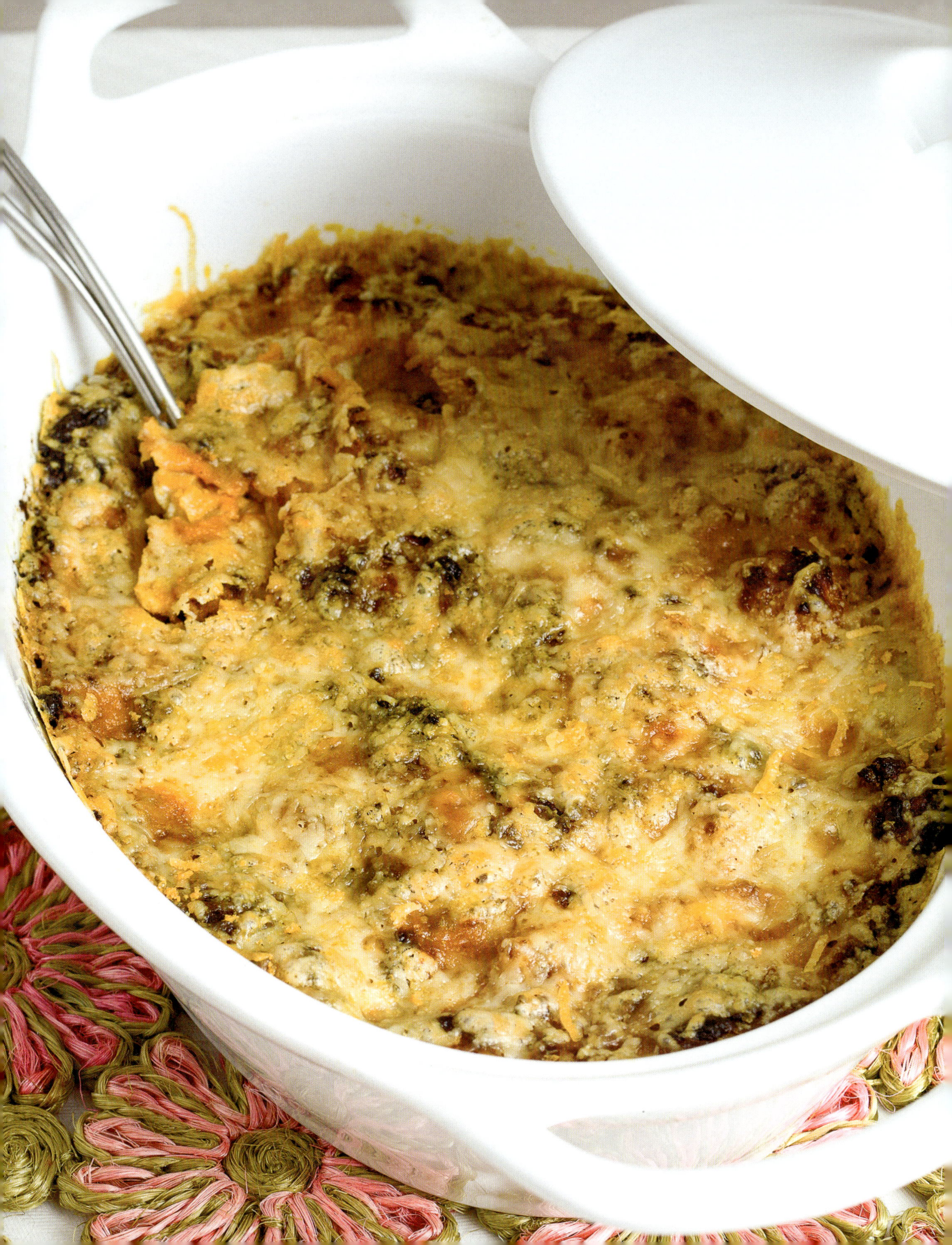

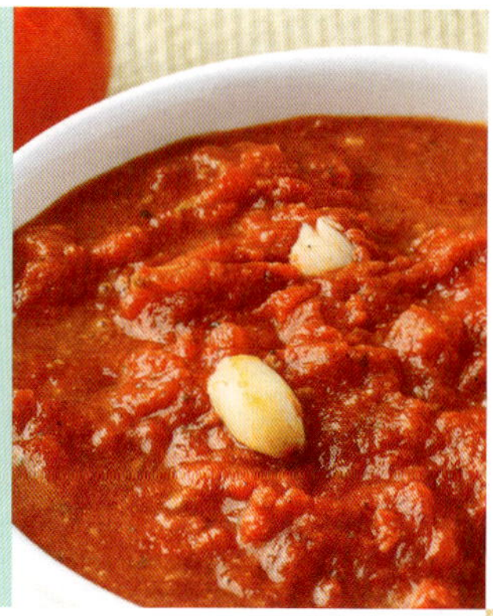
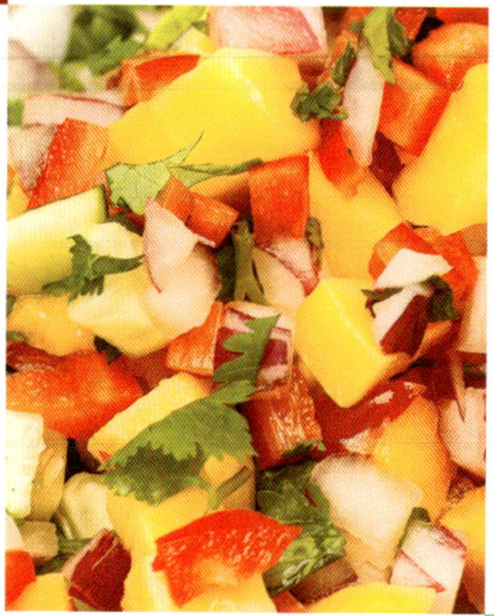
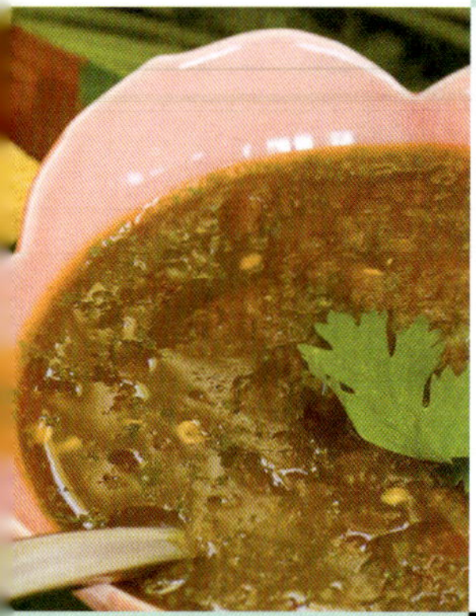
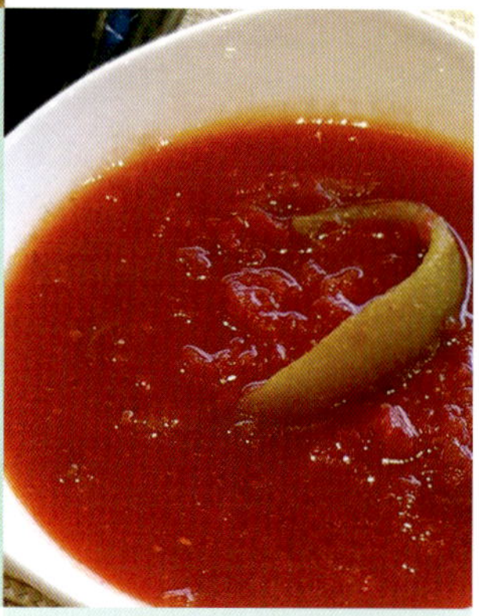
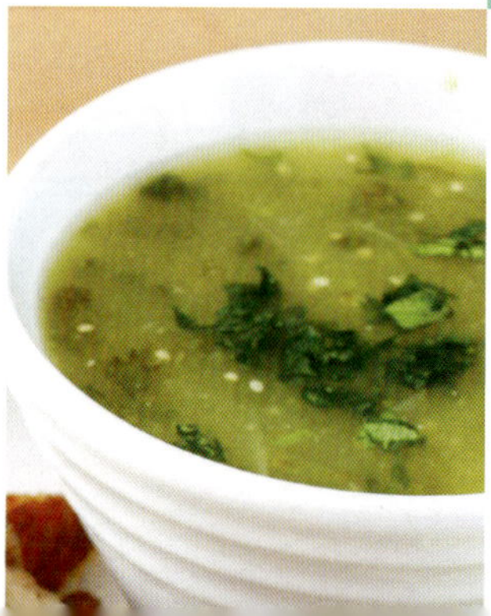

sauces

Sauces add a nice complexity of flavors to different foods. Besides adding flavor, they add moisture and visual appeal to a dish.

KF Denotes that recipe can be made or is keto-friendly.

Basic Marinara Sauce **258**

Mango Salsa **263**

Ranchero Sauce **260**

Red Hot Salsa **261**

Tomatillo Salsa **262**

basic marinara sauce

2 28-ounce cans San Marzano Whole Peeled Tomatoes

5 tablespoons butter

1 onion, peeled and cut in half

4 garlic cloves

Sea salt and ground black pepper to taste

Pinch of basil, oregano, or other Italian herbs, to taste (optional)

KF *Ah, the simplicity of this marvelous tasting sauce! I never quite understood the reason behind adding so much sugar to the tomato sauces found in the grocery store. This sauce is based on Marcella Hazan's tomato sauce. Having a freshly made, zesty tomato sauce adds a versatile ingredient to vegetable-based pasta dishes, pizzas, chicken, beef, pork, and fish. Here's a quick and simple way to make one.*

Pour the whole peeled tomatoes into a 3-quart pot or saucepan.

Place over medium heat and bring to a simmer. Add the peeled onion and garlic.

Cook uncovered for about one hour, stirring occasionally.

Mash any large pieces of tomatoes with a spoon, and add sea salt and pepper as needed. You may discard the onion and cloves of garlic, if desired.

You may add basil, oregano, and/or other herbs of your choice during the cooking time.

tip: This sauce freezes well in Mason jars.

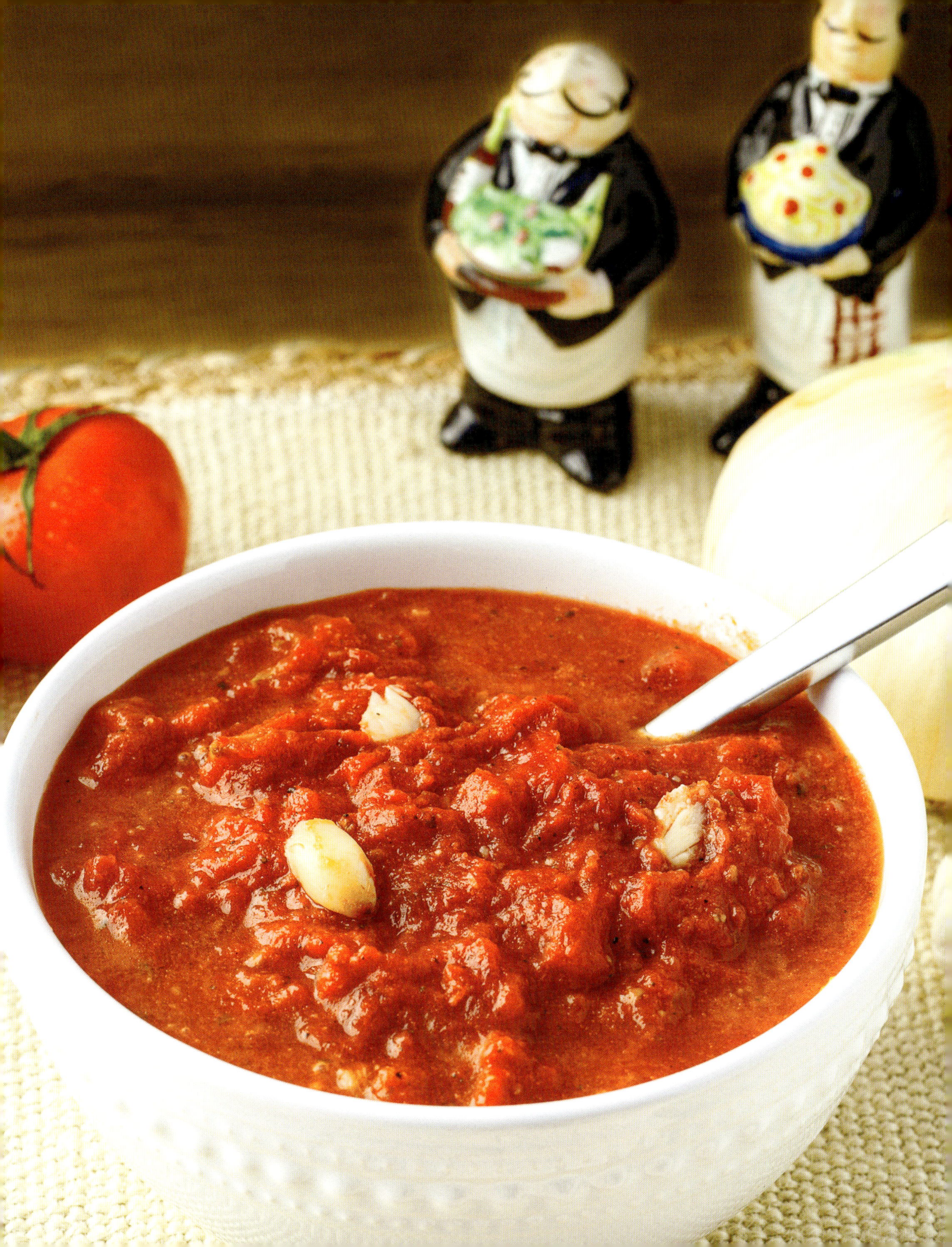

ranchero sauce

- 1 28-ounce can whole tomatoes
- 1 clove garlic
- 2 serrano peppers (add more if you like your ranchero sauce spicier)
- 2 poblano peppers (roasted, peeled, and shredded)
- 1 teaspoon sea salt
- 1 cup tomato juice
- 2 tablespoons olive oil
- ½ cup water

If you love huevos rancheros, this sauce is for you. It is versatile, delicious, and spicy. You can also use it with fish, shrimp, steak, or chicken.

Blend the garlic clove and serrano peppers in the water in blender at high speed. Heat oil in saucepan and once hot, add garlic-serrano blend.

In the same blender cup, add the whole cooked tomatoes and blend lightly to leave a chunky consistency. Add to saucepan.

Bring to a boil and add tomato juice, salt, and chili strips. Boil for about 10 more minutes.

This sauce can be used over different meats and can also be used as a base for cooking with seafood.

If you want to roast your poblano peppers, follow these instructions:

Wash and char the peppers on the stove top over medium heat. If you can use a charring screen, even better.

After cooling to the touch (2–3 minutes), place in a plastic bag to steam for about 10 minutes. This allows you to peel the skin easily and also softens the pepper.

Remove peppers from bag and peel the skin. Shred peppers into strips by hand into a cup or small bowl.

Be sure to devein the peppers as you shred. The fewer the seeds, the milder the sauce will become.

tip: If you want to buy the chili strips already prepared, you'll find them under the Ortega brand in the Mexican food aisle in your grocery store.

red hot salsa

KF *Not to be confused with Pico de Gallo (see Side Dishes), this salsa will spice up your life in a very hot way.*

Preheat oven to 325°F (163°C).

Place the whole dry red peppers on a small baking sheet or sheet of aluminum foil and roast for 5 minutes.

In a cloth napkin or clean kitchen towel, wrap the serrano peppers and cook in the microwave for 3 minutes.

In a blender, add the water, peppers, garlic, and salt, and blend on high (or liquify) for 10–15 seconds.

Add the cilantro and pulse the blender 3–4 times until the cilantro appears chopped.

Add the tomatoes and pulse the blender another 3–4 times.

Pour into bowl and serve with chips.

- 1 28-ounce can whole tomatoes
- 12 dry red chile peppers (Japanese chiles or chile de arbol), no stems
- 18 serrano peppers, no stems
- 1 clove garlic
- ½ bunch cilantro, thoroughly rinsed
- ½ teaspoon sea salt
- 1 cup water

tip: Add more red peppers or serrano peppers if you desire more heat.

261   sauces

tomatillo salsa

1 pound green tomatillos

2 cups water

6 serrano peppers

1 clove garlic

¼ cup onion, chopped

½ bunch cilantro, chopped

1 teaspoon sea salt

½ teaspoon baking soda

KF *This tangy and verdant salsa combines well with meat, poultry, fish or with your favorite grain-free chip.*

Soak tomatillos in cold water for 15 minutes and remove the leaf surrounding it.

Cut the tomatillos in half and place in a saucepan with 2 cups of water.

Bring to a boil and add the 6 serrano peppers (remove the stems prior to cooking), add salt and let simmer for 10 minutes.

Remove from heat and add baking soda, stirring until foam dissolves.

Allow to cool for 30 minutes and remove serrano peppers.

Place serrano peppers in blender with garlic and a cup of the liquid from the tomatillos. Blend well.

Then, add tomatillos with the balance of the liquid, cilantro, and onion to blender and blend lightly.

Pour in a bowl for serving.

tip: Pour balance of the sauce in a Mason jar and store in fridge. Good for about one week.

mango salsa

A great side accompaniment for many dishes. Very versatile and tasty too.

serves 4–6

½ cup cucumber, diced

2 semi-ripe mangos, cubed

1 bunch cilantro, chopped

¾ cup red onion, diced (about ½ of an onion)

1 red bell pepper, diced

Juice of 1 lemon or lime

Put all ingredients into a medium mixing bowl and mix together.

Let it sit in the refrigerator for about 30 minutes and serve chilled.

sauces

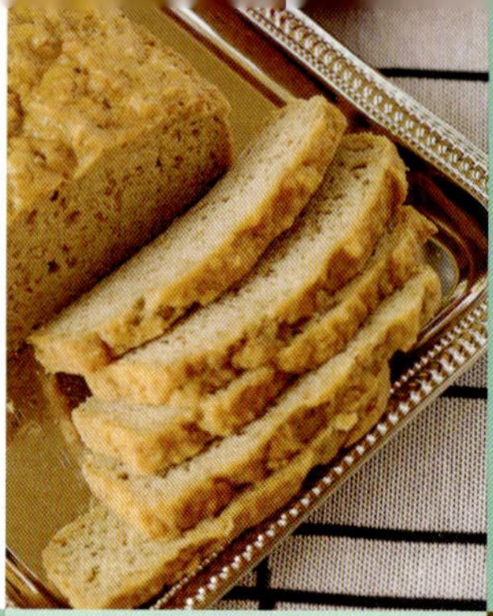
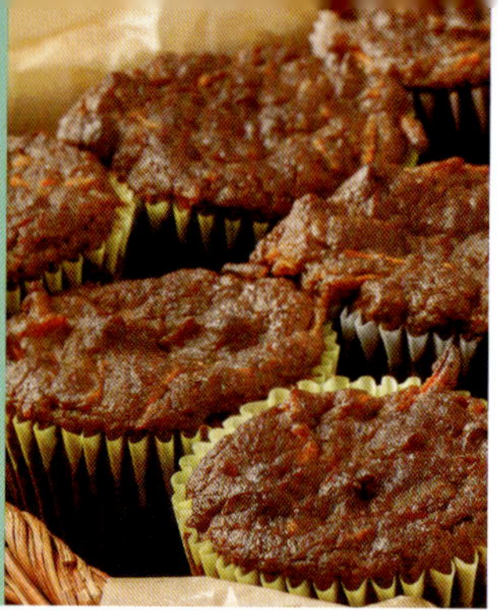
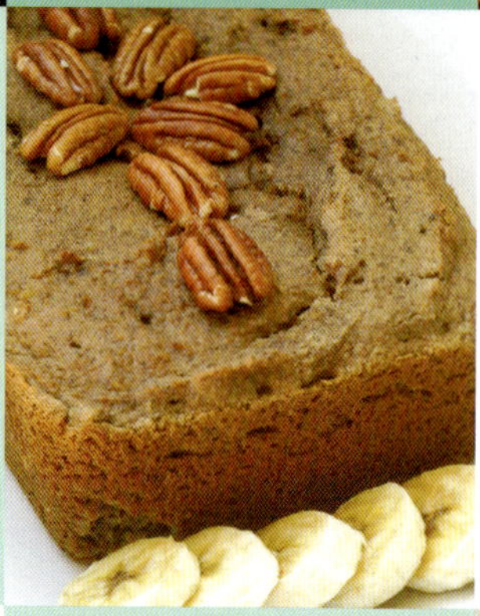
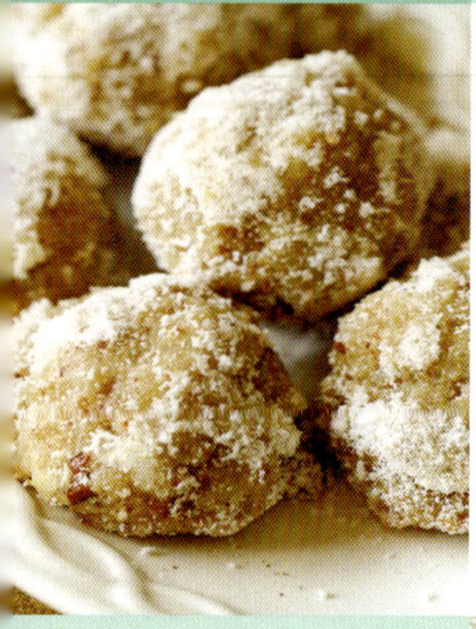
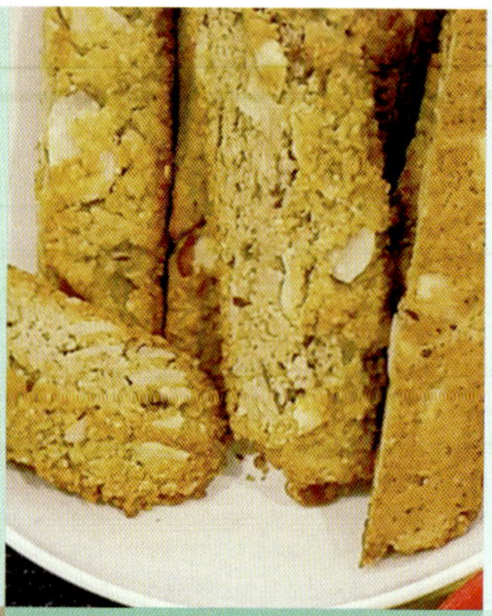
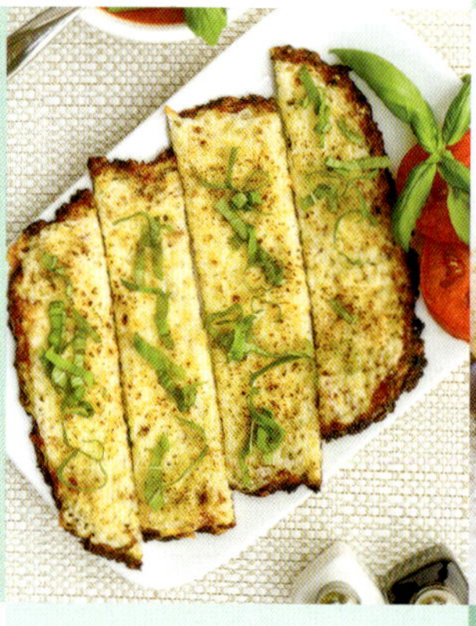
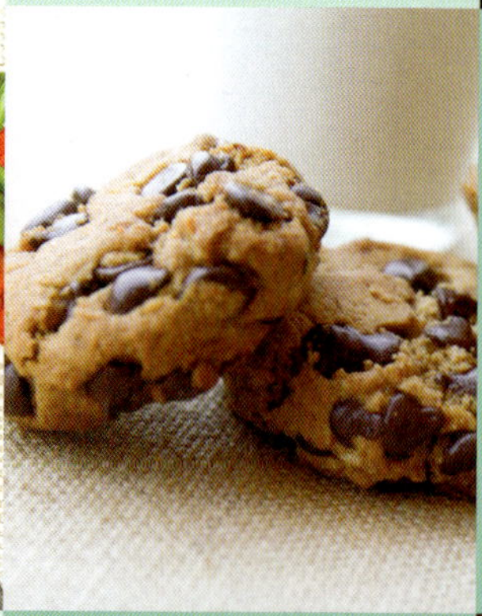
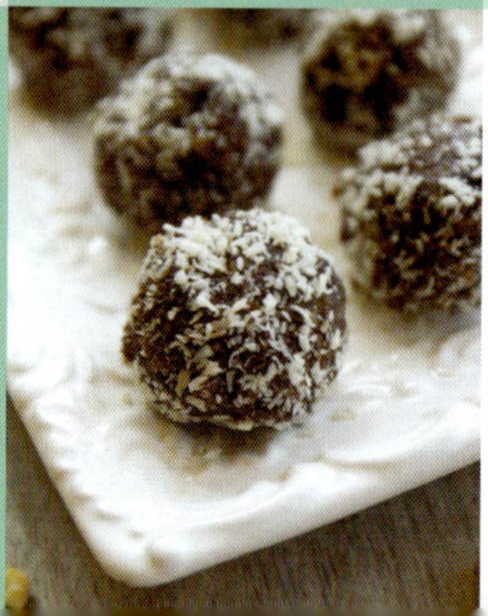

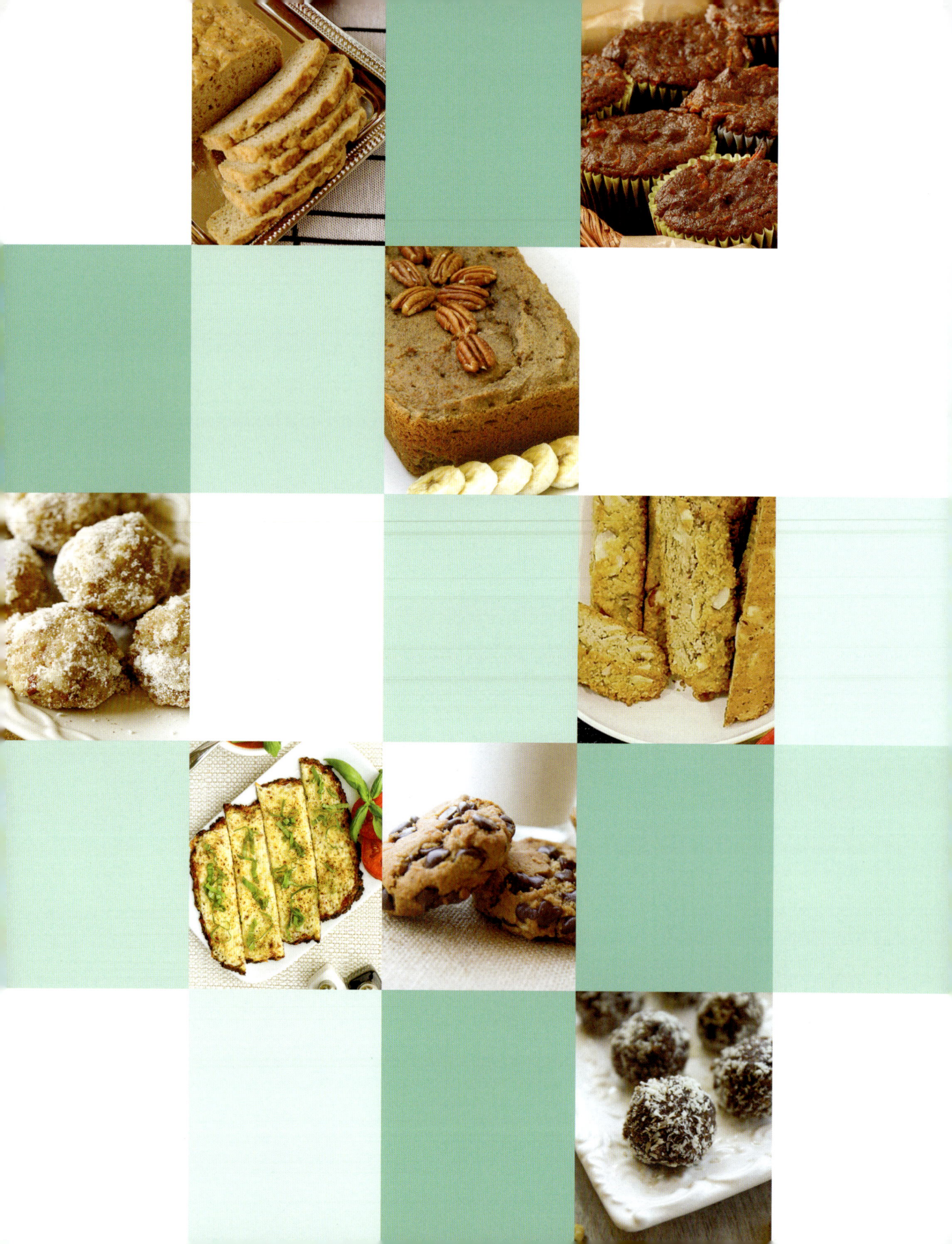

baked goods

Baking without wheat and white flour has been one of the biggest challenges in replacing grains. Luckily, we have almond flour, coconut flour, tapioca flour, arrowroot flour, and a host of other replacements that provide wonderful options in baking almost anything.

The recipes in this section were carefully tested, and some had multiple experiments in refining the flavor.

KF Denotes that recipe can be made or is keto-friendly.

ABC Bread 268

Almond Biscotti 274

Almond Chocolate Chip Cookies 275

Almond Crescent Cookies 276

Banana Blueberry Muffins 278

Banana Carrot Muffins 279

Banana Keto Bread 270

Banana Nut Bread 271

Banana Zucchini Walnut Bread 272

Barb's Sandwich Bread 273

Butter Pecan Cookies 266

Carrot Coconut Cookies with Almond 267

Cauliflower Cheese Bread 280

Cheesy Onion Bialys 286

Cocoa Balls 284

Coconut Chocolate Chip Cookies 290

Dark Chocolate Walnut Cake Brownies 293

Double Chocolate Nut Cookies 294

Flatbread 295

French Bread 282

Ginger Cookies 285

Gooey Chocolate Chip Cookies 288

Maple Pecan Shortbread Cookies 292

Pumpkin Bread with Pecans 296

Scone Loaf Bread 298

butter pecan cookies

makes 18–22 servings

8 tablespoons butter

1½ cups almond flour

1 cup pecans, chopped

½ cup erythritol or Swerve

1 teaspoon vanilla extract

1 teaspoon maple extract

¼ teaspoon sea salt

Erythritol or Swerve to sprinkle on cookies (optional)

KF Did you know that butter pecan cookies originated from Danish bakers? It is a chunky cookie with a twist of both soft and crunchy ingredients in each bite, as well as the sweet and salty uniqueness that only this cookie brings.

Place all ingredients into a mixing bowl and beat with hand mixer until batter forms a ball.

Line a baking sheet with aluminum foil or parchment paper.

Use a cookie scoop or with your hands, make 18–22 mounds.

Place each mound on baking sheet.

Place in freezer for 20–30 minutes.

After 15 minutes, preheat oven to 350°F (177°C).

Place in oven for 15 minutes or until golden around edges.

Allow to cool slightly. Place in freezer again for about 20 minutes.

Take from freezer.

If powdering with sweetener, sprinkle sweetener over cookies on cooled baking sheet.

Place on serving dish and share.

carrot coconut cookies with almond

KF OPTIONAL *Cookies so good, you'll make more for everyone to enjoy.*

makes approximately 12 cookies

Preheat oven to 350°F (177°C).

Prepare a baking sheet with aluminum foil and apply cooking spray.

Using a standing mixer or hand mixer, add maple syrup, almond extract, salt, baking soda, and cinnamon to a mixing bowl and combine thoroughly.

Add ½ cup of almond flour to the mixer and combine. Once combined, add another ½ cup. Repeat the process until 2 cups are combined.

Next add 1 tablespoon of coconut oil and mix slowly. Repeat for the next 2 tablespoons of oil.

Finally, fold in the coconut flakes and carrots to the mixture by hand.

Using a medium-sized ice cream scooper, scoop out 12 cookies onto the baking sheet.

Gently press cookies with the palm of your hand down onto the baking sheet to flatten as these will not spread.

Bake 12–15 minutes.

Remove from oven and allow cookies to cool on baking sheet 10 minutes prior to removing and placing on a cooling rack.

Store in the refrigerator so that cookies maintain their structure or freeze them before serving.

tip: I use ⅛ cup of maple syrup and three packets of monk fruit to cut down on the sugar impact. To make Keto-friendly, use erythritol syrup. Recipe on page 15.

Cooking spray
- ⅓ cup maple syrup (or ⅓ cup erythritol syrup to make keto-friendly, recipe on page 15)
- 2 teaspoons almond extract
- ½ teaspoon sea salt
- ½ teaspoon baking soda
- 2 teaspoons cinnamon
- 2 cups almond flour
- 3 tablespoons coconut oil, melted
- ½ cup coconut flakes, unsweetened
- 1 cup carrots, finely chopped

baked goods

abc bread

makes 10–12 servings

I decided to make a triple delicious bread that combines apples, bananas, and carrots. It's really great with coffee as a morning starter before breakfast.

Cooking spray

½ cup coconut flour

6 eggs

⅓ cup maple syrup

⅓ cup coconut oil

⅓ cup cashews, crushed

2 bananas, finely chopped

½ apple, finely chopped

½ cup carrot, shredded

1 tablespoon vanilla

1 teaspoon baking soda

1 tablespoon cinnamon

½ cup raisins

¼ teaspoon sea salt

Preheat oven to 350°F (177°C).

Grease a loaf pan with cooking spray.

Add all your ingredients in a bowl and mix all together or beat with hand mixer on low until well combined. Make sure to not overmix.

Pour into your loaf pan and place in oven.

Bake 55–60 minutes or until a toothpick comes out clean from the center of the bread loaf.

Place on cooling rack and let cool 10–15 minutes before extracting out of the pan.

Slice and serve.

tips: Be sure to grease the loaf pan well, especially the bottom. So many times, it sticks to the bottom.

Use a butter knife to unstick ends and sides, wiggling slightly as you unstick so that the bottom loosens up too.

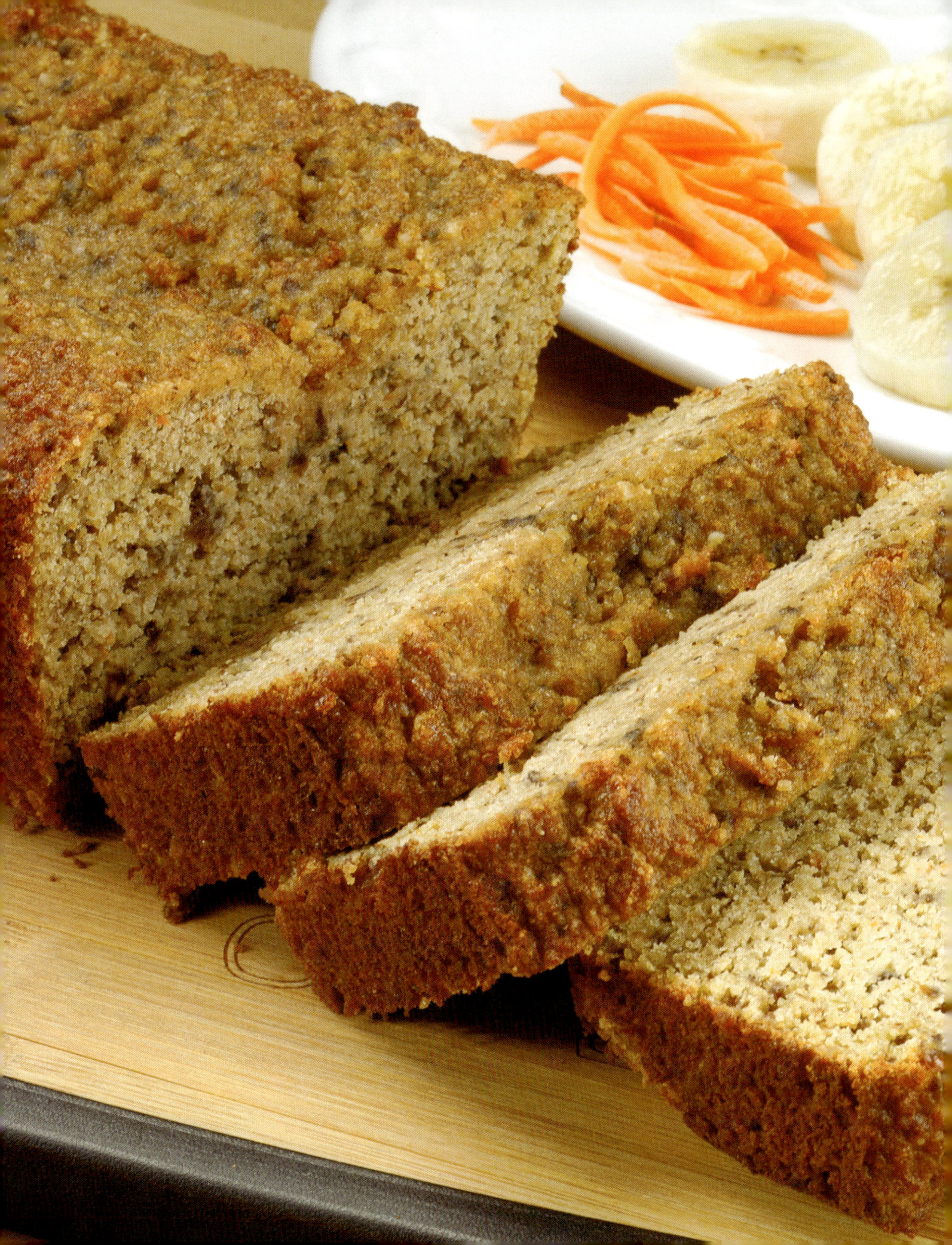

banana keto bread

serves 8–10

2 cups almond flour

¼ cup coconut flour

2 teaspoons baking powder

2 teaspoons cinnamon

¼ teaspoon sea salt

6 tablespoons butter, softened; may use coconut oil

½ cup erythritol

4 large eggs

¼ cup almond milk, unsweetened

2 teaspoons banana extract

tip: The longer you let it sit before slicing, the better it will hold together.

If you are following a keto diet, I figured out how to make a banana bread with reduced sugar to make it keto-friendly. Now you can enjoy this any time of day.

Preheat oven to 350°F (177°C).

Line a 9 x 5 loaf pan with parchment paper so the paper hangs over the sides for easy removal later.

In a medium bowl, mix the almond flour, coconut flour, baking powder, cinnamon, and sea salt together.

In a separate large bowl, beat butter and erythritol until fluffy. Beat in the eggs, stir in the banana extract and almond milk.

Add the dry ingredients to the wet ingredients and mix until a real batter forms.

Transfer the batter into the lined loaf pan and press evenly to make a smooth top.

Bake for 50–60 minutes or until a knife inserted in the center comes out clean.

Cool completely before removing from the loaf pan.

banana nut bread

Monkey-approved, delicious grain-free Banana Nut Bread. This recipe will delight any banana connoisseur.

Preheat oven to 350°F (177°C).

Combine your bananas, eggs, nut butter, and butter in either a blender, food processor, or mixing bowl.

Mix well (if using a mixing bowl, you need a good hand mixer).

Once all of your ingredients are blended, add in your coconut flour, cinnamon, baking soda, baking powder, vanilla, sea salt, and maple syrup, if desired, and mix well.

Stir in your nuts of choice.

Pour your batter in a loaf pan and spread it evenly. Just grease your loaf pan well with cooking spray

Place in oven and bake for 55–60 minutes or until a toothpick inserted into the center comes out clean.

Remove from the oven and flip your bread out onto a cooling rack.

Once cooled, slice and serve.

makes 8–10 servings

- 4 bananas, the riper the better, about 2½ cups, mashed
- 4 eggs
- ½ cup almond butter or any nut butter of your choice
- 4 tablespoons butter, melted
- ½ cup coconut flour
- 1 tablespoon cinnamon
- 1 teaspoon baking soda
- 1 teaspoon baking powder
- 1 teaspoon vanilla
- 2–3 tablespoons maple syrup or honey for added sweetness (optional)
- ½ cup walnuts or pecans, chopped
- Pinch sea salt
- Cooking spray

tip: You can also substitute butter with coconut oil.

Coconut flour can be replaced with almond flour or macadamia nut meal.

banana zucchini walnut bread

makes 12 slices

I learned the combination of bananas and zucchinis made the taste of this bread much more satisfying. A zucchini has about 295 grams of potassium, and bananas 422 grams.

- 2 bananas (2½ cups mashed)
- 2 zucchini, shredded
- 4 eggs
- ½ cup almond butter (or coconut, sunflower seed, or any nut butter of choice)
- 4 tablespoons butter, melted (can substitute coconut oil)
- ½ cup coconut flour
- 1 tablespoon cinnamon
- 1 teaspoon baking soda
- 1 teaspoon baking powder
- 1 teaspoon vanilla
- ½ cup walnuts or pecans, chopped
- Pinch sea salt
- Cooking spray

Preheat oven to 350°F (177°C).

Combine your mashed bananas, shredded zucchini, eggs, nut butter, and butter into a blender, food processor, or mixing bowl, and mix well. If you are using a mixing bowl, you need a good hand mixer.

Once all of your ingredients are blended, add in your coconut flour, cinnamon, baking soda, baking powder, vanilla, chopped walnuts, and sea salt, and mix well.

Pour the batter in a loaf pan heavily greased with cooking spray and spread it evenly.

Place in your preheated oven and bake for 50–60 minutes or until a toothpick inserted into the center comes out clean.

Remove from oven and flip your bread out onto a cooling rack; let cool for about 10 minutes. Once cooled, slice and serve.

tip: If using a metallic bread loaf pan, you can lightly dust your loaf pan with almond flour once greased.

barb's sandwich bread

Baking my own sandwich bread was the best thing I ever did. I can toast it, grill it, or make French toast with it—and best of all—it's grain-free!

makes 12 slices

Cooking spray

2 cups almond flour

6 tablespoons arrowroot flour

4 tablespoons golden flaxseed meal

2 tablespoons tapioca flour

¾ teaspoon fine sea salt

¾ teaspoon baking soda

4 tablespoons butter, melted or coconut oil

4 large eggs, lightly beaten

½ cup almond milk, unsweetened

1½ teaspoons apple cider vinegar

Preheat oven to 350°F (177°C).

Generously grease an 8½- by 4½-inch loaf pan with cooking spray.

Whisk together the almond flour, arrowroot flour, flaxseed meal, tapioca flour, salt, and baking soda in a medium bowl and set aside.

In a large bowl, whisk together the butter or coconut oil, eggs, almond milk and vinegar.

Add the dry ingredients and stir until well combined, being careful not to overmix.

Immediately pour the batter into the greased loaf pan and bake until a toothpick inserted into the center comes out clean, about 40–45 minutes.

Once done, take out of the pan and place bread on a wire rack to cool before slicing.

Once sliced, you can wrap your bread in plastic wrap or in an airtight container in the fridge for up to 5 days.

almond biscotti

makes 4–6 servings.

A favorite for coffee. I found a way to get that wonderfully mild sweet almond taste without the wheat and created this toasty treat to enjoy.

- 1 cup almond flour
- 1 tablespoon coconut flour
- 1 tablespoon ground golden flaxseed
- ½ tablespoon arrowroot flour
- ½ teaspoon baking soda
- ¼ teaspoon sea salt
- 1 cup sliced almonds
- 1 teaspoon almond extract
- 2 eggs
- 2 tablespoons apple cider vinegar
- 1 tablespoon raw honey or maple syrup
- 3–5 tablespoons almond paste
- Cooking spray (optional)

Preheat oven to 350°F (177°C).

Line a baking sheet with parchment paper or aluminum foil. If using foil, grease with cooking spray.

In a small bowl, sift together the dry ingredients except for the sliced almonds. In another small bowl, combine the wet ingredients, whisking well. Add dry ingredients to wet and mix. Fold in the sliced almonds with a spatula to form a thick batter. Divide batter in half and shape each half into a log, making two logs, each about three inches wide on your baking sheet. Transfer to oven and bake 18–20 minutes or until golden and a toothpick inserted into the center comes out clean.

Once baked, take out and increase heat to 400°F (204°C).

When the logs have cooled (about 8 minutes), use a finely serrated bread knife and slice the logs diagonally about the thickness of a biscotti, about an ¾ to 1 inch thick. Place each slice on your cookie sheet and bake for 10–12 minutes until crispy.

Let cool about five minutes and serve with coffee. You can also add butter or preserves. Store cooled biscotti in an airtight container so it lasts in the refrigerator for up to 7 days.

almond chocolate chip cookies

KF OPTIONAL *My version of these is versatile enough that you can replace the sugar with erythritol to make them keto-friendly.*

Preheat oven to 350°F (177°C).

In a medium mixing bowl, add butter, salt, and sweetener together and beat until well blended.

Add almond extract and vanilla and beat well.

Add almond and coconut flours and combine well.

Add in chocolate chips and mix for even distribution.

Line a baking sheet with aluminum foil and grease with cooking spray.

Place about a tablespoon of dough in the palm of your hand and roll into a small ball, and place onto the prepared baking sheet, mashing down to form your cookies and separate about one inch apart.

Bake for 10–12 minutes until lightly golden brown.

Remove from oven, let cool for 10 minutes on the baking sheet, and serve!

makes 10–12 cookies

1 stick butter, softened

⅛ teaspoon sea salt

¾ cup coconut sugar (or erythritol if doing keto)

1 teaspoon almond extract

1 teaspoon vanilla

1½ cups almond flour

½ cup coconut flour

½ cup chocolate chips, (I use Lily's made with stevia.)

Cooking spray

almond crescent cookies

makes 10–12 cookies

> **KF** *These cookies were inspired by my friend, Gail Margaritas. I brought these cookies to a Jack Canfield seminar and received rave reviews. Thank you, Gail!*

1 stick butter, softened

⅛ teaspoon sea salt

¾ cup erythritol or Swerve

1 teaspoon almond extract

1 teaspoon vanilla

1½ cups almond flour

½ cup coconut flour

½ cup almonds, sliced for topping

¼ cup butter

Cooking spray

Preheat oven to 350°F (177°C).

In a medium mixing bowl, add butter, salt, and sweetener together, and beat until well blended.

Add almond extract and vanilla and beat well.

Add almond and coconut flours and combine well.

Form into 10–12 small logs and roll so that the ends get a bit pointy, about 3 inches long. Place on a parchment lined cookie sheet.

Place the sliced almonds on a plate.

In a microwave safe measuring cup, heat the ¼ cup butter and brush the cookies with the butter.

Roll cookies into the sliced almonds and shape into crescents. Place on greased, aluminum foil-lined baking sheet.

Bake for 10–12 minutes.

Remove from oven and let cookies cool for 10 minutes on the baking sheet before placing on a plate to serve.

tip: These cookies have a tendency to want to fall apart. Keep at it, shaping and keeping your crescent cookies together.

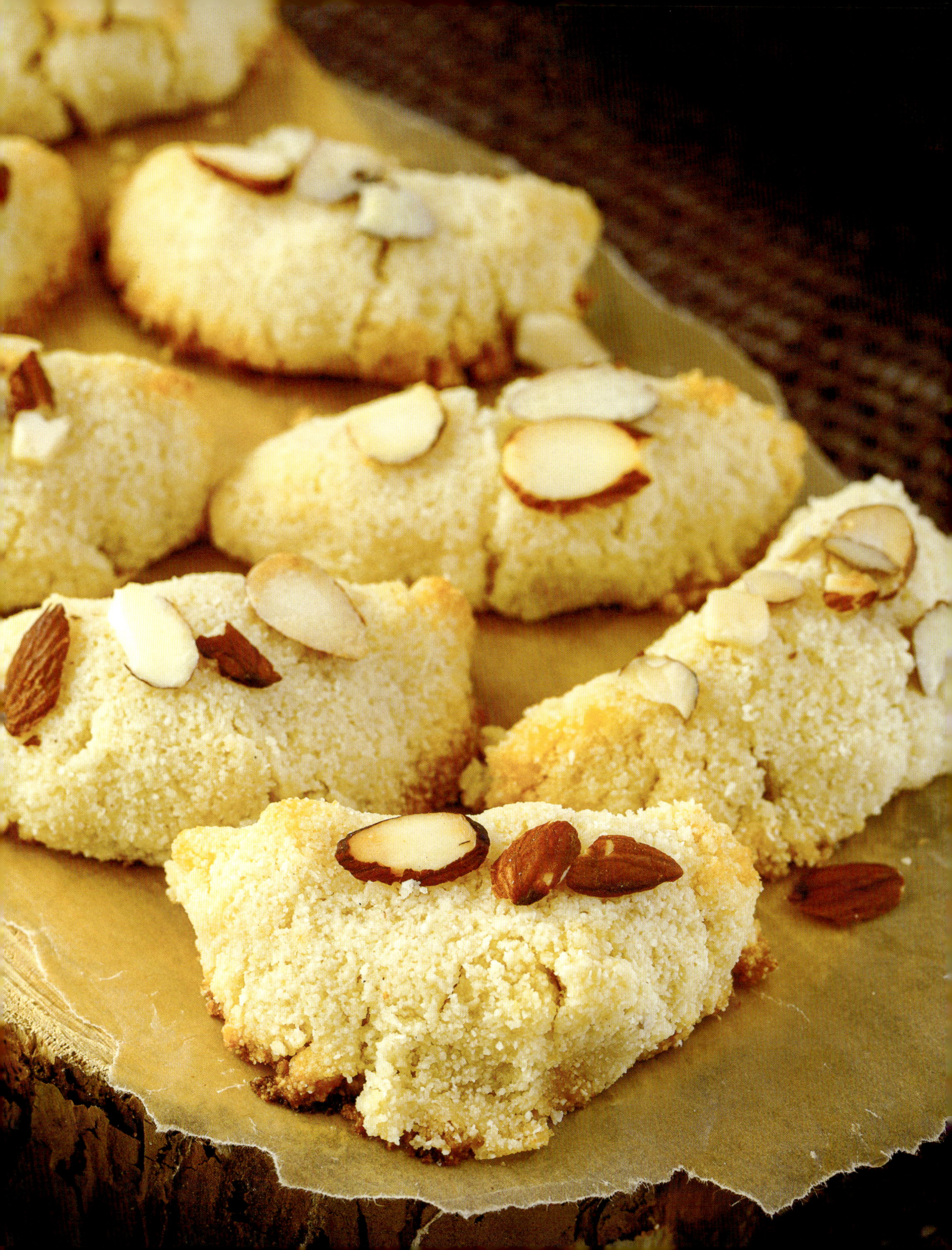

banana blueberry muffins

makes 12

Soothing and sweet, these muffins are great for breakfast or midday snack.

2 tablespoons olive or coconut oil

3 large eggs

2 very ripe bananas, mashed (about 1 cup)

¾ cup almond flour

¼ cup coconut flour

¾ teaspoon baking soda

¼ teaspoon sea salt (about a pinch)

¼ cup maple syrup or honey

½ cup fresh or frozen blueberries

tip: You can store covered at room temp for 2–3 days in an airtight container, in the refrigerator for a few weeks, or in the freezer for a few months.

Preheat oven to 350°F (177°C).

Prepare a muffin pan with paper muffin liners.

Mix the almond flour, coconut flour, baking soda, and salt together in a bowl.

Add coconut oil, eggs, mashed bananas, and maple syrup to the dry ingredients and blend well with a stand or hand-held mixer.

Let the batter sit for a few minutes and mix one more time gently.

Add the blueberries and give it a couple of stirs to even the mix.

Pour the batter, ¾ full per, into the muffin liners.

Bake for 25 minutes or until a toothpick inserted in the middle of a muffin comes out clean.

Let cool before serving.

banana carrot muffins

Good morning sunshine! A great way to start your day is with my Banana Carrot Muffins.

Preheat oven to 350°F (177°C).

In a large bowl combine flour, baking soda, salt, and cinnamon.

In a food processor, combine dates, bananas, eggs, vinegar, and oil.

Add dry mixture in the large bowl with moist ingredients from food processor to combine thoroughly.

Fold in carrots and nuts.

Spoon mixture into paper-lined muffin tins.

Bake for 25 minutes.

Let cool before removing paper from muffins.

makes 12–16

2 cups almond flour

2 teaspoons baking soda

½ teaspoon sea salt

1 tablespoon cinnamon

1 cup dates, pitted

3 medium bananas

3 large eggs

1 teaspoon apple cider vinegar

¼ cup coconut oil, melted

1½ large carrots, shredded (1½ cups)

¾ cup walnuts, (or nuts of choice), finely chopped

Paper muffin liners; if no liners, grease muffin pan with cooking spray

baked goods

cauliflower cheese bread

makes 10–12 servings

KF *I found this to be a nice alternative to regular cheese bread and fun to make as well. Great for dipping in my basic marinara sauce! It really creates a tasty blend of cauliflower, herbs, and cheese.*

- 1 large cauliflower head (7–8 inches wide) or already-riced cauliflower (You can find already-riced cauliflower in the grocery store.)
- ¼ cup egg whites (from 2 large eggs, generally)
- 1¼ cups mozzarella, Tex-Mex, or cheddar cheese, shredded
- 1 teaspoon Italian herb seasoning or any dried herbs like rosemary, basil, parsley
- ¼ teaspoon freshly ground black pepper
- Pinch sea salt
- Cooking spray
- Marinara sauce for dipping (Find my recipe for Basic Marinara Sauce on page 258.)

tip: Refrigerate covered for up to 2 days. You can also freeze, tightly wrapped in plastic, for up to 1 month. Thaw on a counter or in a microwave.

Preheat oven to 375°F (191°C).

Rinse cauliflower, remove outer leaves and separate into florets with a paring knife. Place cauliflower florets in a food processor and process until "rice" texture. Some coarse chunks are fine. If you have the already riced, follow directions on the package for preparation. If using, packaged riced cauliflower is uncooked, so once prepared, skip the next step and work on cooling it down before eliminating liquid.

When using fresh cauliflower that you have riced, place in an ovenproof baking dish (I use a Pyrex pie dish) and bake for 20 minutes. Remove cooked cauliflower from the oven and transfer to a bowl lined with a tea towel (paper towel works well too).

Let the cauliflower cool down a bit until it is safe to touch, about 15 minutes. Fold the towel, holding the ends, and squeeze the liquid out. I squeezed out 1 cup of liquid. Do this a few times until barely any liquid comes out of cauliflower "ball." Be patient.

Increase oven to 450°F (232°C). Transfer cauliflower to mixing bowl along with egg whites, ½ cup cheese, herb seasoning, black pepper, pinch of salt, and mix to combine.

Place the cauliflower mixture onto a well-greased aluminum foil-lined baking sheet. Flatten with your hands into an approximately 9 x 7-inch rectangle and ¼-inch thick. Bake for 18 minutes; remove from the oven, and top with remaining ¾ cup cheese.

Bake for another 5 minutes and then broil until cheese turns golden brown. Cut into 12 sections and serve hot with warm marinara sauce, if desired.

baked goods

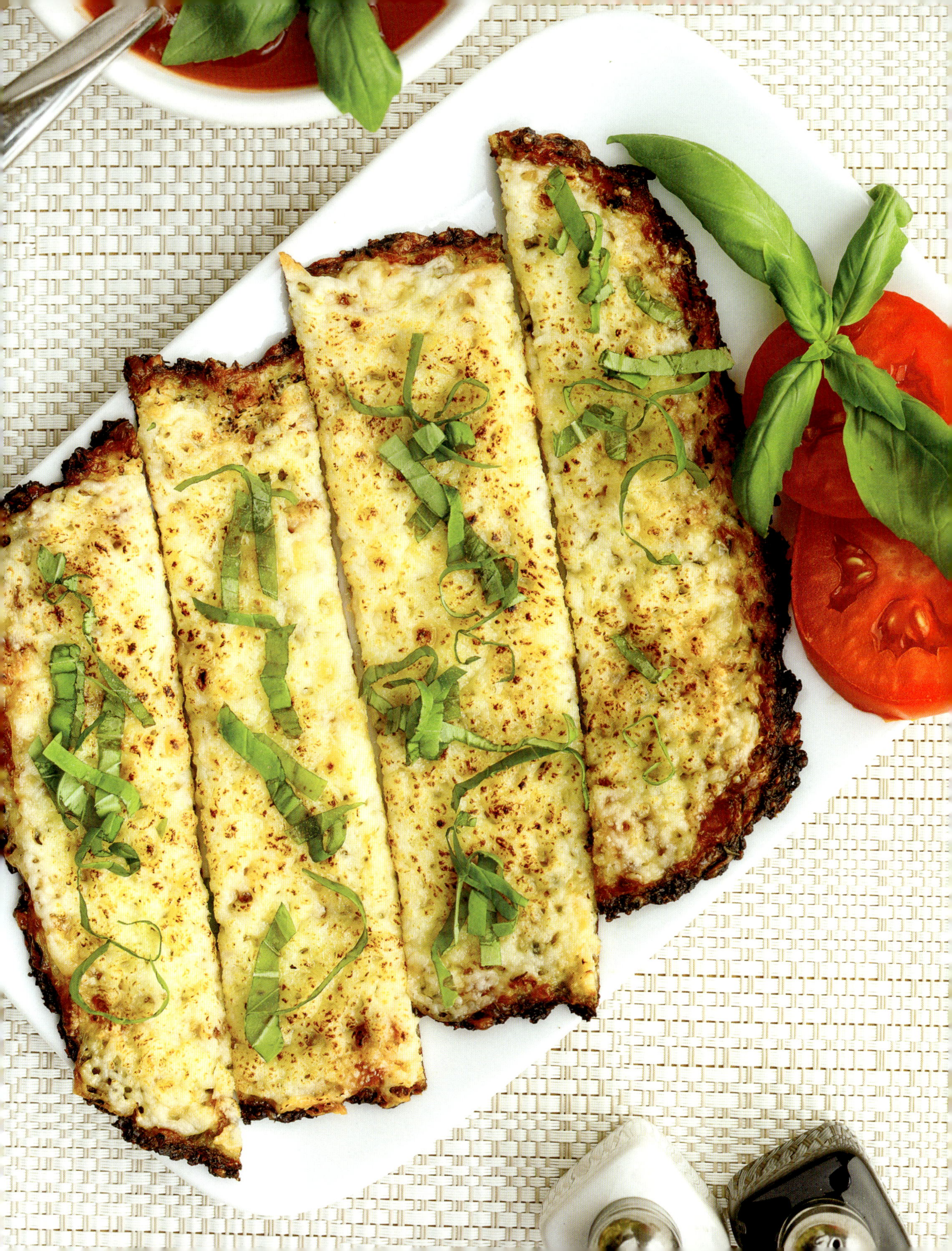

french bread

serves 6–8

½ cup warm water

2 tablespoons maple syrup

1 package active dry yeast

1 ⅓ cups cassava flour

1 ⅓ cups arrowroot flour

1 teaspoon sea salt

4 teaspoons butter, sliced

4 eggs, beaten

Cooking spray

tip: If the bottom seems a bit moist, you can put the loaf directly on the oven rack without the pan for 5 minutes at 400°F (204°C) to harden the bottom.

Everybody loves bread! I don't think I've ever met a bad one. They're all terrific: French baguette, San Francisco sourdough—remember that one—and how about a ciabatta bread? My recipe takes the guilt out of having bread.

Preheat oven to 400°F (204°C).

Mix warm water, maple syrup, and 1 package of active yeast in a bowl and set aside. Wait 10–15 minutes until it's frothy and doubled in size. It typically takes about 10 minutes.

In a mixing bowl, add the 2 flours and the salt, and stir to combine.

Add the butter into the flour mixture and mix on medium until the butter crumbles.

Add the beaten eggs and yeast mixture, and blend. The mixture will be very sticky.

Grease a baking pan with cooking spray.

Take out your bread dough, using some cassava flour on your hands, and shape it into a French loaf on the greased baking pan. Let the loaf rise for about 40 minutes before baking.

After rising, bake for 25–30 minutes. Remove from oven and let cool for 10 minutes.

Slice and serve with butter or cheese.

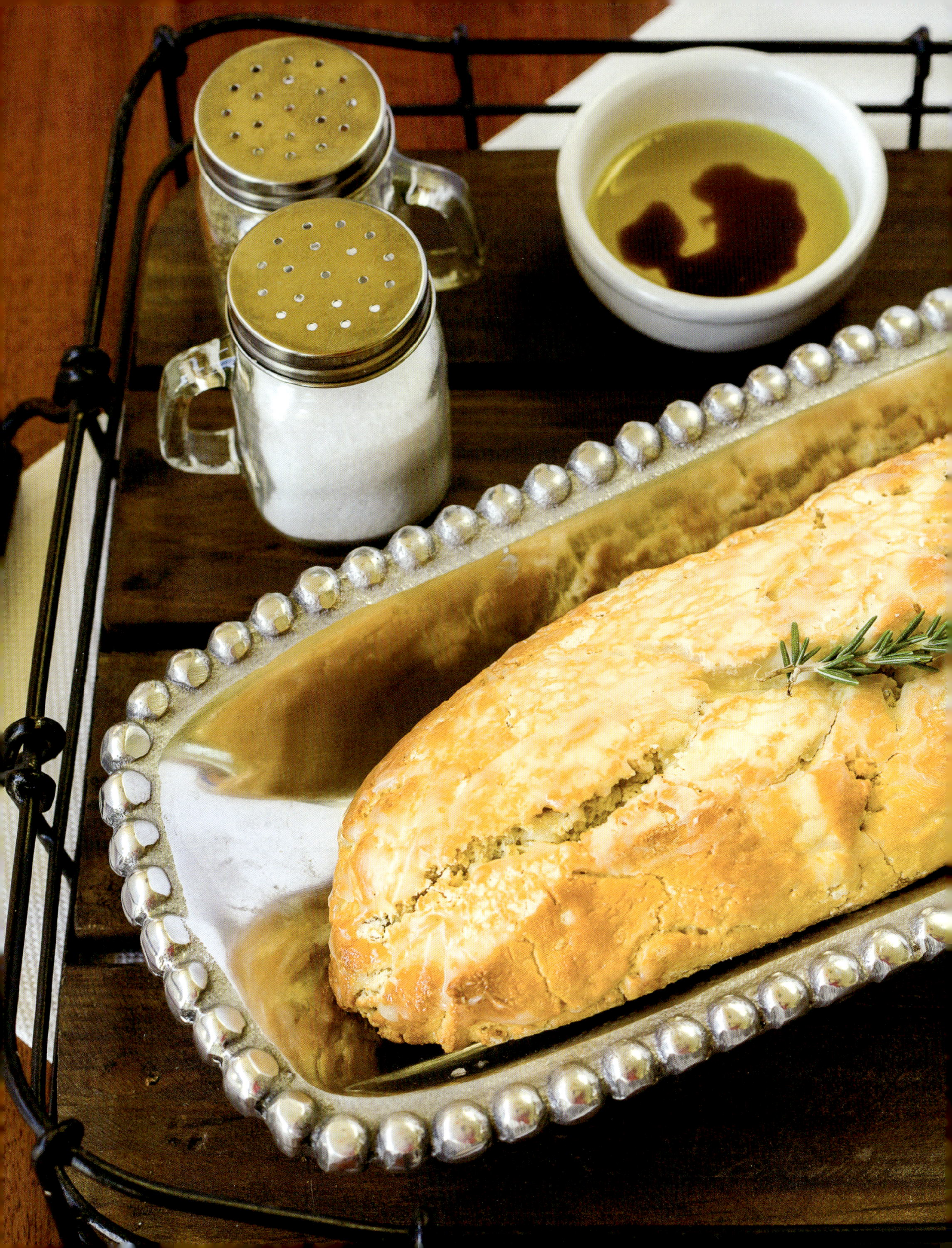

cocoa balls

makes 12–14 cocoa balls

KF *Chocolate—what more can I say? Yummy chocolate grain-free delights!*

- 2 tablespoons Hershey's Chocolate (100% cacao)
- ⅓ cup cocoa powder, unsweetened
- ¼ cup coconut oil
- ¼ cup canned coconut cream, full-fat
- 1 tablespoon chia seeds
- ½ cup shredded coconut, unsweetened
- 1 teaspoon vanilla extract
- 1 ½ tablespoons coconut milk, unsweetened

Add 1 ½ tablespoons of milk and the chia seeds in a small bowl and set aside until the seeds soften.

Add cacao, cocoa powder, coconut oil, coconut cream, ¼ cup of shredded coconut, and vanilla extract to a mixing bowl and mix well until all thoroughly combined. Leave some of the shredded coconut for rolling.

Place in the fridge for an hour to help in the molding.

Use a spoon to scoop out the chocolate and mold into balls, roll over shredded coconut, and place on a dessert tray or cookie sheet until ready to serve. Easy peasy!

ginger cookies

Did you know that ginger provides possible health benefits like relieving nausea, loss of appetite, motion sickness, and pain? Get your dose with these delicious cookies.

makes about 8–10 cookies

½ cup butter, melted

¾ cup coconut sugar

1 egg

1 tablespoon molasses

1 teaspoon vanilla extract

2½ teaspoons ginger

1 teaspoon cinnamon

½ teaspoon pumpkin spice

½ teaspoon cloves

½ teaspoon nutmeg

½ teaspoon sea salt

2 teaspoons baking soda

1 cup almond flour

1 cup arrowroot flour

Cooking spray

Preheat oven to 350°F (177°C).

In a processor or mixer, combine butter and sugar, then add vanilla, molasses, and egg. Pulse or mix to combine. Add spices, salt, baking soda, almond flour, and arrowroot, pulse or mix to combine. Dough will come together in a big ball.

Transfer cookie dough to a bowl. Cover and refrigerate at least 30–60 minutes.

Take out your cookie dough and make 1½ inch balls of dough, rolling them in your hands.

Place the doughballs on a greased aluminum-lined baking sheet and flatten slightly. Cookies will spread, so place them about two inches from each other.

Bake for 10–12 minutes, or until golden around the edges.

Let cookies cool 2–3 minutes on baking sheet before transferring to a cooling rack.

tip: For best results, use a large baking sheet to keep these apart for adequate spacing. Too close, and they stick to each other.

baked goods

cheesy onion bialys

serves 4—6

3 cups mozzarella cheese, shredded

4 tablespoons cream cheese

1½ cups almond flour

2 teaspoons xanthan gum

2 eggs, room temperature

2 teaspoons dried yeast, approximately 1 packet

2 tablespoons warm water

3 tablespoons butter, unsalted, melted

1 tablespoon onion flakes or dried minced onion

1 teaspoon sesame seeds, poppy seeds, and/or dried garlic flakes (optional)

Cooking spray for greasing

tip: I put them in a toaster after they have been frozen or just out of the refrigerator. They are quite yummy!

KF *Oh, the goodness of a morning bread with coffee or tea. Here is my take on a cheesy bialy that is grain and gluten free, so it won't leave you bloated.*

Preheat oven to 400°F (204°C).

In a microwave safe dish, place the mozzarella cheese and cream cheese and microwave in 30 second increments, stirring in between, until fully melted and almost liquid.

Dissolve the yeast in a bowl of warm water and allow it to sit and activate for 2 minutes.

Place the almond flour and xanthan gum in a large bowl and mix well.

Add to the bowl the eggs, yeast mixture, and 1 tablespoon of the melted butter and mix well.

Add the hot melted cheese and knead the dough until all the ingredients are fully combined, around 5–10 minutes. I just use a large spoon and keep mixing. The dough is easiest to work with while it is warm.

Place the 6 balls on the lined cookie sheet after greasing generously. Form them into bialy shapes. Using your finger make a hole in the middle to form a bialy shape. Brush bialys with melted butter and add the dried onion flakes or minced dried onion, poppy seeds, sesame seeds, and/or dried garlic if desired.

Bake in the oven for 12–15 minutes or until golden brown.

When the bialys are golden brown, remove them from the oven. They are best eaten that day, but they do freeze well. They taste great with butter or cream cheese.

baked goods

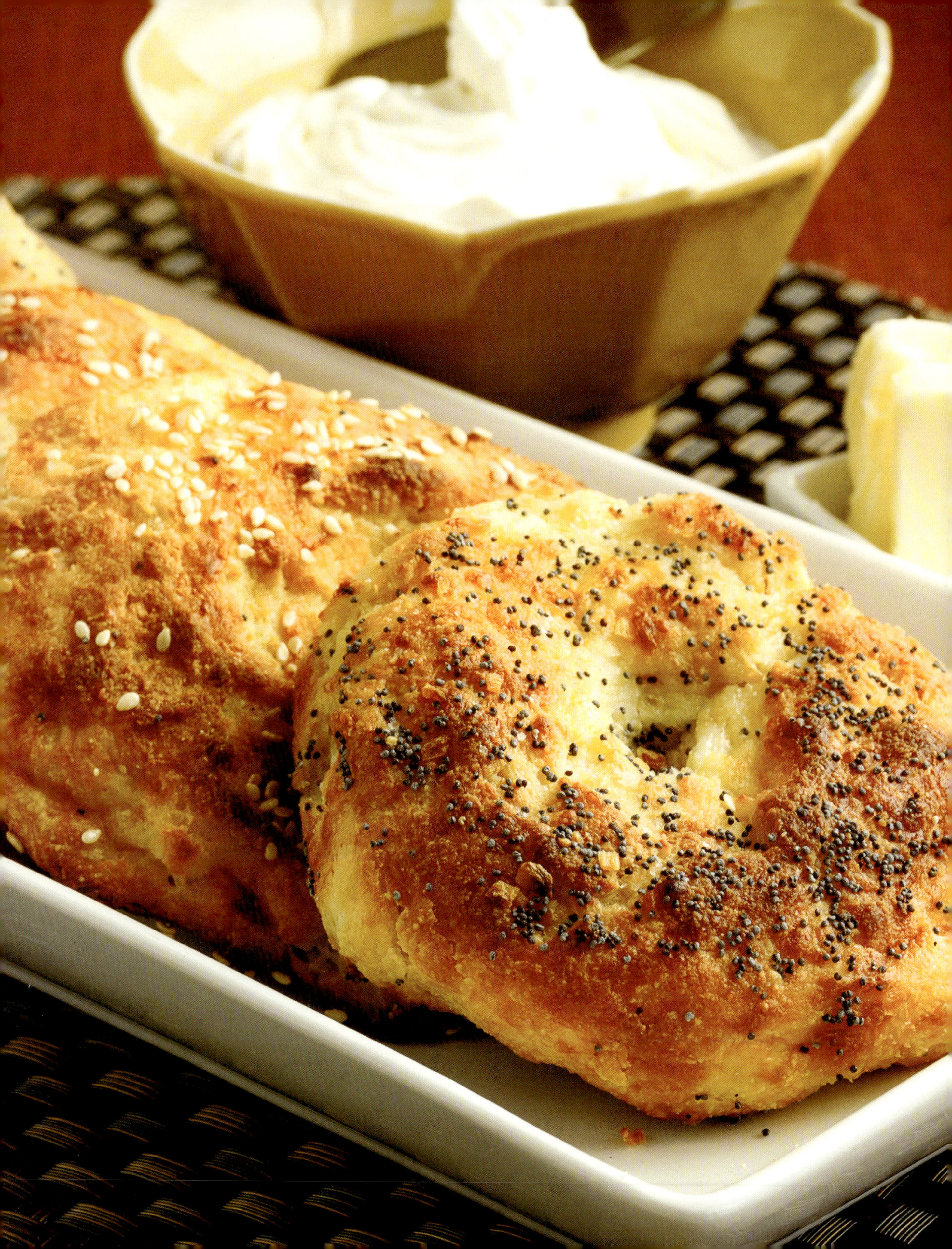

gooey chocolate chip cookies

makes approximately 24 cookies

I do love my chocolate. This healthful recipe brings together the goodness of being grain free with the yumminess of chocolate.

Cooking spray

¾ cup almond flour

¼ cup coconut flour

½ cup cocoa powder, unsweetened

1 teaspoon baking soda

¼ teaspoon sea salt

7 tablespoons coconut oil (You may substitute with unsalted butter.)

¾ cup coconut sugar

6 tablespoons natural cashew butter (You may use almond butter. Cashew butter is creamier.)

1½ teaspoons vanilla extract

1 large egg, room temperature

1 cup semisweet chocolate chips, (I use Lily's made with stevia.)

tip: Put coconut oil in fridge for 10-20 minutes to firm up like soft butter to ensure dough doesn't become too oily.

Use cashew or almond butter at room temperature for ease of mixing.

Preheat oven to 350°F (177°C).

Line a baking sheet with aluminum foil and grease with cooking spray.

In a medium mixing bowl, stir together the almond flour, coconut flour, cocoa powder, baking soda, and salt. Set aside.

In a large mixing bowl with an electric hand mixer or using a stand mixer, beat together the coconut oil and coconut sugar at medium speed until well combined, about 1 minute.

Beat in the cashew or almond butter and vanilla extract on medium speed and mix until combined.

Beat in the egg on low and mix until well incorporated. Stir in the flour mixture until well combined.

Then stir in 1 cup of chocolate chips.

You may want to place the mixture into the refrigerator to harden a bit so the chips won't melt before baking, about ½ hour.

Take the cookie dough out, roll 2 tablespoons of dough in your hands to form dough balls for your cookies. This helps keep the chips from falling out.

Place cookies on the baking sheet about 2–3 inches apart. Press the cookies down lightly with the palm of your hand to flatten slightly.

Bake for 10–12 minutes, making sure the surface of the center of the cookies no longer appears wet. Do not overbake!

Remove from the oven and let them cool completely on the baking sheet. They'll be very soft but will continue to harden as they sit on the cookie sheet.

Store in an airtight container for up to 3 days or in the freezer for up to a month.

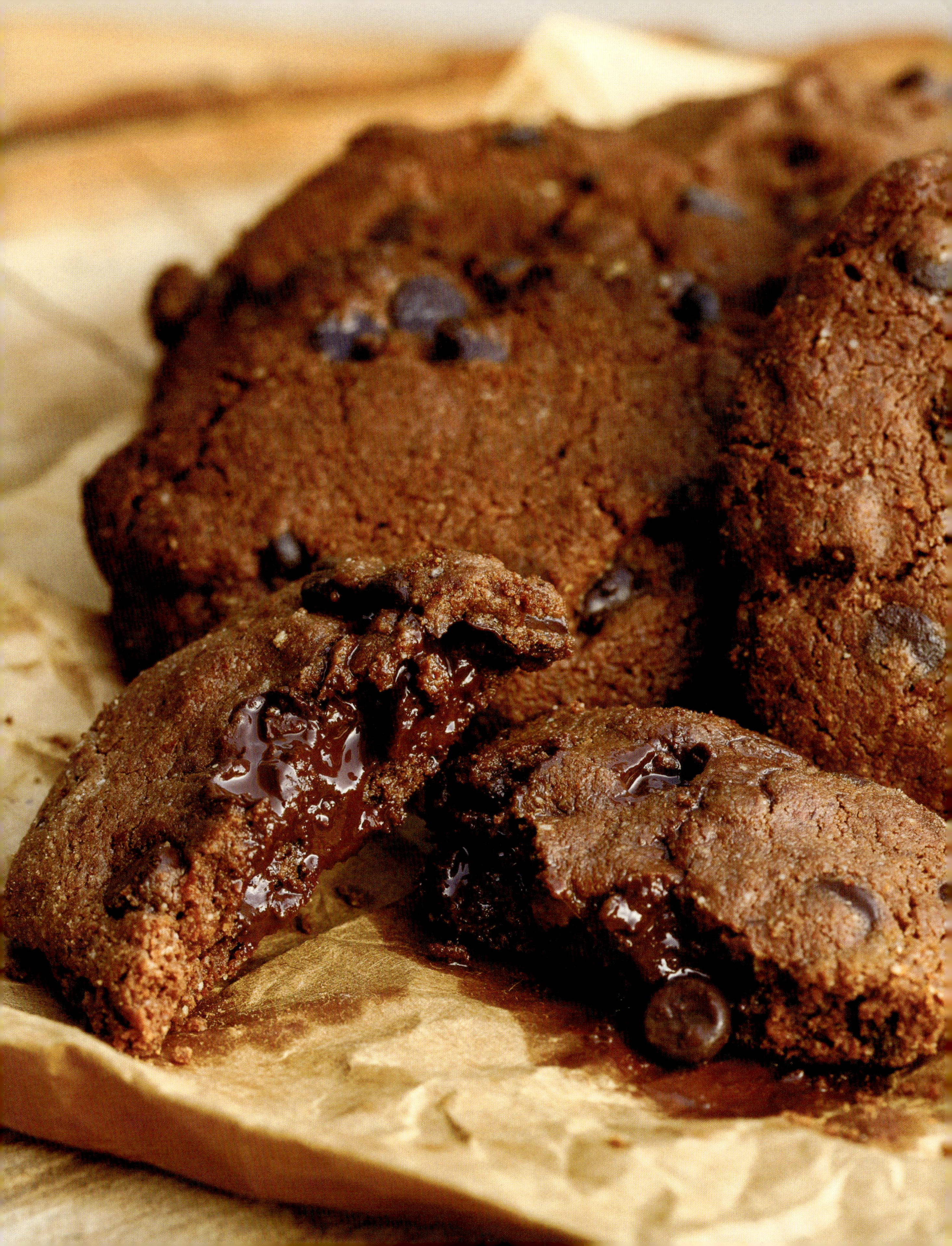

coconut chocolate chip cookies

makes 10–12 cookies

KF OPTIONAL *Rich, decadent chocolate chip cookies are sure to be a hit with any chocolate lover.*

½ cup chocolate chips, (I use Lily's made with stevia.)

½ cup coconut oil

½ cup raw honey (or if doing keto, use erythritol syrup, recipe on page 15)

4 eggs

½ teaspoon vanilla extract

⅛ teaspoon sea salt

1 cup coconut flour

½ cup shredded coconut, unsweetened

Preheat oven to 375°F (191°C).

To make your life easier, in a small bowl, combine the raw honey and coconut oil and soften in the microwave for about 30 seconds. In a large bowl, combine coconut oil, raw honey, eggs, vanilla extract, and sea salt and mix well.

Add in your coconut flour, stir in the shredded coconut and chocolate chips, and mix well.

On parchment-lined baking sheet, drop heaping tablespoons of cookie dough.

Make sure you form them to look like the cookies you want for a final product, as these do not rise or spread like conventional cookies. You can place more on a baking sheet without worrying about them touching.

Bake for 12 minutes or until golden brown. Remove from the oven, transfer to a cooling rack, and let cool.

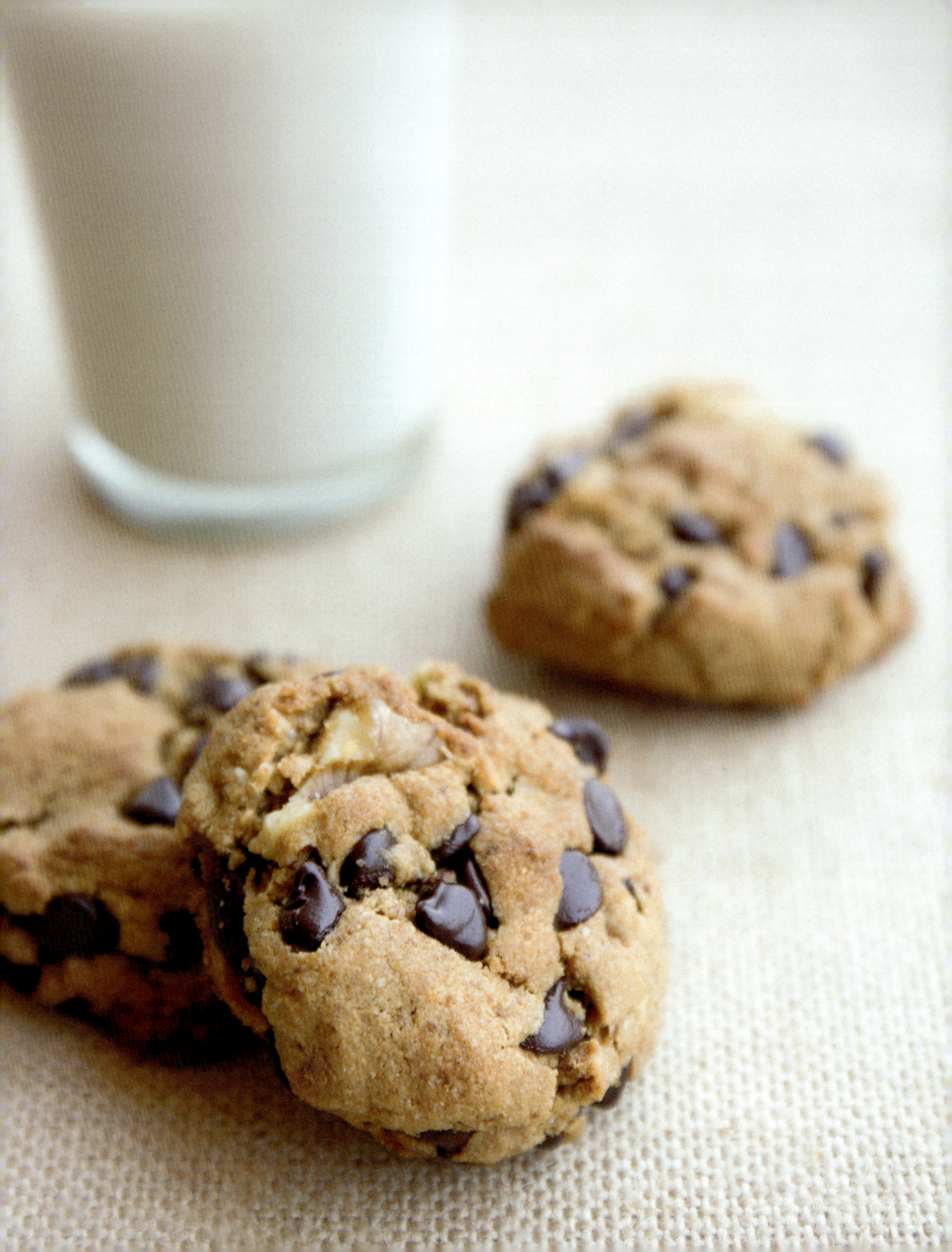

maple pecan shortbread cookies

Shortbread is great with tea or a coffee drink. Perfect for dipping and sipping.

makes 12–16 cookies.

2 cups almond flour

½ cup raw pecans, chopped

½ teaspoon baking soda

Pinch sea salt

¼ cup maple syrup

¼ cup coconut oil, melted and cooled (butter works as well)

1 teaspoon vanilla extract

Preheat oven to 350°F (177°C).

In a mixing bowl, add the first four ingredients and stir together. Add the wet ingredients and mix until a sticky dough forms.

Make a square or log out of the dough, pressing it together, then place it on a sheet of aluminum foil so you can cut it in two so that the logs are easier to manage or less delicate.

Wrap each log tightly in aluminum foil and place in the freezer for 30 minutes or in the refrigerator for 2 hours.

When ready to bake, unwrap the cookie dough, place it on a cutting board, and slice ¼-inch thick slices to form cookie shapes.

Place cookies on a baking sheet lined with parchment paper and bake for 10–15 minutes, or until edges are golden brown.

Remove cookies from the oven and allow them to sit for 15 minutes before removing them from the baking sheet with a spatula.

dark chocolate walnut cake brownies

Alice B. Toklas has got nothing on these brownies. Let your mind wander with this chocolate goodness and best of all—no grain-based flour!

serves 10–12

- 3 ounces baking chocolate, unsweetened
- 5 large eggs
- ¾ cup honey
- ⅓ cup coconut flour, sifted
- ¼ cup cocoa powder, unsweetened
- 1 teaspoon vanilla extract
- ¾ teaspoon baking soda
- ¼ cup dark chocolate chips (Lily's works well.)
- 1 packet stevia
- ½ cup walnuts, chopped
- ½ cup coconut oil, plus a little more for greasing the pan

Preheat oven to 325°F (163°C).

Lightly grease a 9 x 13-inch baking pan with the coconut oil.

Place the ½ cup coconut oil and baking chocolate in a small bowl over a pot of simmering water and whisk until melted and smooth. Make sure not to boil. Set aside.

Place the eggs and honey in a bowl; either blend in a blender or beat with a mixer on medium.

Add the coconut flour, cocoa powder, vanilla, baking soda, packet of stevia, and salt. Beat on low until incorporated then on high until smooth.

Add the melted chocolate mixture and beat on medium until batter thickens, about 15 seconds.

Stir in the chocolate chips by hand and then the nuts.

Pour the batter evenly into the prepared pan, smoothing the top with the back of the spoon.

Bake for 30–35 minutes until a toothpick inserted into the center comes out clean.

Cool in a pan for 10 minutes.

double chocolate nut cookies

makes 12 Cookies

Mmmm! Who doesn't love chocolate? These are so good you'll want to grab your favorite latte and munch away.

⅓ cup honey

⅓ cup stevia

5 teaspoons almond flour

½ cup cocoa powder, unsweetened

1 teaspoon baking soda

1 cup smooth almond butter

2 large eggs

2 teaspoons vanilla extract

½ cup chocolate chips, (Lily's works well.)

Preheat oven to 350°F (177°C).

Line a baking sheet with parchment paper.

In a medium-sized bowl, whisk together the stevia, honey, almond flour, cocoa powder, and baking soda until no more cocoa powder lumps remain.

Stir in the almond butter, eggs, vanilla extract, and chocolate chips until a stiff dough forms.

Use a tablespoon to scoop about 2 tablespoons of cookie dough and roll dough into a ball.

Place the dough ball on the prepared baking sheet and flatten slightly with the palm of your hand to form cookies.

Bake for 8–10 minutes or until crunchy on the edges, but still soft and fudgy in the middle.

Remove cookies and place on a plate or baking rack to let cookies cool completely.

tip: You can freeze any leftover cookies for another day!

flatbread

This delightful treat can be made for a snack, an appetizer, or as a side dish.

Preheat oven to 425°F (218°C) and line a baking sheet with aluminum foil and grease with cooking spray.

Place tapioca flour into a large bowl. Set aside.

In a saucepan, bring milk, butter, and salt to a boil and turn off heat.

Pour milk mixture over tapioca flour and mix until well incorporated into your dough.

Allow dough to rest for 10 minutes to cool.

Combine eggs and cheese into dough and mix until uniform.

Using your hands, make a long rectangle or square shape, making it a thin as possible on the baking sheet.

Transfer baking sheet to oven and decrease oven temperature to 375°F (191°C).

Bake until golden on the edges, 22–25 minutes.

Remove from oven and serve.

Cut into 2-inch-long strips.

tip: I like to serve in long strips with olive oil and herbs. So yummy!

serves 3–4

Cooking spray

2 cups tapioca flour

¾ cup almond or coconut milk, unsweetened

⅓ cup butter

1 teaspoon sea salt

2 eggs, beaten

1 cup Parmesan cheese, grated

Garlic salt to taste

Red pepper flakes for heat

baked goods

pumpkin bread with pecans

Pumpkin has always been a favorite of mine, and now I can enjoy it without the triple "g's"—gluten, grains, and guilt.

makes 6–8 slices

Cooking spray

½ cup pecans, crushed

½ cup coconut flour

1 tablespoon pumpkin pie spice

1 teaspoon cinnamon

½ teaspoon baking soda

¼ teaspoon baking powder

½-1 teaspoon ground nutmeg

¼ teaspoon sea salt

4 eggs

1 cup canned pure pumpkin purée (not pumpkin pie filling)

½ cup maple syrup

1 teaspoon vanilla extract

Preheat oven to 350°F (177°C).

Set up an oven rack right below the middle rung in the oven (should be third rung).

Prepare a loaf pan by generously spraying with cooking spray. Set aside.

In a medium mixing bowl, whisk coconut flour, crushed pecans, pumpkin pie spice, cinnamon, baking soda, baking powder, ground nutmeg, and salt, breaking apart any lumps in the coconut flour.

In a large mixing bowl, whisk the eggs. Add pumpkin, maple syrup, and vanilla extract, and whisk very well to combine all ingredients. There may be a few small clumps of coconut oil that do not totally dissolve—this is okay!

Slowly pour the dry ingredients into the bowl of wet ingredients. Using a rubber spatula or wooden spoon, slowly stirring all ingredients until combined. Batter may be slightly lumpy. Do not overmix. Pour batter into prepared loaf pan.

Bake for 38–45 minutes, or until toothpick inserted into the center comes out clean, or with just a couple of moist crumbs attached.

Set pan on a wire rack to cool for about 15–20 minutes.

Using a plastic knife carefully scrape along the sides of the pan around the loaf to detach bread from sides of pan.

Carefully remove loaf from pan and allow to cool completely on wire rack before slicing, about 10–15 minutes.

tip: Store pumpkin bread in the refrigerator for up to one week. Bread freezes well for up to a month. If freezing, slice into individual pieces and store in separate plastic sandwich bags. To serve, you can toast or microwave for about 30 seconds or less.

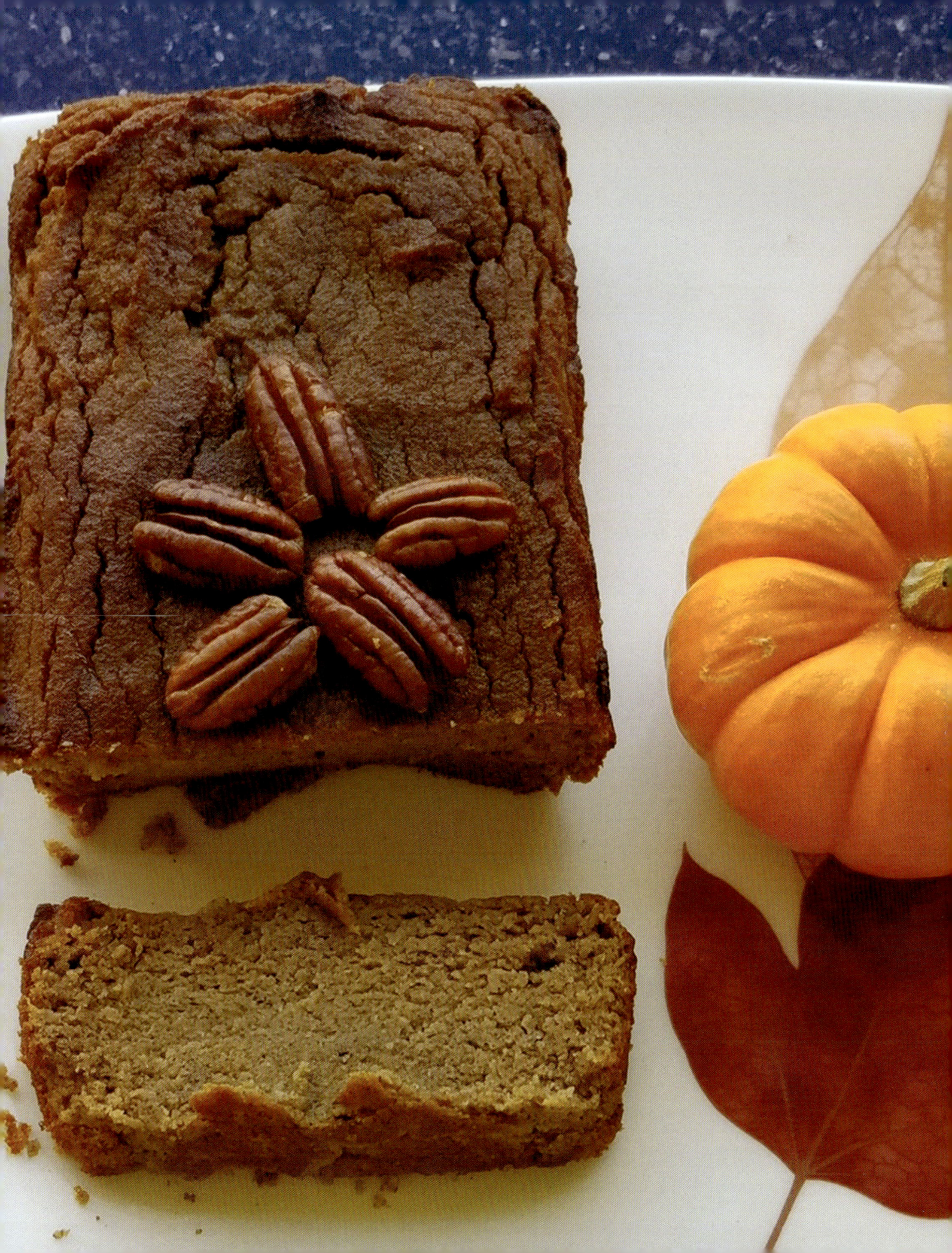

scone loaf bread

makes 4–6 servings

Full of flavor, a scone is the perfect accompaniment to any topping—sweet or savory.

½ cup olive oil or coconut oil

½ cup water

1 teaspoon sea salt

¾ cup tapioca flour

1 large egg

¼ cup coconut flour

Cooking spray

Preheat oven to 350°F (177°C).

In a small saucepan, combine the olive oil, water, and sea salt, and bring to a boil.

Remove from heat, then add the tapioca flour. Mix thoroughly and let it rest for 5 minutes.

Add the egg, mix in the coconut flour, and then knead the dough for 1 minute.

Make it into a small baguette or mini-French bread loaf. Place the loaf on an aluminum-foiled lined baking sheet greased with cooking spray.

Make several cuts on top of the loaf with a butter knife.

Bake for 35–45 minutes.

tips: Sometimes the bread can be a bit gummy. Make sure your cuts are deep on the bread, and if it is gummy, just put it back in the oven for a few more minutes.

I love this, it is so delicious with butter and honey or jam.

If you toast the bread the next day, it may become gummy. I suggest that you thinly slice it and bake in the oven for 8–10 minutes at 400°F (204°C). It is best served fresh!

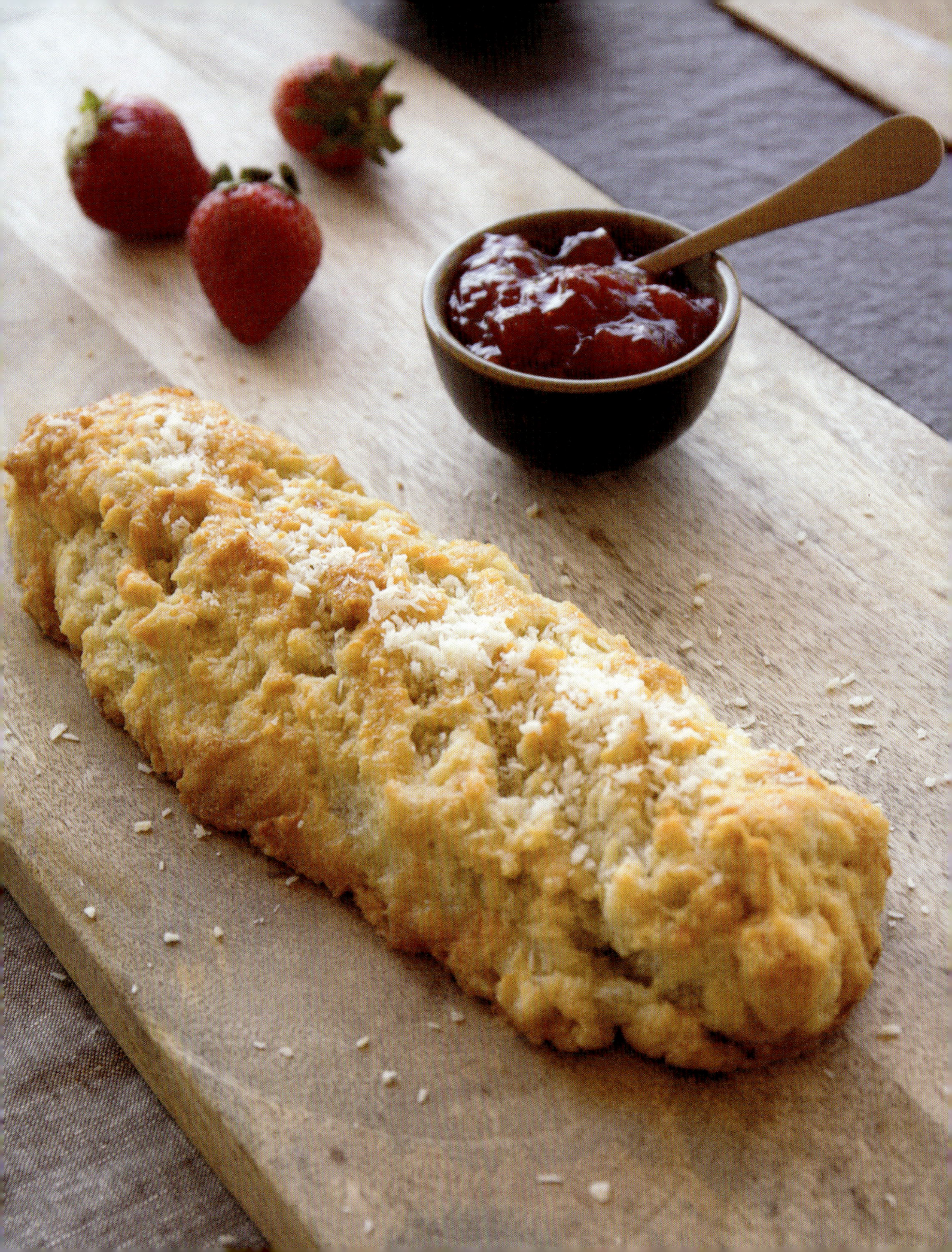

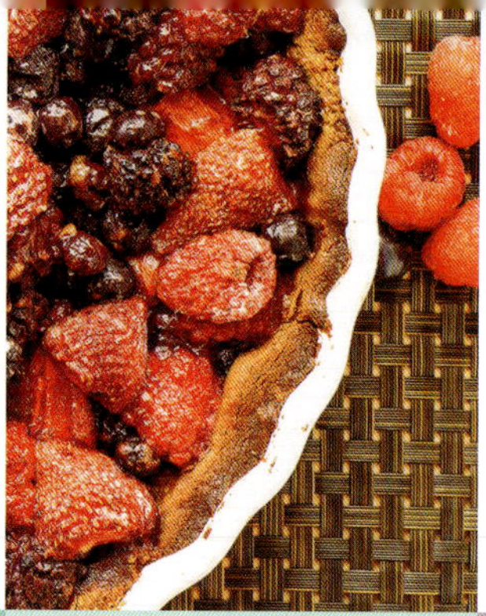
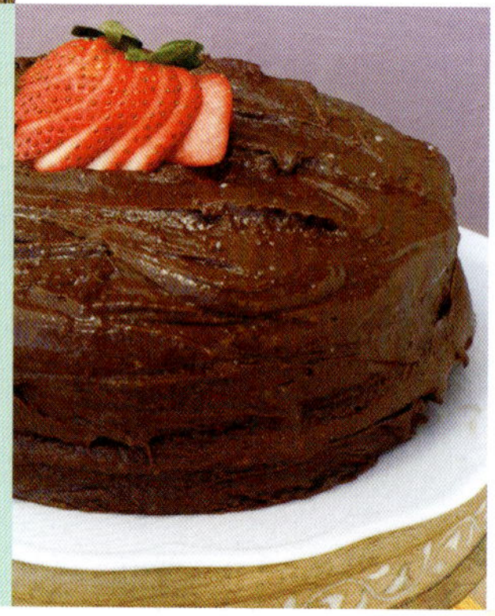
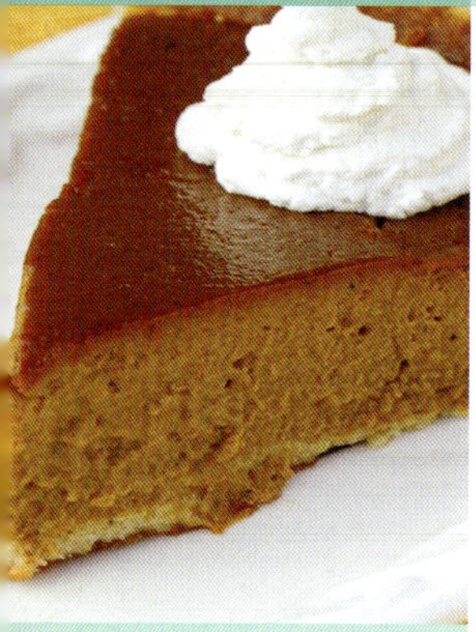
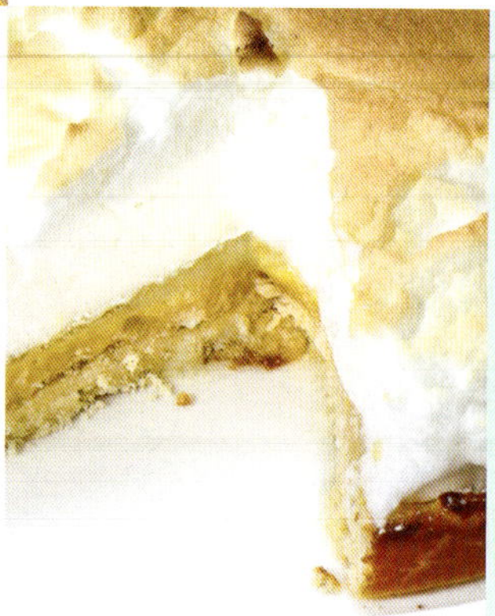
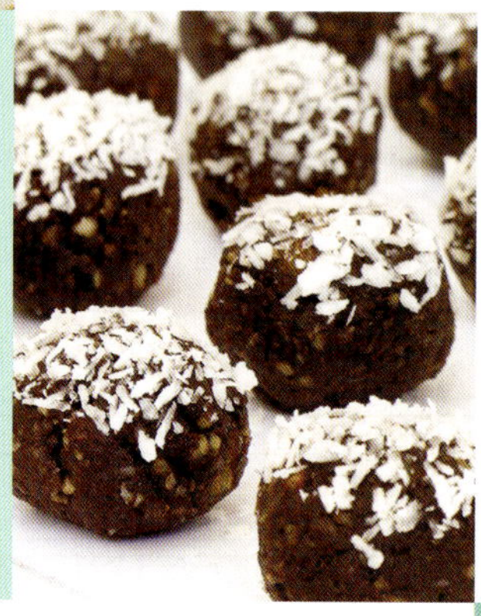
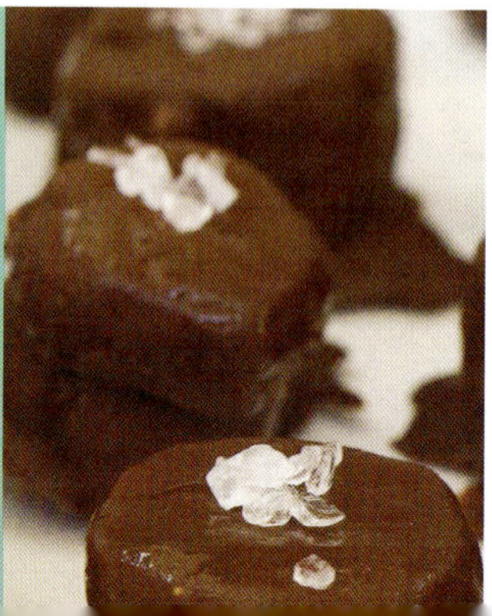

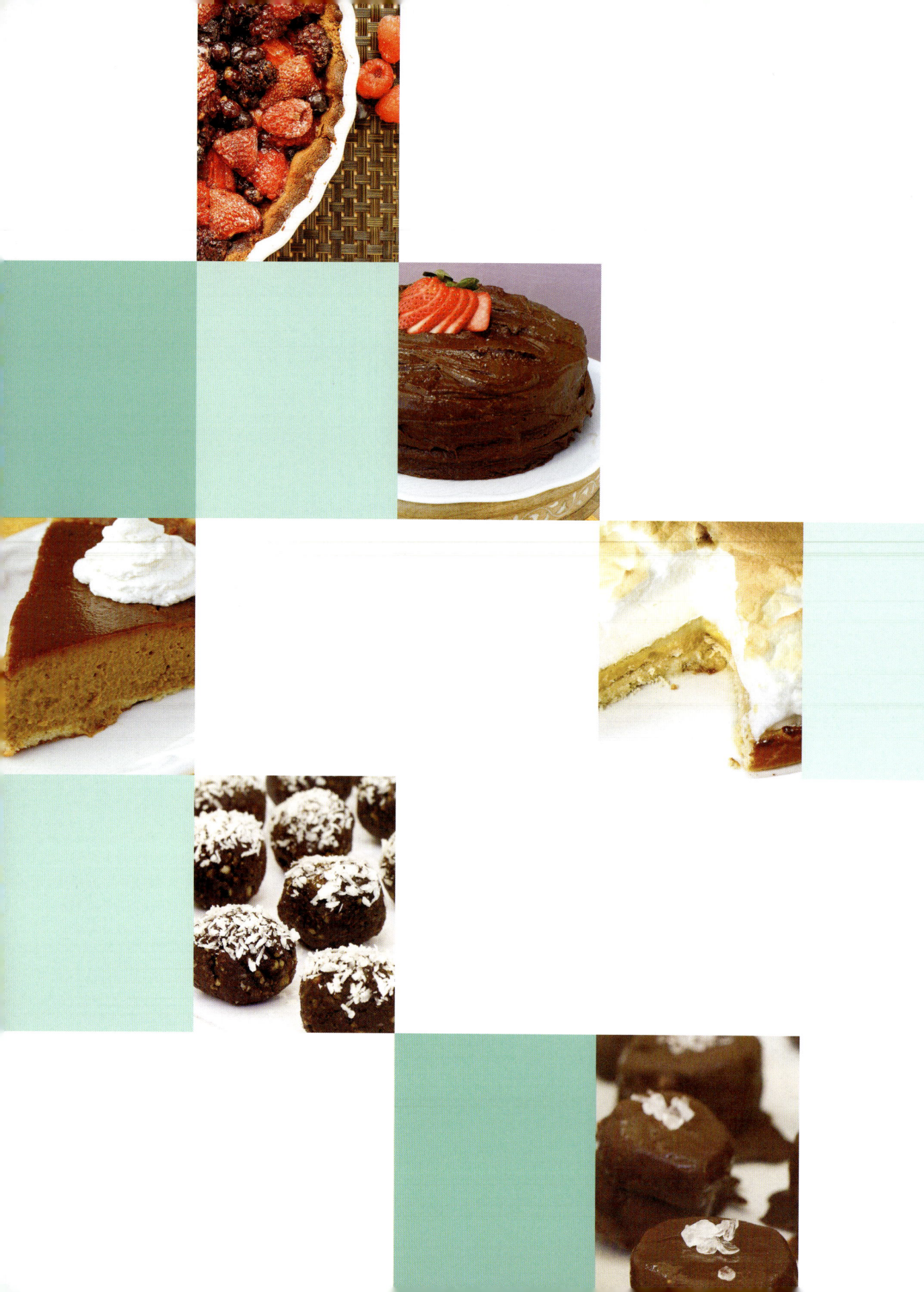

desserts

Dessert is just so much fun to make, serve, and share. Nothing brings a smile to the belly more than to have a dessert that can actually be good for you. I have experimented and created recipes here that use sweeteners other than sugar. Plant-based sweeteners like stevia, monk fruit, or erythritol are excellent, as they will not spike blood sugar levels.

KF Denotes that recipe can be made or is keto-friendly.

Carrot Raisin Frosted Cake 302

Chocolate Cake 306

Chocolate Covered Banana and Almond Butter Bites 320

Chocolate Chip Cookie Dough Bites 316

Chocolate Covered Strawberries 304

Chocolate Nut and Fruit Treats 305

Chocolate Nut Butter Pudding 308

Chocolate Nut Clusters 309

Pumpkin Pie 310

Raspberry Coconut Delight 312

Raw Brownie Bites 315

Rustic Lemon Meringue Pie 318

Soft Chocolate Ice Cream 314

Very Berry Pie 322

carrot raisin frosted cake

makes 12–14 servings

1 ¼ cups almond flour

¼ cup coconut flour

⅓ cup tapioca flour

1 teaspoon baking soda

¼ teaspoon sea salt

1 ½ tablespoons ground cinnamon

½ teaspoon ground ginger

Pinch nutmeg

4 eggs, room temperature

½ cup pure maple syrup

⅓ cup coconut oil, melted and cooled to almost room temperature

¼ cup almond milk, unsweetened

1 tablespoon apple cider vinegar

2 teaspoons pure vanilla extract

2 ½ cups carrots, shredded or grated (I use my food processor shredding attachment)

½ cup raisins

½ cup pecans, finely chopped

With sweet goodness and the spiciness of cinnamon, this is a crowd pleaser. When I was a youngster, I actually thought carrot cake was healthy because it had carrots in it. I laugh at that now, but growing up, it was one of my favorites. It was always so moist and flavorful, and making it from scratch was a labor of love! A birthday comes but once a year, and all of us are entitled to a decadent delight.

Preheat oven to 350°F (177°C).

Line two 8-inch round cake pans with circles of parchment paper to fit in the bottom of each cake pan.

In a medium bowl, combine the dry ingredients: almond, coconut and tapioca flours; baking soda, salt and spices. Set aside.

In a larger bowl, with an electric hand mixer, beat together the eggs, maple syrup, almond milk, cider vinegar, coconut oil, and vanilla on low/medium speed.

Add the dry mixture to the wet ingredients and beat on low speed until fully combined and a thick batter begins to form.

Remove the mixer and gently fold in the shredded carrots, nuts and the raisins.

Divide the batter equally between the two cake pans, scraping the bowl to use all the batter.

Bake both cake pans for 22–25 minutes or until toothpick comes out clean.

Cool in the cake pans for 30 minutes. Carefully remove cake from the pans (use the parchment to help) and transfer to wire racks to cool completely to room temperature before frosting. Be sure the cake has completely cooled before frosting, which usually takes 30 minutes.

cream cheese frosting

Blend all together using a hand mixer. If you refrigerate for up to two hours, the frosting seems to thicken.

Apply a layer of frosting on one of the cake layers. Place the second cake layer on top. Apply frosting on the top layer or if you like more, frost the sides too. Garnish with shaved carrots and pecans if using.

16 ounces cream cheese at room temperature

¾ cup heavy cream

6 tablespoons maple syrup

1–2 teaspoons pure vanilla extract

chocolate covered strawberries

Here's a real treat! Did you know that besides the delightful aroma, bright red color, juicy texture, and sweetness, strawberries could have beneficial effects from vitamin C, fiber, and antioxidants.

makes 14 strawberries, roughly

14 strawberries

½ cup chocolate chips (I recommend Lily's brand made with stevia.)

2 tablespoons cocoa butter or coconut oil

Optional: ¼ cup coconut, shredded, unsweetened, chopped nuts, or mini chocolate chips

Wash and dry the strawberries but leave on their stem for easier grabbing.

In a small bowl, add cocoa butter or coconut oil and chocolate chips, and place in a saucepan filled halfway with water.

Place saucepan over medium-low heat to melt bowl contents in simmering water or use a double boiler until melted. Stir until completely smooth.

One at a time, insert a skewer in the center of each strawberry and dip in the chocolate, twirling around to coat.

Place them on a parchment- or wax paper-lined baking sheet.

Coat all strawberries once, then coat a second time.

Sprinkle on any toppings of choice and let strawberries set in the refrigerator at least for 10 minutes to harden.

chocolate nut and fruit treats

KF *If you are feeling like you want something chocolaty but not sure what, this is the perfect dessert for you. Chocolate treats with berries and nuts will satisfy your desires.*

Put chocolate in a bowl and microwave the chocolate on high 1 minute; let it rest 30 seconds.

Microwave another minute. The chocolate should be melted by then, but if it isn't, microwave for 30-second increments, stirring in between until melted and smooth. You may always add some coconut oil if the chocolate is difficult to melt.

Arrange 12 mini-cupcake liners on a plate or use a muffin pan, greased with cooking spray or coconut oil.

Pour about 2 tablespoons of melted chocolate to fill cups, almost to the top.

Add the fruit, nuts, and mint leaves to each cup before the chocolate sets. You can mix and match any combination you prefer, pushing down lightly to insert into chocolate.

Refrigerate about 45–60 minutes to set the chocolate treats.

Take out of the refrigerator and peel the paper cups off the hard chocolate. If using the muffin pan without the paper cups, take the chocolate cups out of the muffin tins and arrange the treats on a platter.

makes 12

8 ounces Lily's Dark Chocolate made with stevia

12 fresh raspberries

12 fresh blueberries

12 almonds

12 pecans

2 sprigs of fresh mint leaves, stripped from their stems (optional)

Cooking spray or coconut oil

chocolate cake

Who doesn't like moist chocolate cake? This is not only gluten-free, it's also densely packed with iron, magnesium, and antioxidants from the raw cacao. It has more calcium than cow's milk and has been found to help with issues such as depression, stress, blood pressure, and heart health.

makes approximately 12 slices

- 2 cups almond flour
- ¾ cup tapioca flour
- ⅛ cup coconut flour
- 2 cups Swerve or erythritol
- 1 cup raw cacao powder, unsweetened
- 1 teaspoon baking soda
- ⅔ teaspoon espresso powder
- ⅔ teaspoon sea salt
- 3 large eggs
- 1 cup canned coconut milk, full-fat
- ⅔ cup water
- ¼ cup coconut oil
- ⅔ tablespoon apple cider vinegar
- 1½ teaspoons vanilla extract
- Cooking spray

Chocolate Frosting
- 1½ cups Lily's chocolate chips, made with stevia
- 1 can coconut cream, full-fat
- 2 tablespoons cream cheese
- 2 tablespoons raw cacao powder, unsweetened
- 4 tablespoons erythritol

Frosting

You'll want to make the frosting first, either early in the day you are making this cake or the night before. It really makes a difference.

Add all ingredients to a bowl and mix on low for 60 seconds with a hand mixer until smooth. Mixing by hand won't work because of the consistency of the cream cheese. After mixing, let stand in refrigerator, covered with plastic wrap up to 4–5 hours. After removing from refrigerator, mix again until soft peaks form, for about 2–3 minutes.

Baking

Preheat oven to 350°F (177°C).

Grease two 8-inch cake pans and then line the bottom with parchment paper. This helps with removing the layers of cake from the pans more easily. I prefer to grease my pans with coconut oil or any cooking spray.

Set these aside.

Place all of the dry ingredients into a medium mixing bowl and whisk together.

Add all of the wet ingredients to a separate large mixing bowl and whisk together. Then, pour the dry ingredients into the wet and whisk together for 1–2 minutes until well combined.

When using the two baking pans, evenly divide the batter between the two and bake for 35–45 minutes, or until a toothpick comes out clean. Check the cakes earlier, at 23–24 minutes, if your oven tends to bake fast or if you're using a convection oven.

Set pans aside after baking to let cool completely. Once the cakes have completely cooled, remove cake layers from pans and assemble the cake by adding the chocolate frosting between the layers and frosting the outside.

Remember to make sure your cake is 100% cool before frosting.

chocolate nut butter pudding

serves 2–3

Having cravings for that chocolate pudding you grew up with? Here's a delicious and healthy alternative that will bring back sweet memories.

- 2 overripe bananas, peeled and frozen
- ¼ cup nut or almond butter
- ⅓ cup cocoa powder, unsweetened
- 1 tablespoon chocolate protein powder of your choice (I use JJ Virgin's Protein Powder.)
- ¼ teaspoon vanilla extract
- ⅛ teaspoon sea salt
- ½ teaspoon cinnamon
- ¼ cup canned coconut milk, full-fat
- 1–2 packets stevia (optional)

Take your frozen bananas and slice a few pieces for topping your pudding. Set aside.

Put all ingredients, including the rest of the banana, into a blender and mix until smooth.

Pour mixture into small pudding dishes and refrigerate 30–45 minutes.

Wonderful!

tip: Make sure your bananas are nice and ripe, almost brown. If not, then you will need the stevia for added sweetness. Be sure and peel the bananas before you freeze them. It just makes it so much easier.

chocolate nut clusters

KF OPTIONAL *Chocolate has never tasted so decadently good. This is a wonderful sugar-free treat, but you'll feel like you're being so bad.*

serves 8–10

1 tablespoon coconut oil

1 cup mixed raw nuts, your choice

¼ cup raisins (if doing keto, eliminate the raisins)

Pinch sea salt

1 cup chocolate chips, melted (I recommend Lily's brand made with stevia.)

½ cup shredded coconut, unsweetened (optional)

Mix coconut, mixed nuts, raisins, and salt in a bowl until well combined. Set aside.

In a separate bowl, mix the coconut oil with chocolate chips and microwave until melted, about 1 minute.

Combine both bowls into one and mix well with plastic spatula or wooden spoon.

Pour mixture into 8-10 mini-cupcake liners, filling almost to the top.

Place in freezer for 30-plus minutes until set. I leave them in the freezer until I am ready to eat them.

Use a sharp knife to pop out each chocolate cluster. It makes a great chocolate treat!

tip: If freezing overnight, make sure they are placed in a sealed container to eliminate any freezer burn. Remove 5 minutes before eating to help soften the chocolate.

pumpkin pie

serves 8–10

Crust
- ¾ cup almond flour
- ⅓ cup coconut flour
- ½ teaspoon pumpkin spice
- ½ teaspoon xanthan gum
- ¼ teaspoon kosher salt
- ½ teaspoon orange zest
- 1 stick cold butter, unsalted
- ⅔ cup cream cheese
- 1 egg, lightly beaten
- 2 teaspoons apple cider vinegar
- ½ teaspoon cinnamon
- Egg wash (for glossy finish, optional)

KF OPTIONAL *After seven years of living grain-free, my cravings for desserts have diminished. I mostly indulge in dark chocolate, but every autumn, I slip back into yearning for those dense, satisfying, and rich desserts, like the classic, pumpkin pie. I yearn for those wonderful pumpkin spices that can be found in coffee, muffins, frozen yogurt, breads, and of course, pie. I tried many different recipes. This one I think you'll like!*

Add almond flour, coconut flour, cinnamon, pumpkin spice, xanthan gum, salt, and zest in a food processor. Pulse until evenly combined.

Add butter and cream cheese and pulse for just a few seconds until crumbly. Add in egg and vinegar and pulse until the dough just begins to come together but stop before it forms a ball. Make sure not to overmix.

Turn out the dough onto plastic wrap and set into a round ball.

Refrigerate for at least one hour, or up to 2 days.

Lightly butter a 9-inch pie pan.

Roll out pie crust into a roughly 13-inch circle, between two sheets of parchment paper. Feel free to lightly dust with coconut flour as needed.

Transfer to the pan, using the parchment paper as an aid.

Crimp the edge with a greased dinner fork (or simply trim).

If you get any cracks, you can patch them up by pinching the dough together. If at any point, the crust becomes unmanageable, simply pop it in the freezer for 5–10 minutes before finishing.

Otherwise, refrigerate and preheat oven to 400°F (204°C) while you make the filling.

Filling

In a small bowl, mix the sweetener, salt, and spices together and set aside.

In a large bowl, lightly beat the eggs and add in the pumpkin purée, heavy cream, and vanilla extract. Continue to beat until thoroughly incorporated.

Add in the mixed sweetener, salt, and spices, and combine well.

Place the refrigerated pie pan on a baking tray and cover the edges with aluminum foil (to prevent over browning).

Pour in the pumpkin filling and bake for 15 minutes at 400°F (204°C); then reduce heat to 350°F (177°C), and bake for another 40 minutes, uncovering the edges after 25 minutes.

Continue baking.

The filling didn't begin to rise for me until after 35 total minutes.

The pie filling will be jiggly until it sets during cooling.

Remove from oven and place on stove to cool for 10–15 minutes before refrigerating and serving.

Filling

- ¾ cup golden coconut sugar or maple sugar (if doing keto, use erythritol)
- ½ teaspoon kosher salt
- 1½ teaspoons cinnamon
- ½ teaspoon pumpkin pie seasoning
- 1 teaspoon ginger
- ½ teaspoon nutmeg
- Pinch ground cloves
- Pinch ground black pepper
- 3 eggs
- 1 15-ounce can pumpkin purée
- 1 cup heavy cream
- 1 teaspoon vanilla extract

tips: You can make your dough the day before. Alternatively, you can freeze the pie dough and thaw out as needed.

Important, make sure you reduce your heat down to 350°F after 15 minutes. This will allow the crust to harden in the baking process.

If using egg wash, take an egg and beat with 2 tablespoons of water. Lightly brush onto crust edge before covering with aluminum foil.

desserts

raspberry coconut delight

serves 6–8

1½ cups frozen raspberries

1 can coconut cream, full-fat

1 teaspoon maple syrup, optional (if doing keto, replace with erythritol syrup, recipe on page 15)

Up to ¼ cup coconut water from the can of coconut milk

Shredded coconut

KF OPTIONAL *I was actually on a mission to make raspberry ice cream, but it flopped. The taste was so good, but it was not quite up to par because the consistency was lacking: It was not hard enough for ice cream, even after trying several times. That's when the lights went on. I decided that the taste was there, soft and creamy like velvet, so I came up with my newly named dessert: Raspberry Coconut Delight.*

Place frozen raspberries, coconut cream, and maple syrup (if desired) in a high-speed blender or food processor. Add coconut water, a tablespoon at a time, if blender has trouble blending ingredients.

Do not exceed more than ⅓ of a cup of coconut water.

Garnish with a sprinkle of shredded coconut.

Serve immediately or store in freezer for up to 2 weeks.

tips: The Raspberry Coconut Delight tastes best when eaten right away. You can, however, freeze it. Place the dessert in a dish and press parchment or wax paper onto the dessert to prevent ice crystals from forming. There are no thickening agents or starches added to this dessert, so it won't stay soft in the freezer. Therefore, allow adequate time for the dessert to defrost. Beware that each time this is thawed and then frozen again, it will get harder.

Adding maple syrup is entirely optional. This all depends on personal preference and the sweetness/tartness of the raspberries being used. If you prefer other berries, you can replace with blackberries, blueberries, boysenberries, or strawberries.

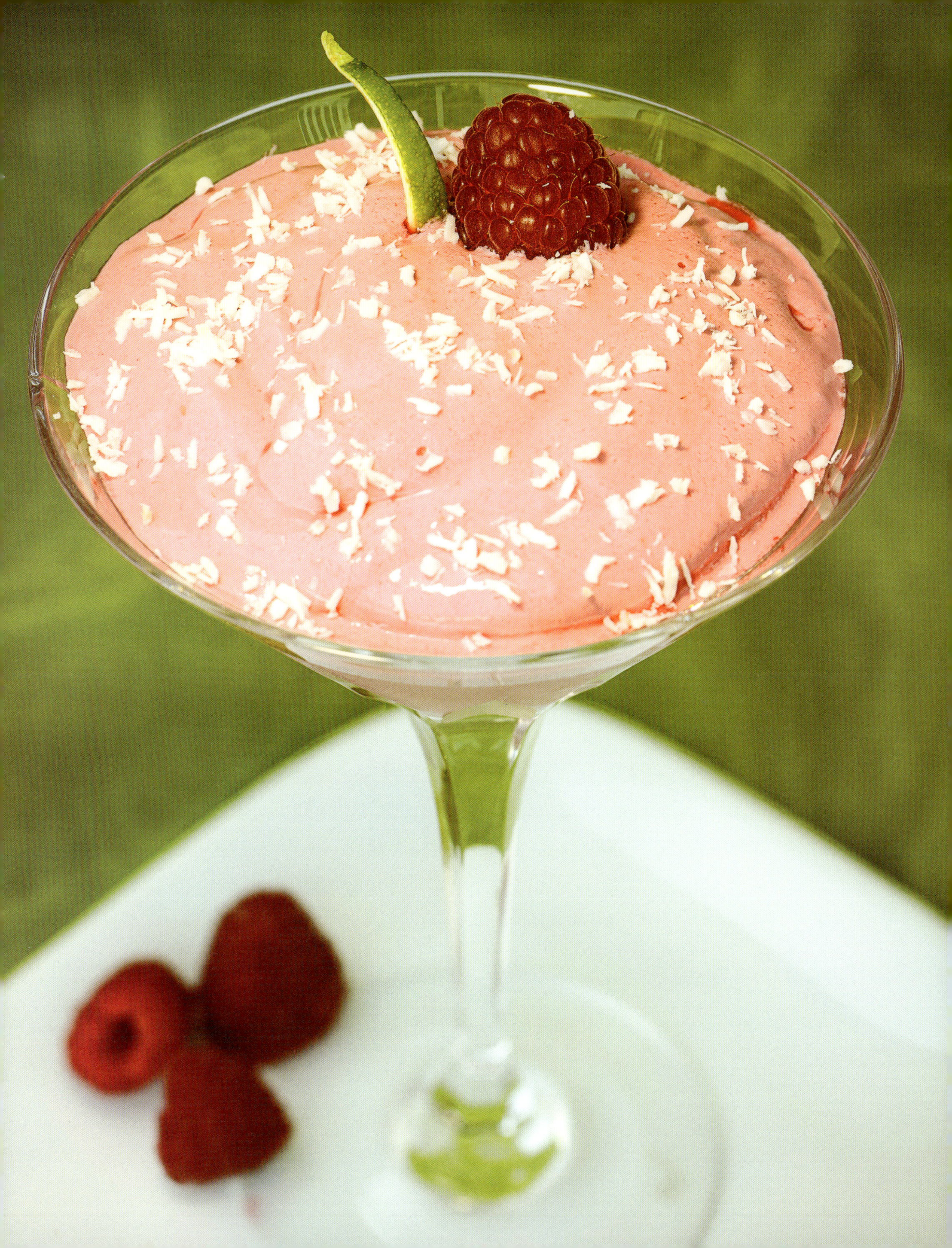

soft chocolate ice cream

serves 2–4

I scream, you scream, we all scream for ice cream! This is a good close cousin to the real thing.

¾ cup heavy cream

¼ cup canned coconut cream, full-fat

2 tablespoons erythritol

1–2 tablespoons cocoa powder, unsweetened

1–2 tablespoons almond butter (optional)

1 teaspoon pure vanilla extract (I like to use a vanilla bean and scrape the bean)

2 tablespoons Lily's Dark Chocolate Chips made with stevia

Put all ingredients in a bowl, except the chips, and use your mixer to mix them all together, about 4–5 minutes. Mix until it all becomes fluffy.

Mix in the chips and transfer to a covered container.

Freeze until set, about 3–4 hours.

Best served immediately once set.

tip: Freezing again is fine, except it may harden too much for your liking. I like the soft consistency from being stored in the refrigerator.

raw brownie bites

These tasty morsels have the right balance of crunch, texture, and sweetness without a ton of sugar. Your mouth will say wow!

Add the walnuts and salt to a blender or food processor. Mix until the walnuts are chopped.

Add the dates, vanilla, and cocoa powder to the blender and mix well until everything is combined.

With the blender still running, add a couple of drops of water at a time to make the mixture stick together into a thick dough.

Transfer the mixture into a bowl, using a spatula, and form it into a big ball.

Use your hands to shape round brownie bites by rolling them in your palms and placing them directly onto your serving dish.

makes 20–24

1½ cups walnuts, chopped

1 cup fresh dates, pitted

1 teaspoon vanilla

⅓ cup cocoa powder, unsweetened

Pinch sea salt

Water

tips: You may add chopped coconut (unsweetened) and lightly roll balls in it at the end, if desired.

You can store in an airtight container in the refrigerator for up to a week.

chocolate chip cookie dough bites

makes roughly 10–14 cookies

1 ¼ cups almond flour

¼ cup arrowroot or tapioca flour

½ teaspoon baking soda

¼ teaspoon sea salt

¼ cup coconut oil, softened

¼ cup smooth nut butter, either almond or cashew (Cashew is better because it's creamier.)

3 tablespoons pure maple syrup

3 tablespoons pure maple sugar or coconut sugar

½ tablespoon pure vanilla extract

1 flaxseed egg (a flaxseed egg is 1 tablespoon ground flaxseed, not flaxseed meal and 3 tablespoons warm-hot water)

¾ cup dark chocolate chips (I use Lily's; they are made with stevia.)

Remember when we were kids and we used to eat half the cookie dough before the cookies were baked? This ought to put a big happy face on your belly. These cookie dough bites are a great dessert without the gluten or refined sugar.

Line a baking sheet with aluminum foil. Set aside.

In a medium mixing bowl, whisk together the almond and arrowroot flours, baking soda, and salt. Set aside.

In a separate bowl with an electric mixer or whisk, cream together the nut butter and coconut oil until smooth, then add the maple syrup, maple sugar, and vanilla. Continue to mix until very smooth. I just do this by hand.

Combine the ground flaxseeds with the water. Refrigerate for 10 minutes before using. After the 10 minutes, add to mixture and continue to whisk or mix by hand (or beat on low) until fully combined.

Slowly stir in the flour mixture with a spoon until a sticky cookie dough forms.

Fold in the chocolate chips; chill the mixture in the refrigerator for 10–15 minutes. This is an important step, so the chips do not melt!

Use an ice cream scoop or a spoon to take out the dough. Use your hands to form doughballs about an inch in diameter.

Place on a baking sheet about an inch apart.

Chill in the refrigerator for 30 minutes and enjoy!

tip: Since this recipe is not cooked, I use a flaxseed egg. Why the flaxseed egg? The basic ratio is one tablespoon of flax seeds and three tablespoons of water to replace one egg. There is some controversy about eating raw cookie dough. I think this is safe since we aren't using a chicken egg or grain flour. Always keep refrigerated.

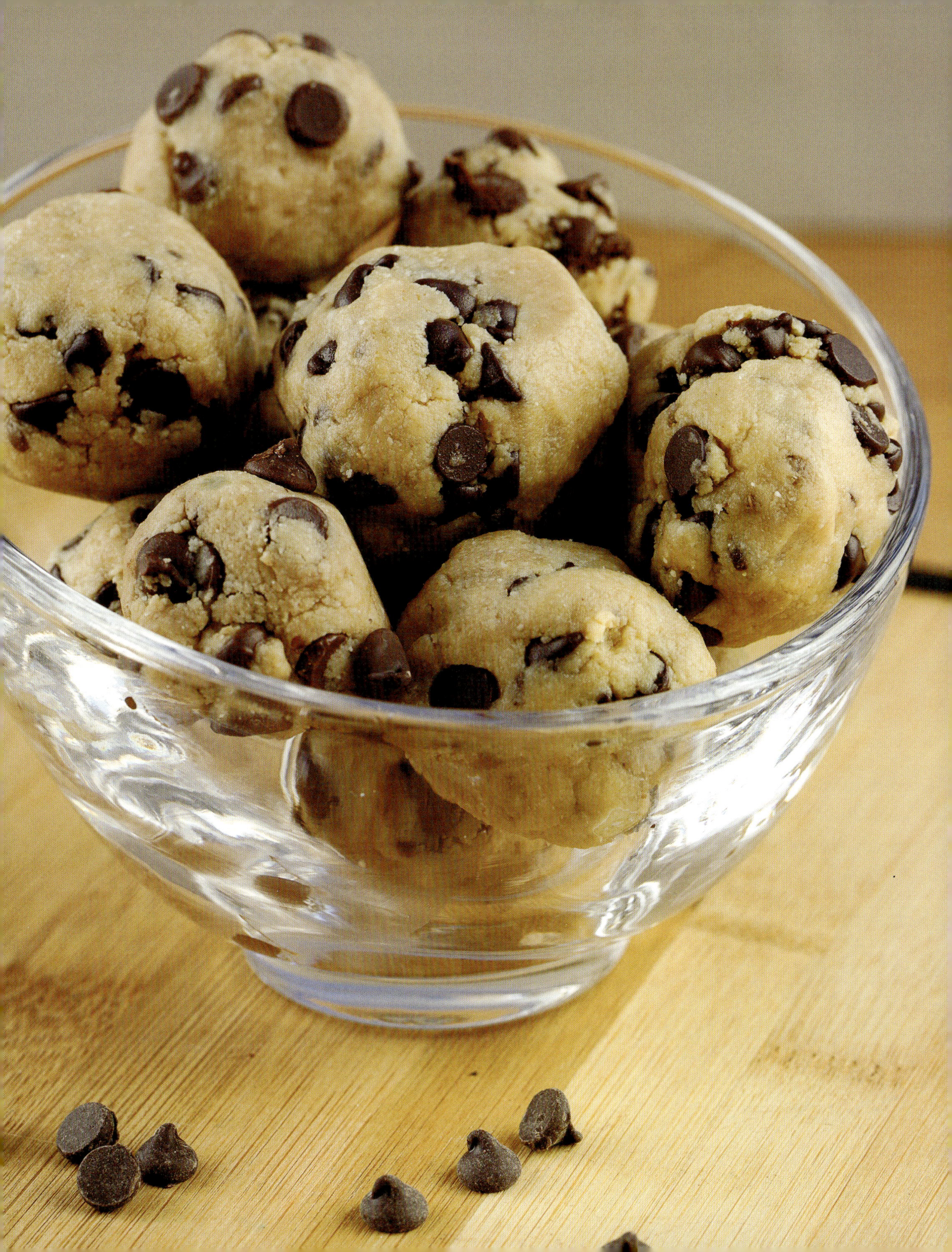

rustic lemon meringue pie

This pie is so good you'll want a large piece and won't want to share. However, I recommend you do share so others can indulge in this delicious dessert.

serves 8–10

Pie Crust

- 1 cup almond flour
- 2 tablespoons coconut flour
- ⅔ cup tapioca flour
- ½ cup coconut oil or butter
- 2 teaspoons maple sugar or coconut sugar
- ½ teaspoon sea salt
- 1 large egg

Preheat oven to 375°F (191°C).

Add all ingredients except the egg in a bowl of a food processor and pulse to create thick crumbs, then add the egg until mixed.

Press the dough with your hands into the pie tin. Keep pressing until it's thin and even all over.

You can chill the dough until ready to use, leaving it in its pie tin covered with foil.

Prick the dough all over with a fork so it won't bubble up during cooking. Bake the crust for 15 minutes or until lightly browned.

You can use a foil tent to prevent the edges from browning too much.

Lemon Filling (Curd)

- 4 eggs
- 4 egg yolks
- ½ cup raw honey
- ¾ cup lemon juice from fresh lemons
- Zest of four lemons (make sure this is very thin)
- ½ cup coconut oil
- Pinch sea salt

In a small pot, whisk together the eggs, honey, lemon juice, zest, and a pinch of salt.

Add the coconut oil and turn on the heat to medium low, whisk constantly until curd thickens, about eight minutes.

Strain the curd through a sieve and pour onto the prepared crust.

Let it cool slightly and refrigerate one hour to allow the curd to set even more.

Meringue

- 4–6 egg whites, (I use 6 egg whites for a fluffy high meringue, but 4 egg whites will work fine.)
- 2 teaspoons stevia

In a large glass or metal bowl, whip egg whites until foamy. Add stevia gradually and continue to whip until stiff peaks form. Spread meringue over pie, sealing the edges at the crust. Broil for 5 minutes, watching closely, or until meringue browns.

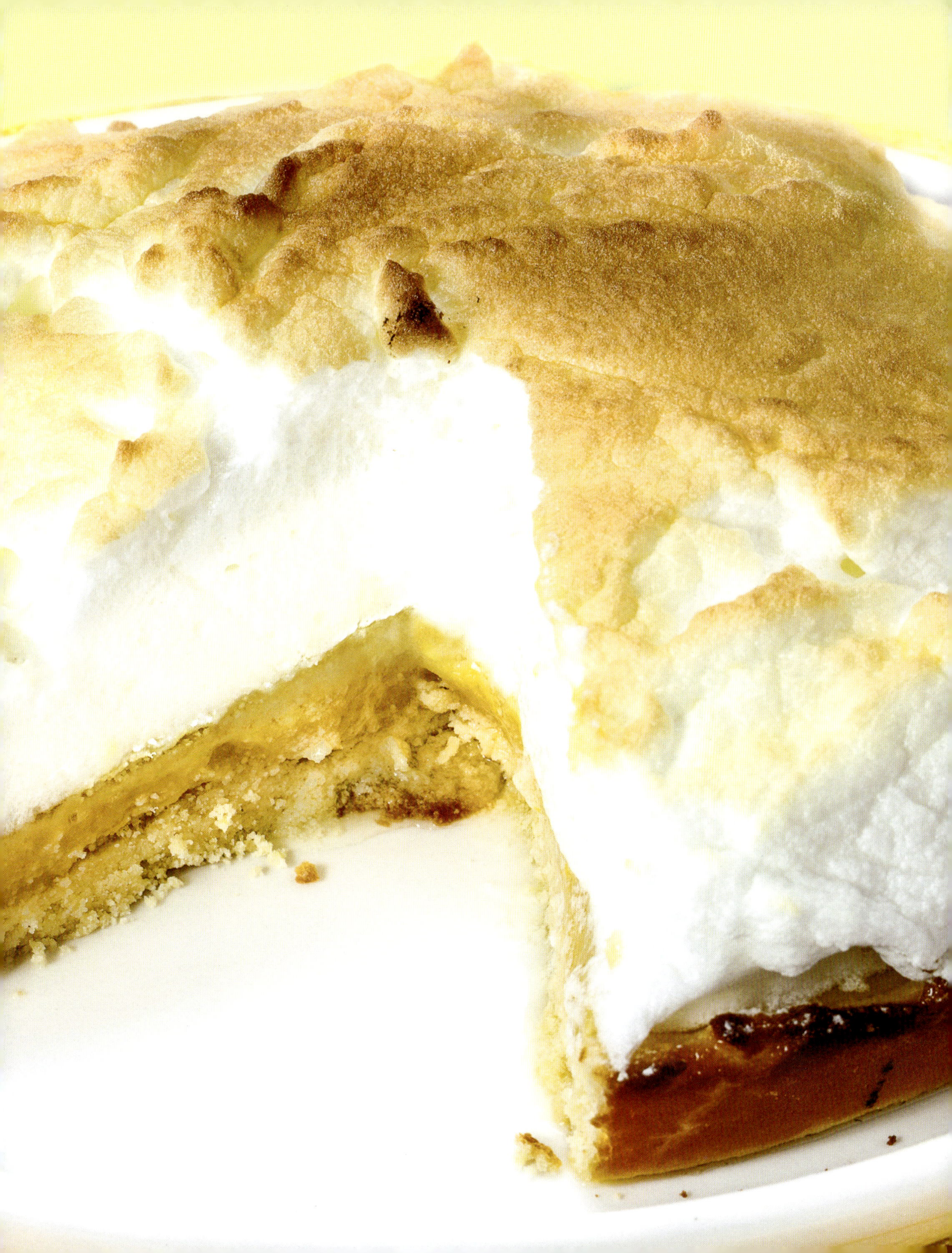

chocolate covered banana and almond butter bites

makes roughly 20 bite-sized pieces

This dessert is fun to share with family and friends. Your taste buds will smile!

2 large bananas, peeled and sliced into ¼-inch rounds

½ cup creamy almond butter

2 cups bittersweet chocolate chips (I use Lily's; they are made with stevia.)

Sea salt (coarse)

Almonds, chopped fine (optional)

tip: If you don't want to boil water, you can microwave chocolate chips with 2 tablespoons of coconut oil in 10-second intervals, stirring between each interval until they are completely melted.

If your chocolate starts to thicken during the coating process, reheat the water in the saucepan or place measuring cup with the chocolate in the microwave in 10-second intervals, and stir to a saucy consistency before continuing to coat your banana bites.

Line a baking sheet or cutting board with a piece of parchment paper. Just make sure the board fits into your freezer.

Place half of the banana rounds onto the parchment paper and set the rest aside.

Mix the almond butter in a bowl with a spoon to soften. Scoop approximately ½ teaspoon of the almond butter mixture onto each banana round you previously placed on the parchment paper.

Top with the banana rounds you set aside and gently press down so they form little banana sandwiches.

Place the cutting board/baking sheet into the freezer and freeze for at least 2 hours.

Once the rounds are frozen, put chocolate chips in a 2-cup glass measuring cup.

Boil 2–3 cups of water in a medium saucepan. Place measuring cup in the boiling water and lower flame to medium.

Remove the baking sheet/cutting board from the freezer and place on counter near stove if possible.

Place saucepan of hot water with the measuring cup holding your chocolate sauce, and using a teaspoon, you can either scoop a spoonful of chocolate and pour over each bite or use your spoon to dip a frozen bite/sandwich into the melted chocolate, coating it thoroughly.

Place back on the parchment paper and repeat for each one.

If using sea salt, sprinkle some flakes on top of the chocolate-covered banana bite/sandwich before the chocolate hardens. Repeat one by one with the remaining frozen banana sandwiches.

If using chopped walnuts, sprinkle some on top to your liking.

desserts

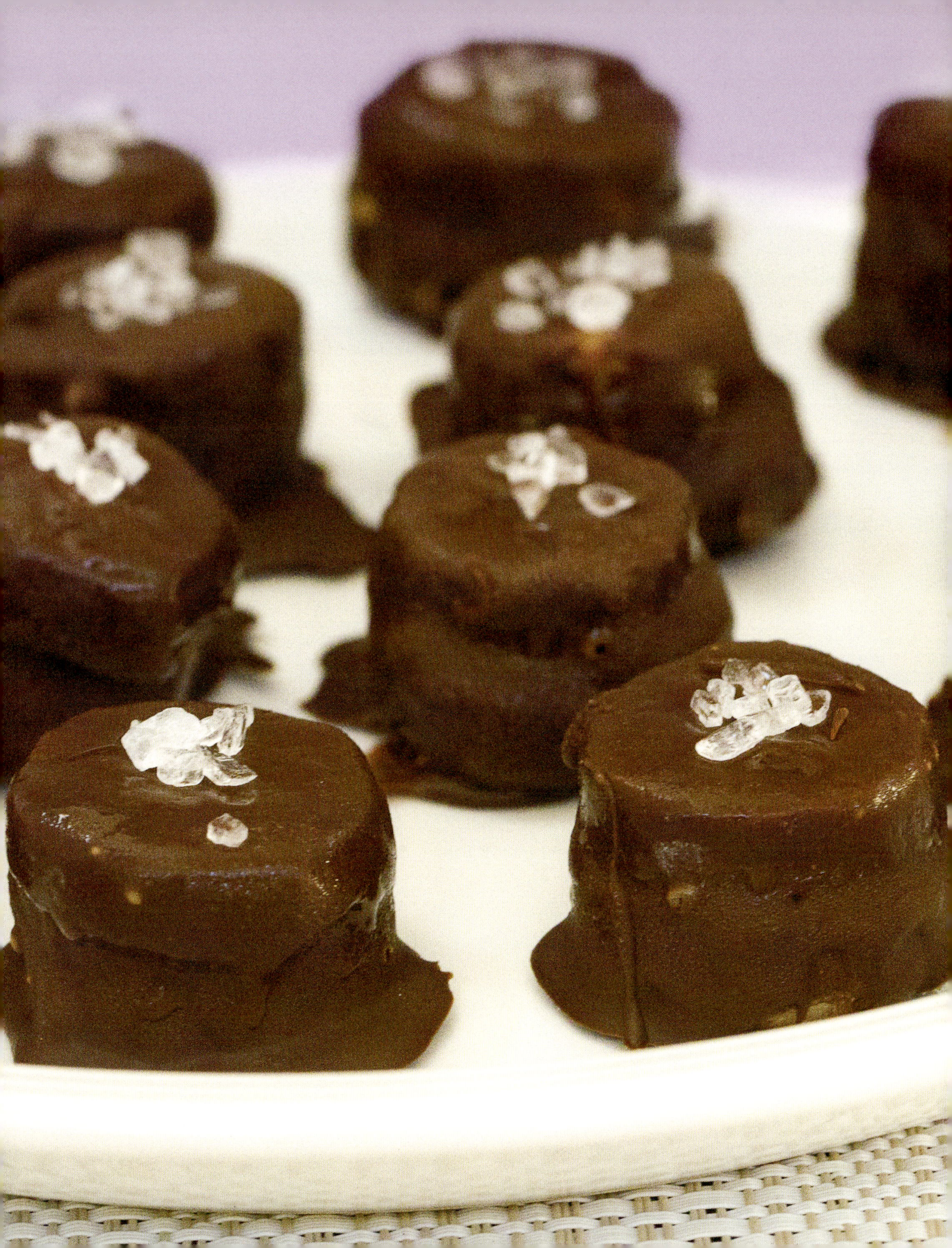

very berry pie

serves: 8–10

Sweet, tart and altogether yummy! Berries are full of antioxidants and in this pie, I am packing them in for your delight.

Crust Ingredients

1 cup nut and seed butter (Recipe on page 250) or almond butter

1 egg

6–8 dates, pitted

Pinch sea salt, if the nut butter is unsalted

Cooking spray or coconut oil

Filling Ingredients

4 cups fresh or frozen berries (one cup each of blueberries, raspberries, strawberries, and blackberries)

1 tablespoon arrowroot flour

2 packets stevia

1 teaspoon ground cinnamon

Preheat oven to 350°F (177°C).

Grease a pie pan with coconut oil or cooking spray.

Place crust ingredients in a blender or food processor and blend all together. This may take a while since it's so thick; just be patient. It is so worth it!

After blending, pour into pie pan. Make sure you flatten and push all sides up about ¼-½-inch.

For the filling, spoon ingredients in a bowl. Make sure the strawberries and blackberries are cut into smaller pieces or mashed somewhat since the other berries are so much smaller in comparison. Mix well.

Fill the pie pan with your very berry mix and spread out evenly.

Place in oven for approximately 45 minutes.

Halfway through baking, use aluminum foil to cover so the crust does not overbrown.

Take out the pie and let it cool, then place in the refrigerator for 2 hours before slicing.

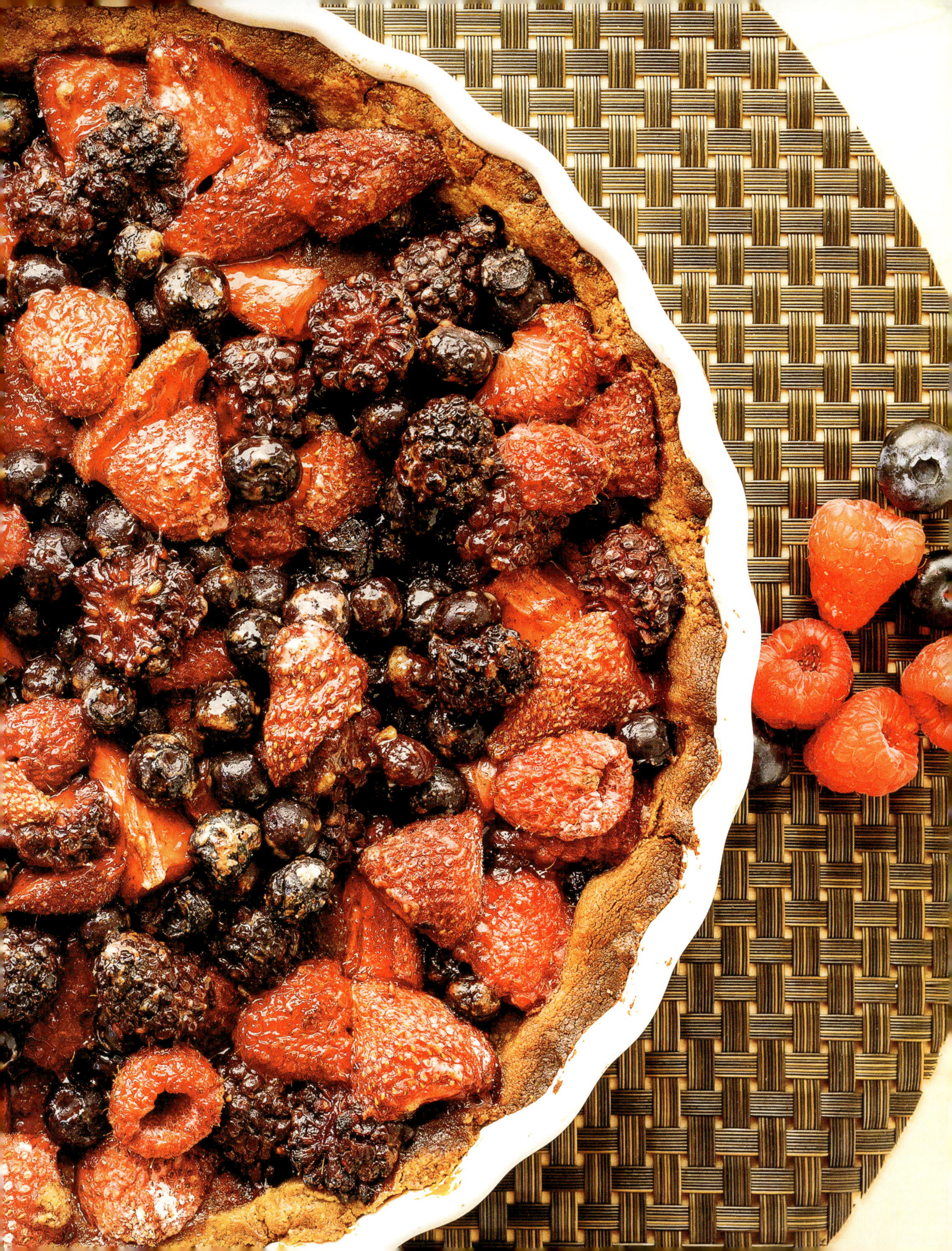

endnotes

[1] CDC, National Center for Chronic Disease Prevention and Health Promotion (NCCDPHP)-Fact Sheet, 2018; https://www.cdc.gov/chronicdisease/resources/publications/factsheets/diabetes-prediabetes.htm, page 5.

[2] Harvard University, Glycemic index for 60+ foods; https://www.health.harvard.edu/diseases-and-conditions/glycemic-index-and-glycemic-load-for-100-foods, page 7.

[3] Buettner, Dan. (2008) "Blue Zones: Lessons for Living Longer from The People Who've Lived the Longest by Dan Buettner." *National Geographic,* page 18.

[4] Di Noia, Jennifer. "Defining Powerhouse Fruits and Vegetables: A Nutrient Density Approach." Centers for Disease Control, https://www.cdc.gov/pcd/issues/2014/13_0390.htm, page 20.

[5] National Institutes of Health, National Library of Medicine, https://pubmed.ncbi.nlm.nih.gov/10502528/ Smith DA, Germolec DR. Introduction to immunology and autoimmunity. Environ Health Perspect. 1999 Oct;107 Suppl 5(Suppl 5): 661-5. doi: 10.1289/ehp.99107s5661. PMID: 10502528; PMCID: PMC1566249, page 23.

[6] Bredesen, Dale. *The End of Alzheimer's,* New York, Avery, 2017, page 25.

index

A

ABC bread, 268

Ahi poke twist, 56

Ahi tuna, 56, 222

Almond biscotti, 274

Almond butter, 34, 271, 272, 288, 294, 308, 314, 316, 320, 322

Almond butter cereal, 34

Almond chocolate chip cookies, 275

Almond crescent cookies, 276

Almond extract, 267, 274, 275, 276

Almond flour, 45, 46, 62, 68, 77, 107, 114, 120, 136, 138, 144, 162, 170, 188, 208, 220, 240, 248, 252, 254, 266, 267, 270, 271, 272, 273, 274, 275, 276, 278, 279, 285, 286, 288, 292, 294, 302, 306, 310, 316, 318

Almond milk, 34, 37, 38, 41, 42, 44, 118, 144, 192, 193, 270, 273, 295, 302

Almond paste, 274

Almonds, 40, 250, 274, 276, 305, 320

Alzheimer's disease, 6, 25–26

Anaheim peppers, 176

Anchovy paste, 94

Appetizers, 56–84
- ahi poke twist, 56
- avocado, mango, and shrimp cocktail, 58
- bacon cheddar chips, 59
- bacon-wrapped artichoke hearts, 60
- bacon-wrapped Brussels sprouts, 61
- bacon-wrapped pears, 64
- baked Parmesan zucchini chips, 65
- BBQ bacon-wrapped meatballs, 62
- bruschetta with French bread, 66
- caprese meatballs, 68
- cauliflower popcorn, 70
- chicken meatballs, 71
- crustless mini-quiche, 82
- excellent artichoke dip, 72
- maple bacon shrimp, 76
- melon, Manchego, and prosciutto di Parma skewers, 74
- mock tortilla chips, 77
- prosciutto rollups, 75
- roasted candied nuts, 79
- sautéed sweet peppers with toasted garlic and capers, 78
- seasoned jicama, pineapple, and watermelon, 81
- spicy lime chicken wings, 80
- spicy sriracha chicken wings, 85
- spicy turkey patty with mango salsa, 84

Apple BBQ sauce, 62, 159

Apple cider vinegar, 42, 92, 128, 156, 159, 273, 274, 279, 302, 306, 310

Apple juice, 194

Apples, 186, 248, 268

Applesauce, 159

Appliances, 29

Arrowroot flour, 45, 67, 125, 138, 144, 170, 254, 273, 274, 282, 285, 316, 322

Artichoke hearts, 60, 72

Artichokes, 226

Arugula, 75, 90, 92, 96, 104, 109, 132

Arugula and roasted pear salad, 90

Asian turkey stir fry, 156

Asparagus, 198

Atkins diet, 3, 16

Autoimmune disease, 9, 23–24
foods contributing to, 12, 24

Avocado, 36, 56, 58, 75, 84, 96, 98, 100, 128, 166, 222, 245

Avocado and sweet red onion, 128

Avocado cheese breakfast soufflé, 36

Avocado, fennel, and orange salad, 98

Avocado, mango, and shrimp cocktail, 58

Avocado oil, 21, 178, 228

B

Baby back rib racks, 158

Baby back ribs with apple BBQ sauce, 158

Baby spinach and arugula salad with berries, 92

Bacon, 12–13, 49, 51, 59, 60, 61, 62, 64, 71, 76, 100, 102, 130, 160, 162, 192, 196, 244
preparing, 19, 51

Bacon cheddar chips, 59

Bacon-wrapped artichoke hearts, 60

Bacon-wrapped Brussels sprouts, 61

Bacon-wrapped cauliflower steak, 160

Bacon-wrapped meatloaf, 162

Bacon-wrapped pears, 64

Baked artichokes, 226

Baked goods recipes
- ABC bread, 268
- almond biscotti, 274
- almond chocolate chip cookies, 275
- almond crescent cookies, 276
- banana blueberry muffins, 278
- banana carrot muffins, 279
- banana keto bread, 270
- banana nut bread, 271
- banana zucchini walnut bread, 272
- Barb's sandwich bread, 273
- butter pecan cookies, 266
- carrot coconut cookies with almond, 267
- cauliflower cheese bread, 280

cheesy onion bialys, 286
cocoa balls, 284
coconut chocolate chip cookies, 290
dark chocolate walnut cake brownies, 293
double chocolate nut cookies, 294
flatbread, 295
French bread, 282
ginger cookies, 285
gooey chocolate chip cookies, 288
maple pecan shortbread cookies, 292
pumpkin bread with pecans, 296
scone loaf bread, 298

Baked Parmesan zucchini chips, 65
Balsamic honey salad dressing, 93
Balsamic vinegar, 66, 74, 90, 93, 95, 96, 104, 108, 110
Bananas, 37, 38, 45, 268, 270, 271, 272, 278, 279, 308, 320
Banana and egg pancakes, 45
Banana blueberry muffins, 278
Banana carrot muffins, 279
Banana coconut pancakes with lavender sprinkles, 38
Banana extract, 270
Banana keto bread, 270
Banana nut bread, 271
Banana zucchini walnut bread, 272
Barbara's nutty bark, 42
Barb's sandwich bread, 41, 273
Basic marinara sauce, 68, 145, 148–149, 152, 177, 183, 191, 192, 258, 280
Basic paleo mayo, 72, 94, 100, 102, 103, 140, 206, 217, 222, 244
Basil (fresh), 66, 68, 74, 95, 104, 110, 111, 132, 134, 145, 147, 148, 152, 177, 191, 193, 212, 220
Bay leaf, 165
BBQ bacon-wrapped meatballs, 62
BBQ citrus salmon, 202
BBQ shrimp with lemon sauce, 206
Beef, 11, 49, 62, 114, 162
  brisket, 165
  prime rib, 164, 184

Beef broth/stock (consommé), 124, 165
Beets, 96
Beet and arugula salad, 96
Bell peppers, 46, 58, 62, 78, 84, 140, 162, 198, 248
Berries, 322
Beverage recipes
  guiltless margarita, 87
  sugarless train wreck mojito, 87
  thin Lizzy cosmo, 87
Blackberries, 322
Black olives, 103, 166, 174
BLT avocado salad, 100
Blueberries, 92, 110, 278, 305, 312, 322
Blue cheese dressing, 102
Breakfast, 34–52
  almond butter cereal, 34
  avocado cheese breakfast soufflé, 36
  banana and egg pancakes, 45
  banana coconut pancakes with lavender sprinkles, 38
  Barbara's nutty bark, 42
  cinnamon craisin breakfast bread, 42
  coconut flour pancakes, 44
  country hash brown mock potatoes, 46
  fig and strawberry jam, 48
  French toast, 41
  green chile and egg casserole, 49
  homemade breakfast sausage, 50
  maple candied bacon, 51
  pumpkin smoothie, 37
  waffles, 52
Brisket of beef, 165
Broiled lobster tails, 208
Broiled salmon fillets, 209
Bruschetta with French bread, 66
Brussels sprouts, 61
Buffalo mozzarella balls, 95
Burrata mozzarella, 177
Butter pecan cookies, 266

Butternut squash, 116, 144, 183, 230, 233, 242, 248
Butternut squash fries, 230
Butternut squash mac and cheese, 144
Butternut squash pizza rounds, 183
Butternut squash purée, 233

C

Cabbage, 145, 148, 166
Cabbage enchiladas, 166
Cabbage lasagna, 145
Cabbage or zucchini pasta Bolognese, 148
Cacao, 284
Cacao powder, 306
Caesar salad dressing, 94
Cantaloupe, 134
Capers, 78, 188
Caprese meatballs, 68
Caprese salad with prosciutto and mozzarella, 95
Caprese salad with tomato and basil, 104
Carne asada, 168
Carnitas, 164
Carrot coconut cookies with almond, 267
Carrot raisin frosted cake, 302
Carrots, 116, 122, 123, 162, 175, 267, 268, 279, 302
Cashews, 42, 52, 147, 150, 250, 268,
Cashew butter, 288, 316
Cassava flour, 67, 125, 228, 282
Cassava flour tortillas, 228
Cauliflower, 46, 70, 82, 103, 114, 118, 160, 172, 190–191, 210, 222, 232, 234, 238, 254, 280
Cauliflower cheese bread, 280
Cauliflower coconut rice, 234
Cauliflower crust pepperoni pizza, 190
Cauliflower dreaming, 172

Cauliflower popcorn, 70
Celery, 81, 103, 122, 123, 162, 175, 186, 248
Celery root, 235
Celery root purée, 235
Celiac disease, 6, 25
Cheese. *See also* Cottage cheese; Cream cheese
  blue, 90, 102, 109
  brie, 66
  burrata, 104, 177, 193
  cheddar, 59, 62, 82, 130, 138, 144, 146, 166, 174, 176, 196, 244, 280
  feta, 66, 108, 110, 111, 134
  fontina, 198
  goat, 92, 96
  gouda, 124
  Gruyère, 36, 144, 236, 254
  Manchego, 74
  Mexican blend, 196
  Monterey Jack, 49, 166, 176, 244
  mozzarella, 68, 71, 72, 75, 95, 145, 152, 174, 177, 191, 192, 193, 240, 242, 280, 286
  Parmesan, 46, 60, 61, 65, 66, 71, 111, 138, 144, 148, 150, 152, 177, 191, 192, 193, 226, 236, 238, 242, 247, 295
  parmigiano reggiano, 94, 136–137, 188
  provolone, 136
  ricotta, 145, 152
  Roquefort, 109
  Tex-Mex, 280
Cheese soufflé, 236
Cheesy cheese bread, 240
Cheesy onion bialys, 286
Cheesy spaghetti squash casserole, 146
Cherry tomatoes, 95, 220
Chia seeds, 40, 284
Chicken, 14, 71, 80, 85, 122, 148, 150–151, 166, 170, 174, 175, 178, 180, 181, 186, 188
Chicken broth/stock, 116, 117, 118, 120, 150, 170, 212, 232

Chicken marsala, 170
Chicken meatballs, 71
Chicken sausage, 148
Chicken-stuffed poblano peppers, 174
Chicken tetrazzini, 150
Chicken with sautéed fennel, 175
Chile relleno casserole, 176
Chipotle chile powder, 172
Chipotle pepper, 168, 233
Chocolate cake, 306
Chocolate chip cookie dough bites, 316
Chocolate chips, 275, 288, 290, 293, 294, 304, 306, 309, 314, 316, 320
Chocolate covered banana and almond butter bites, 320
Chocolate covered strawberries, 304
Chocolate nut and fruit treats, 305
Chocolate nut butter pudding, 308
Chocolate nut clusters, 309
Chocolate protein powder, 308
Cinnamon craisin breakfast bread, 42
Citrus rotisserie chicken, 180
Cocoa balls, 284
Cocoa butter, 304
Cocoa powder, 284, 288, 293, 294, 308, 314, 315
Coconut, 40, 44, 267, 284, 290, 302, 304, 309, 315
Coconut aminos, 56, 156, 213
Coconut chocolate chip cookies, 290
Coconut cream, 181, 254, 284, 306, 312, 314
Coconut flakes, 40, 44, 267
Coconut flour, 38, 42, 44, 49, 52, 82, 236, 268, 270, 271, 272, 274, 275, 276, 278, 288, 290, 293, 296, 298, 302, 306, 310, 318
Coconut flour pancakes, 44
Coconut milk, 34, 37, 38, 41, 44, 52, 77, 116, 117, 118, 144, 192, 193, 210, 232, 234, 235, 236, 284, 295,

306, 308, 312
Coconut nectar, 56
Coconut oil, 38, 40, 44, 45, 52, 67, 70, 71, 82, 107, 108, 111, 118, 138, 150, 166, 183, 196, 210, 230, 234, 248, 250, 252, 267, 268, 270, 271, 272, 273, 278, 279, 284, 288, 290, 292, 293, 298, 302, 304, 305, 306, 309, 316, 318, 320, 322
Coconut sugar, 79, 275, 285, 288, 311, 316
Coconut water, 312
Cookware, 29
Coleslaw, 156
Cottage cheese, 49
Country hash brown mock potatoes, 46
Craisins, 42
Cranberries, 90, 96, 108, 248. *See also* Craisins
Cream, heavy whipping, 102
Cream cheese, 72, 130, 166, 240, 244, 286, 303, 306, 310
Cream cheese frosting, 303
Creamy mushroom soup, 117
Crème fraiche, 36
Crustless mini-quiche, 82
Cucumber, 56, 58, 81, 84, 105, 132, 222, 263
Cucumber radish salad, 105

D
Dark chocolate, 293, 305, 314, 316
Dark chocolate walnut cake brownies, 293
Date night chicken, 178
Dates, 279, 315, 322
Desserts
  carrot raisin frosted cake, 302
  chocolate cake, 306
  chocolate chip cookie dough bites, 316
  chocolate covered banana and almond butter bites, 320

chocolate covered strawberries, 304
chocolate nut and fruit treats, 305
chocolate nut butter pudding, 308
chocolate nut clusters, 309
pumpkin pie, 310
raspberry coconut delight, 312
raw brownie bites, 315
rustic lemon meringue pie, 318
soft chocolate ice cream, 314
very berry pie, 322

Diet
   types of, 3, 9, 16–19

Dijon mustard, 51, 90, 94, 100, 103, 109, 188, 206, 217, 222

Double chocolate nut cookies, 294

Dry mustard, 165

E

Easy creamy cauliflower mash, 238

Egg drop soup, 120

Eggplant, 136–137, 177

Eggplant Parmesan, 177

Eggplant sandwich, 136

Eggs, 36, 38, 41, 42, 44, 45, 46, 49, 52, 62, 67, 68, 71, 79, 82, 94, 100, 103, 107, 114, 120, 125, 136, 138, 145, 146, 150, 152, 162, 176, 181, 188, 191, 192, 193, , 196, 198, 206, 222, 236, 240, 242, 248, 252, 268, 270, 271, 272, 273, 274, 278, 279, 280, 282, 285, 286, 288, 290, 293, 294, 295, 296, 298, 302, 306, 310, 311, 318, 322

Enchilada sauce, 166

Erythritol, 15, 17, 42, 79, 88, 92, 93, 108, 250, 266, 267, 270, 274, 275, 276, 290, 306, 311, 312, 314
   preparing syrup, 21

Espresso powder, 306

Excellent artichoke dip, 72

F

Fat (health effects of), 13, 17

Fennel, 98, 175

Fig and strawberry jam, 48

Fig chutney, 239

Figs, 109, 239. *See also* Mission figs

Fish and seafood, 14
   ahi tuna, 56
   king crab, 216
   lobster, 208
   mercury in, 14
      salmon, 202, 204, 205, 209, 217, 218, 220
   shellfish, 14
   shrimp, 58, 76, 140, 206, 210
   sushi, 222
   swordfish, 213
   as substitutes for meat, 18
   trout, 214
   wild-caught seafood, 20

Flatbread, 295

Flatbread, heirloom tomato, and basil pizza, 193

Flatbread meat lover's pizza, 192

Flax seeds, 34, 250

Flaxseed, ground, 274, 316

Flaxseed meal, 273

French bread, 66, 67, 124, 125, 282, 298

French onion soup, 124

French toast, 41

Fried chicken, 181

G

Garlic, 62, 66, 78, 80, 90, 94, 107, 111, 114, 117, 118, 130, 132, 140, 145, 146, 147, 148, 152, 156, 159, 164, 168, 175, 178, 182, 196, 205, 209, 210, 212, 216, 220, 226, 232, 233, 247, 258, 260, 261, 262

Garlic flakes, 240, 286

Garlic powder, 50, 68, 85, 107, 159, 165, 191, 202, 213, 238, 244, 252. *See also* Herbs, spices, and seasonings: garlic salt

Garlic shrimp with cauliflower coconut rice, 210

Ginger (fresh), 120, 123, 156, 205

Ginger cookies, 285

Gluten, 5–6, 24
   definition of, 5
   effects on body, 6, 7, 9, 23, 24
   gliadin, 5
   glutenin, 5
   sources of, 5

Glycemic index (GI), 7–9

Gooey chocolate chip cookies, 288

Grain-free croutons, 107

Grape tomatoes, 100

Greek yogurt, 102, 166

Green chile and egg casserole, 49

Green chiles, 49

Green onions, 59, 102, 103, 105, 120, 138, 156, 205, 252. *See also* Scallions

Grilled Caesar salad, 106

Grilled swordfish steaks, 213

Ground beef, 49, 62, 114, 162

Guiltless margarita, 87

H

Ham, 136

Hearty Mexican chicken soup, 124

Heavenly butternut squash casserole, 242

Heavy cream, 118, 123, 176, 196, 198, 220, 303, 311, 314

Heavy whipping cream, 102, 181, 238

Hemp seeds, 37

Herb-roasted lamb chops, 182

Herbs, spices, and seasoning
   basil, 66, 68, 71, 74, 92, 95, 104, 110, 111, 118, 132, 134, 145, 147, 148, 149, 150, 152, 162, 177, 191, 193, 212, 220, 258, 280
   bay leaf, 165
   cayenne pepper, 123, 136, 217, 236, 239, 253
   chili powder, 72, 116, 159, 165, 168, 172
   cilantro, 58, 84, 85, 114, 122, 156, 166, 168, 205, 210, 234, 245, 246, 261, 263
   cloves, 37, 285, 311

cream of tartar, 228
   cumin, 98, 116, 168
   dill, 105, 202, 209, 230
   garlic salt, 46, 72, 93, 95, 135, 150, 158, 160, 162, 170, 172, 181, 184, 192, 193, 194, 209, 218, 242, 295
   ginger, 120, 123, 156, 205, 285, 302, 311
   Italian herb seasoning, 177, 191, 280
   lemon pepper, 46, 93, 135, 140, 150, 156, 158, 160, 170, 172, 178, 181, 194, 202, 213, 217, 218, 233, 242
   liquid smoke, 206
   mint leaves, 87, 95, 110, 114, 132, 134, 305
   nutmeg, 37, 79, 144, 236, 285, 296, 302, 311
   oregano, 62, 114, 168, 170, 177, 181, 191, 216, 258
   paprika, 65, 84, 130, 134, 135, 158, 159, 168, 178, 206, 208, 236,
   parsley, 62, 71, 102, 103, 107, 114, 118, 132, 145, 147, 162, 170, 188, 198, 212, 216, 220, 226, 236, 280
   pumpkin pie spice, 285, 296, 310
   rosemary, 175, 182, 186, 188, 248, 280
   sage, 50, 248, 254
   Spike seasoning, 102, 107, 117, 140, 150, 156
   sriracha sauce, 76, 85, 156, 204
   tajín, 81, 134
   tarragon, 206
   thyme, 50, 107, 114, 117, 146, 162, 175, 182, 186, 187, 188, 216, 248
Homemade breakfast sausage, 46, 50
Homemade ketchup, 159
Honey, 15, 37, 38, 40, 44, 48, 52, 80, 85, 92, 93, 95, 96, 108, 109, 239, 271, 274, 278, 290, 293, 294, 318
Honeydew melon, 74, 134

I
Iceberg wedge salad, 102
Infused king crab legs, 216
Ingredients (replacing), 10–15
Italian sausage, 49, 192, 196, 212, 248

J
Japanese chile peppers (dry red chiles), 261
Jalapeño bacon cheese poppers, 130
Jalapeño bacon queso, 244
Jalapeño peppers, 58, 70, 76, 84, 130, 132, 196, 244, 245
Jalapeño juice, pickled, 36, 245
Jean's tabbouleh, 132
Jicama, 81, 92

K
Kalamata olives, 178
Ketchup, homemade, 159
Keto diet, 16–17
   defined, 16
   differences from paleo diet, 16–18
   potential drawbacks, 17
Keto-friendly/keto-optional recipes
   appetizers
      ahi poke twist, 56
      avocado, mango, and shrimp cocktail, 58
      bacon cheddar chips, 59
      bacon-wrapped artichoke hearts, 60
      bacon-wrapped Brussels sprouts, 61
      baked Parmesan zucchini chips, 65
      BBQ bacon-wrapped meatballs, 62
      caprese meatballs, 68
      cauliflower popcorn, 70
      chicken meatballs, 71
      crustless mini-quiche, 82
      excellent artichoke dip, 72
      prosciutto rollups, 75
      roasted candied nuts, 79
      sautéed sweet peppers with toasted garlic and capers, 78
      seasoned jicama, pineapple, and watermelon, 81
      spicy lime chicken wings, 80
      spicy sriracha chicken wings, 85
      spicy turkey patty with mango salsa, 84

baked goods
   almond chocolate chip cookies, 275
   almond crescent cookies, 276
   banana keto bread, 270
   butter pecan cookies, 266
   carrot coconut cookies with almond, 267
   cauliflower cheese bread 280
   cheesy onion bialys, 286
   cocoa balls, 284
   coconut chocolate chip cookies, 290
breakfast
   almond butter cereal, 34
   avocado cheese breakfast soufflé, 36
   cinnamon craisin breakfast bread, 42
   country hash brown mock potatoes, 46
   green chile and egg casserole, 49
   homemade breakfast sausage, 50
desserts
   chocolate covered strawberries, 304
   chocolate nut and fruit treats, 305
   chocolate nut clusters, 309
   pumpkin pie, 310
   raspberry coconut delight, 312
   soft chocolate ice cream, 314
main dishes
   Asian turkey stir fry, 156
   baby back ribs with apple BBQ sauce, 158
   bacon-wrapped cauliflower steak, 160
   bacon-wrapped meatloaf, 162
   brisket of beef, 165
   butternut squash pizza rounds, 183
   cabbage enchiladas, 166
   cauliflower crust pepperoni pizza, 190
   cauliflower dreaming, 172
   chicken marsala, 170
   chicken-stuffed poblano peppers, 174
   chicken with sautéed fennel, 175

chile relleno casserole, 176
date night chicken, 178
eggplant Parmesan, 177
fried chicken, 181
herb-roasted lamb chops, 182
oven-roasted crispy chicken, 186
parmigiano reggiano chicken, 188
salt-encrusted prime rib, 184
smoked pork roast, 194
spinach and mushroom crustless quiche, 196
vegetable frittata, 198

pasta dishes
butternut squash mac and cheese, 144
cabbage lasagna, 145
cabbage or zucchini pasta Bolognese, 148
cheesy spaghetti squash casserole, 146
chicken tetrazzini, 150
zucchini pesto pasta, 147
zucchini ravioli, 152

salads
baby spinach and arugula salad with berries, 92
balsamic honey salad dressing, 93
BLT avocado salad, 100
Caesar salad dressing, 94
caprese salad with prosciutto and mozzarella, 95
caprese salad with tomato and basil, 104
cucumber radish salad, 105
grilled Caesar salad, 106
iceberg wedge salad, 102
no potato salad, 103
strawberry spinach salad, 108
warm fig and arugula salad, 109
watermelon, blueberry, and feta cheese salad, 110
zucchini noodles with red onion and feta, 111

sauces
basic marinara sauce, 68, 145, 148–149, 152, 177, 183, 191, 192, 258, 280
ranchero sauce, 260
red hot salsa, 261
tomatillo salsa, 262

seafood and fish
BBQ shrimp with lemon sauce, 206
broiled lobster tails, 208
broiled salmon fillets, 209
garlic shrimp with cauliflower coconut rice, 210
grilled swordfish steaks, 213
infused king crab legs, 216
lemon pepper salmon, 217
pecan-encrusted trout, 214
salmon rellenos with caramelized onions, 218
spicy California sushi stack, 222
steamed Manila clams, 212
Tuscan salmon, 220

side dishes
baked artichokes, 226
butternut squash fries, 230
butternut squash purée, 233
cauliflower coconut rice, 234
celery root purée, 235
cheese soufflé, 236
cheesy cheese bread, 240
easy creamy cauliflower mash, 238
heavenly butternut squash casserole, 242
jalapeño bacon queso, 244
killer guacamole dip, 245
mock garlic mashed potatoes, 232
nut and seed butter, 250
pico de gallo, 246
pumpkin cauliflower gratin, 254
sautéed Swiss chard with Parmesan cheese, 247
zucchini pancakes, 252

small plates
avocado and sweet red onion, 128
eggplant sandwich, 136
jalapeño bacon cheese poppers, 130
Jean's tabbouleh, 132
roasted mushroom medley, 135
shrimp-stuffed yellow chile peppers, 140
zucchini grilled cheese melt, 138

soups
creamy mushroom soup, 117
egg drop soup, 120
French onion soup, 124
hearty Mexican chicken soup, 122
pumpkin ginger soup with toasted pepitas, 123
sopa de albondigas (Mexican meatball soup), 114
zucchini cauliflower soup, 118
Killer guacamole dip, 245
King crab legs, 216

L

Lamb, 182
Lemon, 48, 84, 85, 94, 100, 114, 118, 128, 132, 134, 140, 147, 168, 172, 180, 188, 202, 204, 206, 208, 209, 213, 214, 217, 222, 226, 247, 263, 318
Lemon pepper, 46, 156, 158, 160, 170, 172, 178, 181, 194
Lemon pepper salmon, 217
Lettuce, 75, 100, 102
Lobster tail, 208
Lime, 58, 80, 81, 84, 87, 98, 114, 168, 245, 246, 263

M

Macadamia nuts, 40, 250
Macadamia nut meal, 271
Main dishes
Asian turkey stir fry, 156
baby back ribs with apple BBQ sauce, 158
bacon-wrapped cauliflower steak, 160
bacon-wrapped meatloaf, 162
butternut squash pizza rounds, 183
brisket of beef, 165
cabbage enchiladas, 166
carne asada, 168
carnitas, 164
cauliflower crust pepperoni pizza, 190
cauliflower dreaming, 172
chicken marsala, 170
chicken-stuffed poblano peppers, 174

index 330

chicken with sautéed fennel, 175
chile relleno casserole, 176
citrus rotisserie chicken, 180
date night chicken, 178
eggplant Parmesan, 177
flatbread, heirloom tomato and basil pizza, 193
flatbread meat lover's pizza, 192
fried chicken, 181
herb-roasted lamb chops, 182
oven-roasted crispy chicken, 186
parmigiano reggiano chicken, 188
salt-encrusted prime rib, 184
smoked pork roast, 194
spinach and mushroom crustless quiche, 196
vegetable frittata, 198

Mango, 58, 84, 263
Mango salsa, 84, 94, 263
Manila clams, 212
Maple bacon shrimp, 76
Maple candied bacon, 51
Maple pecan shortbread cookies, 292
Maple sriracha salmon, 204
Maple syrup, 38, 41, 44, 45, 51, 52, 67, 76, 80, 90, 95, 96, 108, 109, 125, 134, 159, 204, 250, 267, 268, 271, 274, 278, 282, 292, 296, 302, 303, 312, 316
Marinara. *See* Basic marinara sauce
Marsala wine, 170
Mayonnaise, 72, 94, 102, 103, 140, 206, 217, *See also* Basic paleo mayo
Mediterranean diet, 23
Melon, Manchego, and prosciutto di Parma skewers, 74
Mint leaves, 87, 95, 98, 110, 114, 132, 134, 305
Mission figs, 48
Mock garlic mashed potatoes, 232
Mock tortilla chips, 77
Molasses, 285
Monk fruit sweetener, 164, 267
Mushrooms, 82, 117, 120, 135, 148, 150, 170, 172, 196

N
No potato salad, 103
Nut and seed butter, 250
Nut butter, 271, 272, 308, 316
Nuts, 304, 309
  almonds, 40, 250, 274, 276, 305, 320
  cashews, 42, 52, 147, 150, 250, 268
  macadamia, 40, 250
  pecans, 34, 40, 79, 92, 108, 214, 250, 266, 271, 272, 292, 302, 305
Nutrient-dense foods, 20–21

O
Oils, plant-based vs. seed-based, 15
Onion flakes, 240, 286
Onion, minced, 240, 286
Onion powder, 50, 150, 159, 165, 181
Onions, 46, 62, 82, 114, 116, 117, 118, 122, 123, 124, 140, 145, 150, 156, 159, 162, 166, 175, 178, 186, 196, 198, 210, 216, 218, 220, 233, 234, 235, 242, 245, 246, 248, 254, 258, 262. *See also* Green onions, Red onion
Orange juice, 98, 164, 168, 180, 202
Oranges, 98, 310
Oven roasted crispy chicken, 186

P
Paleo diet, 16–17, 26
Pancetta, 170
Parmigiano reggiano chicken, 188
Pasta
  butternut squash mac and cheese, 144
  cabbage lasagna, 145
  cabbage or zucchini pasta Bolognese, 148
  cheesy spaghetti squash casserole, 146
  chicken tetrazzini, 150
  zucchini pesto pasta, 147
  zucchini ravioli, 152
Pears, 64, 90, 186
Pecan-encrusted trout, 214
Pecans, 34, 40, 79, 92, 108, 214, 250, 266, 271, 272, 292, 296, 302, 303, 305
Pepperoni, 191, 192
Pescatarian diet, 18. *See also* Seafood and fish
Pico de gallo, 246
Pineapple, 56, 81, 205
Pineapple salmon, 205
Pine nuts, 90
Pizza crust, 183, 191, 192, 193
Poblano peppers, 174, 176, 212, 218, 260
Poppy seeds, 108, 240, 286
Pork, 11, 50, 148, 162, 164, 194
Pork rinds, 136, 181
Pork sausage, 148
Prosciutto, 74, 75, 95, 134
Prosciutto rollups, 75
Powerhouse foods. *See* Nutrient-dense foods
Pumpkin, 37, 123, 254, 296, 310–11
Pumpkin bread with pecans, 296
Pumpkin cauliflower gratin, 254
Pumpkin ginger soup with toasted pepitas, 123
Pumpkin purée, 123, 296, 311
Pumpkin smoothie, 37
Pumpkin seeds, 40, 123, 250
Pumpkin pie, 310
Pumpkin pie seasoning, 311
Pumpkin spice, 310

R
Radish, 105
Raisins, 248, 268, 302, 309
Ranchero sauce, 260
Raspberries, 92, 305, 312, 322
Raspberry coconut delight, 312
Raspberry vinaigrette, 92
Raw brownie bites, 315
Red hot salsa, 261

331 index

Red onion, 58, 84, 95, 98, 103, 105, 111, 128, 132, 247, 252, 263

Red pepper flakes, 52, 70, 111, 120, 136, 181, 192, 193, 196, 205, 210, 295

Red wine vinegar, 128

Roasted butternut squash soup, 116

Roasted candied nuts, 79

Roasted mushroom medley, 135

Romaine lettuce, 106

Rum (white), 87

Rustic lemon meringue pie, 318

S

Salads
- arugula and roasted pear salad, 90
- avocado, fennel, and orange salad, 98
- baby spinach and arugula salad with berries, 92
- balsamic honey salad dressing, 93
- beet and arugula salad, 96
- BLT avocado salad, 100
- Caesar salad dressing, 94
- caprese salad with prosciutto and mozzarella, 95
- caprese salad with tomato and basil, 104
- caprese salad with tomato and mozzarella, 95
- cucumber radish salad, 105
- grilled Caesar salad, 106–107
- iceberg wedge salad, 102
- no potato salad, 103
- strawberry spinach salad, 108
- three melon salad with feta and prosciutto, small plate, 134
- warm fig and arugula salad, 109
- watermelon, blueberry, and feta cheese salad, 110
- zucchini noodles with red onion and feta, 111

Salmon, 202, 204, 205, 209, 217, 218, 220

Salmon rellenos with caramelized onions, 218

Salt-encrusted prime rib, 184

Sauces
- basic marinara sauce, 68, 145, 148–149, 152, 177, 183, 191, 192, 258, 280
- mango salsa, 263
- ranchero sauce, 260
- red hot salsa, 261
- tomatillo salsa, 262

Sautéed sweet peppers with toasted garlic and capers, 78

Sautéed Swiss chard with Parmesan cheese, 247

Savory breadless stuffing, 248

Scallions, 75, 100, 132. *See also* Green onions

Scone loaf bread, 298

Seafood and fish recipes
- BBQ citrus salmon, 202
- BBQ shrimp with lemon sauce, 206
- broiled lobster tails, 208
- broiled salmon fillets, 209
- garlic shrimp with cauliflower coconut rice, 210
- grilled swordfish steaks, 213
- infused king crab legs, 216
- lemon pepper salmon, 217
- maple sriracha salmon, 204
- pecan-encrusted trout, 214
- pineapple salmon, 205
- salmon rellenos with caramelized onions, 218
- spicy California sushi stack, 222
- steamed Manila clams, 212
- Tuscan salmon, 220

Seasoned jicama, pineapple, and watermelon, 81

Seed butter, 250, 322

Seeds, 10

Serrano pepper, 117, 246, 260, 261, 262

Sesame oil, 120, 156, 205

Sesame seeds, 40, 56, 156, 222, 240, 286

Shallots, 93, 96

Sherry vinegar, 109, 239

Shishito peppers, 56

Shrimp, 58, 76, 140, 206, 210

Shrimp-stuffed yellow chile peppers, 140

Side dishes
- baked artichokes, 226
- butternut squash fries, 230
- butternut squash purée, 233
- cassava flour tortillas, 228
- cauliflower coconut rice, 234
- celery root purée, 235
- cheese soufflé, 236
- cheesy cheese bread, 240
- easy creamy cauliflower mash, 238
- fig chutney, 239
- heavenly butternut squash casserole, 242
- jalapeño bacon queso, 244
- killer guacamole dip, 245
- mock garlic mashed potatoes, 232
- nut and seed butter, 250
- pico de gallo, 246
- pumpkin cauliflower gratin, 254
- sautéed Swiss chard with Parmesan cheese, 247
- savory breadless stuffing, 248
- zucchini pancakes, 252

Small plate recipes
- avocado and sweet red onion, 128
- eggplant sandwich, 136
- jalapeño bacon cheese poppers, 130
- Jean's tabbouleh, 132
- roasted mushroom medley, 135
- shrimp-stuffed yellow chile peppers, 140
- three melon salad with feta and prosciutto, 134
- zucchini grilled cheese melt, 138

Smoked pork roast, 194

Soft chocolate ice cream, 314

Sopa de albondigas (Mexican meatball soup), 114

Soups
- creamy mushroom soup, 117
- egg drop soup, 120
- French onion soup, 124
- hearty Mexican chicken soup, 122
- pumpkin ginger soup with toasted pepitas, 123

roasted butternut squash soup, 116
sopa de albondigas (Mexican meatball soup), 114
zucchini cauliflower soup, 118
Sour cream, 36, 72, 105, 146, 166, 238, 242, 244, 252
as substitute for crème fraiche, 36
Soy sauce (gluten free), 85, 120, 140, 156, 168, 213, 217, 222
Spaghetti squash, 146, 150
Sparkling black cherry water, 87, 187
Spicy California sushi stack, 222
Spicy lime chicken wings, 80
Spicy sriracha chicken wings, 85
Spicy turkey patty with mango salsa, 84
Spike seasoning, 102, 107, 117, 140, 150, 156
Spinach, 72, 82, 92, 108, 196, 220
baby, 92, 220
Spinach and mushroom crustless quiche, 196
Spring lettuce, 100
Sriracha sauce, 76, 85, 156, 204
Steamed Manila clams, 212
Stevia, 17, 79, 293, 294, 308, 318, 322
Strawberries, 48, 92, 108, 304, 322
Strawberry spinach salad, 108
Sugar
health effects of, 13, 15
hidden sources, 15
substitutes. *See* Erythritol; Stevia; Swerve, Xylitol
Sugar-free cocktails, 86–87
Sugarless train wreck mojito, 87
Sunflower seeds, 34, 114, 250, 272
Sweet chili sauce, 205

Swerve, 21, 52, 266, 276, 306
Swordfish, 260

T
Tapioca flour, 65, 77, 192, 193, 273, 295, 298, 302, 306, 316, 318
Tequila, 87
Thin Lizzy cosmo, 87
Three melon salad with feta and prosciutto, 134
Tomatillos, 262
Tomatillo salsa, 262
Tomatoes, 66, 68, 95, 100, 102, 104, 114, 122, 132, 191, 193, 220, 245, 246, 258, 260, 261
canned, 260, 261
cherry, 95, 220
grape, 100
heirloom, 104, 193
Roma, 66
San Marzano, 258
sun-dried, 68
Tomato paste, 159
Tomato sauce, 162, 177
Triple Sec, 86–87
Trout, 214
Turkey, 49, 68, 84, 136, 145, 156
Tuscan salmon, 220
Type-2 diabetes, 6–7, 23–25

U
Utensils, 29

V
Vegan diet, 18
Vegetable frittata, 198
Vegetable stock/broth, 117, 123, 172

Vegetarian diet, 16
Very berry pie, 322
Vodka, 87

W
Waffles, 52
Walnuts, 34, 40, 79, 96, 109, 250, 271, 272, 279, 293, 315
Warm fig and arugula salad, 109
Watermelon, 74, 81, 110, 134
Watermelon, blueberry, and feta cheese salad, 110
White pepper, 181
White wine, 117, 175, 178, 209, 212, 216, 239, 247
Worcestershire sauce, 94, 209

X
Xanthan gum, 240, 286, 310
Xylitol, 15

Y
Yeast, active dry, 67, 125, 240, 282, 286
Yellow chile peppers, 140

Z
Zucchini, 65, 111, 114, 118, 122, 138, 147, 148, 152, 198, 252, 272
Zucchini cauliflower soup, 118
Zucchini grilled cheese melt, 138
Zucchini noodles with red onion and feta, 111
Zucchini pancakes, 252
Zucchini pesto pasta, 147
Zucchini ravioli, 152